Ext JS in Action, Second Edition

Ext JS in Action, Second Edition

JESUS GARCIA
GRGUR GRISOGONO
JACOB K. ANDRESEN

MANNING

SHELTER ISLAND

Manning Publications Co.
20 Baldwin Road
PO Box 261
Shelter Island, NY 11964

Development editors: Sebastian Stirling, Frank Pohlman
Copyeditor: Tiffany Taylor
Proofreader: Melody Dolab
Typesetter: Dennis Dalinnik
Cover designer: Marija Tudor

ISBN: 9781617290329
Printed in the United States of America
1 2 3 4 5 6 7 8 9 10 – MAL – 19 18 17 16 15 14

brief contents

contents

preface

I started my career in the world of Sencha back in 2006 when the precursor to what is known as Ext JS today (Sencha's desktop JavaScript framework) was something of an experiment. Soon after my introduction, I became addicted to the design patterns that were promoted by the quickly evolving framework. But, more importantly, I fell in love with the thriving community of developers looking to give back.

I was inspired by many of the active members in the community, and decided to become a contributing member myself, spending tens of hours per week answering questions, writing blog posts, and eventually publishing instructional screencasts. Times were certainly interesting back then, as design patterns emerged from the community.

This second edition of *Ext JS in Action*, originally published in 2010, reflects a new era of desktop web front-end development that was ushered in by Ext JS 4.0. This version brought forth an extremely robust class system and offers many capabilities that extend those of JavaScript. Add to that a very well-designed event system, data package, UI, and MVC, and in Ext JS 4.0 you have a powerful framework that will allow you to develop applications to be used for many years to come.

We are delighted to share our knowledge of Ext JS with you and hope you enjoy this journey.

—JAY GARCIA

acknowledgments

The authors would like to thank the following:

- The Sencha Community—Without you, this book would simply not have been possible.

- Sebastian Sterling—The publication of this book has taken a lot longer than we anticipated. As our primary developmental editor at Manning, you challenged our writing and helped us bring out the best content. Thank you for all of your hard work. Thanks also to Frank Pohlman, who helped usher this book through its final stages and hand it off to production.

- The Manning production team—You guys are absolutely amazing! We feel very fortunate to have had the opportunity to work with you, on this book as well as our previous ones, and we value the work you've done through the years. Thank you so very much!

- Our MEAP (Manning Early Access Program) readers—Thank you for your helpful corrections and comments in the Author Online forum.

- Our reviewers—They read the manuscript in its various stages during development and contributed insights and feedback that helped make this a better book. Thanks to Bradley Meck, Brian Crescimanno, Brian Daley, Brian Forester, Chad Davis, Darragh Duffy, Efran Cobisi, Jeet Marwah, John J. Ryan III, Loiane Groner, Mary Turner, Raul Cota, Robby O'Connor, and Todd Hill.

- Doug Warren—Your technical proofread and thorough review of the chapters and the code during production has proved invaluable to us. Thank you!

Jay Garcia

Writing this book took a lot of effort on my part, but I certainly wouldn't have been able to do it without the help and contributions of others. I owe each of the following a personal thank you:

- My wife—Erika, this book has been in the works for a few years. When people congratulate me, they often don't recognize that I couldn't have written this book had you not provided the much-needed support for me to do so. I love you with all of my heart and am very grateful to have you in my life.
- My sons—Takeshi, Kenji: I won't forget the constant running around the house as I wrote this book. I thank you for your sacrificed time with me to allow me to complete it. You boys are the reason I work so hard, and I love you very much.
- Mitchell Simoens—I'm grateful to call you my friend. Watching your development both professionally and personally has been something I've taken great pride in. Always remember to push the envelope with your knowledge.
- Abe Elias—I have been amazed to see you evolve as you worked through the many years with Sencha to lead a team of top-notch professional engineers. Whenever I talk about great people, you're one of the names that always comes to mind. Keep staying awesome!
- Grgur Grisogono—Meeting you has changed my life for the better. I'm grateful to your friendship and look forward to many more years.
- Jacob Andresen—Your contributions to this manuscript have been valuable, and I thank you for the hard work you put in to get chapters cranked out.
- Don Griffin—Thank you for allowing me to take part in conversations regarding Sencha Cmd and other Ext JS–related tools.

Grgur Grisogono

I want to thank my loving wife Andrea and kids Laurenco and Paulina for their constant support and encouragement. They provided me with the resources and the love that I needed to generate, channel, and renew energy to write the content for this book. I'm forever indebted to the incredible reviewers who shared their energy and knowhow to make a much better book for the good of the community.

I would also like to extend my gratitude to Modus Create for supporting me and granting me new challenges that have made me a better professional. Special thanks to Sencha and its core team engineers, who have been incredibly helpful, providing insight into the latest and greatest to make the content of this book up to date with the most recent Ext JS and Sencha Cmd upgrades.

The most sincere appreciation is due to two of the most prominent Ext JS community members and tremendous people: my coauthors, Jesus Garcia and Jacob Andresen. They were a tremendous team to work with, the perfect guides and reviewers, and the never-tiring locomotive that constantly pushed the project forward.

And finally, I'm forever indebted to my incredible friend, role model, and co-worker, Jay G. for his amazing support, energy, and patience. His insights have been a constant source of awe, sharp observations, and great ideas.

Jacob Andresen

First of all, I would like to thank Jesus Garcia for allowing me to tag along on the ride. Contributing to this book has given me the opportunity to study the craft of writing and observe how Jesus has curated the amount of technical detail that has gone into this book. I would also like to thank Grgur Grisogono for the effort he put into this book, as well as his work in the international Sencha community.

Speaking of the community, there is no escaping Mats Bryntse, Fredric Berling, and Emil Pennlöv here in Scandinavia—thank you for all the good times.

Most important of all, thanks to my wife Anita for understanding why I spend all those long nights programming.

about this book

The purpose of this book is to inform and educate you about the flexible and powerful desktop framework, Ext JS. This book is designed to walk you through the basics of using this framework all the way through to developing and deploying production applications with Sencha Cmd. After you've read this book, you should be able to develop robust desktop web applications. This revised edition covers the many new features of Ext JS 4.0.

Who should read this book

This book is intended for developers who want to use Ext JS to create rich desktop web applications that feel native. Although Ext JS is themed and highly customized, this book is targeted to those who primarily perform the programming aspect of specification implementation.

We assume that you already have a working understanding of how websites interact with web servers. To be most effective in writing robust and responsive applications, you need a solid background with core technologies like HTML, CSS, JavaScript, and JSON. The only time we talk in detail about these core technologies is in chapter 13, where we discuss prototypal inheritance with JavaScript, a prerequisite to the Ext JS class system.

What you'll need

In the book, we'll walk you through many hands-on examples. In order to get the most out of them, the following items should be set up on your computer:

- *A web server*—We recommend Apache HTTPD or Microsoft IIS.
- *An intelligent IDE*—We recommend Webstorm or Aptana.
- *A copy of Sencha Cmd installed*—It's available at www.sencha.com/products/sencha-cmd/download.

That's pretty much it!

Roadmap

This book is designed to give you a guided tour of Ext JS, updated for version 4.0. Along the way, we'll focus on many of the rich features that Ext JS provides, including UI widgets and supportive classes such as data stores, models, and proxies. This tour consists of 14 chapters.

Chapter 1 is an introductory chapter, focused on getting you familiar with the framework. We'll take a top-down view of the framework and discuss many of the commonly used widgets.

Chapter 2 is designed to get your feet wet with the framework. We'll take a good look at how the framework is delivered to you and identify its contents. We'll also walk through the basics of DOM manipulation and work our way up to using the Ext JS template engines, Template and XTemplate, to render data in the DOM.

Chapter 3 is about Component and Container, both base classes for the Ext JS UI. We'll discuss the component lifecycle and look at how to use Container and its utility methods to manage and query for child components.

Chapter 4 builds on chapter 3. We'll discuss core UI components such as panels, windows, message boxes, and tab panels. These are all fundamental widgets that extend Container and allow you to present your UIs with more functionality than Container provides.

Chapter 5 covers the various layout managers that Ext JS provides, which are used to organize components on screen. After reading this chapter, you'll be able to construct complex user interfaces with the many Ext JS widgets.

Chapter 6 revolves around the form panel and the various input fields. We'll look at how to set up validations with input fields, and you'll learn how to load and save data with form panels.

Chapter 7 focuses on the Ext JS data package. You'll learn about the core data classes—Model, Proxy, Reader, and Store—all of which are used to supply data to various UI components.

Chapter 8 builds on chapter 7, and you'll learn about the grid panel. We'll explore the various classes that support the grid panel, and you'll learn to use many common implementation patterns.

Chapter 9 is the root source for learning about Ext JS tree panels. We'll dive into how to use the data TreeStore class to support hierarchical data to the tree panel widget and end the chapter with tree data manipulation via implementation of an Ext JS menu.

Chapter 10 covers the Ext JS Draw and Charting package. You'll draw simple shapes as we explore how to draw on a canvas using the Ext JS Draw API. Afterward, you'll learn how to implement the many charts that Ext JS provides.

Chapter 11 focuses on direct web remoting with Ext JS. We'll explore what it takes to integrate server-side logic with the client to allow the server code to dictate API calls to the client.

Chapter 12 covers drag-and-drop with Ext JS. We'll look at how to implement the basic drag-and-drop classes and then dive into using drag-and-drop with grids, trees, and data views.

Chapter 13 focuses on the Ext JS class system. We begin by covering basic JavaScript prototypal inheritance and elevate your knowledge up to developing Ext JS classes. You'll learn how to extend Ext JS components and develop plug-ins to the framework.

Chapter 14 will take you through what it's like to develop an application using Sencha Cmd and the Ext JS MVC system. You'll learn how to set up the basic application scaffolding, develop an app using MVC, and then produce testing and production builds.

Code conventions

All source code in this book is in a `fixed-width font like this`, which sets it off from the surrounding text. In many listings, the code is annotated to point out the key concepts. We have tried to format the code so that it fits within the available page space in the book by adding line breaks and using indentation carefully. Sometimes, however, very long lines include line-continuation markers.

Getting the latest examples

The examples in this book are designed to be easy to navigate. Each chapter is its own folder, with each example named according to the listing it corresponds to.

We'll work to keep the examples up to date as the framework is upgraded. To get the latest version of the examples, you can fork the following GitHub repo: https://github.com/ModusCreateOrg/extjs-in-action-examples. You can also download a zip file with the code examples from the publisher's website at www.manning.com/ExtJSinActionSecondEdition.

Author Online

Purchase of *Ext JS in Action, Second Edition* includes free access to a private web forum run by Manning Publications where you can make comments about the book, ask technical questions, and receive help from the authors and from other users. To access the forum and subscribe to it, point your browser to www.manning.com/ExtJSinActionSecondEdition. This page provides information on how to get on the forum once you're registered, what kind of help is available, and the rules of conduct on the forum.

Manning's commitment to our readers is to provide a venue where a meaningful dialog between individual readers and between readers and the authors can take place. It's not a commitment to any specific amount of participation on the part of the authors, whose contribution to the AO remains voluntary (and unpaid). We suggest you ask the authors challenging questions lest their interest stray!

About the authors

Jay Garcia is CTO and cofounder of Modus Create, a company focused on delivering high-end solutions with Sencha products. Jay's involvement with the world of Sencha started in 2006. Since then, Jay has been focused on knowledge sharing through books, blog articles, screencasts, meetups, and conferences. His blog is at http://moduscreate.com/.

Grgur Grisogono is a principal at Modus Create and a web technology evangelist. Grgur has been involved with Ext JS since 2007 and has successfully organized three Sencha-focused conferences in Europe.

Jacob Andresen resides in Germany and is an Ext JS enthusiast. He works on various projects and contributes to the community via blog posts and the Sencha forums.

about the cover illustration

The figure on the cover of *Ext JS in Action, Second Edition* is captioned "Le voyageur," which means a traveling salesman. The illustration is taken from a 19th-century edition of Sylvain Maréchal's four-volume compendium of regional dress customs published in France. Each illustration is finely drawn and colored by hand. The rich variety of this collection reminds us vividly of how culturally apart the world's towns and regions were just 200 years ago. Isolated from each other, people spoke different dialects and languages. In the streets or in the countryside, it was easy to identify where they lived and what their trade or station in life was just by their dress.

Dress codes have changed since then and the diversity by region, so rich at the time, has faded away. It is now hard to tell apart the inhabitants of different continents, let alone different towns or regions. Perhaps we have traded cultural diversity for a more varied personal life—certainly for a more varied and fast-paced technological life.

At a time when it is hard to tell one computer book from another, Manning celebrates the inventiveness and initiative of the computer business with book covers based on the rich diversity of regional life of two centuries ago, brought back to life by illustrations from collections such as this one.

Part 1

Introduction to Ext JS 4.0

This book thoroughly explains and demonstrates how to develop JavaScript applications using the powerful Ext JS framework. The extensive practical examples will help you understand its components and containers, and, even more important, how they can be used together.

Chapter 1 provides an overview of what's new with Ext JS 4.0. It also covers the fundamental concepts and widgets of the framework, and helps you develop a "Hello World" application. Chapter 2 addresses the basics needed for the foundation of any Ext JS application, such as initialization, DOM element manipulation, and injecting HTML fragment templates with Ajax server data. Chapter 3 explores components and the life cycle of UI building blocks such as viewports, panels, menus, tabs, data grids, dynamic forms, and stylized pop-up windows, as well as containers and layout controls that manage child items.

After reading the chapters in part 1, you'll see how Ext JS works from the inside out and be ready to explore the many widgets that compose the Ext JS framework.

A framework apart

Envision a scenario where you're tasked to develop an application with many of the typical user interface (UI) widgets such as menus, tabs, data grids, dynamic forms, and stylized pop-up windows. You want something that allows you to programmatically control the position of widgets, which means it has to have layout controls. You also want detailed and organized centralized documentation to ease your learning curve with the framework. Finally, your application needs to look mature and go into beta phase as quickly as possible, which means you don't have a lot of time to toy with HTML and CSS. Before entering the first line of code for the prototype, you need to decide on an approach for developing the frontend. What are your choices?

You do some recon on the common popular frameworks and libraries on the market and quickly learn that all of them can manipulate the DOM, but only two of them have mature UI widgets: Yahoo! User Interface (YUI) and Ext JS.

With your first glance at YUI, you might think you needn't look any further. You play with the examples and notice that they look mature but aren't exactly professional quality, which means you'll need to modify CSS. No way. Next, you look at the documentation. It's centralized and technically accurate, but it's far from user-friendly. You notice all of the scrolling required to locate a method or class. Some classes are even cut off because the left navigation pane is too small.

In this chapter, we'll take a good look at Ext JS, and you'll learn about some of the widgets that compose the framework. After we finish the overview, you'll download Ext JS and take it for a test drive.

1.1   *Looking at Ext JS*

To develop a rich internet application (RIA) with a set of rich UI controls, you turn to Ext JS and find that, out of the proverbial box, Ext JS provides a rich set of DOM utilities and widgets. Although you can get excited about what you see in the examples page, it's what's under the hood that's most exciting. Ext JS comes with a full suite of layout management tools to give you full control over organizing and manipulating the UI as requirements dictate. One layer down exist what are known as the Component model and Container model, each playing an important role in managing how the UIs are constructed.

> ### Component and Container models
> The Component and Container models play a key role in managing UIs with Ext JS and are part of the reason Ext JS stands out from the rest of the Ajax libraries and frameworks. The Component model dictates how UI widgets are instantiated, rendered, and destroyed in what's known as the *component life cycle*. The Container model controls how widgets can manage (or *contain*) other child widgets. These are two key areas for understanding the framework, which is why we'll spend a lot of time on these two topics in chapter 3.

Almost all UI widgets in the framework are highly customizable, giving you the option to enable and disable features, override functions, and use custom extensions and plug-ins. One example of a web application that takes full advantage of Ext JS is conjoon. Figure 1.1 shows a screenshot of conjoon in action.

conjoon is an open source personal information manager and can be considered the epitome of web applications developed with Ext JS. It uses just about all of the framework's native UI widgets and demonstrates how well the framework can integrate with custom extensions such as YouTubePlayer, LiveGrid, and ToastWindow.

You've learned that Ext JS can be used to create a full-page web application. It's quite easy to see that a lot can be achieved using this framework. As you'll soon learn, the framework is pretty vast, and the API documentation will become your best friend.

Speaking of the API documentation, let's switch gears and take a glance at it.

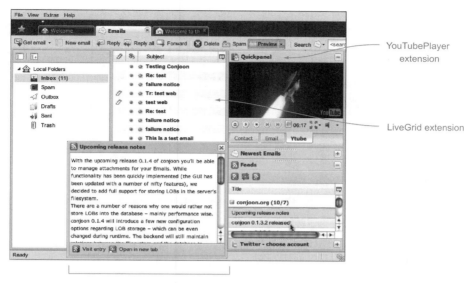

YouTubePlayer
extension

LiveGrid extension

ToastWindow extension

Figure 1.1   conjoon is an open source personal information manager that's a great example of a web application that uses the Ext JS framework to manage a UI which uses 100 percent of the browser's viewport. You can download it at http://conjoon.org/.

1.1.1   Rich API documentation

With the 4.0 version of the framework, the API documentation is new and improved. When opening the API documentation for the first time, you get a sense of the framework's polish. Unlike competing frameworks, the Ext JS API documentation uses its own framework to present a clean and easy-to-use documentation tool that uses Ajax to provide the documentation.

We'll explore all of the features of the API and talk about some of the components used in this documentation tool. Figure 1.2 illustrates some of the components used in the Ext JS API documentation application.

The API documentation tool is chock-full of gooey GUI goodness and incorporates six of the most commonly used widgets, including the text input field, tree panel, tab panel, panel, and toolbar with embedded buttons.

> **History support**
> The Ext JS 4.0 documentation now includes browser history support. This means that you can use the browser's forward and back buttons to walk up and down your API documentation breadcrumbs.

You're probably wondering what all of these are and what they do. Let's take a moment to discuss these widgets before we move on.

Figure 1.2   The Ext JS API documentation contains a wealth of information and is a great resource for learning more about components and widgets.

The text input field is a widget that wraps the native browser text input form control, adding features such as validation. In the API documentation, it's used to perform live searches against the tree panel and is custom styled. We'll talk more about tab panels in chapter 4.

The tree panel widget displays hierarchical data visually in the form of a tree much like Windows Explorer displays your hard drive's folders. The tab panel provides a means to have multiple documents or components on the canvas but allows only one to be active at a time, though in the API documentation, it displays only one item.

The panel is a workhorse of Ext JS. It's flexible and contains many areas to display content, including the dock and the content body. The dock is where items like toolbars are typically placed, and the content body is the area where content or child widgets are typically rendered. In the case of the API documentation, the content body contains the documentation for the framework.

The `Toolbar` class provides a means to present commonly used UI components such as buttons and menus, but it can also contain, as in this case, any of the `Ext.form.Field` subclasses. You can think of the toolbar as a place for the common file-edit-view menus that you see in popular operating systems and desktop applications.

Using the API is a cinch. To view a document, click the class node on the tree. Doing so invokes an Ajax request to fetch the documentation for the desired class. Each document for the classes is an HTML fragment (not a full HTML page).

So the documentation is thorough. But what about rapid application development? Can Ext JS accelerate your development cycles?

1.1.2   *Rapid development with prebuilt widgets*

Ext JS can help you jump from conception to prototype because it offers many of the required UI elements already built and ready for integration. Having these UI widgets prebuilt, instead of having to engineer them, saves you a lot of time. In many cases, the UI controls are highly customizable and can be modified to your application's needs.

1.2   *What you need to know*

Although being an expert in web application development isn't required to develop with Ext JS, developers should have some core competencies before attempting to write code with the framework.

The first of these skills is a basic understanding of Hypertext Markup Language (HTML) and Cascading Style Sheets (CSS). It's important to have some experience with these technologies because Ext JS, like any other JavaScript UI library, uses HTML and CSS to build its UI controls and widgets. Although its widgets may look like and mimic typical modern operating system controls, it all boils down to HTML and CSS in the browser.

Because JavaScript is the glue that holds Ajax together, we recommend you have a solid foundation in JavaScript programming. Again, you needn't be an expert, but you should have a good grasp of key concepts such as arrays, references, and scope. It's a plus if you're familiar with object-oriented JavaScript fundamentals such as objects, classes, and prototypal inheritance. If you're new to JavaScript, you're in luck. Java-Script has existed nearly since the dawn of the internet. An excellent place to start is W3Schools.com, which offers a lot of free online tutorials and even has sandboxes for you to play with JavaScript online. You can visit them at http://w3schools.com/JS/.

If you need to develop code for the server side, you must have a server-side solution for Ext JS to interact with as well as a way to store data. To persist data, you'll need to know how to interact with a database or filesystem via your server-side language of choice.

Naturally, the range of solutions available is quite large. For this book, we won't focus on a specific language. Instead, we'll use online resources at http://ExtJSinaction.com, where we've done the server-side work for you. This way, all you have to focus on is learning Ext JS. Along the way, we'll provide specific API URLs for you to use.

We'll begin our exploration of Ext JS with a bird's-eye view of the framework, where you'll learn about the categories of functionality.

1.3   *A tour of the Ext JS widgets*

The story of Ext JS main codebase begins in early 2010, during the development of Sencha Touch, the world's first HTML5 mobile framework (released in November 2010). Sencha Touch brought forth the base underpinnings, known as Sencha Platform (see figure 1.3), which contains many of the critical features that Ext JS and Sencha Touch both use. Such common features include DOM and event management, the Component model, and layouts, all of which we'll be diving into later in this book.

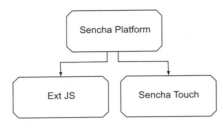

Figure 1.3   Ext JS 4.0 and Sencha
Touch both branch off of Sencha
Platform, a common base for the Sencha
family of HTML5 frameworks.

The Ext JS framework provides not only UI widgets but also a host of other features. These fall into seven major areas of purpose: core, UI components, web remoting, data services, drag-and-drop, draw and charts, and general utilities. Figure 1.4 illustrates the seven areas of purpose.

Knowing what the different areas of purpose are and what they do will give you an edge when developing applications, so we'll take a moment to discuss them.

CORE
The first feature set is the Ext JS core, which comprises many basic features such as Ajax communication, DOM manipulation, and event management. Everything else is dependent on the core of the framework, but the core isn't dependent on anything else.

UI COMPONENTS
The UI components contain all of the widgets that interface with the user.

WEB REMOTING
Web remoting is a means for JavaScript to remotely execute method calls that are defined and exposed on the server, which is commonly known as a remote procedure call (RPC). It's convenient for development environments where you'd like to expose your server-side methods to the client and not worry about all of the fuss of Ajax method management. This package is known as Ext Direct.

DATA SERVICES
The data services section takes care of all your data needs, which include fetching, parsing, and loading information into stores. With the Ext JS data services classes you can read Array, XML, and JavaScript Serialized Object Notation (JSON), which is a

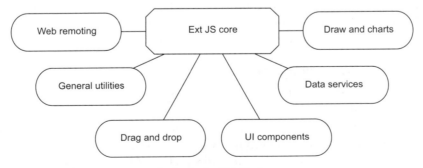

Figure 1.4   The seven areas of purpose for Ext JS classes

data format that's quickly becoming the standard for client-to-server communication. Stores typically feed UI components.

DRAW AND CHARTS

This all-new package encompasses the Ext JS cross-browser drawing engine compatible with Vector Markup Language (VML) and Scalable Vector Graphics (SVG). With Draw, you can generate your own data visualizations, but its primary purpose is to act as a foundation for the Charting package. The Charting package comes complete with many popular charts including Cartesian (Bar, Line, Column, and so on), Pie, Area, Scatter, and others.

> **Get your JSON on!**
> Even though JSON has been around for many years, if this is the first time you've heard of it we encourage you to visit http://json.org, the go-to source for information on this ubiquitous data exchange format. If you're interested in learning how to implement JSON in your server-side language of choice, there are a ton of JSON implementations, most of which are documented and explained online. We suggest searching Google using a query like "PHP JSON."

DRAG-AND-DROP

Drag-and-drop is like a mini-framework inside Ext JS, where you can apply drag-and-drop capabilities to an Ext JS component or any HTML element on the page. It includes all the necessary members to manage the entire gamut of drag-and-drop operations. Drag-and-drop is a complex topic; we'll spend the entirety of chapters 13 and 14 on this subject alone.

UTILITIES

The utilities section consists of cool utility classes that help you more easily perform some of your routine tasks. An example is `Ext.util.Format`, which allows you to format or transform data easily. Another neat utility is the CSS singleton, which lets you create, update, swap, and remove style sheets as well as request the browser to update its rule cache.

Now that you have a general understanding of the framework's major areas of functionality, let's look at commonly used UI widgets that Ext JS has to offer.

1.3.1 Containers and layouts at a glance

Even though we'll cover these topics in detail in chapter 3, let's spend a little time here talking about containers and layouts. The terms *container* and *layout* are used extensively throughout this book, and we want to make sure you have at least a basic understanding of them before we continue. Afterward, we'll begin our exploration of visual components of the UI library.

CONTAINERS

Containers are widgets that can manage one or more child items. A child item is generally any widget or component that's managed by a container or parent; thus the parent-child paradigm. You've already seen this in action in the API. The tab panel is a

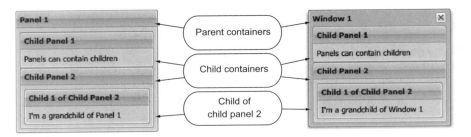

Figure 1.5   Here you see two parent `Containers`, `Panel` (left) and `Window` (right), managing child items, which include nested children.

container that manages one or more child items, which can be accessed via tabs. Please remember this term, because you'll use it a lot when you start to learn more about how to use the UI portion of the framework.

LAYOUTS

Layouts are implemented by a container to visually organize the child items in the container's content body. Ext JS has a whopping 33 layouts in the library! The good news is that you only have to learn 13 of them, which we'll go into in great detail about in chapter 5, where we show the ins and outs of each layout.

Now that you have a high-level understanding of containers and layouts, let's look at some containers in action. In figure 1.5 you see two subclasses of `Container`—`Panel` and `Window`—each engaged in parent-child relationships, demonstrating the power of the `Container` class and various layouts.

The `Panel` (left) and `Window` (right) in figure 1.5 each manage two child items. Child Panel 1 of each parent container contains HTML. The children with the title Child Panel 2 manage one child panel each using AutoLayout, which is the default container layout. This parent-child relationship is the crux of all the UI management of Ext JS and will be reinforced and referenced repeatedly throughout this book.

You learned that containers manage child items and use layouts to visually organize them. Now that you have these important concepts down, we'll see and discuss other containers in action.

1.3.2   *Other containers in action*

You saw the `Panel` and `Window` subclasses used when you learned about `Containers`. Figure 1.6 shows some other commonly used subclasses of `Container`.

In figure 1.6 you see the form panel, tab panel, window, toolbar, and field container widgets. The form panel works with the `Basic Form` class to wrap fields and other child items with a `form` element. All of these widgets are contained by an instance of `Ext.window.Window`.

You'll spend some time building a complex UI in chapter 6, where you'll learn more about form panels. For now, let's move on to see what data-presentation widgets the framework has to offer.

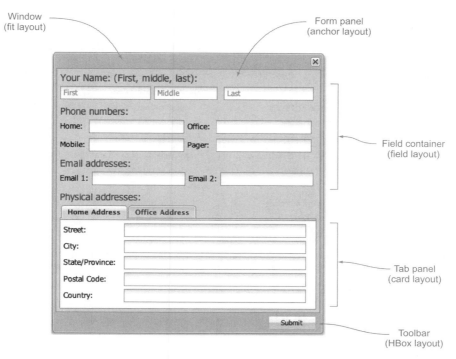

Figure 1.6 Commonly used subclasses of `Container`—`FormPanel`, `TabPanel`, `FieldContainer`, and `Toolbar`—and the layouts used to compose this UI window. We'll build this in chapter 6, when you learn about forms.

1.3.3   *Data-bound views*

You've already learned that the data services portion of the framework is responsible for the loading and parsing of data. Ext JS 4.0 has a lot of widgets that are bound to data stores, known as *views*. Many of the views that you'll deploy include the data view, grid panel, and tree panel. If your application requires charts, you'll be pleased to learn that all of the charts in the framework are also considered views and are bound to data stores. Figure 1.7 shows the Ext JS grid panel in action.

The newly refactored `GridPanel` is a subclass of `Panel` and presents data in a table-like format, but its functionality extends far beyond that of a traditional table, offering sortable, resizable, and movable column headers and selection models such as `RowSelectionModel` and `CellSelectionModel`. You can customize its look and feel and couple it with a paging toolbar to allow large datasets to be segmented and displayed in pages. It contains many features and plug-ins, allowing you to do tasks such as edit by row or cell, or lock a column. The data view shown in figure 1.8 renders photos and other bits of data for various phones on the market.

The `DataView` class consumes data from a store, paints it onscreen using a class known as `XTemplate`, and provides a simple selection model. The Ext JS XTemplate is an HTML fragment-generation utility that allows you to create a template with

Last Name	DOB	Email
Avery	08/28/1942	ultrices.a@luctus.org
Ballard	01/06/1976	sem@infaucibusorci.edu
Bradshaw	11/09/1974	facilisis.facilisis@Aeneane...
Callahan	06/22/1949	cursus@vitaemauris.com
Carrillo	03/14/1988	cursus.Nunc.mauris@vellec...
Charles	11/16/1973	molestie@convallis.edu
Chavez	05/17/1970	risus.In.mi@nonlacinia.edu
Chen	12/22/1975	Sed.congue.elit@pedeNunc...
Christian	10/27/1960	sollicitudin.orci@enimEtia...
Cline	11/29/1958	sed.pede@Integertincidunt...
Colon	06/29/1975	felis.Nulla@convallis.edu
Dillon	10/05/1942	quam.elementum@elitelit...

Figure 1.7   The grid panel as seen in the Buffered Grid example in the Ext JS SDK

Figure 1.8   The data view as demonstrated in the Ext JS SDK examples

placeholders for data elements, which can be filled in by individual records in a store and stamped out on the DOM.

Gone is the list view widget!

If you're coming from Ext JS 3, you may wonder where the list view widget is. The simple answer is that the list view, providing faster table rendering in Ext JS 3.0, was removed from 4.0, in favor of refactoring the grid panel for much faster performance.

The grid panel and data view are essential tools for painting data onscreen, but they do have one major limitation: they can show only lists of records and can't display hierarchical data. This is where the tree panel fills the gap.

Figure 1.9 An Ext JS tree, which is an example from the Ext JS SDK

1.3.4 *Make like a tree panel and leaf*

The tree panel widget is an exception to the list of UI widgets that consume data in that it doesn't consume data from a data store. Instead, it consumes hierarchical data via the use of the `TreeStore` class. Figure 1.9 shows an example of an Ext JS tree panel widget. Here, the tree panel is being used to display the parent-child data inside the directory of an installation of the framework.

For Ext JS 4.0, it has been completely rebuilt and is now a close cousin to the grid panel. Figure 1.10 demonstrates the versatility of the new tree panel.

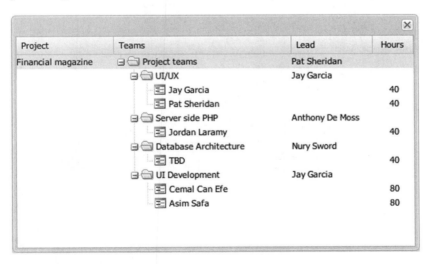

Figure 1.10 A tree panel with columns

You already saw text fields when we discussed containers. Next, we'll look at some of the other input fields that the framework has to offer.

1.3.5 Form input fields

Ext JS has a palette of eight input fields. They range from simple text fields, as you've already seen, to complex fields such as the ComboBox and the HTML Editor. Figure 1.11 shows the Ext JS form field widgets available out of the box.

As you can see in figure 1.11, some of the form input fields look like stylized versions of their native HTML counterparts. The similarities end there, though. With the Ext JS form fields, there's much more than meets the eye.

Each of the Ext JS fields (except for the HTML Editor) includes a suite of utilities to perform actions such as getting and setting values, marking the field as invalid, resetting, and performing validations against the field. You can apply custom validation to the field via regex or custom validation methods, giving you complete control over the data being entered into the form. The fields can validate data as it's being entered, providing live feedback to the user.

TEXTFIELD AND TEXTAREA

The `TextField` and `TextArea` classes can be considered extensions of their generic HTML counterparts that include extra features like validation. The `TextField` class is the base for many other complex widgets, such as the ComboBox, Number field, and Time field.

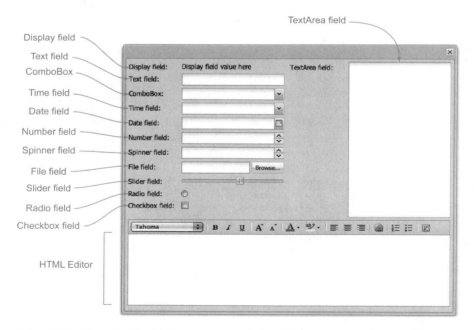

Figure 1.11 The out-of-the-box form elements displayed in an encapsulating window

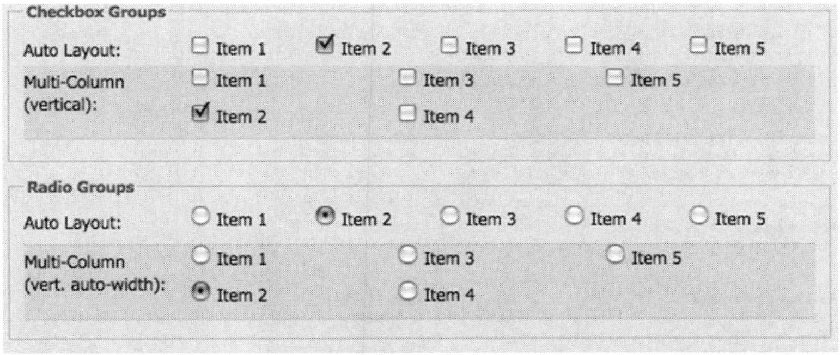

Figure 1.12 An example of the `Checkbox` **and** `RadioGroup` **convenience classes in action with automatic layouts**

RADIO AND CHECKBOX

Like the text field, radio and checkbox fields are extensions of the out-of-the-box HTML radio and checkbox, but they include all of the Ext JS element management goodness and have convenience classes to assist with the creation of checkbox and radio groups with automatic layout management. Figure 1.12 shows a small sample of how the Ext JS `CheckboxGroup` and `RadioGroup` classes can be configured with complex layouts.

HTML EDITOR

The HTML Editor is WYSIWYG, like the text area on steroids. The HTML Editor uses existing browser HTML editing capabilities and can be considered somewhat of a black sheep when it comes to fields. There's much more to discuss about this field, which we're going to save for chapter 6. But for now, let's circle back to `ComboBox` and its subclass, `TimeField`.

TRIGGERFIELD FAMILY OF FIELDS

The `TriggerField` class is the base class responsible for rendering a button to the right of a text field. Its subclasses are broken up into two groups, pickers and spinners. Included in the list of pickers are the ComboBox and the date field. The spinners include the spinner and number fields.

The ComboBox is easily the most complex and configurable form input field. It can mimic traditional option drop-down boxes or can be configured to use remote datasets via the data store. It can be configured to autocomplete text (known as *type-ahead*) entered by the user and to perform remote or local filtering of data. It can also be configured to use your own instance of an Ext JS XTemplate to display a custom list in the drop-down area, known as the *bound list*. Figure 1.13 shows an example of a custom ComboBox in action, being used to search the Ext JS forums..

The ComboBox here shows information like the post title, date, and author, and a snippet of the post in the list box. Because some of the dataset ranges are so large, it's configured to use a paging toolbar, allowing users to page through the resulting data.

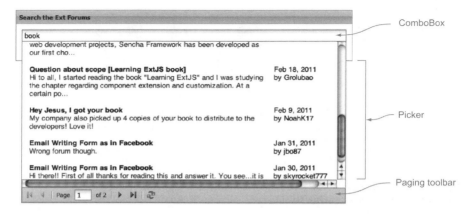

Figure 1.13   A custom ComboBox, which includes an integrated paging toolbar, as shown in the downloadable Ext JS examples

Because the ComboBox is so configurable, you could also include image references to the resulting dataset, which can be applied to the resulting rendered data.

Here we are, on the last stop of our UI tour. Now let's take a peek at some of the other UI components that work anywhere.

1.3.6   *Other widgets*

A bunch of UI controls stand out that aren't major components but that play supporting roles in the grander scheme of a UI. Look at figure 1.14 for a palette of the various widgets rendered onscreen.

You've learned how Ext JS can help you get the job done through a large palette of widgets. You've learned that you could elect to use Ext JS to build an application without touching an ounce of HTML. You also got a top-down view of the framework, which included a UI tour. All of the material discussed thus far existed for Ext JS 3.0. Let's take a moment to discuss what's new in Ext JS 4.0.

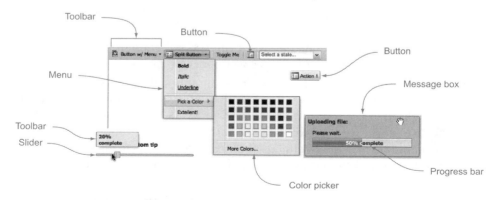

Figure 1.14   Miscellaneous UI widgets and controls

1.4 What's new in Ext JS 4.0

We aren't exaggerating when we say that Ext JS 4.0 is a revolution for JavaScript frameworks. There are so many enhancements to the framework that it's sometimes hard to grasp all that's changed. A lot of the changes are beneath the presentation layer, in the deepest, darkest caverns of the Ext JS codebase, a place where you rarely venture due to its sometimes mind-bending complexity.

Next, we'll look at some of the most drastic transformations that the framework has undergone. If you have experience in version 3.0, you may have wondered why the size of the framework has grown. You'll learn the reason in the next few sections.

1.4.1 Poof goes the adapter layer!

Through the use of an adapter layer, Ext JS 2.0 and 3.0 were able to ride on top of the jQuery, Prototype, and YUI libraries. With Ext JS 4.0, this is no longer the case.

Though heralded by developers migrating from those libraries, the adapter layer has always been a source of contention for a number of reasons. The main issue with the adapter layer has been that the versions of the base libraries would change and introduce bugs into Ext JS.

Another well-known issue is the problem of framework namespace collision. Ext JS 1.0–3.0 added to JavaScript by injecting methods into the Function, String, and Array prototypes. Because other libraries took the same action with similar method names, Ext JS trampled on the changes that the base libraries made.

The Sencha development team made sure to prevent such collisions and sources of tension with other libraries by moving said features into the `Ext.util` namespace as String, Function, and Array singletons. With such changes, the Sencha team decided to remove the adapter layer and make Ext JS work alongside any other library, allowing you to use any version of those libraries without fear that an upgrade of those libraries would cause problems with your Ext JS code.

1.4.2 New class system

Ext JS 4.0 comes with an entirely new class system that includes features such as dependency injection and on-the-fly class loading, a must-have for internet-facing RIAs built with Ext JS 4.0.

Along with dynamic class loading comes the concept of *mixins*, a modern object-oriented programming pattern that allows for multiple inheritance. This concept has allowed the Sencha development team to be much more creative when developing the framework, reducing the amount of duplicate code while increasing the level of functionality and sometimes the ease of use for some classes and widgets.

> **Learn about mixins!**
> If you're new to the concept of mixins, the following article explains this programming concept very well: http://en.wikipedia.org/wiki/Mixin.

Although the new class system provides many new features, it comes at a cost: new patterns. The new class system promotes vastly different patterns compared to those of Ext JS 3.0 when it comes to instantiation or defining a class. These new patterns can make the learning curve for Ext JS 4.0 steeper, but rest assured that they'll allow you to be more creative with your application code.

Speaking of classes, Ext JS 4.0 has a completely refactored data class system, which we discuss next.

1.4.3   *Data package*

The all-new data package in Ext JS 4.0 can trace its origins back to Sencha Touch, which used terms such as *model* in place of *record*. The changes to the data package bring functionality and organization far beyond that of Sencha Touch, however.

The Ext JS 4.0 data package incorporates an explosion of classes, and it includes new members such as the LocalStorage proxy and tree store. The LocalStorage proxy allows data to be stored and retrieved using the browser's local storage feature, whereas the tree store replaces the Ext JS 3.0 tree loader, allowing you to do a lot more with trees than ever before.

The data package comes with added features, such as associations and validations, along with a well-thought-out reorganization of functionality. Figure 1.15 illustrates how features and functions of the data package are segmented and related. We'll be going over this package in greater detail later on; we just wanted to whet your appetite with some detail.

In Ext JS 4.0, models can directly use proxies, whereas they couldn't in previous versions of the framework. Likewise, validations and associations are now performed at the model level.

The data package has seen a lot of attention, but the layout namespace has seen a lot of refactoring love as well.

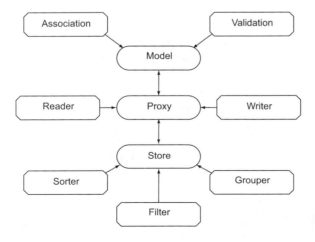

Figure 1.15   The Ext JS 4.0 data package

1.4.4 *Layouts: an explosion of code*

As we discussed earlier, Ext JS 4.0 comes jam-packed with 33 new layout managers, but there are only 13 that you need to be aware of. This is because layouts are broken up into two main areas of functionality: component and container layouts.

The component and container layouts play two completely different roles in the framework. Component layouts are responsible for arranging the HTML for components, whereas container layouts are responsible for managing the location and size of child components.

While we're on the topic of layouts, let's shed some light on the new docking system that Ext JS 4.0 brings to the table.

1.4.5 *New docking system*

Originating in Sencha Touch, panels in Ext JS can have widgets such as toolbars arranged on the outside of the area known as the *content body*, affording more UI arrangement flexibility than ever before with this widget. Figure 1.16 shows three toolbars docked on the top, bottom, and left of a panel. This arrangement wasn't possible with any previous versions of Ext JS without deep nesting of containers and layouts. This is all made possible via the component layout known as Dock.

Though using the Dock layout is something that you might be able to envision taking full advantage of, if your application uses grid panels what we're about to discuss next might excite you.

1.4.6 *Grid panel improvements*

The Sencha development team literally worked night and day on features like the grid panel, and the results show, especially after taking a good look at what's changed since Ext JS 3.0.

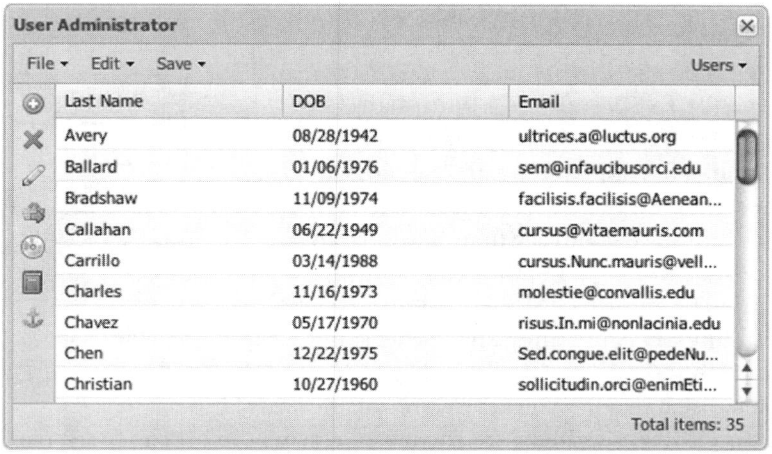

Figure 1.16 Demonstrating the new docking feature of the Ext JS panel

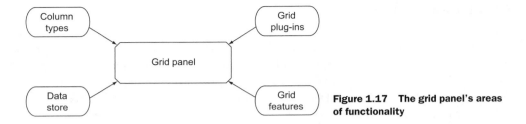

Figure 1.17 The grid panel's areas of functionality

Features new to the grid panel include what's known as the *infinite grid*, which allows you to paginate through large datasets without having to include a paging toolbar. Other new features include a reorganization of the namespace for better grouping of classes (see figure 1.17).

The grid area of code has been segmented by groups of code, including column types, plug-ins, and features. Even though not technically in the grid namespace, data Store is a supporting class for GridPanel, so we included it in figure 1.17.

This level of organization of the grid package means that you have more flexibility in configuring grid panels, allowing Ext JS to implement only code that's required. For instance, if you want to allow cell editing, you include the CellEditing plug-in in your grid panel configuration. Likewise, if you want to include drag-and-drop functionality, include the DragDrop plug-in.

Other bits of functionality were migrated to the so-called *feature namespace*, which is somewhat similar to plug-ins. We don't want to muddy the waters with details of how features work, but it's good to note that grid goodies like row grouping and providing a summary row of your data can be engaged only if you desire them to be.

As you just learned, the grid panel endured a lot of changes. The story of major change doesn't end here. The tree panel has undergone some serious changes as well!

1.4.7 *Tree panel now closer to grids*

The code for the Ext JS tree panel has stayed relatively the same for Ext JS versions 1.0 through 3.0, but the Ext JS 4.0 tree panel code has been completely rewritten. Applying a family tree analogy to the difference between the grid and tree panels in prior Ext JS versions, we could say that they were, at best, third cousins. In Ext JS 4.0, they're siblings!

As illustrated in figure 1.18, the grid and tree panels are siblings because they share the same superclass, meaning they share the same base code. The good news is that once you learn one of the

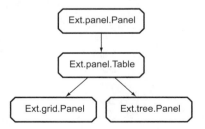

Figure 1.18 The tree and grid panels share the same superclass.

two, the learning curve is reduced for the other. Having the grid and tree panels share the same base code means that you can have things like columns in your tree views.

That said, the tree panel doesn't contain a lot of the functionality that the grid panel sports, such as the summary row plug-in or column locking. In addition, the tree panel must use the `TreeStore` class from the data package to manage and display hierarchical data.

We just covered two of the major data-bound views that have been with the framework since its early days. Next we'll tackle the all-new charting package.

1.4.8 Draw and charts

Charts were first introduced in Ext JS 3.0 with relatively little fanfare. There were two reasons for this. The first is that they were Flash-based charts repackaged from the YUI library. The second is that upgrades to the YUI packaged charts often lagged behind a few revisions, frustrating developers.

With Ext JS 4.0, the YUI charting package was tossed and rebuilt from scratch in two major sections. The first is Ext Draw, which is a mini-framework inside Ext JS that has its roots in lessons learned by RaphaelJS, a Sencha labs project for drawing in the browser using Vector Markup Language (VML), Scalable Vector Graphics (SVG), or Canvas.

The second is the charting package, which uses Ext Draw as a base. With the new charting package come two new graphs: scatter and radar. Figure 1.19 shows the radar chart.

We've discussed many elements from the UI widgets, but there are others under the hood that are worth mentioning.

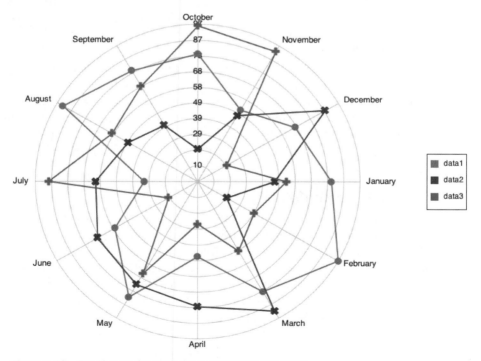

Figure 1.19 Ext JS contains new charts that don't use Flash.

1.4.9 *New CSS styling architecture*

Ext JS uses Sass (Syntactically Awesome Stylesheets) to allow both the Sencha development team and users to create custom themes. This means that if you want to change your entire color scheme, you can do so with relative ease if you know Sass.

> **Learn more about Sass**
>
> Sass has taken the world of style sheet management by storm and has arguably revolutionized how people style their web pages and apps. To learn more about this utility, check out *Sass and Compass in Action* (Manning, 2013).

Custom style sheets and widgets enable you to develop applications with Ext JS. They need something to tie them together, and with Ext JS 4.0, Sencha has delivered such a tool.

1.4.10 *New MVC architecture*

One of the things that Ext JS has lacked is a solid pattern for developing applications with the framework. This isn't the case with Ext JS 4.0. Using the lessons learned with Sencha Touch, Ext JS 4.0 comes with a solid MVC architecture that lets you develop code using the tried-and-true MVC pattern. We'll go over this in great detail in the last two chapters of this book.

The new stuff for Ext JS 4.0 doesn't apply just to what can be used in the browser. The framework comes with other tools that you can use in your application build process.

1.4.11 *Bundled packaging tool*

Earlier, you learned that Ext JS 4.0 comes with a dynamic class-loading system. The class loader is a great solution for internet-based Ext JS applications, but intranet-based applications often have higher demands on response times, which is why Sencha now includes its popular JSBuilder packaging and minification tool, the same tool it uses to build and package Ext JS and Sencha Touch.

We've spent a lot of time looking at what's new in the framework. It's time that you download it and begin using it.

1.5 *Downloading and configuring*

Even though downloading Ext JS is a simple process, configuring a page to include Ext JS isn't as simple as referencing a single file in HTML. Now you'll learn about configuration, the folder hierarchy, and what folders are and what they do.

The first thing you need to do is get the source code. To do so, visit www.sencha .com/products/ExtJS/download/. The downloaded file will be the SDK in zip format, which weighs in at over 30 MB in size. We'll explain why this file is so large in a moment. Now extract the file to a place where you serve JavaScript. To use Ajax and view the documentation without having to visit sencha.com, you're going to need a web server. We typically use Apache configured locally on our computer, which is free and cross-platform, but IIS for Windows will do.

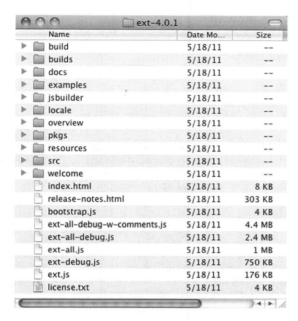

Figure 1.20　A view of the Ext JS SDK contents

If you're like us, you probably checked the size of the files extracted from the downloaded SDK zip file. If your jaw dropped, feel free to pick it back up. Yes, over 30 MB is rather large for a JavaScript framework. Pay no attention to the size for now; figure 1.20 shows what was extracted.

Looking at the contents of the SDK, you see a lot of stuff. The reason there are so many folders and files is that the downloadable package contains a few copies of the entire codebase and CSS. It's done this way because you have the freedom to build or use Ext JS any way you see fit. Table 1.1 explains what each of the folders is and what each one does.

Table 1.1　The contents of the Ext JS SDK

Folder	What it does
build	Contains the necessary scripts to use JSBuilder to concatenate and minify your application code.
builds	Contains three different builds of the Ext JS framework. First is the sandbox version, where you can run Ext JS 4.0 inline with Ext JS 3.0 to mitigate migration risk. The second is the core of the library. The core contains DOM management and various utilities in the framework. The last item is Ext JS foundation, which is the base of the Ext JS framework.
docs, overview, and welcome	The docs folder holds the full API documentation, and the overview directory contains a quick introduction to the framework. The welcome folder contains the necessary resources to support the framework's splash screen, which you make visible by double-clicking index.html.

Table 1.1   The contents of the Ext JS SDK *(continued)*

Folder	What it does
examples	Holds all of the example source code.
jsbuilder	Contains the binaries and source code for JSBuilder.
locale	Contains 45 spoken language translations to replace various texts in the framework.
pkgs	Contains the entire framework, in minified and concatenated chunks to allow for browser consumption over slower connections. It's broken up into foundation, DOM, classes, and extras. Classes is by far the largest of the sets, containing all of the widgets and store code, and extras contains utilities like JSON and the Ext JS MVC application.
resources	Contains the CSS, images, and Sass source code.
ext*.js	There are various ext*.js files in the root of the Ext JS distribution. Know that anything with "-debug" in the name is a nonminified version of that file. These can be broken down into two groups. First are ext.js and ext-debug.js. These two contain the foundation of the framework. Include these when you want to use the Ext JS class loader. The ext-all* files are the entire library packaged into one file. You'll use ext-all-debug for the exercises.

Although there are quite a few files and folders in the distribution, you need only a few of them to get the framework running in your browser. Now is a good time to look at using Ext JS for the first time.

1.6   *Take it for a test drive*

For this exercise you're going to create an instance of `Ext.form.Panel`, which will be rendered inside an `Ext.window.Window`. The form panel will contain two text input fields and a button to provide some feedback once clicked. The following listing demonstrates how you'll bootstrap the application code.

Listing 1.1   Creating hello_world.html

```
<link rel="stylesheet" type="text/css"
    href="/ExtJS/resources/css/ext-all.css" />
<script type="text/javascript"
    src="/ExtJS/ext-all-debug.js"></script>
<script type="text/javascript" src='hello_world.js'>
</script>
```

Listing 1.1 shows the HTML markup for a typical Ext JS–only setup, which includes the concatenated CSS file, ext-all.css, and the required JavaScript file, ext-all-debug.js. Last, it includes your soon-to-be-created hello_world.js file.

The listing uses /ExtJS as the absolute path to the framework code. Be sure to change it if your path is different. Create a script tag pointing to the hello_world.js file, which will contain your main JavaScript code.

Next you're going to create the hello_world.js file in two phases. The first, shown in the next listing, is the construction of the form panel and its related child components.

Listing 1.2 Creating hello_world.js

```
var tpl = Ext.create('Ext.Template', [                    ◄─┐   Creates instance
    'Hello {firstName} {lastName}!',                    ❶   of Template
    ' Nice to meet you!'
]);
var formPanel = Ext.create('Ext.form.FormPanel', {        ◄─┐   Configures
    itemId      : 'formPanel',                          ❷   form panel
    frame       : true,
    layout      : 'anchor',
    defaultType : 'textfield',
    defaults    : {
        anchor     : '-10',
        labelWidth : 65
    },
    items       : [                                        ◄─┐   Sets up two
        {                                               ❸   input fields
            fieldLabel : 'First name',
            name       : 'firstName'
        },
        {
            fieldLabel : 'Last name',
            name       : 'lastName'
        }
    ],
    buttons : [
        {                                               ❹   Configures
            text    : 'Submit',                        ◄─┘   feedback button
            handler : function() {
                var formPanel = this.up('#formPanel'),
                    vals      = formPanel.getValues(),
                    greeting  = tpl.apply(vals);

                Ext.Msg.alert('Hello!', greeting);      ◄─┐   Shows Ext.Msg
            }                                           ❺   alert dialog
        }
    ]
});
```

Listing 1.2 shows the code needed to configure a form panel that contains two input fields and a button. First, you create an instance of `Ext.Template` ❶, which you'll use later to create a dynamic dialog text body. Next, you create an instance of `Ext.form .FormPanel` ❷, which contains two text input fields ❸ and a button ❹. The button is configured with a handler that uses the template you configured earlier and values from the form panel to display an `Ext.Msg` alert dialog ❺.

You're almost done with the "Hello world" example. Your form hasn't been rendered onscreen yet. For this, you need to call `Ext.onReady`. You'll also wrap the form panel inside the window to demonstrate the flexibility of the framework in the next listing.

Listing 1.3   Putting it all together

```
Ext.onReady(function() {

    Ext.create('Ext.window.Window', {
        height    : 125,
        width     : 200,
        closable  : false,
        title     : 'Input needed.',
        border    : false,
        layout    : 'fit',
        items     : formPanel
    }).show();

});
```

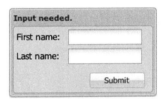

❶ Calls Ext.onReady

❷ Renders window

❸ Includes form panel

Listing 1.3 contains code to render your form panel inside an Ext JS window. You first call `Ext.onReady` ❶ and pass in an anonymous function, which gets executed when Ext JS deems that the browser is ready to have the DOM manipulated. Inside this anonymous function is where you create your `Ext.window.Window` instance ❷, which contains your `FormPanel` instance ❸. Figure 1.21 shows the example rendered with the child form panel.

Figure 1.21   The example window rendering the form panel

Figure 1.22 shows the "Hello world" example rendered onscreen. To exercise the Submit button handler you need to enter data in the two input fields and click the Submit button. If you've done everything correctly, you should see the `Ext.Msg` alert dialog using the data that you placed in the form.

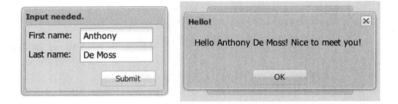

Figure 1.22   The final result of the "Hello world" example

There you have it! You just used Ext JS to render a form panel with related input fields and a button inside an Ext JS window. Though this example was simple in nature, it shows you the power of Ext JS.

1.7   Summary

In this introduction to Ext JS, you learned how it can be used to build robust web applications. You also learned how it measures up against other popular frameworks on the market and that it's the only UI-based framework to contain UI-centric support classes such as the Component, Container, and Layout models.

You explored many of the core UI widgets that the framework provides and learned that the many prebuilt widgets help rapid application development efforts. We also investigated some of the changes that Ext JS 4.0 has implemented, such as all-new non-Flash charts and the MVC package.

Finally, you saw how to download and set up the framework with each base framework. You created a "Hello world" example of how to use an Ext JS window to render a form panel with a button that displays an `Ext.Msg` alert dialog with some simple JavaScript.

In the chapters to follow, you'll explore how Ext JS works from the inside out. This knowledge will empower you to make the best decisions when building well-constructed UIs and better enable you to use the framework effectively. This will be a fun journey.

DOM manipulation

This chapter covers
- Bootstrapping JavaScript code
- Managing DOM elements with `Ext.Element`
- Loading HTML fragments via Ajax
- Achieving a highlight effect on an HTML element
- Implementing templates and XTemplates

When working on applications, you may think metaphorically to help you develop parallels for concepts in your mind. For instance, we like to think of the timing of an application's launch as similar to that of the space shuttle's launch, where timing can mean the difference between success and frustration. Knowing when to initialize your JavaScript is critical when dealing with anything that manipulates the DOM. In this chapter you'll learn how to launch your JavaScript using Ext JS to ensure your application code initializes at the right time on each browser. Then we'll discuss using `Ext.Element` to manipulate the DOM.

As you know, DOM manipulation is one of the tasks that web developers are required to code for most of the time. Whether it's the addition or removal of elements, I'm sure you've felt the pain of performing these tasks with the out-of-the-box

JavaScript methods. After all, DHTML has been at the center of dynamic web pages for ages now.

We'll look at the heart of Ext JS, known as the Ext.Element class, which is a robust, cross-browser, DOM element-management suite. You'll learn to use Ext.Element to add nodes to and remove them from the DOM, and you'll see how it makes this task easier.

Once you're familiar with the Ext.Element class, you'll learn how to use templates to stamp out HTML fragments into the DOM. We'll also dive deep into the use of the XTemplate, and you'll learn how to use it to easily loop through data and inject behavior-modification logic while you're at it. This is going to be a fun chapter. Before you can begin coding, we need to discuss how to bootstrap Ext JS–enabled web applications.

2.1 *Let Ext JS kick off your code*

Since the early days, to initialize JavaScript most developers would add an onLoad attribute to the <body> tag of the HTML page that's loading:

```
<body onLoad="initMyApp();">
```

Although this method of invoking JavaScript works, it's not ideal for Ajax-enabled Web 2.0 sites or applications because the onLoad code is generally fired at different times for different browsers. For instance, some browsers fire this method when the DOM is ready and all content has been loaded and rendered by the browser. For Web 2.0, this isn't a good thing, because the code generally wants to start managing and manipulating DOM elements when the DOM is ready but before any images are loaded. Here's where you can achieve the right balance of timing and performance. We like to call this the "sweet spot" in the page-loading cycle.

Like many things in the world of browser development, each browser generally has its own way of knowing when its DOM nodes can be manipulated.

Native browser solutions are available for detecting that the DOM is ready, but they aren't implemented uniformly across each browser. For instance, Firefox and Opera fire the DOMContentLoaded event. Internet Explorer requires a script tag to be placed in the document with a defer attribute, which fires when its DOM is ready. WebKit fires no event but sets the document.readyState property to complete, so a loop must be executed to check for that property and fire off a custom event to tell your code that the DOM is ready. Boy, what a mess!

Luckily, you have Ext.onReady, which solves the timing issues and serves as the base from which to launch your application-specific code. Ext JS achieves cross-browser compatibility by detecting on which browser the code is executing and managing the detection of the DOM-ready state, executing your code at just the right time.

Ext.onReady is a reference to Ext.EventManager.onDocumentReady and accepts three parameters: the method to invoke, the scope from which to call the method, and any options to pass to the method. The second parameter, scope, is used when you're calling an initialization method that requires execution within a specific scope.

> ### Getting a handle on scope
>
> The concept of scope is something that many JavaScript developers wrestle with early in their careers. It's a concept that every JavaScript developer should master. You'll find a great resource to learn about scope at www.digital-web.com/articles/scope_in_javascript/.

All of your Ext JS–based JavaScript code can be anywhere below (after) the inclusion of the Ext JS script. This positioning is important because JavaScript files are requested and loaded synchronously. Trying to call any Ext JS methods before Ext JS is defined in the namespace will cause an exception, and your code will fail to launch. Here's an example of using `Ext.onReady` to fire up an Ext JS `MessageBox` alert window:

```
Ext.onReady(function() {
    Ext.Msg.alert('Hello', 'The DOM is ready!');
});
```

In the preceding example, you pass what's known as an *anonymous* function to `Ext.onReady` as the only parameter, which will be executed when the DOM is ready to be manipulated. Your anonymous function contains a line of code to invoke an Ext JS `MessageBox`, as shown in figure 2.1.

Figure 2.1 The result of your `Ext.onReady` call, an `Ext.MessageBox` window

An anonymous function is any function that has no variable reference to it or key reference in an object. `Ext.onReady` registers your anonymous function, which is to be executed when the internal `docReadyEvent` event is fired. In short, an event is like a message that something has occurred. A listener is a method that's registered to be executed, or called, when that event occurs, or fires.

Ext JS fires this `docReadyEvent` event when it finds *exactly* the right time (remember the sweet spot) in the page-loading cycle to execute your anonymous method and any other registered listeners. If the concept of events sounds a bit confusing, don't be alarmed. Event management is a complex topic, and we'll cover it later in chapter 3.

We can't stress enough the importance of using `Ext.onReady`. All of the example code *has to be* launched this way. Moving forward, if `Ext.onReady` isn't explicitly detailed in the examples, please assume that you must launch the code with it and wrap the example code in the following manner:

```
Ext.onReady(function() {
  // ... Some code here ...
});
```

Now that you're comfortable with using `Ext.onReady` to launch your code, let's spend some time exploring the `Ext.Element` class. This is essential knowledge that's used everywhere in the framework where DOM manipulation occurs.

2.2 Managing DOM elements with Ext.Element

All JavaScript-based web applications revolve around a nucleus, which is the HTML `Element`. JavaScript's access to the DOM nodes gives you the power and flexibility to perform any action against the DOM you wish. Such actions could include adding, deleting, styling, or changing the contents of any node in the document. The traditional method to reference a DOM node by ID is as follows:

```
var myDiv = document.getElementById('someDivId');
```

The `getElementById` method lets you perform basic tasks such as changing the `innerHTML` or styling and assigning a CSS class. But what if you want to do more with the node, such as manage its events, apply a style on mouse click, or replace a single CSS class? You'll have to manage all of your own code and constantly update to make sure your code is fully cross-browser compatible. We can't think of another thing that we'd want to spend less time on. Thankfully, Ext JS takes care of this for you.

2.2.1 The heart of the framework

Let's turn to the `Ext.Element` class, which is known to many in the Ext JS community as the heart of the framework because it plays a role in every UI widget and can be generally accessed by the `getEl` method or the `el` property.

The `Ext.Element` class is a full DOM element-management suite, which includes a treasure chest of utilities, enabling the framework to work its magic on the DOM and provide the robust UI that we've come to enjoy. This toolset and all of its power are available to you, the end developer.

Because of its design, its capabilities aren't relegated to simple management of DOM elements but to performing complex tasks such as managing dimensions, alignments, and coordinates with relative ease. You can also easily update an element via Ajax, manage child nodes, animate, enjoy full event management, and much more.

2.2.2 Using Ext.Element for the first time

Using `Ext.Element` is easy and makes some of the hardest tasks simple. To take advantage of `Ext.Element`, you need to set up a base page. Set up a page where you include the Ext JS and CSS, as we discussed in chapter 1. Next, include the following CSS and HTML:

```
<style type="text/css">
    .myDiv {
        border: 1px solid #AAAAAA;
        width: 200px;
        height: 35px;
        cursor: pointer;
        padding: 2px 2px 2px 2px;
```

```
        margin: 2px 2px 2px 2px;
    }
</style>
<div id='div1' class='myDiv'> </div>
```

With this code, you're setting the stage for this book's examples by ensuring your target div tags have specific dimensions and a border so you can clearly see them on the page. You include one div with the id of 'div1', which you'll use as a target. If you set up your page correctly, the stylized div should be clearly visible, as shown in figure 2.2. This figure shows the generic HTML box, which you'll use to exercise the fundamental Ext.Element methods.

> **NOTE**   All of the Ext.Element example code will reference the base page you just set up. If you're interested in watching changes to the DOM occur live, we suggest using the multiline Firebug text editor in Firefox with these examples. If you're unfamiliar with Firebug, you can learn about it at http://getfirebug .com/wiki. Or you can place these examples inside generic script blocks. Just be sure to use Ext.onReady.

According to the CSS, any div with the class myDiv is set to 35 pixels high and 200 pixels wide and looks a bit odd. Let's make that element perfectly square by setting the height to 200 pixels:

```
var myDiv1 = Ext.get('div1');
myDiv1.setHeight(200);
```

The execution of the previous two lines is pretty important. The first line uses Ext.get, to which you pass the string 'div1', and returns an instance of Ext.Element referenced by the variable myDiv1. Ext.get uses document.getElementById and wraps it with the Ext JS element-management methods.

Use your newly referenced instance of Ext.Element, myDiv1, and call its set-Height method, passing it an integer value of 200, which grows the box to 200 pixels tall. Alternatively, you could use its setWidth method to change the width of the element, but we'll skip that and jump to something more fun.

"Now it's a perfect square. Big deal!" you say. Well, suppose you change dimensions again; this time you'll use setSize. Make the width and height 350 pixels. Use the already created reference, myDiv1:

```
myDiv1.setSize(350, 350, {duration: 1, easing:'bounceOut'});
```

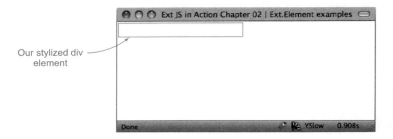

Our stylized div
element

Figure 2.2   Your base page with your stylized div ready for some Ext JS Element action

What happens when you execute this line of code? Does it animate and have a bouncing effect? That's better!

Essentially, the `setSize` method is the composite of `setHeight` and `setWidth`. For this method, you passed the target width and height, and an object with two properties, `duration` and `easing`. A third property, if defined, will make `setSize` animate the size transition of the element. If you don't care for animation, omit the third argument and the box will change size instantly, much like when you set the height.

Setting dimensions is a single facet of the many sides of element management with the `Element` class. Some of `Ext.Element`'s greatest power comes from its ease of use for full CRUD (create, read, update, and delete) of elements.

2.2.3 Creating child nodes

One of the great uses of JavaScript is the ability to manipulate the DOM, which includes the creation of DOM nodes. JavaScript provides many methods natively that give you this power. Ext JS conveniently wraps many of these methods with the `Ext.Element` class. Let's have some fun creating child nodes.

To create a child node, use `Element`'s `createChild` method:

```
var myDiv1 = Ext.get('div1');
myDiv1.createChild('Child from a string');
```

This code adds a string node to the `innerHtml` of your target `div`. What if you wanted to create an element? Easy as pie:

```
myDiv1.createChild('<div>Element from a string</div>');
```

This use of `createChild` will append a child `div` with the string `'Element from a string'` to the `innerHtml` of `div1`. We don't like to append children this way because we find the string representation of elements to be messy. Ext JS helps you with this problem by accepting a configuration object instead of a string:

```
myDiv1.createChild({
    tag  : 'div',
    html : 'Child from a config object'
});
```

Here, you're creating a child element by using a configuration object. You specify the `tag` property as `'div'` and `html` as a string. This technically does the same thing as the prior `createChild` implementation but is cleaner and self-documenting. What if you wanted to inject nested tags? With the configuration object approach, you can achieve this with ease:

```
myDiv1.createChild({
    tag        : 'div',
    id         : 'nestedDiv',
    style      : 'border: 1px dashed; padding: 5px;',
    children   : {
        tag    : 'div',
        html   : '...a nested div',
```

```
    style  : 'color: #EE0000; border: 1px solid'
  }
});
```

In this code you're creating one last child, with an id, a bit of styling applied, and a child element, which is a div with some more styling. Figure 2.3 illustrates what the changes to the div look like. You see all of the additions to myDiv1, including the live DOM view from Firebug, showing that you added a string node and three child divs, one of which has its own child div.

If you wanted to inject a child at the top of the list, you'd use the convenience method insertFirst, like this:

```
myDiv1.insertFirst({
    tag  : 'div',
    html : 'Child inserted as node 0 of myDiv1'
});
```

Element.insertFirst will always insert a new element at position 0, even when no child elements exist in the DOM structure.

If you want to target the insertion of a child node at a specific index, the create-Child method can take care of that task. All you need to do is pass it the reference of where to inject the newly created node, like this:

```
myDiv1.createChild({
    tag  : 'div',
    id   : 'removeMeLater',
    html : 'Child inserted as node 2 of myDiv1'
}, myDiv1.dom.childNodes[3]);
```

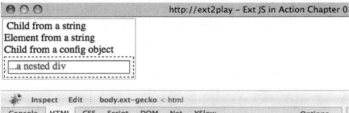
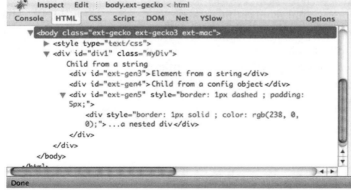

Figure 2.3 A composite of the element additions using `myDiv1.createChild`

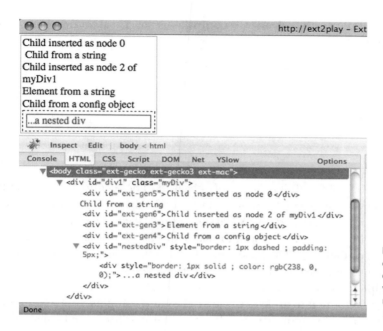

Figure 2.4   The results of the targeted DOM element insertions with `createChild` using an index and `insertFirst`

In this code, you're passing two arguments to `createChild`. The first is the configuration object representation of the newly created DOM element, and the second is the DOM reference of the target child node that `createChild` will use as the target to inject the newly created node. Please keep in mind the id that you set for this newly created item; you'll use it in a bit.

Notice that you're using `myDiv1.dom.childNodes`. `Ext.Element` gives you the opportunity to use all of the generic browser element-management goodness by means of the `dom` property.

> **NOTE** The `Element.dom` property is the same DOM object reference that's returned by `document.getElementById()`.

Figure 2.4 shows what the inserted nodes look like in both the page view and the DOM hierarchy using the Firebug DOM inspection tool. As you can see, the node insertions functioned as intended. You used `insertFirst` to inject a new node at the top of the list and `createChild` to inject a node above child node 3. Remember always to start with the number 0 instead of 1 when counting child nodes.

Adding is something that you do often as a web developer. After all, this is part of what DHTML is all about. But it's equally important to know how to remove something. Let's see how to remove some of the child elements using `Ext.Element`.

2.2.4   *Removing child nodes*

Removing nodes could be considered much easier than adding them. All you need to do is locate the node with Ext JS and call its `remove` method. To test out removal of child nodes, you'll start with a clean and controlled slate. Create a new page with the following HTML:

```
<div id='div1' class="myDiv">
    <div id='child1'>Child 1</div>
    <div class='child2'>Child 2</div>
    <div class='child3'>Child 3</div>
    <div id='child4'>Child 4 </div>
    <div>Child 5</div>
</div>
```

Examining this HTML, you find a parent div with the id of 'div1'. It has five direct descendants, the first of which has the id of 'child1'. The second and third children have no ids, but they have CSS classes of 'child2' and 'child3'. The fourth child element has an id of 'child4' and a CSS class of 'sameClass'. Likewise, it has a direct child with an id of "nestedChild1" and the same CSS class as its parent. The last child of div1 has no id or CSS class. The reason you have all this stuff going on is that you're going to start to use CSS selectors as well as directly target the ids of the elements.

In the examples where you add child nodes, you always reference the parent div (id='div1') by wrapping it in an Ext.Element class and using its create methods. To remove a child node, the approach is different. You need to specifically target the node that's to be removed. Using the new DOM structure, let's practice a few ways of doing this.

The first approach removes a child node from an already-wrapped DOM element. You'll create an instance of Ext.Element wrapping div1 and then use it to find its first child node using a CSS selector:

```
var myDiv1 = Ext.get('div1');
var firstChild = myDiv1.down('div:first-child');
firstChild.remove();
```

In this example, you create a reference to div1 using Ext.get. You then create another reference, firstChild, to the first child using the Element.down method. You pass a pseudo class selector, which causes Ext JS to query the DOM tree within the context of div1 for the first child, which is a div, and wrap it within an instance of Ext.Element.

The Element.down method queries the first-level DOM nodes for any given Ext.Element. It so happens that the element that's found is the one with the div id of 'child1'. You then call firstChild.remove, which removes that node from the DOM.

Here's how you could remove the last child from the list using selectors:

```
var myDiv1 = Ext.get('div1');
var lastChild = myDiv1.down('div:last-child');
lastChild.remove();
```

This example works similarly to the previous one. The biggest difference is that you use the selector 'div:last-child', which locates the last childNode for div1 and wraps it in an instance of `Ext.Element`. After that, you call `lastChild.remove`, and it's gone.

> **NOTE** CSS selectors are a powerful way of querying the DOM for items. Ext JS supports the CSS3 selector specification. If you're new to CSS selectors, we advise visiting the following W3C page, which has a plethora of information on selectors: http://mng.bz/0vmd.

What if you want to target an element by an `id`? You can use `Ext.get` to do your dirty work. This time, you'll create no reference and instead use *chaining* to take care of the job:

```
Ext.get('child4').remove();
```

Executing this code removes the child node with the `id` of `'child4'` and its child node. Always remember that removing a node with children will also remove its child nodes.

> **NOTE** If you'd like to read more about chaining, Dustin Diaz, an industry-leading developer, has an excellent article on his site at www.dustindiaz.com/javascript-chaining/.

The last task we'll look at is using `Ext.Element` to perform an Ajax request to load remote HTML fragments from the server and inject them into the DOM.

2.2.5 *Using Ajax with Ext.Element*

The `Ext.Element` class has the ability to perform an Ajax call to retrieve remote HTML fragments and inject those fragments into its `innerHTML`. You'll need to first write an HTML snippet to load:

```
<div>
    Hello there! This is an HTML fragment.
    <script type="text/javascript">
        Ext.getBody().highlight();
    </script>
</div>
```

In this HTML fragment, you have a simple `div` with an embedded script tag, which performs an `Ext.getBody` call. It uses chaining to execute the results of that call, to execute its `highlight` method. `Ext.getBody` is a convenient method to get a reference to the `document.body` wrapped by `Ext.Element`. Save this file as htmlFragment.html.

Next, you'll perform the load of this snippet:

```
Ext.getBody().load({
    url     : 'htmlFragment.html',
    scripts : true
});
```

In this snippet, you call the `load` method of the result of the `Ext.getBody` call; pass a configuration object specifying the `url` to fetch, which is the htmlFragment.html file; and set `scripts` to `true`. What happens when you execute this code? See figure 2.5.

Figure 2.5 Loading an HTML fragment into the document body

When you execute this code snippet, you'll see that the document body performs an Ajax request to retrieve your htmlFragment.html file. While the file is being retrieved, it shows a loading indicator. Once the request is complete, the HTML fragment is injected into the DOM. You then see the entire body element highlighted in yellow, which is an indication that your JavaScript was executed. Now you see that using the `Ext.Element.load` utility method is a great convenience compared to manually coding an `Ext.Ajax.request` call.

And there you have it. Adding elements to and removing elements from the DOM is a cinch when using `Ext.Element`. Ext JS has another way to make adding elements even simpler, especially if you have repeatable DOM structures to be placed in the DOM. We explore the `Template` and `XTemplate` utility classes next.

2.3   *Using templates and XTemplates*

The `Ext.Template` class is a powerful core utility that allows you to create an entire DOM hierarchy with slots that can be filled in later with data. Once you define a template you can use it to replicate one or more of the predefined DOM structures, with your data filling in the slots. Mastering templates will help you master UI widgets that use templates, such as the grid panel, data view, and ComboBox.

2.3.1   *Using templates*

You'll start out by creating an extremely simple template, and then you'll move on to create one that's much more complex:

```
var myTpl = Ext.create('Ext.Template' , "<div>Hello {0}.</div>");
myTpl.append(document.body, ['Marjan']);
myTpl.append(document.body, ['Michael']);
myTpl.append(document.body, ['Sebastian']);
```

In this example, you create an instance of `Ext.Template` and pass it a string representation of a `div` with a slot, which is marked in curly braces, and you store a reference in the variable `myTpl`. You then call `myTpl.append` and pass it a target element, `document.body`, and data to fill in the slots, which in this case happens to be a single-element array that contains a first name.

Do this three consecutive times, which results in three `div`s being appended to the DOM, with each different first name filling in a slot. Figure 2.6 shows the result from your `append` calls.

Figure 2.6 Using your first template to append nodes to the DOM, shown in the exploded view in Firebug

As you can see, three `divs` were appended to the document body, each with a different name. The benefits of using templates should now be clear. You set the template once and apply it to the DOM with different values.

In the previous example, the slots were integers in curly braces, and you passed in single-item arrays. Templates can also map object key/values from plain objects. The following listing shows how to create a template that uses such syntax.

Listing 2.1 Creating a complex template

```
var myTpl = Ext.create('Ext.Template', [                     Creates
    '<div style="background-color: {color}; margin: 10px;">',   complex
        '<b> Name :</b> {name}<br />',                      ❶ template
        '<b> Age :</b> {age}<br />',
        '<b> DOB :</b> {dob}<br />',
    '</div>'
]);

                              ❷  Compiles template
myTpl.compile();                  for faster speed

myTpl.append(document.body,{
    color : "#E9E9FF",
    name  : 'John Smith',            Appends template
    age   : 20,                  ❸  to document body
    dob   : '10/20/89'
});

myTpl.append(document.body,{
    color : "#FFE9E9",
    name  : 'Naomi White',
    age   : 25,
    dob   : '03/17/84'
});
```

When creating this complex template ❶ the first thing you'll probably notice is that you pass in quite a few arguments. You do this because, when creating a template, it's much easier to view the pseudo HTML in a tab-delimited format rather than a long string. The Ext JS developers were keen on this idea, so they programmed the Template constructor to read all of the arguments being passed, no matter how many there might be.

In the Template pseudo HTML, slots are included for four data points. The first is color, which will be used to style the background of the element. The three other data points are name, age, and dob, which will be directly visible when the template is appended.

The next step is to compile ❷ your template, which speeds up the template merging data with the HTML fragment by eliminating regular expression overhead. For these two operations you don't technically need to compile it because you wouldn't see the speed benefits; but for larger applications where many templates are stamped out, compiling has a clear benefit. To be safe, we always compile templates after instantiating them.

Last, you perform two append calls ❸ where you pass in the reference element and a data object. Instead of passing an array as you did in your first exploration of templates, you pass in a data object, which has keys that match the template slots. Figure 2.7 shows the result of the complex template with a DOM view in Firebug.

By using the template, you were able to get two differently styled HTML structures in the DOM. What if you had an *array* of objects? For instance, what if an Ajax request returned an array of data objects, and you needed to apply a template for each data object? One way to handle this is to loop through the array, which is easily done with a generic for loop or the more robust Ext.each utility method. I say nay to that approach. I'd use XTemplates instead, which makes the code much cleaner.

Figure 2.7   The result of the complex template with a DOM view in Firebug

2.3.2 Looping with XTemplates

XTemplates technically can be used for single data objects, but they especially make life much easier when you have to deal with looping through arrayed data to stamp out HTML fragments onscreen. The `XTemplate` class extends `Template` and offers much more functionality. You'll start your exploration by creating an array of data objects, and then you'll create an XTemplate, which you'll use to stamp out HTML fragments, as shown in the next listing.

Listing 2.2 Using an XTemplate to loop through data

```
var tplData = [{
    color : "#FFE9E9",                          ① Adds data
    name  : 'Naomi White',
    age   : 25,
    dob   : '03/17/84',
    cars  : ['Jetta', 'Camry', 'S2000']
},{
    color : "#E9E9FF",
    name  : 'John Smith',
    age   : 20,
    dob   : '10/20/89',
    cars  : ['Civic', 'Accord', 'Camry']
}];
                                                ② Instantiates
var myTpl = Ext.create('Ext.XTemplate', [         new XTemplate
    '<tpl for=".">',
        '<div style="background-color: {color}; margin: 10px;">',
            '<b> Name :</b> {name}<br />',
            '<b> Age :</b> {age}<br />',
            '<b> DOB :</b> {dob}<br />',
        '</div>',
    '</tpl>'
]);

myTpl.compile();                                ③ Appends HTML
myTpl.append(document.body, tplData);             fragments
```

In listing 2.2 you first set up an array of data objects ①, which are like the data objects you used in your last template exploration, with the addition of a `cars` array, which you'll use in the next example.

Next, you instantiate an instance of `XTemplate` ②, which looks much like the last `Template` configuration, except you encapsulate the `div` container with a custom `tpl` element with the attribute `for`, which contains the value `"."` ③. The `tpl` tag is like a logic or behavior modifier for the template and has two operators, `for` and `if`, which alter the way the XTemplate generates the HTML fragments. In this case, the value of `"."` instructs the XTemplate to loop through the root of the array for which it's passed and construct the fragment based on the pseudo HTML encapsulated inside the `tpl` element. When you look at the rendered HTML, you'll see no `tpl` tags rendered to the DOM. The results of your efforts are identical to the template example, as shown in figure 2.8.

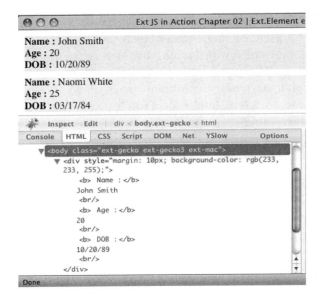

Figure 2.8   The result of using XTemplate with an exploded DOM view from Firebug

Remember, the advantage of using XTemplates in this case is that you don't have to write code to loop through the array of objects. You let the framework do the dirty work for you. The capabilities of XTemplates extend far beyond merely looping through arrays, which increases its usability exponentially.

2.3.3   *Advanced XTemplate usage*

You can configure XTemplates to loop through arrays within arrays and even have conditional logic. The example in the next listing will flex some XTemplate muscle and demonstrate many of these advanced concepts. Some of the syntax you're about to see will be foreign to you. Don't get discouraged. We'll explain every bit. We'll use the previous `tplData` from listing 2.2 for this advanced XTemplate usage.

Listing 2.3   Advanced XTemplate usage

```
var myTpl = Ext.create('Ext.XTemplate', [
    '<tpl for=".">',
        '<div style="background-color: {color}; margin: 10px;">',
            '<b> Name :</b> {name}<br />',
            '<b> Age :</b> {age}<br />',
            '<b> DOB :</b> {dob}<br />',
            '<b> Cars : </b>',
            '<tpl for="cars">',
                '{.}',
                '<tpl if="this.isCamry(values)">',
                  '<b> (same car)</b>',
                '</tpl>',
                '{[ (xindex < xcount) ? ", " : "" ]}',
            '</tpl>',
            '<br />',
```

❶ Loops through cars data

❷ Displays current data

❸ Executes this.isCamry method

❹ Tests for end of array

```
        '</div>',
      '</tpl>',
    {
        isCamry : function(car) {          ◁─┐    Adds
            return car === 'Camry';          ❺   method
        }
    }
]);
myTpl.compile();
myTpl.append(document.body, tplData);
```

This use of XTemplate demonstrates quite a few advanced concepts, the first of which is looping within a loop ❶. Remember, the for attribute instructs the XTemplate to loop through a list of values. In this case, the for attribute has the value of 'cars', which differs from the value that's set for the first for attribute, ".". This attribute instructs the XTemplate to loop through this block of pseudo HTML for each car. Remember that cars is an array of strings.

Inside this loop is a string with "{.}" ❷, which instructs the XTemplate to place the value of the array at the current index of the loop. In simple terms, the name of a car will be rendered at this position.

Next, you see a tpl behavior modifier with an if attribute ❸, which executes this.isCamry and passes values. The this.isCamry method is generated at the end of the XTemplate ❺. We'll talk more about this in a bit. The if attribute is more like an if condition, where the XTemplate will generate HTML fragments *if* the condition is met. In this case, this.isCamry must return true for the fragment that's encapsulated inside this tpl flag to be generated.

The values property is an internal reference of the values for the array you're looping through. Because you're looping through an array of strings, it references a single string, which is the name of a car.

In the next line you're arbitrarily executing JavaScript code ❹. Anything encapsulated in curly braces and brackets ({ [... JS code ...] }) will be interpreted as generic JavaScript; it has access to some local variables that are provided by the XTemplate and can change with each iteration of the loop. In this case, you're checking to see if the current index (xindex) is less than the number of items in the array (xcount) and returning either a comma with a space or an empty string. Performing this test inline will ensure that commas are placed exactly between the names of cars.

The last item of interest is the object that contains your isCamry method ❺. Including an object (or reference to an object) with a set of members with the passing arguments to the XTemplate constructor will result in those members being applied directly to the instance of XTemplate itself. This is why you called this.isCamry directly in the if condition of one of the tpl behavior modifier pseudo elements. All of these member methods are called within the scope of the instance of XTemplate for which they're being passed. This concept is extremely powerful but can be dangerous, because you can override an existing XTemplate member. So please try to make your methods or properties unique. The isCamry method uses JavaScript shorthand to test

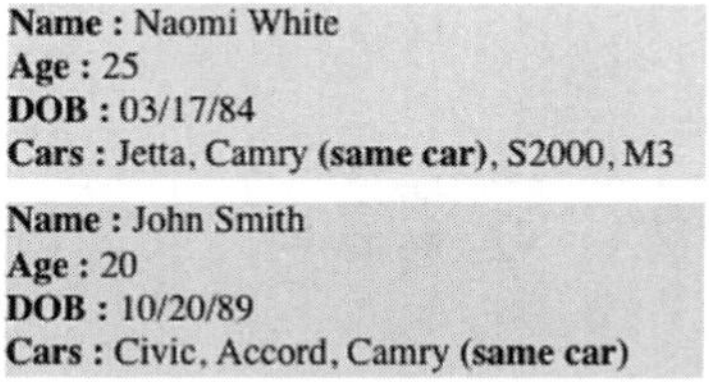

Name : Naomi White
Age : 25
DOB : 03/17/84
Cars : Jetta, Camry (**same car**), S2000, M3

Name : John Smith
Age : 20
DOB : 10/20/89
Cars : Civic, Accord, Camry (**same car**)

Figure 2.9   The results of the advanced XTemplate example

whether the passed string, car, is equal to "Camry" and will return true if it is; otherwise, it will return false. Figure 2.9 shows the results of the advanced XTemplate example.

The results show that all of your behavior injections worked as planned. All of the cars are listed, and there's proper comma placement. You can tell that your arbitrary JavaScript injection worked because the string "(same car)" is placed to the right of the Camry name.

As you can see, templates and XTemplates have numerous benefits compared to generic DOM injections using Ext.Element to stamp out HTML fragments with data. We encourage you to look over the template and XTemplate API pages for more details and examples of how to use these utilities. Your next exposure to templates will be when you learn how to create a custom ComboBox.

2.4   *Summary*

In this chapter we talked about how JavaScript application logic was launched in the old days with the onLoad handler of the <body> element. Remember that browsers typically have their own way of publishing when the DOM is ready for manipulation, which causes a code-management nightmare. In working with Ext.onReady, you learned that it takes care of launching your application code at just the right time for each browser so you can concentrate on the important stuff: application logic.

You then took an in-depth look at the Ext.Element class, which wraps and provides end-to-end management for DOM nodes. You explored a few of the management utilities for DOM nodes by adding and removing elements. All UI widgets use the Ext.Element, making it one of the most-used components of the core framework. Each widget's element can be accessed via the public getEl method or the private el property, but only after it's been rendered.

Last, you learned about using the Template class to inject HTML fragments into the DOM. You also jumped into advanced techniques with XTemplates and learned how to embed behavioral modifying logic into the template definition itself, producing results depending on the data provided.

Looking forward, you'll focus on the UI side of the framework and delve right into the core concepts and models that drive the framework.

Components
and containers

This chapter covers

- Getting to know the Component model and life cycle
- Exploring the Ext JS Container model
- Managing parent-child relationships of widgets
- Implementing the Container model utility methods

I (Jay) recall my early days with the Ext framework, when I learned by toying with the examples and reading the API documentation. I spent many hours on some of the most important core UI concepts, such as adding user interaction, reusing widgets, and understanding how one widget can contain or control another. For instance, how would I make clicking an anchor tag display an Ext window? Sure, there's a generic JavaScript way to attach an event handler, but I wanted to use Ext JS. Likewise, I needed to know how to get widgets to communicate with each other. For example, how would I reload a grid panel when a row of another grid panel was clicked? Also, how would I add child items dynamically to and remove them dynamically from a panel? How could I find a particular field within a form panel based on the type field?

In this chapter you'll explore the deep caverns of the fundamental UI building block, the `Component` class, and learn how it serves as the central model for all UI widgets by implementing a template for standard behaviors known as the *component life cycle.*

We'll also discuss the `Container` class, and you'll get an in-depth look at how widgets can manage child items. You'll learn how to dynamically add items to and remove them from widgets like the panel, which can be used as a building block for dynamically updating UIs.

3.1 *The Component model*

The Ext JS Component model is a centralized model that provides many of the essential component-related tasks, including a set of rules, known as the component life cycle, that dictate how the component instantiates, renders, and is destroyed. We'll cover the component life cycle in section 3.2.

All UI widgets are subclasses of `Ext.Component`, which means that all of the widgets conform to the rules dictated by the model. Figure 3.1 partially depicts what types of widgets subclass the `Component` class.

Knowing how each UI widget is going to behave introduces stability and predictability into the framework. The Component model also supports direct instantiation of classes, or deferred instantiation, known as *XTypes*. Knowing which to use when can enhance the responsiveness of your application. This section discusses three introductory features of the Component model.

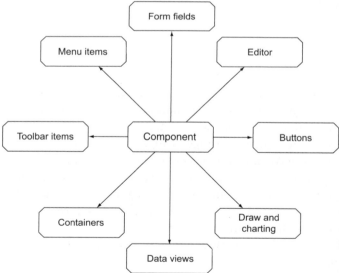

Figure 3.1 The Ext JS Component class plays a major role in every UI widget in the framework.

3.1.1 *XTypes and ComponentManager*

Ext 2.0 introduced a radical new concept known as an XType, which allows for lazy instantiation of components. XTypes can speed up the class instantiation of complex user interfaces and clean up your code quite a bit.

In short, an XType is nothing more than a plain JavaScript object, which generally contains an xtype property with a string value denoting which class the XType is for. Here's a quick example of an XType in action:

```
var myPanel = {
    xtype  : 'panel',
    height : 100,
    width  : 100,
    html   : 'Hello!'
};
```

Here myPanel is an XType configuration object that would be used to configure an Ext.Panel widget. This works because just about every widget is registered to the Ext.ComponentManager class with a unique string key and a reference to that class, which is then referred to as an *XType*. In each UI class in the framework, you'll find an alias declaration that is prefixed with 'widget.'—the Ext JS class system automatically registers the widget's XType with ComponentManager because of the prefix.

Here's what it would look like to register an XType for a custom class:

```
Ext.define('MyApp.CustomClass', {
    extend: 'Ext.panel.Panel',
    alias: 'widget.myCustomComponent'
});
```

Once registration is complete, you can specify your custom component as an XType:

```
new Ext.Panel({
    ...
    items : {
        xtype : 'myCustomComponent',
        ...
    }
});
```

When a visual component that can contain children is initialized, it looks to see if it has this.items and will inspect this.items for XType configuration objects. If any are found, it'll attempt to create an instance of that component using ComponentManager .create. If the xtype property isn't defined in the configuration object, the visual component will use its defaultType property when calling ComponentManager.create.

This concept may sound a tad confusing at first. To better understand it, you'll create a window with an accordion layout that includes two children, one of which won't contain an xtype property. First, create your configuration objects for two of the children:

```
var panel1 = {
    xtype : 'panel',
```

```
      title : 'Plain Panel',
      html  : 'Panel with an xtype specified'
};
var panel2 = {
      title : 'Plain Panel 2',
      html  : 'Panel with <b>no</b> xtype specified'
};
```

Notice that panel1 has an explicit xtype value of 'panel', which in turn will be used to create an instance of Ext.Panel. Objects panel1 and panel2 are similar, but they have a distinct difference: object panel1 has an xtype specified, and panel2 doesn't.

Next, create your window, which will use these xtypes:

```
Ext.create('Ext.window.Window',{
    width: 200,
    height : 150,
    title  : 'Accordion window',
    border : false,
    layout : {
        type     : 'accordion',
        animate : true
    },
    items : [
        panel1,
        panel2
    ]
}).show();
```

In your new instantiation of an Ext JS window, you pass items, which are an array of references to the two configuration objects you created earlier. The rendered window should look like the one in figure 3.2. Clicking a collapsed panel will expand it and collapse any other expanded panels, and clicking an expanded panel will collapse it.

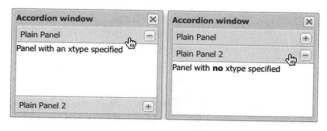

Figure 3.2   The results of the XType example: an Ext JS window, which has two child panels derived from XType configuration objects

One of the lesser-known advantages of using XTypes is developing somewhat cleaner code. Because you can use plain object notation, you can specify all of your XType child items inline, resulting in streamlined code. Here's the previous example reformatted to include all of its children inline:

```
Ext.create('Ext.window.Window',{
    width          : 200,
    height         : 150,
    title          : 'Accordion window',
    layout         : 'accordion',
```

```
    border       : false,
    layoutConfig : {
        animate : true
    },
    items : [
        {
            xtype : 'panel',
            title : 'Plain Panel',
            html  : 'Panel with an xtype specified'
        },
        {
            title : 'Plain Panel 2',
            html  : 'Panel with <b>no</b> xtype specified'
        }
    ]
}).show();
```

As you can see, this code includes all of the child configuration items inline with the Window configuration object. The performance enhancements from using XTypes can't be seen with such a simple example. The biggest XType-based performance gains come in bigger applications, where there are a rather large number of components to be instantiated.

Components also contain another performance-enhancing feature: lazy rendering. Lazy rendering means that a component is rendered only when necessary.

3.1.2   Component rendering

The Ext.Component class supports both direct and lazy (on-demand) render models. Direct rendering can happen when a subclass of Component is instantiated with either the renderTo or applyTo attribute, where renderTo points to a reference from which the component renders itself and applyTo references an element that has HTML structured in such a way that it allows the component to create its own child elements based on the referenced HTML. You'll typically use these parameters when you want a component to be rendered upon instantiation, as in this example:

```
var myPanel = Ext.create('Ext.panel.Panel',{
    renderTo : document.body,
    height   : 50,
    width    : 150,
    title    : 'Panel rendered immediately',
    frame    : true
});
```

The result of this code would be the immediate render of the Ext.panel.Panel, which sometimes is favorable and other times isn't. The times where it's not favorable can be when you want to *defer* rendering to another time in code execution or the component is a child of another.

If you want to defer the rendering of the component, omit the renderTo and applyTo attributes and call the component's render method when you (or your code) deem it necessary:

```
var myPanel = Ext.create('Ext.panel.Panel',{
    height : 50,
    width  : 150,
    title  : 'Lazy rendered Panel',
    frame  : true
});
// ... some business logic...
myPanel.render(document.body);
```

In this example you instantiate an instance of Ext.panel.Panel and create a reference to it, myPanel. After some hypothetic application logic, you call myPanel.render and pass a reference to document.body, which renders the panel to the document body.

You could also pass an ID of an element to the render method:

```
myPanel.render('someDivId');
```

When passing an element ID to the render method, the component will use that ID with Ext.get to manage that element, which gets stored in its local el property. If this rings a bell, you may recall the Ext.Element discussion from the previous chapter, where you learned that you can access a widget's el property or use its *accessor* method, getEl, to obtain the reference.

There's one major exception to this rule: you *never* specify applyTo or renderTo when the component is a child of another. Components that *contain* other components have a parent-child relationship, which is known as the *Container model*. If a component is a child of another component, it's specified in the items attribute of the configuration object, and its parent will manage the call to its render method when required. This is known as *lazy* or *deferred* rendering.

We'll investigate containers later in this chapter, where you'll learn more about the parent-child relationship that components can have. But first you need to understand the component life cycle, which details how components are created, rendered, and eventually destroyed. Learning how each phase works will better prepare you for building robust and dynamic interfaces and can assist in troubleshooting issues.

3.2   *The component life cycle*

Ext JS components, like everything in the real world, have a life cycle where they're created, used, and destroyed. This life cycle is broken up into three major phases: initialization, render, and destruction, as shown in figure 3.3.

To better utilize the framework, you must understand in finer detail how the life cycle works. This is especially important if you'll be building extensions, plug-ins, or composite components. Quite a few steps take place at each phase of the life cycle, which is controlled by the base class, Ext.Component.

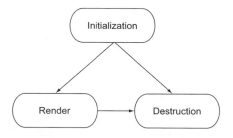

Figure 3.3   **The Ext JS component life cycle always starts with initialization and always ends with destruction. The component needn't enter the render phase to be destroyed.**

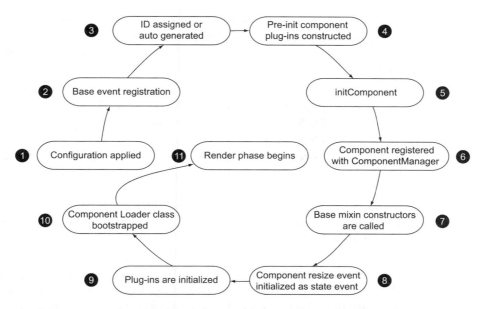

Figure 3.4 The initialization phase of the component life cycle executes important steps such as event and component registration, as well as calling the `initComponent` method. It's important to remember that a component can be instantiated but may not be rendered.

3.2.1 Initialization

The initialization phase is when a component is born. All of the necessary configuration settings, event registration, and prerender processes take place in this phase, as illustrated in figure 3.4.

Let's explore each step of the initialization phase:

1 *The configuration is applied.* When instantiating an instance of a component, you pass a configuration object, which contains all of the necessary parameters and references to allow the component to do what it's designed to do. This is done within the first few lines of the `Ext.Component` widget base class.

2 *Base component events are registered.* Per the Component model, each subclass of `Ext.Component` has, by default, a set of core events that is fired from the base class. These are fired before and after some behaviors occur: enable/disable, show, hide, render, destroy, state restore, and state save. The before events are fired and tested for a successful return of a registered event handler and will cancel the behavior before any real action has taken place. For instance, when `myPanel.show` is called, it fires the `beforeshow` event, which will execute any methods registered for that event. If the `beforeshow` event handler returns `false`, `myPanel` doesn't show.

3 *The component ID is assigned or autogenerated.* If you haven't configured a static ID for a component, it'll automatically generate one by combining the component's

XType with an autogenerated numeric value, beginning with 1000. For example, creating an instance of `Ext.panel.Panel` without configuring it with a static ID will result in the component having a self-generated ID of something similar to "panel-1001."

4   *Pre-`initComponent` plug-ins are constructed.* In this step, any plug-ins that are defined before the `initComponent` method is executed are constructed. This allows plug-ins like the grid panel editors to perform operations extremely early, such as initializing the editor fields.

5   `initComponent` *is executed.* The `initComponent` method is where a lot of work occurs for subclasses of `Component`, like registration of subclass-specific events, references to data stores, and creation of child components. `initComponent` is used as a supplement to the constructor and is typically used as the main point to extending `Component` or any subclass thereof. We'll elaborate on extending with `initComponent` later on.

6   `ComponentManager` *is registered.* Each component that's instantiated is registered with the `ComponentManager` class with a unique Ext JS–generated string ID. You can choose to override the Ext JS–generated ID by passing an `id` parameter in the configuration object passed to a constructor. The main caveat is that if a registration request occurs with a nonunique registration ID, the newest registration will override the previous one. Be careful to use unique IDs if you plan to use your own ID scheme.

7   *Base mixin constructors are called.* Components make use of two mixin classes to provide low-level functionality. `Ext.util.Observable` is responsible for providing components with the ability to listen to and fire events, and `Ext.state.Stateful` is responsible for handling state-specific events for components.

8   *The resize state event is initiated.* At this point `Component` registers its base resize event as a state-specific event. This means that you can expect any subclass of `Component` to be state-aware for sizing.

9   *Plug-ins are initialized.* If plug-ins are passed in the configuration object to the constructor, their `init` method is called, with the parent `Component` passed as a reference. It's important to remember that the plug-ins are called upon in the order in which they're referenced.

10 *The component's* `loader` *is bootstrapped.* If the component is configured with a `loader` configuration property, it's used to construct an instance of `Component-Loader`. This class is responsible for fetching data for a component via Ajax and employs an HTML, a data, or a component renderer to display the data. See the `Ext.ComponentLoader` documentation for details.

11 *The component is rendered.* If the `renderTo` or `applyTo` parameter is passed into the constructor, the render phase begins at this time; otherwise, the component lies dormant, awaiting its `render` method to be called either by your code or by a parent component.

This phase of a component's life is usually the fastest because all of the work is done in JavaScript. It's particularly important to remember that the component doesn't have to be rendered to be destroyed.

3.2.2 Render

The render phase is the one where you get visual feedback that a component has been successfully initialized. If the initialization phase fails for whatever reason, the component may not render correctly or at all. For complex components, this is where a lot of CPU cycles get eaten up, where the browser is required to paint the screen, and computations take place to allow all of the items for the component to be properly laid out and sized. Figure 3.5 illustrates the steps of the render phase.

If `renderTo` or `applyTo` isn't specified, a call to the `render` method must be made, which triggers this phase. If the component isn't a child of another Ext JS component, your code must call the `render` method, passing a reference of the DOM element:

```
someComponent.render('someDivId');
```

If the component is a child of another component, its `render` method will be called by the parent component. Let's explore the different steps of the render phase:

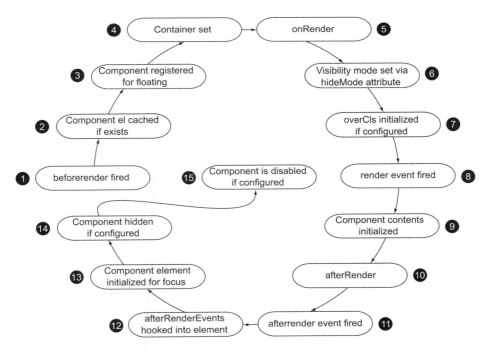

Figure 3.5 The render phase of a component's life can utilize a lot of CPU because it requires elements to be added to the DOM and calculations to be performed to properly size and manage them.

1 beforerender *is fired.* The component fires the beforerender event and checks the return of any of the registered event handlers. If a registered event handler returns false, the component halts the rendering behavior. Recall that step 2 of the initialization phase registers core events for subclasses of Component and that "before" events can halt execution behaviors.

2 *The component's element is cached.* If you configured a component with an el property, it wraps an instance of Ext.Element around that element.

3 *The component is registered with floating.* If the component is configured to be floatable, it'll register itself with WindowManager to enable z-index and focus management. This step is important for classes like Window and Menu, where they're designed to be positioned (float) above other UI widgets.

4 *The container is set.* A component needs a place to live, and that place is known as its container. If you specify a renderTo reference to an element, the component adds a single child div element to the referenced element, its container, and renders the component inside that newly appended child. If an applyTo element is specified, the element referenced in the applyTo parameter becomes the component's container, and the component appends to the referenced element only those items that are required to render it. The DOM element referenced in applyTo will then be fully managed by the component. You generally pass neither when the component is a child of another component, in which case the container is the parent component. It's important to note that you should pass only renderTo or applyTo, not both. We'll explore renderTo and applyTo later on when you learn more about widgets.

5 onRender *is executed.* This is a crucial step for subclasses of Component, where all of the DOM elements are inserted to get the component rendered and painted onscreen. Each subclass is expected to call its superclass's onRender first when extending Ext.Component or any subclass thereafter, which ensures that the Ext.Component base class can insert the core DOM elements needed to render a component.

6 *Visibility mode is configured.* The component's element is instructed to set its visibility mode according to how the component's hideMode property is set. Generally you don't have to worry about what to configure hideMode to, but it's good to get some exposure to what's available to you in case you create a custom component with special HTML requirements. By default it's set to 'display' (CSS display : none;), but other valid options are 'visibility' (CSS visibility: hidden;) and 'offsets'. A hideMode of 'offsets' will absolutely position the element for the component and push it −1000 pixels in the X and Y coordinate space.

7 overCls *is initialized if configured.* If you configure a component with an overCls property, the component will instruct its element to add that CSS class on its mouseover event and set the removeOverCls property on the mouseout event.

8 *The* render *event is fired.* At this point all necessary elements have been injected into the DOM and styles applied. The render event is fired, triggering any registered event listeners.

9 *The component's contents are initialized.* If a component is configured with contentEl, html, and/or a combination of tpl (Template) and data properties, it'll render that content as children of its own element. AbstractComponent is modeled so that you can use one, two, or all three if you wish. html will get rendered first, contentEl second, tpl third, and data last.

10 afterRender *is executed.* afterRender is a crucial postrender method that's automatically called by the render method. This method is responsible for configuring the size of the component, aligning and positioning the component, and adding some styling to the HTML content. It's also responsible for initializing an instance of Resizable (if configured), setting the component's element to scroll (if configured via autoScroll), and making the component draggable if it's configured as such. Finally, if the component is configured for Accessible Rich Internet Applications (ARIA) compliancy, the widget is initialized as such. It's important to note that all subclasses of Component that have their own afterRender method are expected to call their superclass's afterRender method.

11 *The* afterrender *event is fired.* This event is critical for classes to be aware that all critical render operations have completed and the component is ready to have its element modified. This event is typically the best to listen to so that your subclasses can perform DOM manipulations.

12 *The* afterRenderEvents *are hooked.* If the component is set with an afterRenderEvents configuration object, it'll use that configuration object to hook element listeners to available widget-specific element references, such as el for Component and body for Panel.

13 *The component's element is initialized for focus.* Components that are configured to be focusable and have focusable elements will be bound to the internal onFocus handler. This necessary plumbing is responsible for components being able to fire their own custom focus and blur events after managing their underlying elements' focus and blur events.

14 *The component is hidden.* If the component is configured with hidden set to true, the element's hide method is executed. This hides the component via the configured hideMode attribute.

15 *The component is disabled.* If the component is configured with disabled set to true, the component's disable method is executed, effectively disabling the widget. It's important to note that the widget is disabled without firing the disable event.

The render phase is generally where a component spends most of its life until it meets its demise in the destruction phase.

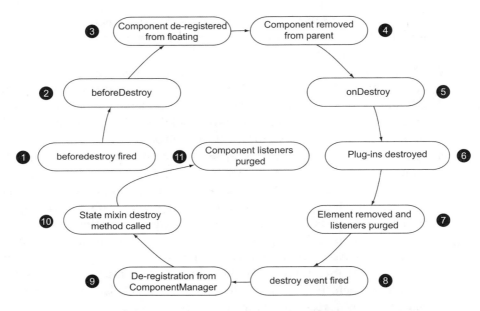

Figure 3.6 The destruction portion of a component's life is equally as important as its initialization because event listeners and DOM elements must be de-registered and removed, reducing overall memory usage.

3.2.3 Destruction

As in real life, the death of a component is a crucial phase in its life. Destruction of a component performs critical tasks, such as removing itself and any children from the DOM tree, de-registration of the component from the ComponentManager class, and de-registration of event listeners, as shown in figure 3.6.

The component's destroy method could be called by a parent container or by your code. Here are the steps in this final phase of a component's life:

1 beforedestroy *is fired.* This, like many before<action> events, is a cancelable event, preventing the component's destruction if its event handler returns false.

2 beforeDestroy *is called.* This method is first to be called within the component's destroy method and is the perfect opportunity to remove any noncomponent items, such as toolbars or buttons. Any subclass of Component is expected to call its superclass's beforeDestroy method.

3 *The component is de-registered from floating.* If a component is floating, it's de-registered with FloatingManager.

4 *The component is removed from the parent container.* If a component is a child of a parent container, it's removed from its parent.

5 onDestroy *is called.* The onDestroy method is charged with quite a few tasks. The first is the destruction of any configured drag-and-drop proxy, immediately

followed by the destruction of a `Resizer` if it's configured. Next, if a focus `DelayedTask` is registered, it's removed from the component. If the component is configured to monitor the browser's resize event, the resize event handler is removed. Finally, the `ComponentLayout`, the `loadMask`, and any floating child items are destroyed if the component is configured with the same.

6 *Registered plug-ins are destroyed.* At this point in the destruction phase all registered plug-ins are looped through, each with its `destroy` method being called.

7 `Element` *and* `Element` *listeners are purged.* If a component has been rendered, any handlers registered to its `Element` are removed and the `Element` is removed from the DOM.

8 *The* `destroy` *event is fired.* Any registered event handlers are triggered by this event, which signals that the component is no longer in the DOM.

9 *The component is unregistered from* `ComponentManager`. The reference for this component in the `ComponentManager` class is removed.

10 *The state mixin is destroyed.* Here the state mixin is called upon to be destroyed, de-registering any state-specific component events.

11 *The component's event handlers are purged.* All event handlers are de-registered from the component.

And there you have it, an in-depth look at the component life cycle, one of the features that makes the Ext JS framework so powerful and successful.

Don't dismiss the destruction portion of a component's life cycle if you plan on developing your own custom components. Many developers have gotten into trouble when they've ignored this crucial step and have code that has left artifacts behind, such as bound data stores that continuously poll web servers or event listeners that are expecting an element to be in the DOM. If these aren't cleaned properly they can cause exceptions and halt the execution of a crucial branch of logic.

Next we'll look at the `Container` class, which is a subclass of `Component` and gives components the ability to manage other components in a parent-child relationship.

3.3 Containers

`Container` is a behind-the-curtains class that provides a foundation for components to manage their child items, and it's often overlooked by developers. This class provides a suite of utilities, which includes `add`, `insert`, and `remove` methods, along with some child `query`, `bubble`, and `cascade` utility methods. These methods are used by most of the subclasses, including `Panel`, `Viewport`, and `Window`. It's also common to use these methods in your application.

3.3.1 Building a container with child items

In order for you to learn how these tools work, you need to build a container with some child items for you to use, as shown in the next listing.

Listing 3.1   Building your first container

```
var panel1 = {
    html   : 'I am Panel1',
    id     : 'panel1',
    frame  : true,
    height : 100
};
var panel2 = {
    html   : '<b>I am Panel2</b>',
    id     : 'panel2',
    frame  : true
};

var myWin = Ext.create('Ext.window.Window',{
    id     : 'myWin',
    height : 400,
    width  : 400,
    items  : [
        panel1,
        panel2
    ]
});
myWin.show();
```

① Configures panels

② Creates window

Take a gander at listing 3.1. The first thing you do is create two vanilla panels ①, and then you create myWin ②, an instance of Ext.window.Window that contains the previously defined panels. The rendered UI should look like figure 3.7.

You leave some room at the bottom of myWin, which will come in handy when you add items. Each container stores references to its children via an items property, which can be accessed via someContainer.items and is an instance of Ext.util .MixedCollection.

MixedCollection is a utility class that allows the framework to store and index a mixed collection of data, which includes strings, arrays, and objects, and provides a nice collection of handy utility methods.

Now that you've rendered your container, let's add children to it.

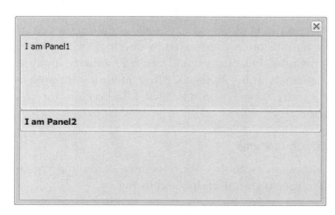

Figure 3.7   The rendered container UI from listing 3.1

3.3.2 *Dealing with children*

As in the real world, dealing with children can lead to frustration and many gray hairs, so you must learn to use the tools that are available to you. Mastering these utility methods will enable you to dynamically update your UI, which is in the spirit of Ajax web pages.

Adding components is a simple task, in which you're provided two methods: add and insert. The add method only *appends* a child to the container's hierarchy, but insert allows you to inject an item into the container at a particular index.

Let's add to the container that you created in listing 3.1. For this you'll use the handy Firebug JavaScript console:

```
Ext.getCmp('myWin').add({
    title : 'Appended Panel',
    id    : 'addedPanel',
    html  : 'Hello there!'
});
```

Running this code adds the item to the container; see figure 3.8.

Appending children is handy, but sometimes you need to be able to insert items at a specific index. Using the insert method easily accomplishes this task:

```
Ext.getCmp('myWin').insert(1, {
    title : 'Inserted Panel',
    id    : 'insertedPanel',
    html  : 'It is cool here!'
});
```

You insert a new panel at index 1, which is right under Panel1. The result should look like figure 3.9.

As you can see, adding and inserting child components is a cinch. Removing items is just as easy; it requires two arguments, the first of which is a reference to the component or the component ID from which you want the child to be removed. The second parameter, though, specifies whether or not the destroy method should be called for that component, which gives you incredible flexibility by allowing you to move

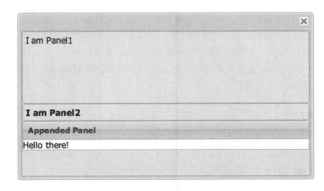

Figure 3.8 Adding a panel to the window from listing 3.1

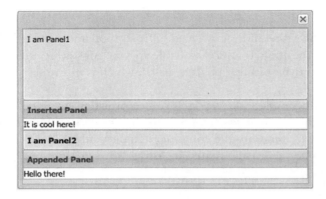

Figure 3.9   The rendered results of the dynamically added and inserted child panels

components from one container to another if you so desire. Here's how you'd remove one of the child panels that you recently added using your handy Firebug console:

```
var panel = Ext.getCmp('addedPanel');
Ext.getCmp('myWin').remove(panel);
```

After you execute this code, you'll notice that the panel immediately disappears. This is because you didn't specify the second parameter, which is `true` by default. You can override this default parameter by setting `autoDestroy` to `false` on a parent container. When removing a component, the component's `destroy` method is called, initiating its destruction phase and deleting its DOM element.

If you want to move a child to a different container, you specify `false` as `remove`'s second parameter and then add or insert it into the parent, like this:

```
var panel = Ext.getCmp('insertedPanel');
Ext.getCmp('myWin').remove(panel, false);
Ext.getCmp('otherParent').add(panel);
```

The preceding code snippet assumes that you already have another parent container instantiated with the ID of `'otherParent'`. You create a reference to your previously inserted panel and perform a nondestructive removal from its parent. Next you add it to its new parent to perform the DOM-level move operation of the child's element into the new parent's content body element.

The utilities offered by the `Container` class extend beyond the addition and removal of child items. They provide you with the ability to descend deep into the container's hierarchy to search for child components, which becomes useful if you want to gather a list of child items of a specific type or that meet special criteria and perform an operation on them.

3.4   *Querying for components*

Ext JS 4.0 comes with a new `ComponentQuery` class that has a selector engine similar to that of the browser's selector engine. This means that you can use familiar query constructs when searching for components. Because `ComponentQuery` was modeled after the browser's selector engine, you can perform lookups using any source node as a root.

To illustrate this, we've created an example that contains deeply nested panels. To view this tool, go to the following URL: http://extjsinaction.com/v4/examples/ch03/ using_ComponentQuery.html. In figure 3.10 we're using Firefox with Firebug in multi-line console mode.

This online tool contains child components nested four levels deep, starting with a viewport using the fit layout and rendering a single "master" panel. This master panel has an itemId of master_panel and contains three child panels. The child panels moving forward have their itemIds published in either their title or content body. The deepest nested components have a grandchild property set to Boolean true. As you'll see, any of these known properties can be used to home in on any targetComponent that you wish. Finally, each child component has a unique property named unique that's randomly generated and will change with each page refresh.

You'll begin by obtaining a reference to the topmost panel. For this and the rest of the example you'll use the Firebug console, so please keep it open and available as you read along.

NOTE If you don't have Firebug, we've included a toolbar that'll perform a query for you. All you need to do is supply the query parameters and click the Submit button. Any components found will fade out and back in again to indicate that they've been discovered.

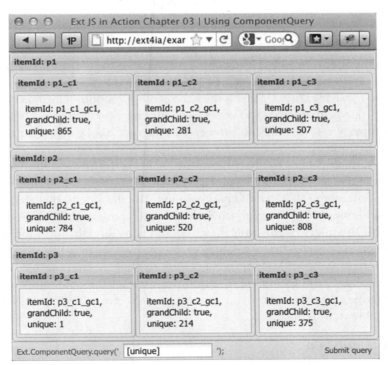

Figure 3.10 The tool you'll use in the ComponentQuery example

Enter the following code in Firebug's JavaScript console, and execute it. You'll find that the entire app fades out and fades in:

```
var results = Ext.ComponentQuery.query('#master_panel'),
    panel   = results[0];
panel.body.fadeOut().fadeIn();
```

In this snippet you first create a `results` reference pointing to the results of the query call. The query you've configured will search for and return any registered component with the id or itemId of `master_panel`.

Next you set the `panel` reference to the first item of the returning result set. By default, `ComponentQuery`'s query method will return an array no matter how many items have been found. This means that to test whether the query was successful, you'll need to inspect the returning result set's number of items to see if it's greater than 0.

If you plan on searching for a unique item, you can also collapse the first two lines into one like this:

```
var panel = Ext.ComponentQuery.query('#master_panel')[0];
```

The query that you just performed was global; Ext JS searched against all registered components on the page, and it was relatively high-level. But you can go much deeper by just searching for any component with a particular attribute.

For example, you can query for one of the deeply nested panels using this type of global query mechanism:

```
var panel = Ext.ComponentQuery.query('#p2_c3')[0];
```

There are other patterns as well. For example, if you want to search for the presence of an attribute, you can do that. To search for the presence of the `grandchild` attribute, query for `[grandchild]`. Or if you want to search for a unique property, such as the random `unique` property that you've set, you can query for `[unique="784"]`. Even though the property is technically an integer, you instruct Ext JS to test for the value by wrapping it in quotes.

Containers have the ability to query down the chain via the `down` method. Doing so allows you to use the `ComponentQuery` mechanism, forcing the scope of the search to be within the container itself and child components. The flip side to the `down` method is `up`. Child components can query up their parent hierarchy using `ComponentQuery`, but the scope of the query begins with the child and goes directly up to the topmost parent container.

By now you have the core knowledge necessary to manage child items. Let's shift focus and flex some Ext JS UI muscle by exploring some of the commonly used subclasses of `Container`. You'll see how you can use Ext JS to create a UI using all of the browser's available viewing space.

3.5   *The viewport container*

The `Viewport` class is the foundation on which all web applications that depend solely on Ext JS are built. It manages 100% of the browser's—you guessed it—viewport, or display area. Weighing in at a tad over 20 lines, this class is extremely lightweight and efficient. Because it's a direct subclass of the `Container` class, all of the child management and layout ability is available to you. To use the viewport, try the following example code:

```
Ext.create('Ext.container.Viewport', {
    layout : 'border',
    items  : [
        {
            height : 75,
            region : 'north',
            title  : 'Does Santa live here?'
        },
        {
            width  : 150,
            region : 'west',
            title  : 'The west region rules'
        },
        {
            region : 'center',
            title  : 'No, this region rules!'
        }
    ]
});
```

The rendered viewport from the code uses the entire browser's viewport and displays three panels organized by the border layout. If you resize the browser window you'll notice that the center panel is resized automatically, which demonstrates how the viewport listens and responds to the browser's window `resize` event (see figure 3.11). The `Viewport` class provides the foundation for all Ext JS–based applications that use the framework as a complete web-based UI solution for their RIAs.

Many developers run into a brick wall when they attempt to create more than one viewport in a fully managed Ext JS page to display more than one screen. To get around this you can use the card layout with the viewport and flip through different

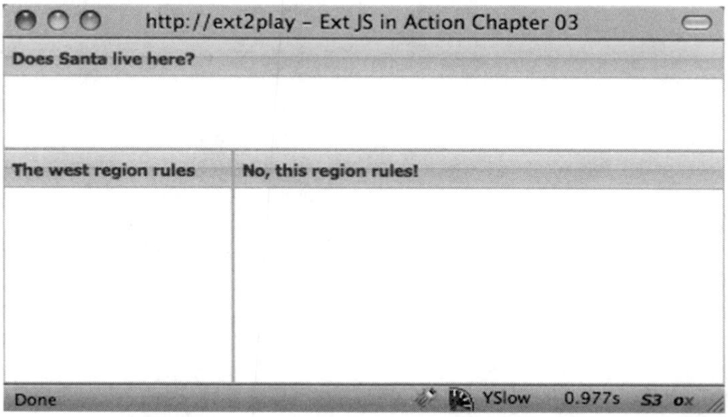

Figure 3.11 Your first viewport, which takes up 100% of the browser's available viewing space

application screens, which are resized to fit the viewport. We'll dive into layouts in chapter 5, where you'll learn key terms like *fit* and *flip* in the context of layouts.

3.6 *Summary*

This chapter took an in-depth look at the Component model, which gives the Ext JS framework a unified method of managing instances of components. The component life cycle is one of the most important concepts for the UI portion of the framework, which is why we covered it before we went too deep into the many widgets.

Next you explored the world of containers and saw how they're used to manage child components. You also learned about the `Viewport` class and how it's the foundation for web applications that are based entirely on Ext JS.

You now have the foundation that will help propel you forward as you start to exercise the framework's UI machinery. Next we'll explore the panel, which is the most commonly used UI widget to display content.

Part 2

Ext JS components

At this point, you're ready to examine the various widgets included with the Ext JS framework. In this part of the book, you'll also have an opportunity to look at how data-driven views work.

Chapter 4 covers core UI components that display user-interactive content such as panels, windows, message boxes, tabs, toolbars, and buttons, as well as container life cycles to manage child items. Chapter 5 explores layouts used for visual organization such as Fit, Card, and Border. Chapter 6 investigates forms and various input fields such as text fields, text areas, numbers, and combo boxes, in addition to validation and related data stores and views.

Chapter 7 explains data stores for persistence of array, JSON, and XML data; advanced user interaction for data-driven views including data models, proxies, readers, and writers; and associations, validations, grid panels, and editor plug-ins. Chapter 8 discusses the grid panel for rapid data entry in a tabular form and visualizing and manipulating large datasets with features like menus, interaction, editing, paging, and scrolling. Chapter 9 addresses trees for displaying hierarchical data including remote data loading, editing node data, and custom context menus. Chapter 10 deals with drawing and charting for visualizing data representations along with their chart types, shapes, themes, and legends.

Chapter 11 examines direct remote method invocation for server data exchanges with data stores, grids, trees, forms, and templates. Chapter 12 discusses using the drag-and-drop workflow to move items around the screen with mouse gestures, as well as associated override methods, the drag-and-drop life cycle, and plug-ins for grid and tree panels.

By the end of this part, you'll have a solid foundation in how Ext JS widgets work and how to use them effectively.

Core UI components

This chapter covers

- Exploring the panel
- Implementing panel content areas
- Displaying an `Ext.Window`
- Using `Ext.MessageBox`
- Creating tab panels

When developers start to experiment or build applications with Ext JS, they often start by copying examples from the downloadable SDK. Although this approach is good for learning how a particular layout was accomplished, it falls short in explaining how the stuff works, which leads to those throbbing forehead arteries. In this chapter you'll learn about core topics that are the building blocks of developing a successful UI deployment.

You'll also dive into how the panel works and explore the areas where it can display content and UI widgets. You'll then explore windows and the message box, which float above all other content on the page. You'll also learn about tab panels in this chapter.

When you finish this chapter you'll have the ability to manage the full CRUD (create, read, update, and delete) life cycle for containers and their child items, which you'll depend on as you develop your applications.

4.1   *The panel*

Panel, a subclass of Container, is considered a workhorse of the framework because it's what many developers use to present UI widgets. A fully loaded panel is divided into six areas for content, as shown in figure 4.1. Recall that Panel is also a subclass of Component, which means that it follows the component life cycle. Moving forward, we'll use the term *container* to describe any subclass of Container. This is because we want to reinforce the notion that Panel is a subclass of Container.

The panel's title bar is a busy place that offers both visual and interactive content for the end user. As in Microsoft Windows, you can place an icon at the top left of the panel, offering your users a visual cue as to what type of panel they're seeing. In addition to the icon you can display a title on the panel.

On the rightmost area of the title bar is a section for tools, which is where miniature icons can be displayed that will invoke a handler when clicked. Ext JS provides many icons for tools, which include many common user-related functions like help, print, and save. To view all of the available tools, visit the type property of the tool API.

Of the six content areas, the panel body is arguably the most important. It's where the main content or child items are housed. As dictated by the Container class, a layout must be specified upon instantiation if you don't want to use the container's default layout. If a layout isn't specified, an AutoLayout default layout manager is used. One important attribute about layouts is that one layout can't be swapped for another dynamically.

Let's build a complex panel, with top and bottom toolbars, with two buttons each.

Figure 4.1   An example of a fully loaded panel, which has a title bar with an icon and tools, top and bottom toolbars, and a button bar on the bottom

4.1.1 Building a complex panel

Because the toolbar will have buttons, it's a good idea to have a method to be called when they're clicked to give you visual feedback. This is known as a *handler*.

```
var myBtnHandler = function(btn) {
  Ext.MessageBox.alert('You Clicked', btn.text);
}
```

This method will be called when a button on any toolbar is clicked. The toolbar buttons will call handlers, passing themselves as a reference, called `btn`. Next, define your toolbars, as shown in the next listing.

Listing 4.1 Building toolbars for use in a panel

```
var myBtnHandler = function(btn) {                              Adds click
        Ext.MessageBox.alert('You Clicked', btn.text);      ❶  handler
    },
    fileBtn =  Ext.create('Ext.button.Button', {             Adds File
        text    : 'File',                                ❷  button
        handler : myBtnHandler
    }),
    editBtn = Ext.create('Ext.button.Button', {
        text    : 'Edit',
        handler : myBtnHandler
    }),
    tbFill = new Ext.toolbar.Fill();

var myTopToolbar = Ext.create('Ext.toolbar.Toolbar', {          Instantiates
    items : [                                            ❸  top toolbar
        fileBtn,
        tbFill,
        editBtn
    ]
});
var myBottomToolbar = [
    {                                                       Configures bottom
        text    : 'Save',                                ❹  toolbar
        handler : myBtnHandler
    },
    '-',
    {
        text    : 'Cancel',
        handler : myBtnHandler
    },
    '->',
    '<b>Items open: 1</b>'
];
```

Listing 4.1 provides two ways of defining a toolbar and its child components. First you define `myBtnHandler` ❶. By default, each button's handler is called with two arguments: the `Button` object itself and the browser event wrapped in an `Ext.Event` object. You use the passed `Button` reference (`btn`) and pass that text to `Ext.Message-Box.alert` to provide the visual confirmation that a button was clicked.

Next you instantiate the File ❷ and Edit buttons and the "greedy" toolbar spacer, which will push all toolbar items after it to the right. You assign myTopToolbar to a new instance of Ext.Toolbar ❸, referencing the previously created buttons and spacer as elements in the new toolbar's items array.

That was a lot of work for a relatively simple toolbar. We had you do it this way so you'd "feel the pain" of doing things the old way and better appreciate how much time (and end developer code) the Ext JS shortcuts and XTypes save.

The myBottomToolbar ❹ reference is a simple array of objects and strings, which Ext JS translates into the appropriate objects when its parent container deems it necessary to do so. You'd use these two methods to add or remove items dynamically to or from either toolbar. Next you'll create your panel body:

```
var myPanel = Ext.create('Ext.panel.Panel', {
    width        : 200,
    height       : 150,
    title        : 'Ext Panels rock!',
    collapsible : true,
    renderTo     : Ext.getBody(),
    tbar         : myTopToolbar,
    bbar         : myBottomToolbar,
    html         : 'My first Toolbar Panel!'
});
```

You've created panels before, so just about everything here should look familiar except for the tbar and bbar properties, which reference the newly created toolbars. Also, there's a collapsible attribute; when collapsible is set to true, the panel creates a toggle button at upper right on the title bar. Rendered, the panel should look like the one in figure 4.2. Remember, clicking any of the toolbar buttons will result in an Ext.MessageBox displaying the button's text, giving you visual confirmation that the click handler was called.

The toolbars rendered in figure 4.2 are placed above and below the content body. The process in which this occurs is called *docking* and is managed by the Dock component layout class. We'll dive deeper into docking items in section 4.1.2.

Figure 4.2 The rendered results of listing 4.1, where you create a complex collapsible panel with top and bottom toolbars that each contain buttons

4.1.2 Adding buttons and tools

Toolbars are great places to put content, buttons, or menus that are outside the panel body. There are two areas you still need to explore: buttons and tools. To do so, you'll add to the `myPanel` example in the following listing, but you'll do it using the Ext JS shortcuts with XTypes inline with all of the other configuration options.

Listing 4.2 Adding buttons and tools to your existing panel

```
var myPanel = Ext.create('Ext.panel.Panel', {
    // height, weight and renderTo go here
    buttonAlign : 'left',                              ❶ Adds
    buttons     : [                                        buttons
        {
            text    : 'Press me!',
            handler : myBtnHandler
        }
    ],                                                 ❷ Configures
    tools       : [                                        tools
        {
            type    : 'gear',
            handler : function(evt, toolEl, panel) {
                var toolClassNames = toolEl.className.split(' ');
                var toolClass      = toolClassNames[1];
                var toolId         = toolClass.split('-')[2];

                Ext.MessageBox.alert('You Clicked', 'Tool ' + toolId);
            }
        },
        {
            type    : 'help',
            handler : function() {
                Ext.MessageBox.alert('You Clicked', 'The help tool');
            }
        }
    ]
});
```

In listing 4.2 you add to the previous set of config options and include two shortcut arrays: one for buttons and the other for tools. Because you specified a `buttons` array ❶, when the panel renders it'll create a new instance of `Ext.Toolbar` with a special CSS class, `x-toolbar-footer-docked-bottom`, and render it to the newly created footer `div`. The Press Me! button will be rendered in the newly created footer toolbar, and when clicked it'll invoke your previously defined `myBtnHandler` method.

If you look at the `myBottomToolbar` shortcut array in listing 4.1 and the `buttons` shortcut array in listing 4.2 you'll see some similarities. All of the panel toolbars (`tbar`, `bbar`, and `buttons`) can be defined using the same shortcut syntax because they'll all get translated into instances of `Ext.Toolbar` and rendered to their appropriate position in the panel.

You also specify a `tools` array ❷ configuration object, which is somewhat different than the way you define the toolbars. Here, to set the icon for the tool you must

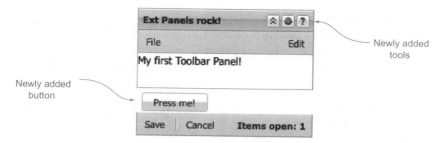

Figure 4.3   The rendered results from listing 4.2, which adds a button in the button bar and tools to the title bar

specify the id of the tool, such as `'gear'` or `'help'`. For every tool that's specified in the array, an icon will be created in the tools. The `Panel` class will assign a click event handler to each tool, which will invoke the handler specified in that tool's configuration object. The rendered version of the newly modified `myPanel` should look like the one in figure 4.3.

You can see the button you configured for the panel, but there's something wrong. The bottom toolbar is rendered *below* the button bar and is in need of serious repair. This gives us an excellent opportunity to dive right into how the `Panel` class uses the Dock component layout to render items above, below, and even to the left and right of the content body.

4.1.3   Docking items to a panel

The Dock layout is exclusively used by the `Panel` class and is responsible for rendering one or more components on either side of the panel's content body. When you configured the `tbar` and `bbar` attributes for your panel in listing 4.2, the panel *technically* pushed the configurations into what are known as `dockedItems` internally. The Dock layout is responsible for arranging each of those widgets based on a property known as `weight`. You'll explore `weight` in just a moment, but first we want to show you how flexible component docking is.

Instead of configuring the `tbar` and `bbar` (or `lbar` and `rbar`) attributes for a panel, you can just configure `dockedItems` as an array of toolbar configuration options. Doing so will allow you to keep all of the docked items in a single configuration collection.

The next listing demonstrates how you can dock a single top-docked toolbar to a panel using `dockedItems` instead of `tbar`. We're going to keep things as simple as possible.

Listing 4.3   Top-docking a single toolbar

```
var buttons = [
    { text : 'Btn 1' },
    { text : 'Btn 2' },
```

❶ Adds buttons

```
        { text : 'Btn 3' }
];

var topDockedToolbar = {                          Configures top-
    xtype   : 'toolbar',                       ❷ docked toolbar
    dock    : 'top',
    items   : buttons
};

var myPanel = Ext.create('Ext.panel.Panel', {
    width       : 350,
    height      : 250,
    title       : 'Ext Panels rock!',
    renderTo    : Ext.getBody(),
    html        : 'Content body',              ❸ Adds
    buttons     : {                               buttons
        items : buttons
    },
    dockedItems : [                            Sets up
        topDockedToolbar                    ❹ docked items
    ]
});
```

In listing 4.3 you first set up a reusable collection of button configuration objects ❶. Doing so allows you to render buttons easily when you add more toolbars later.

Next you create a top-docked `Toolbar` configuration object ❷. What makes this dock to the top is the `dock` property that you've set. As you'll see later, other possible values are `bottom`, `left`, and `right`.

Finally, render a panel, configuring it with a `buttons` configuration object ❸ and a `dockedItems` array ❹ containing a single element, `topDockedToolbar`. Rendered onscreen, your panel should look like figure 4.4.

So far you haven't seen anything new outside of configuring `tbar` and `buttons` properties for a panel. So next you'll add the left-, right-, and bottom-docked toolbars. You'll have to inject code *above* your panel:

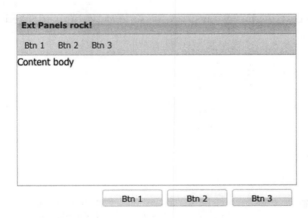

Figure 4.4 Your panel with a top-docked toolbar

```
var bottomDockedToolbar = {
    xtype   : 'toolbar',
    dock    : 'bottom',
    items   : buttons
};
var leftDockedToolbar = {
    xtype   : 'toolbar',
    vertical : true,
    dock    : 'left',
    items   : buttons
};
var rightDockedToolbar = {
    xtype   : 'toolbar',
    vertical : true,
    dock    : 'right',
    items   : buttons
};
```

In looking at this code snippet, you should be able to see patterns emerge. The dock property dictates where the toolbar will be docked. You set vertical to true so that the toolbar knows to use the VBox layout (vertical organization of components) instead of the default HBox layout (horizontal organization of components).

Next you'll add the toolbars to the dockedItems property of the panel:

```
dockedItems : [
    topDockedToolbar,
    bottomDockedToolbar,
    leftDockedToolbar,
    rightDockedToolbar
]
```

Modifying the dockedItems in this way will result in your panel rendering as shown in figure 4.5.

You've docked items on all four sides of your panel's content body, but the button bar is in the wrong place. Also, you want the bottom-docked toolbar to be the same width as the top-docked toolbar.

To fix these issues you'll need to adjust what's known as the *weight* of the docked items.

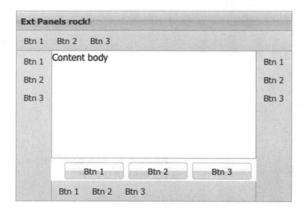

Figure 4.5   Rendering docked toolbars to all four quadrants of the panel

4.1.4 *Weight matters!*

The reason you had the problems you did with sizing is because the framework is rendering and sizing the docked items based on the default weight of each docked item. To understand how this all works, you need to think about how gravity works in the real world.

The more weight an object has, the closer it is to the source of gravity. With the Dock layout, the components with the most weight will be rendered closer to the content body and be sized smaller, giving the lighter docked items higher priority in sizing.

For completion's sake, in the following listing we'll show you the entire code base that includes the button bar and four docked toolbars, because you'll be making incremental changes along the way.

Listing 4.4 Your panel with four docked toolbars and a button bar

```
var buttons = [
    { text : 'Btn 1' },
    { text : 'Btn 2' },
    { text : 'Btn 3' }
];

var topDockedToolbar = {
    xtype    : 'toolbar',
    dock     : 'top',
    items    : buttons
};

var bottomDockedToolbar = {
    xtype    : 'toolbar',
    dock     : 'bottom',
    items    : buttons
};

var leftDockedToolbar = {
    xtype    : 'toolbar',
    vertical : true,
    dock     : 'left',
    items    : buttons
};

var rightDockedToolbar = {
    xtype    : 'toolbar',
    vertical : true,
    dock     : 'right',
    items    : buttons
};

var myPanel = Ext.create('Ext.panel.Panel', {
    width    : 350,
    height   : 250,
    title    : 'Ext Panels rock!',
    renderTo : Ext.getBody(),
    html     : 'Content body',
    buttons  : buttons,
```

```
dockedItems : [
    topDockedToolbar,
    bottomDockedToolbar,
    leftDockedToolbar,
    rightDockedToolbar
]
});
```

The first problem that you'll attack is the button bar being sized and positioned improperly. To fix this you'll have to change the way the buttons property is configured for the panel:

```
buttons : {
    weight : -1,
    items  : buttons
},
```

Here you're wrapping the buttons array reference in an object that contains a weight property of –1. When the panel initializes, it'll recognize that the buttons property is an object and use it to create a new instance of a toolbar for you, applying the custom weight attribute. Because you gave it a value of –1, it's considered *extremely light* and therefore will be rendered below the bottom-docked toolbar. Figure 4.6 shows what it looks like rendered.

The next problem you'll tackle is the left- and right-docked toolbar sizing issue. Rather than making the bottom-docked toolbar lighter, you'll make the left- and right-docked toolbars heavier. To do so, add the following property to the leftDockedToolbar and rightDockedToolbar configuration objects:

```
weight   : 10,
```

Adding the newly configured weight property to the left- and right-docked toolbar configuration objects ensures that your bottom-docked toolbar will render properly sized, as illustrated in figure 4.7. As you can see, adding weight : 10 to the left- and right-docked toolbar configuration objects allows the bottom-docked toolbar to take 100% of the width of the panel.

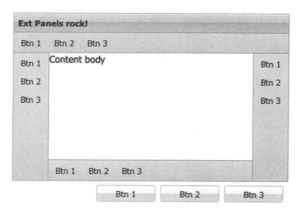

Figure 4.6   Rendering the docked items properly

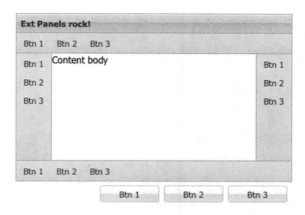

Figure 4.7 Fixing the bottom-docked button bar

The magic 10?

You're probably asking why you set the `weight` property of the left- and right-docked toolbars to 10 and not some other number, like 50 or 100. The reason you use 10 is because each quadrant where items are docked has a default weight. Top is 1, left is 3, right is 5, and bottom is 7. You use 10 because it's a nice round number that's larger than 7 (bottom dock).

We encourage you to play around with this code and add more than one docked item in each section, adjusting the weights. As you do that, remember that you can dock other `Component` subclasses to panels.

Now that you have some experience with the `Panel` class, let's look at one of its close descendants, `Window`, which you can use to float content above everything else on the screen and to replace the traditionally lame browser-based pop-up.

4.2 Displaying window dialogs

The window UI widget builds on the panel, providing you with the ability to float UI components above all the other content on the page. With windows you can provide a modal dialog box that masks the entire page, forcing the user to focus on the dialog box, and prevents any mouse-based interaction with anything else on the page. Figure 4.8 shows how you can use this class to focus the user's attention and request input.

Working with the `Window` class is a lot like working with the `Panel` class, except you have to consider issues such as whether you want to disable resizing or want the window to be constrained within the boundaries of the browser's viewport.

4.2.1 Building a window

Let's look into how you can build a window. For this, you'll need a vanilla Ext JS page with no widgets loaded, as shown in the next listing.

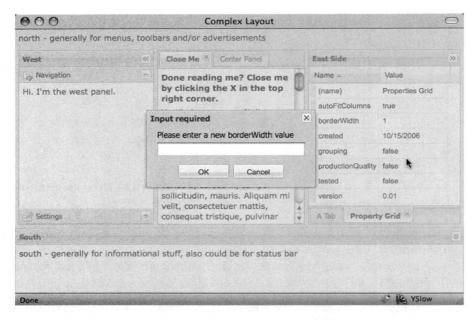

Figure 4.8   An Ext JS modal window, which masks the browser's viewport

---

Listing 4.5   Building an animated window

```
var win;
var newWindow = function(btn) {                          ◁——  Creates new
    if (!win) {                                          ❶    window
        win = Ext.create('Ext.window.Window', {
            animateTarget : btn.el,
            html          : 'My first vanilla Window',
            closeAction   : 'hide',
            id            : 'myWin',
            height        : 200,
            width         : 300,                         ◁——  Constrains
            constrain     : true                         ❷    Window instance
        });
    }
    win.show();
}
new Ext.Button({                                         ◁——  Creates
    renderTo : Ext.getBody(),                            ❸    button
    text     : 'Open my Window',
    style    : 'margin: 100px',
    handler  : newWindow
});
```

In this listing you do things a little differently in order to see the animation for your window's `close` and `hide` method calls. The first thing you do is create a global variable, `win`, for which you'll reference the soon-to-be-created window. You create a

Figure 4.9 The rendered results from listing 4.3, where you create a window that animates from the button's element when clicked

method, newWindow ❶, that will be the handler for your future button and is responsible for creating the new window.

Let's take a moment to examine some of the configuration options for your window. One of the ways you can instruct the window to animate upon show and hide method calls is to specify an animateEl property, which is a reference to some element in the DOM or the element ID. If you don't specify the element in the configuration options, you can specify it when you call the show or hide methods, which take the same arguments. In this case you're launching the button's element. Another important configuration option is closeAction, which defaults to close and destroys the window when the close tool (x) is clicked. You don't want that in this instance, so you set it to hide, which instructs the close tool to call the hide method instead of close. You also set the constrain parameter ❷ to true, which instructs the window's drag-and-drop handlers to prevent the window from being moved from outside the browser's viewport.

Last, you create a button ❸ that, when clicked, will call your newWindow method, resulting in the window animating from the button's element. Clicking the close tool will result in the window hiding. The rendered results look like figure 4.9.

Because you don't destroy the window when the close tool is clicked, you can show and hide the window as many times as you wish, which is ideal for windows that you plan to reuse. Whenever you deem that it's necessary to destroy the window, you can call its destroy or close method. Now that you have experience in creating a reusable window, you can begin exploring other configuration options to further alter the behavior of the window.

4.2.2 *Further window configuration*

There are times when you need to make a window behave to meet requirements of your application. In this section you'll learn about some of the commonly used configuration options.

Sometimes you need to produce a window that's modal and rigid. To do so you need to set a few configuration options, as shown in the following listing.

Listing 4.6   Creating a rigid modal window

```
var win = Ext.create('Ext.window.Window', {
    height     : 75,
    width      : 200,
    modal      : true,                               ❶ Ensures page
    title      : 'This is one rigid window',            is masked
    html       : 'Try to move or resize me. I dare you.',
    plain      : true,
    border     : false,                              ❷ Prevents
    resizable  : false,                                 resizing
    draggable  : false,
    closable   : false,                                 Disables window
    buttonAlign : 'center',                          ❸ movement
    buttons    : [
        {
            text    : 'I give up!',                  ❹ Prevents
            handler : function() {                      window closure
                win.close();
            }
        }
    ]
})
win.show();
```

In listing 4.6 you create an extremely strict modal window. You have to set quite a few options. The first of these, modal ❶, instructs the window to mask the rest of the page with a semitransparent div. Next you set resizable ❷ to false, which prevents the window from being resized via mouse actions. To prevent the window from being moved around the page, you set draggable ❸ to false. You want only a single center button to close the window, so you set closable ❹ to false, which hides the close tool. Last, you set some cosmetic parameters, plain, border, and buttonAlign. Setting plain to true will make the content body background transparent. When coupled with setting the border to false, the window appears to be one unified cell. Because you want to have the single button centered, you specify the buttonAlign property to be 'center'. The rendered example should look like figure 4.10.

Other times you want to relax the restrictions on the window. For instance, there are situations where you need a window to be resizable but not less than specific dimensions. For this, you allow resizing (resizable) and specify minWidth and min-Height parameters. Unfortunately, there's no easy way to set boundaries as to how large a window can grow.

Although there are many reasons for creating your own windows, sometimes you need something quick and dirty—for instance, to display a message or prompt for user data. The Window class has a stepchild known as MessageBox to fill this need.

4.3   *MessageBox*

MessageBox is a reusable, yet versatile, singleton class that gives you the ability to replace some of the common browser-based message boxes such as alert and prompt

Figure 4.10   Your first strict modal window rendered in the Ext JS SDK feed viewer example

with a simple method call. The most important thing to know about the `MessageBox` class is that it *does not* stop JavaScript execution like traditional alerts or prompts do, which we consider an advantage. While the user is digesting or entering information, your code can perform Ajax queries or even manipulate the UI. If specified, `Message-Box` will execute a callback method when the window is dismissed.

4.3.1   *Alerting your users*

Before you start to use the `MessageBox` class, let's create a callback method. You'll need this later on:

```
var myCallback = function(btn, text) {
    console.info('You pressed '  + btn);
    if (text) {
        console.info('You entered : ' + text)
    }
}
```

Your `myCallback` method will use Firebug's console to echo the button that was clicked and the text entered, if any. `MessageBox` will pass only two parameters to the callback method: the button ID and any entered text. Now that you have your callback, let's launch an alert message box:

```
var msg   = 'Your document was saved successfully';
var title = 'Save status:'
Ext.MessageBox.alert(title, msg);
```

Here you call the `MessageBox.alert` method, which will generate a window (see figure 4.11, left) and will dismiss when OK is clicked. If you want `myCallback` to get executed upon dismissal, add it as the third parameter.

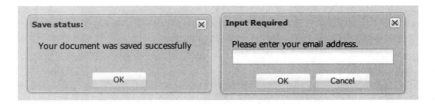

Figure 4.11 `MessageBox`'s alert (left) and prompt (right) modal dialog windows

Now that we've looked at alerts, let's see how you can request user input with the `Mes-sageBox.prompt` method:

```
var msg   = 'Please enter your email address.';
var title = 'Input Required'
Ext.MessageBox.prompt(title, msg, myCallback);
```

You call the `MessageBox.prompt` method, which you pass the reference of your callback method; it'll look like figure 4.11 (right). Enter some text, and click Cancel. In the Firebug console you'll see the button ID pressed and the text entered.

And there you have it, `MessageBox` alert and prompt windows at a glance. We find these handy, because we don't have to create our own singleton to provide these UI widgets. Remember them when you need to implement a `Window` class to meet a requirement.

We have to confess a little secret. The `alert` and `prompt` methods are actually shortcut methods for the much larger and highly configurable `MessageBox.show` method. Next up is an example of how you can use the `show` method to display an icon with a multiline text area input box.

4.3.2 *Advanced MessageBox techniques*

The `MessageBox.show` method provides an interface to display the `MessageBox` using any combination of the 24 available options. Unlike the previously explored shortcut methods, `show` accepts the typical configuration object as a parameter. Let's display a multiline text area input box along with an icon:

```
Ext.Msg.show({
    title     : 'Input required:',
    msg       : 'Please tell us a little about yourself',
    width     : 300,
    buttons   : Ext.Msg.OKCANCEL,
    multiline : true,
    fn        : myCallback,
    icon      : Ext.MessageBox.INFO
});
```

When the preceding example is rendered, it'll display a modal dialog box like the one in figure 4.12 (on the left). Next, let's see how to create an alert box that contains an icon and three buttons:

```
Ext.Msg.show({
    title       : 'Hold on there cowboy!',
    msg         : 'Are you sure you want to reboot the internet?',
    width       : 300,
    buttons     : Ext.Msg.YESNOCANCEL,
    fn          : myCallback,
    icon        : Ext.MessageBox.ERROR
});
```

The preceding code example will display your tributton modal alert dialog window, like the one in figure 4.12 (on the right).

Although everything in these two custom `MessageBox` examples should be self-explanatory, we think it's important to highlight two of the configuration options that pass references to `MessageBox` public properties.

The `buttons` parameter is used as a guide for the singleton to know which buttons to display. Although you pass a reference to an existing property, `Ext.Message-Box.OKCANCEL`, you can display no buttons by setting `buttons` to an empty object, such as {}.

If you want to just show buttons but not customize the text, the singleton already has a set of predefined popular combinations: `CANCEL`, `OK`, `OKCANCEL`, `YESNO`, and `YESNOCANCEL`.

Otherwise, you can customize which buttons you want to display. But instead of setting `buttons` as a property, you set `buttonText`. For example, to display Yes and Cancel buttons, set `buttonText` to { yes : 'Sure thing!', cancel : 'No way! '}, where the key to the object is the button ID and the string is the display text for the button.

The `icon` parameter works in the same way as the `buttons` parameter, except it's a reference to a string. The `MessageBox` class has three predefined values: `INFO`, `QUESTION`, and `WARNING`. These are references to strings that are CSS classes. If you wish to display your own icon, create your own CSS class and pass the name of your custom CSS class as the `icon` parameter. Here's an example of a custom CSS class:

```
.icon-add {
    background-image: url(/path/to/add.png) !important;
}
```

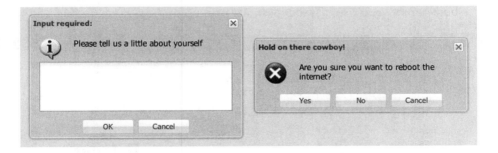

Figure 4.12   A multiline input box with an icon (left) and a tributton icon alert box (right)

Figure 4.13   A simple animated `MessageBox` wait dialog where the progress bar is looping infinitely at a predetermined fixed interval (left) and a similar message box with text in the progress bar (right)

Now that you have your feet wet with some advanced `MessageBox` techniques, we can explore how to use `MessageBox` to display an animated dialog box, which can offer the user live and updated information regarding a particular process.

4.3.3   *Showing an animated wait message box*

When you need to stop a particular workflow, you must display some sort of modal message box, which can be as simple and boring as a modal dialog box with a "Please wait" message. We prefer to introduce some spice into the application and provide an animated "wait" dialog box. With the `MessageBox` class you can create a seemingly effortless and infinitely looping progress bar:

```
Ext.MessageBox.wait("We're doing something...", 'Hold on...');
```

This code will produce a wait box like the one shown in figure 4.13 (on the left). If the syntax seems a little strange, it's because the first parameter is the message body text, with the title as the second parameter. It's exactly the opposite of the alert and prompt calls. Let's say you want to display text in the body of the animating progress bar itself. You could pass a third parameter with a single text property, such as {`text: 'loading your items'`}. Figure 4.13 (on the right) shows what it looks like if you add progress bar text to your dummy wait dialog box.

Although this may seem cool at first, it's not interactive because the text is static and you're not controlling the progress bar status. You can customize the wait dialog box by using the handy `show` method and passing in some parameters. Using this method, you now have the leeway to update the progress bar's advancement as you see fit. To create an auto-updating wait box, you need to create a rather involved loop (shown in the next listing), so please stay with us on this.

Listing 4.7   Building a dynamically updating progress bar

```
Ext.MessageBox.show({
    title        : 'Hold on there cowboy!',
    msg          : "We're doing something...",
    progressText : 'Initializing...',
    width        : 300,
    progress     : true,                           Shows
    closable     : false                        ❶ ProgressBar
});
var updateFn = function(num){
```

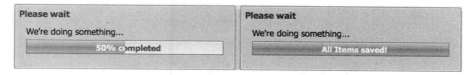

Figure 4.14 Your automatically updating wait message box (left), and the same box with the final update before automatic dismissal (right)

```
    return function(){
        if(num == 6){
            Ext.MessageBox.updateProgress(100,
                'All Items saved!');
            Ext.Function.defer(Ext.MessageBox.hide,
                1500, Ext.MessageBox);
        }
        else{
            var i = num/6;
            var pct = Math.round(100 * i);
            Ext.MessageBox.updateProgress(i,                  ❷ Updates
                pct + '% completed');                            percentage, text
        }
    };
};
for (var i = 1; i < 7; i++){                               ┌─
    setTimeout(updateFn(i), i * 500);                      ❸ Adds looping
}                                                             .5 second timeout
```

In listing 4.7 you create a message box, with the progress option ❶ set to true, which will show your progress bar. Next you define a rather involved updater function, aptly named updateFn, which is called at a predefined interval. In that function, if the number passed equals your limit of 6, you update the progress bar to 100% wide and show the completion text. You also defer the dismissal of the message box by one and a half seconds. Otherwise, you'll calculate a percentage completed and update the progress bar width and text accordingly ❷. Last, you create a loop that calls setTimeout ❸ six consecutive times, which delays your calls of updateFn by the iteration times one half second. The results of this rather lengthy example will look like figure 4.14. With some effort, you can dynamically update your users on the status of operations that are taking place before they can move on.

In this section you learned how to create both flexible and extremely rigid windows to get the user's attention. You also explored a few ways of using one of Ext JS's super singletons, the Ext JS MessageBox class. Let's now shift focus to the TabPanel class, which provides a means to allow a UI to contain many screens but display them only one at a time.

4.4   Components can live in tab panels too

The TabPanel class builds on Panel to create a robust tabbed interface, which gives the user the ability to select any screen or UI control associated with a particular tab.

Figure 4.15   Exploring top- and bottom-positioned tabs

Tabs within the tab panel can be unclosable, closable, disabled, and even hidden, as illustrated in figure 4.15.

Unlike other tab interfaces, the Ext JS tab panel supports only a top or bottom tab strip configuration. This is mainly because a lot of browsers still don't support CSS to a point where vertical text is possible. The tab panel uses the Card layout, which renders complex UIs quickly because it makes use of a common technique called lazy or deferred rendering for its child components. The deferred rendering feature of the tab panel is controlled by the deferredRender parameter, which is set to true by default.

Deferred render means that only cards that get activated are rendered. It's fairly common for tab panels to have multiple children that have complex UI controls, such as the one in figure 4.16, which can require a significant amount of CPU time to render. Deferring the render of each child until it's activated accelerates the tab panel's initial rendering and gives the user a more efficiently responsive widget.

Now you'll construct your first tab panel.

4.4.1   *Building your first tab panel*

TabPanel is a direct descendant of Panel and makes clever use of CardLayout. The tab panel's main job is to manage tabs in the tab strip. Management of child components is performed by the Container class, and the layout management is performed by CardLayout. The next listing shows how to build your first tab panel.

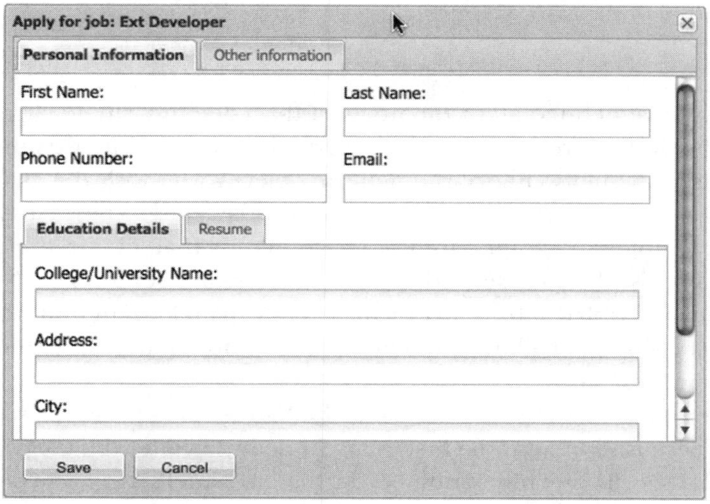

Figure 4.16 A tab panel with children that have complex layouts

---

Listing 4.8 Exploring a tab panel

```
var simpleTab = {                                        Introduces
    title  : 'Simple tab',                          ❶   static tab
    html   : 'This is a simple tab.'
};
                                                         Creates
var closableTab = {                                 ❷   closable tab
    title    : 'I am closable',
    html     : 'Please close when done reading.',
    closable : true
};

var disabledTab = {                                      Adds
    title    : 'Disabled tab',                      ❸   disabled tab
    itemId   : 'disabledTab',
    html     : 'Peekaboo!',
    disabled : true,
    closable : true
};

var tabPanel = Ext.create('Ext.tab.Panel', {             Instantiates
    activeTab : 0,                                  ❹   tab panel
    itemId    : 'myTPanel',
    items     : [
        simpleTab,
        closableTab,
        disabledTab
    ]
});

Ext.create('Ext.window.Window', {                        Renders
    height : 300,                                   ❺   tab panel
    width  : 400,
```

```
    layout : 'fit',
    items  : tabPanel
}).show();
```

Although you could've defined all of the items in this code in a single large object, we thought it'd be best to break it up so that everything is clear. The first three variables define your tab panel's children in generic object form, with the assumption that the `defaultType` (XType) for the `TabPanel` class is `Panel`. The first child is a simple and nonclosable tab ❶. One thing to note here is that all tabs are nonclosable by default. This is why your second tab ❷ has `closable` set to `true`. Next, you have a closable *and* disabled tab. Each of these child panel configuration objects has its own `itemId`, which will allow you to home in on it to do some operations such as enable, hide, and disable.

You then go on to instantiate your tab panel ❸. You set the `activeTab` parameter to 0. You do this because you want the first tab to be activated after the tab panel ❹ is rendered. You can specify any index number in the tab panel's `items` mixed collection. Because the mixed collection is an array, the first item always starts with 0. Last, your tab panel's `items` array has your three tabs specified.

Next, you create a container for your tab panel, an instance of `Ext.Window` ❺. You specify a Fit layout for the window and set the tab panel reference as its single item. The rendered code should display the tab panel shown in figure 4.17.

Now that you've rendered your first tab panel, you can start to have fun with it. You've probably closed the "I am closable" tab, which is okay. If you haven't done so, feel free to explore the rendered UI control and close out the only closable tab when you're comfortable doing so, which will leave only two tabs available: "My first tab" and "Disabled tab."

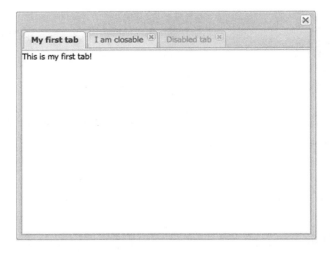

Figure 4.17 Your first tab panel rendered inside a window

4.4.2 *Tab management methods you should know*

Because the `TabPanel` class is a descendant of `Container`, all of the common child-management methods are available to use. These include `add`, `remove`, and `insert`. There are a few other methods, though, that you'll need to know to take full advantage of the `TabPanel` class.

The first of these is `setActiveTab`, which activates a tab as if the user had selected the item on the tab strip and accepts either the index of the tab or the component ID:

```
var tPanel = Ext.ComponentQuery.query('#myTPanel')[0];
tPanel.add({
    title  : 'New tab',
    itemId : 'myNewTab',
    html   : 'I am a new Tab'
});
tPanel.setActiveTab('myNewTab');
```

Executing this code will result in a new tab with the title of "New tab," which gets activated automatically. Calling `setActiveTab` after an `add` operation is akin to calling `doLayout` on a generic container. You also have the capability to enable and disable tabs at runtime, but this requires a different approach than simply calling a method on the tab panel.

The tab panel doesn't have `enable` and `disable` methods, so in order to enable or disable a child you need to call those methods of the child items themselves. You can use listing 4.8 to enable your disabled tab. With the `tPanel` reference you created a bit ago, you can query for the disabled child item and enable it as such:

```
tPanel.down('#disabledTab').enable();
```

Yes, that's all there is to it. The tab strip item (tab UI control) now reflects that the item is no longer disabled. This happens because the tab panel subscribes to the child item's—you guessed it—`enable` and `disable` events to manage the associated tab strip items.

In addition to enabling and disabling tabs, you can hide them. To hide a tab, you have to access the `tab` property of the tab panel's child items. To illustrate this, you'll hide the disabled tab and then show it:

```
tPanel.down('#disabledTab').tab.hide();
```

To make it reappear, execute the following code:

```
tPanel.down('#disabledTab').tab.show();
```

You've now seen how easy it is to create and manage a tab panel.

4.5 *Summary*

We covered a lot of material about the Swiss Army knife of UI display widgets, the panel, which is enough to make just about any developer's head spin. In exploring the `Panel` class, you saw how it provides a plethora of options to display user-interactive content, including toolbars, buttons, title bar icons, and miniature tools.

You used the `Window` class as a general container and mastered the art of adding and removing children dynamically, providing you with the ability to dynamically and drastically change an entire UI or a single widget or control.

In exploring the `Window` class and its cousin, `MessageBox`, you learned how you can replace the generic alert and prompt dialog boxes to get your user's attention to display information or request user input. You also had some fun fooling with the animated wait `MessageBox`.

Finally you examined the tab panels, learning how to dynamically manage tab items, as well as a few of the usability pitfalls that the UI control brings.

In the next chapter you'll explore the many Ext JS layout schemes, and you'll learn the common uses and pitfalls of these controls.

Exploring layouts

This chapter covers
- Using layout systems
- Exploring the `Layout` class inheritance model
- Understanding the Card layout

When building an application, many developers struggle with how to organize their UI and which tools to use to get the job done. In this chapter you'll gain the necessary experience to be able to make these decisions in an educated manner. We'll start by introducing component layouts that are new to Ext JS 4 and go on to explore the numerous container layout models and identify best practices as well as common issues you'll encounter.

The container layout management schemes are responsible for the visual organization of widgets onscreen. They include simple layout schemes such as Fit, where a single child item of a container will be sized to fit the container's body, and complex layouts such as the Border layout, which splits a container's content body into five manageable slices or regions.

We'll have some lengthy explorations of container layouts accompanied by some long examples that can serve as a great springboard for your own layouts. But before we continue our journey with in-depth descriptions of each container layout management scheme, let's talk about how layout managers work and introduce the new component layouts.

5.1   How layout managers work

As mentioned earlier, the layout management schemes are responsible for the visual organization of widgets onscreen. To do this, they keep track of how the individual child items are placed in relation to one another. The strategy used for placement depends on which layout manager you use. The layout managers are divided into two groups: component and container layouts.

5.1.1   Component layouts

Component layouts are new to Ext JS 4 and are used to lay out the internal items of components. For everyday use, you should be familiar with the Dock component layout. The Dock layout is responsible for managing docked items like toolbars and gives you the option of adding several top and bottom toolbars, as well as adding left and right toolbars (feel free to take a look back at section 4.2 now, if you need to brush up on the details of how to dock items).

If you're implementing your own components and want to implement your own component layout management scheme, then we encourage you to familiarize yourself with the existing hierarchy of component layouts and choose a relevant class to extend.

If you've been using Ext JS 3 or earlier versions, then you may remember the Form layout as cumbersome and complex to use. In Ext JS 4 the Form layout is no longer needed due to the introduction of the Field component layout and its descendants, along with the associated functionality in the code base.

Remember that all the standard components already have their corresponding component layout, so for your everyday programming tasks you don't need detailed knowledge of each component layout. We'll focus on container layouts in this chapter.

5.1.2   Container layouts

Container layouts let you manage the position and size of child components within a container. When you add a component to or remove a component from a container, the container communicates with the parent container and resizes sibling containers or components depending on the layout management scheme.

All of the container layout managers share common functionality available from `Ext.layout.container.Container`. We'll explore each layout manager in detail.

We'll start our journey through container layouts by taking a look at the Auto layout, which is the default layout for containers. The Auto layout is the most basic layout manager, and it shares common functionality with the Container layout.

5.2   The Auto layout

As you may recall, the Auto layout is the *default* layout for any instance of a container. It places items on the screen, one on top of another. Although the Auto layout doesn't

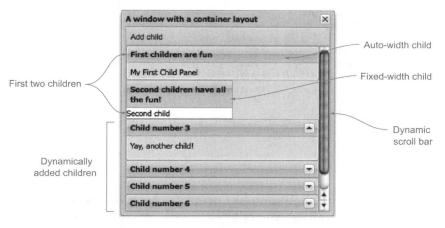

Figure 5.1   The results of your first implementation of the Auto layout

explicitly resize child items, a child's width may conform to the container's content body if it isn't constrained.

An Auto layout is the easiest to implement, requiring only that you add and remove child items. To see this you need to set up a dynamic example, using quite a few components, as shown in the next listing. When you're done, the layout will look like figure 5.1.

Listing 5.1   Implementing the Auto layout

```
var childPnl1 = {                          ❶ Configures
    frame  : true,                            first child
    height : 50,
    html   : 'My First Child Panel',
    title  : 'First children are fun'
};
var childPnl2 = {                          ❷ Configures
    width  : 150,                             second panel
    html   : 'Second child',
    title  : 'Second children have all the fun!'
};
var myWin = Ext.create("Ext.Window", {     ❸ Creates
    height     : 300,                         Window
    width      : 300,
    title      : 'A window with a container layout',
    autoScroll : true,                     ❹ Sets
    items      : [                            scrollable
        childPnl1,                         ❺ Adds child
        childPnl2                             panels
    ],
    tbar : [                               ❻ Configures
        {                                     toolbar
            text    : 'Add child',
            handler : function() {
```

```
        var numItems = myWin.items.getCount() + 1;
        myWin.add({
            title      : 'Child number ' + numItems,
            height     : 60,
            frame      : true,
            collapsible : true,
            collapsed  : true,
            html       : 'Yay, another child!'
        });
      }
    }
  ]
});
myWin.show();
```

In listing 5.1, the first thing you do is instantiate object references using XTypes for the two child items that'll be managed by a window: childPnl1 ❶ and childPnl2 ❷. These two child items are static. Next, you begin your myWin ❸ reference, which is an instance of Ext.Window. You also set the autoScroll property ❹ to true. This tells the container to set the CSS attributes overflow-x and overflow-y to auto, which instructs the browser to show the scroll bars only when it needs to.

Notice that you set the child items ❺ property to an array. The items property for any container can be an instance of an array used to list multiple children *or* an object reference for a single child. The window contains a toolbar ❻ that has a single button that, when clicked, adds a dynamic item to the window. Note that before Ext JS version 4, you could benefit from calling doLayout on the parent container after removing or adding an item; this should no longer be necessary due to the bidirectional communication in the component/container hierarchy. In earlier versions you would've called myWin.doLayout after adding one or more child items. If you're performing bulk updates of your component, then you set suspendLayout to true on the container to avoid calling doLayout. The rendered window should look like the one in figure 5.1.

Although the Auto layout provides little to manage the size of child items, it's not completely useless. It's lightweight relative to its subclasses, which makes it ideal if you want to display child items that have fixed dimensions. There are times, though, when you'll want to have the child items dynamically resize to fit the container's content body. This is where the Anchor layout can be useful.

5.3   *The Anchor layout*

The Anchor layout is similar to other container layouts in that it stacks child items one on top of another, but it adds dynamic sizing into the mix using an anchor parameter specified on each child. This anchor parameter is used to calculate the size of the child item relative to the parent's content body size and is specified as either a pair of percentages or a pair of offsets, which are integers. The anchor parameter is a string, using the following format:

```
anchor : "width, height" // or "width height"
```

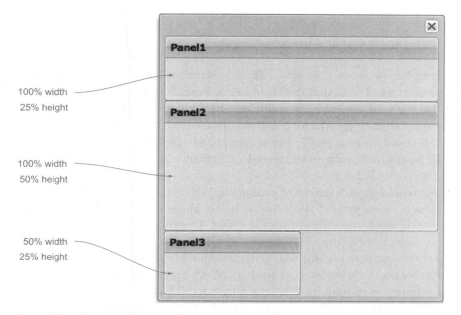

100% width
25% height

100% width
50% height

50% width
25% height

Figure 5.2   The rendered results of your first implementation of the Anchor layout in listing 5.2

Figure 5.2 shows what you'll be constructing.

In the following listing you'll take your first stab at implementing an Anchor layout using percentages.

Listing 5.2   The Anchor layout using percentages

```
var myWin = Ext.create("Ext.Window", ({        ◁─┐  Creates
    height     : 300,                           ❶  window
    width      : 300,
    layout     : 'anchor',                      ◁─┐  Sets
    border     : false,                         ❷  layout
    anchorSize : '400',
    items      : [
        {
            title  : 'Panel1',                  ❸  Sets
            anchor : '100%, 25%',               ◁──  dimensions
            frame  : true
        },
        {
            title  : 'Panel2',                  ❹  Configures
            anchor : '0, 50%',                  ◁──  dimensions
            frame  : true
        },
        {
            title  : 'Panel3',                  ❺  Sets
            anchor : '50%, 25%',                ◁──  size
            frame  : true
```

```
        }
    ]
}));
myWin.show();
```

In listing 5.2 you instantiate `myWin` ❶, an instance of `Ext.Window`, specifying the layout as `'anchor'` ❷. The first of the child items, `Panel1`, has its anchor parameter ❸ specified as 100% of the parent's width and 25% of the parent's height. `Panel2` has its anchor parameter ❹ specified a little differently, where the `width` parameter is 0, which is shorthand for 100%. You set `Panel2`'s height to 50%. `Panel3`'s anchor parameter ❺ is set to 50% relative `width` and 25% relative `height`. The rendered item should look like figure 5.2.

Relative sizing with percentages is great, but you also have the option to specify offsets, which allows greater flexibility with the Anchor layout. Offsets are calculated as the content body dimension plus the offset. In general, offsets are specified as negative numbers to keep the child item in view. Let's put on our algebra hats for a second and remember that adding a negative integer is exactly the same as subtracting an absolute integer. Specifying a positive offset would make the child's dimensions greater than the content body's, requiring a scroll bar.

We'll explore offsets by using the previous example, modifying only the child item XTypes from listing 5.2:

```
items : [
  {
    title     : 'Panel1',
    anchor    : '-50, -150',
    frame     : true
  },
  {
    title     : 'Panel2',
    anchor    : '-10, -150',
    frame     : true
  }
]
```

The rendered panel from the preceding layout modification should look like figure 5.3. We reduced the number of child items to two to more easily illustrate how offsets work and how they can cause you a lot of trouble.

It's important to dissect what's going on, which will require you to do a little math. By inspecting the DOM with Firebug, you learn that the window's content body is 285 pixels high and 288 pixels wide. Using simple math, you can determine what the dimensions of `Panel1` and `Panel2` should be:

```
Panel1 Width  = 288px - 50px  = 238px
Panel1 Height = 285px - 150px = 135px
Panel2 Width  = 288px - 10px  = 278px
Panel2 Height = 285px - 150px = 135px
```

You can easily see that both child panels fit perfectly within the window. If you add the height of both panels, you see that they fit, with a total of only 270 pixels. But what

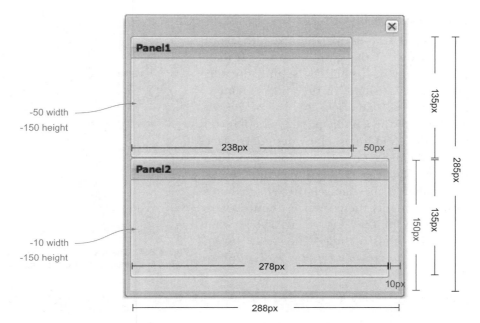

Figure 5.3 Using offsets with an Anchor layout with sizing calculations

happens if you resize the window vertically? Notice anything strange? Increasing the window's height by more than 15 pixels results in Panel2 being pushed offscreen and scroll bars appearing in the windowBody.

Recall that with this layout, the child dimensions are relative to the parent's content body plus a *constant*, which is the offset. To combat this problem, you can mix anchor offsets with fixed dimensions. To explore this concept, modify Panel2's anchor parameter and add a fixed height:

```
{
    title   : 'Panel2',
    height  : 150,
    anchor  : '-10',
    frame   : true
}
```

This modification makes Panel2's height fixed at 150 pixels. The newly rendered window can now be resized to virtually any size, and Panel1 will grow to the window content body minus 150 pixels, which leaves just enough vertical room for Panel2 to stay onscreen. One neat thing about this is that Panel2 still has the relative width.

Anchors are used for a multitude of layout tasks. The Anchor layout is used by the Ext.form.Panel class by default, but it can be used by any container or subclass that can contain other child items, such as Panel or Window.

There are times when you need complete control over the positioning of the widget layout. The Absolute layout is perfect for this requirement.

5.4   *The Absolute layout*

Next to the Auto layout, the Absolute layout is by far one of the simplest to use. It fixes the position of a child by setting the CSS 'position' attribute of the child's element to 'absolute' and sets the top and left attributes to the x and y parameters that you set on the child items. Many designers place HTML elements as a position: absolute with CSS, but Ext JS uses JavaScript's DOM-manipulation mechanisms to set attributes to the elements themselves, without having to muck with CSS. Figure 5.4 shows what you'll be constructing. The next listing shows how to create a window with an Absolute layout.

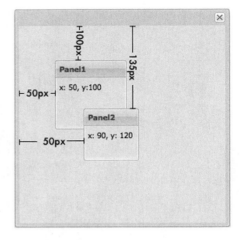

Figure 5.4   **The results of your Absolute layout implementation from listing 5.3**

Listing 5.3   AbsoluteLayout in action

```
var myWin = Ext.create("Ext.Window", {
    height     : 300,
    width      : 300,
    layout     : 'absolute',            ❶ Sets
    autoScroll : true,                     layout
    border     : false,
    items      : [
        {
            title  : 'Panel1',          ❷ Sets child
            x      : 50,                   coordinates
            y      : 50,
            height : 100,
            width  : 100,
            html   : 'x: 50, y:50',
            frame  : true
        },
        {
            title  : 'Panel2',          ❸ Sets child
            x      : 90,                   coordinates
            y      : 120,
            height : 75,
            width  : 100,
            html   : 'x: 90, y: 120',
            frame  : true
        }
    ]
});
myWin.show();
```

By now, most of this code should look familiar to you, but there are a few new parameters. The first noticeable change is that the window's layout ❶ parameter is set to 'absolute'. You attach two children to this window. Because you're using the Absolute layout, you need to specify the X and Y coordinates.

The first child, Panel1, has its X ❷ (CSS left attribute) coordinate set to 50 pixels and Y (CSS top attribute) coordinate set to 50. The second child, Panel2, has its X ❸ and Y coordinates set to 90 pixels and 120 pixels, respectively. The rendered code should look like figure 5.4.

One obvious detail in this example is that Panel2 overlaps Panel1. Panel2 is on top because of its placement in the DOM tree. Panel2's element is below Panel1's element, and because Panel2's CSS position attribute is set to 'absolute' as well, it's going to show above Panel1. Always keep the risk of overlapping in mind when you implement this layout. Also, because the positions of the child items are fixed, the Absolute layout isn't an ideal solution for parents that resize.

If you have one child item and want it to resize with its parent, the Fit layout is the best solution.

Figure 5.5 Using the Fit layout (listing 5.4)

5.5 *The Fit layout*

The Fit layout forces a container's single child to "fit" to its body element and is another remarkably simple layout. Figure 5.5 illustrates the end results of this exercise, as shown in the next listing.

Listing 5.4 The Fit layout

```
var myWin = Ext.create("Ext.Window", {
    height    : 200,
    width     : 200,
    layout    : 'fit',              ❶ Configures layout
    border    : false,
    items     : [
        {
            title : 'Panel1',
            html  : 'I fit in my parent!',   ❷ Adds child
            frame : true
        }
    ]
});
myWin.show();
```

In listing 5.4 you set the window's layout property to 'fit' ❶ and instantiate a single child, an instance of Ext.Panel ❷. The child's XType is assumed by the window's defaultType property, which is automatically set to 'panel' by the window's prototype. The rendered panels should look like figure 5.5.

The Fit layout is a great solution for a seamless look when a container has one child. Often, though, multiple widgets are housed in a container. All other layout-management schemes are generally used to manage multiple children. One of the

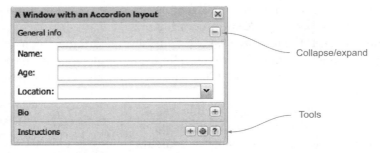

Figure 5.6   The Accordion layout is an excellent way to present the user with multiple items as a single visible component.

best-looking layouts is the Accordion layout, which allows you to vertically stack items that can be collapsed, showing the user one item at a time.

5.6   *The Accordion layout*

The Accordion layout, shown in the following listing, is a direct subclass of the VBox layout. It's useful when you want to display multiple panels vertically stacked, where only a single item can be expanded or contracted. Figure 5.6 shows the end result.

Listing 5.5   The Accordion layout

```
var myWin = Ext.create("Ext.Window", {
    height          : 200,
    width           : 300,
    border          : false,
    title           : 'A Window with an Accordion layout',    ❶ Creates
    layout          : 'accordion',                               delegate
    layoutConfig : {                                             instance
        animate     : true                          ❷ Configures
    },                                                 layout
    items           : [
        {                                   ❸ Adds first
            xtype           : 'form',         child item
            title           : 'General info',
            bodyStyle       : 'padding: 5px',
            defaultType     : 'field',
            fieldDefaults : {
                labelWidth: 50
            },
            labelWidth  : 50,
            items       : [
                {
                    fieldLabel : 'Name',
                    anchor     : '-10'
                },
                {
                    xtype      : 'field',
                    fieldLabel : 'Age',
```

```
            size       : 3
        },
        {
            xtype      : 'combo',
            fieldLabel : 'Location',
            anchor     : '-10',
            store      : [ 'Here', 'There', 'Anywhere' ]
        }
    ]
},
{
    xtype  : 'panel',                          Creates
    title  : 'Bio',                        ④  text area
    layout : 'fit',
    items  : {
        xtype : 'textarea',
        value : 'Tell us about yourself'
    }
},
{
    title : 'Instructions',                    Adds panel
    html  : 'Please enter information.',    ⑤  with tools
    tools : [
        {id : 'gear'}, {id:'help'}
    ]
}
    ]
});
myWin.show();
```

Listing 5.5 demonstrates the usefulness of the Accordion layout. The first thing you do is instantiate a window, myWin, which has its layout property set to 'accordion' ❶. A configuration option you haven't seen thus far is layoutConfig ❷. Some layout schemes have specific configuration options, which you can define as configuration options for a component's constructor.

These layoutConfig parameters can change the way a layout behaves or functions. In this case, you set layoutConfig for the Accordion layout, specifying animate: true, which instructs the Accordion layout to animate the collapse and expansion of a child item. Another behavior-changing configuration option is activeOnTop, which, if set to true, will move the active item to the top of the stack. When you're working with a layout for the first time, we suggest consulting the API for all the options available to you.

Next you start to define child items, which build on some of the knowledge you've gained so far. The first child is FormPanel ❸, which uses the anchor parameters you learned about earlier in this chapter. Next you specify a panel ❹ that has its layout property set to 'fit' and contains a child TextArea. You then define the last child item ❺ as a vanilla panel with some tools. The rendered code should look like figure 5.6.

Another way to configure layouts

Instead of using both the `layout` (`String`) as well as the `layoutConfig` (`Object`) configurations, you can set the `layout` configuration to an `Object` that contains both the layout type and any options for that layout. For example:

```
layout  : {
    type    : 'accordion',
    animate : true
}
```

It's important to note that the Accordion layout can only function well with an `Ext.panel.Panel` and two of its subclasses, `Ext.grid.Panel` and `Ext.tree.Panel`. This is because `Panel` (and the two specified subclasses) has what's required for the Accordion layout to function properly. If you need anything else inside an Accordion layout, such as a tab panel, wrap a panel around it and add that panel as a child of the container that has the Accordion layout.

Although the Accordion layout is a good solution for having more than one panel onscreen, it has limitations. For instance, what if you needed to have 10 components in a particular container? The sum of the heights of the title bars for each item would take up a lot of valuable screen space. The Card layout is perfect for this requirement, because it allows you to show and hide or flip through child components.

5.7   *The Card layout*

The Card layout ensures that its children conform to the size of the container. Unlike the Fit layout, the Card layout can have multiple children under its control. This tool gives you the flexibility to create components that mimic wizard interfaces.

Except for the initial active item, the Card layout leaves all of the flipping to the end developer with its publicly exposed `setActiveItem` method. To create a wizard-like interface, you need to create a method to control the card flipping:

```
var handleNav = function(btn) {
    var activeItem  = myWin.layout.activeItem,
        index       = myWin.items.indexOf(activeItem),
        numItems    = myWin.items.getCount(),
        indicatorEl = Ext.getCmp('indicator').el;

    if (btn.text == 'Forward' && index < numItems - 1) {
        index++;
        myWin.layout.setActiveItem(index);
        index++;
        indicatorEl.update(index + ' of ' + numItems);
    }
    else if (btn.text == 'Back' && index > 0) {
        myWin.layout.setActiveItem(index - 1);
        indicatorEl.update(index + ' of ' + numItems);
    }
}
```

Here you control the card flipping by determining the active item's `index` and setting the active item based on whether the Forward or Back button is clicked. You then update the indicator text on the bottom toolbar. Next let's implement your Card layout. The code example in the next listing is rather long and involved, so please stick with us.

Listing 5.6   The Card layout in action

```
var myWin = Ext.create("Ext.Window", {
    height       : 200,
    width        : 300,
    border       : false,
    title        : 'A Window with a Card layout',      ❶ Sets card layout
    layout       : 'card',
    activeItem   : 0,                                   ❷ Configures active item
    defaults     : { border : false },
    items        : [
        {
            xtype       : 'form',
            title       : 'General info',
            bodyStyle   : 'padding: 5px',
            defaultType : 'field',
            labelWidth  : 50,
            items       : [
                {
                    fieldLabel : 'Name',
                    anchor     : '-10',
                },
                {
                    xtype      : 'numberfield',
                    fieldLabel : 'Age',
                    size       : 3
                },
                {
                    xtype      : 'combo',
                    fieldLabel : 'Location',
                    anchor     : '-10',
                    store      : [ 'Here', 'There', 'Anywhere' ]
                }
            ]
        },
        {
            xtype  : 'panel',
            title  : 'Bio',
            layout : 'fit',
            items  : {
                xtype : 'textarea',
                value : 'Tell us about yourself'
            }
        },
        {
            title : 'Congratulations',
            html  : 'Thank you for filling out our form!'
```

```
            }
        ],
        dockedItems : [
            {
                xtype : 'toolbar',
                dock  : 'bottom',
                items : [
                    {
                        text    : 'Back',
                        handler : handleNav
                    },
                    '-',
                    {
                        text    : 'Forward',
                        handler : handleNav
                    },
                    '->',
                    {
                        type  : 'component',
                        id    : 'indicator',
                        style : 'margin-right: 5px',
                        html  : '1 of 3'
                    }
                ]
            }
        ]
    });
    myWin.show();
```

❸ Adds navigation buttons

❹ Adds indicator component

Listing 5.6 details the creation of a window that uses the Card layout. Although most of this should be familiar to you, we should point out a few things. The first obvious item is the `layout` property ❶, which is set to `'card'`. Next is the `activeItem` property ❷, which the container passes to the layout at render time. You set this to 0 (zero), which tells the layout to call the child component's `render` method when the container renders.

Next you define the bottom toolbar, which contains the Forward and Back ❸ buttons, which call your previously defined `handleNav` method and a generic component ❹ that you use to display the index of the current active item. The rendered container should look like the one in figure 5.7.

Clicking Forward or Back will invoke the `handleNav` method, which will take care of the card flipping and update the indicator component. Remember that with the

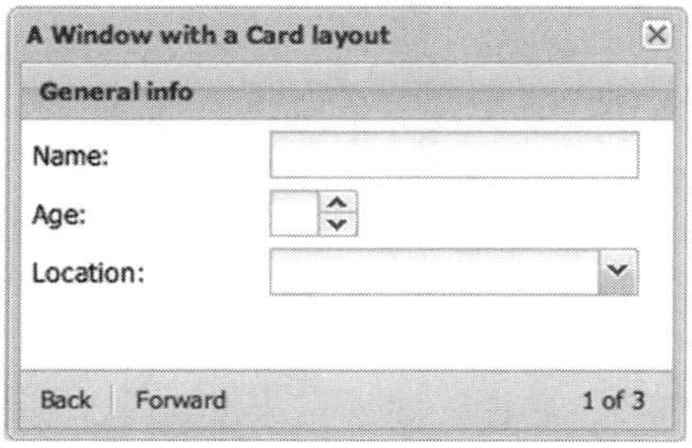

Figure 5.7   Your first Card layout implementation with a fully interactive navigation toolbar (listing 5.6)

Card layout, the logic of the active item switching is completely up to the end developer to create and manage.

In addition to the previously discussed layouts, Ext JS offers a few more schemes. The Column layout is one of the favorite schemes among UI developers for organizing UI columns that can span the entire width of the parent container.

5.8 The Column layout

Organizing components into columns allows you to display multiple components in a container side by side. Like the Anchor layout, the Column layout allows you to set the absolute or relative width of the child components. There are some things to look out for when using this layout. We'll highlight these in a bit, but first let's construct a Column layout window, as shown in the following listing.

Listing 5.7 Exploring the Column layout

```
var myWin = Ext.create("Ext.Window", {
    height      : 200,
    width       : 400,
    autoScroll  : true,                                 ❶ Sets
    id          : 'myWin',                                 scrollable
    title       : 'A Window with a Column layout',
    layout      : 'column',                             ❷ Configures
    defaults    : {                                        layout
        frame : true
    },
    items       : [
        {
            title       : 'Col 1',
            id          : 'col1',
            columnWidth : .3                            ❸ Sets relative
        },                                                 width
        {
            title       : 'Col 2',
            html        : "20% relative width",
            columnWidth : .2
        },
        {
            title : 'Col 3',
            html  : "100px fixed width",
            width : 100                                 ❹ Fixes width
        },                                                 to 100 pixels
        {
            title       : 'Col 4',
            frame       : true,
            html        : "50% relative width",
            columnWidth : .5                            ❺ Configures
        }                                                  relative width
    ]
});
myWin.show();
```

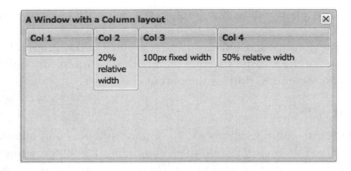

Figure 5.8   Your first Column layout, which uses relative column widths with a fixed-width entity

In a nutshell, the Column layout is easy to use. Declare child items and specify relative or absolute widths or a combination of both, as you do here. In listing 5.7, you set the autoScroll property ❶ of the container to true, which ensures that scroll bars will appear if the composite of the child component dimensions grows beyond those of the container. Next you set the layout property to 'column' ❷. You then declare four child components, the first of which has its relative width set to 30% via the columnWidth ❸ property. Set the second child's relative width to 20%. You mix things up a bit by setting a fixed width for the third child of 100 pixels ❹. Last, you set a relative width ❺ of 50% for the last child. The rendered example should look like figure 5.8.

If you tally up the relative widths, you'll see that they total up to 100%. How can that be? Three components, taking 100% width, *and* a fixed-width component? To understand how this is possible you need to dissect how the Column layout sets the sizes of all of the child components. Put your math cap back on for a moment.

The meat of the Column layout is its onLayout method, which calculates the dimensions of the container's body, which in this case is 388 pixels. It then goes through all of its direct children to determine the amount of available space to give to any of the children with relative widths.

To do this, it first subtracts the width of each of the absolute-width child components from the known width of the container's body. In this example, you have one child with an absolute width of 100 pixels. The Column layout calculates the difference between 388 and 100, which is 288 (pixels).

Now that the Column layout knows exactly how much horizontal space it has left, it can set the size of each of the child components based on the percentage. It goes through each of the children and sizes each one based on the known available horizontal width of the container's body. It does this by multiplying the percentage (decimal) by the available width. Once complete, the sum of the widths of relatively sized components turns out to be about 288 pixels.

Now that you understand the width calculations for this layout, let's change our focus to the height of the child items. Notice how the height of the child components doesn't equal the height of the container body; this is because the Column layout doesn't manage the height of the child components. This causes an issue with child items that may grow beyond the height of their containers' bodies. This is precisely why you set `autoScroll` to `true` for the window. You can exercise this theory by adding an extra-large child to the `'Col 1'` component. Enter the following code inside Firebug's JavaScript input console. Make sure you have a virgin copy of listing 5.7 running in your browser:

```
Ext.getCmp('col1').add({
    height : 250,
    title  : 'New Panel',
    frame  : true
});
```

You should now see a panel embedded into the `'Col 1'` panel with its height exceeding that of the window's body. Notice how scroll bars appear in the window. If you didn't set `autoScroll` to `true`, your UI would look cut off and might have its usability reduced or halted. You can scroll vertically and horizontally. The reason you can scroll vertically is that `Col1`'s overall height is greater than that of the window's body. That's acceptable. The horizontal scrolling is the problem in this case. Recall that the Column layout calculated only 288 pixels to properly size the three columns with relative widths. Because the vertical scroll bar is now visible, the physical amount of space in which the columns can be displayed is reduced by the width of the vertical scroll bar. In Ext JS 4, the parent's `doLayout` method is automatically called when adding a component to any of the direct children (in earlier versions you would have to call `doLayout` on the parent to keep your UIs looking great).

As you can see, the Column layout is great for organizing your child components in columns. With this layout, you have two limitations. All child items are always left-justified, and their heights are unmanaged by the parent container. Ext JS offers the HBox layout to help overcome the limitations of the Column layout and extend it far beyond its capabilities.

5.9 The HBox and VBox layouts

The HBox layout's behavior is similar to that of the Column layout because it displays items in columns, but it allows for much greater flexibility. For instance, you can change the alignment of the child items both vertically and horizontally. Another great feature of this layout scheme is the ability to allow the columns or rows to stretch to their parent's dimensions if required.

Let's dive into the HBox layout, shown in the next listing, where you'll create a container with three child panels to manipulate. But first, check out figure 5.9 to see what you're trying to accomplish.

> **Listing 5.8   HBox layout: exploring the packing configuration**

```
Ext.create("Ext.Window", {
    layout         : 'hbox',           ◁──┐  Sets layout
    height         : 300,                 ❶  to 'hbox'
    width          : 300,
    title          : 'A Container with an HBox layout',
```

```
    layoutConfig : {
        pack : 'start'
    },
    defaults : {
        frame : true,
        width : 75
    },
    items : [
        {
            title  : 'Panel 1',
            height : 100
        },
        {
            title  : 'Panel 2',
            height : 75,
            width  : 100
        },
        {
            title  : 'Panel 3',
            height : 200
        }
    ]
}).show();
```

Specifies layout
❷ configuration

In listing 5.8 you set layout to 'hbox' ❶ and specify the layoutConfig ❷ configuration object. You create the three child panels with irregular shapes, allowing you to properly exercise the different layout configuration parameters. Of these you can specify two, pack and align, where pack means "vertical alignment" and align means "horizontal alignment." Understanding the meanings for these two parameters is important because they're flipped for the HBox layout's cousin, the VBox layout. The pack parameter accepts three possible values: 'start', 'center', and 'end'. In this context, we like to think of them as left, center, and right. Modifying that parameter in listing 5.8 will result in one of the rendered windows in figure 5.9. The default value for the pack attribute is 'start'.

The align parameter accepts four possible values: 'top', 'middle', 'stretch', and 'stretchmax'. Remember that with the HBox layout, the align property specifies vertical alignment.

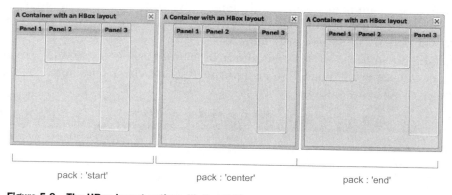

Figure 5.9   The HBox layout options (listing 5.8)

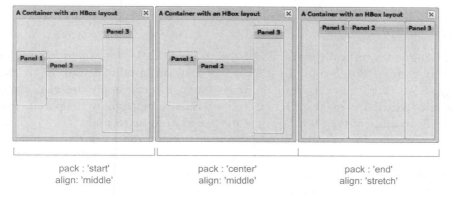

| pack : 'start' | pack : 'center' | pack : 'end' |
| align: 'middle' | align: 'middle' | align: 'stretch' |

Figure 5.10 The `'stretch'` alignment will always override any height values specified by the child items.

The default parameter for align is `'top'`. To change how the child panels are vertically aligned, you need to override the default by specifying it in the `layoutConfig` object for the container. Figure 5.10 illustrates how you can change the way the children are sized and arranged based on a few different combinations.

Specifying a value of `'stretch'` for the align attribute instructs the HBox layout to resize the child items to the height of the container's body, which overcomes one limitation of the Column layout.

The last configuration parameter that we must explore is `flex`, which is similar to the `columnWidth` parameter for the Column layout and gets specified on the child items. Unlike the `columnWidth` parameter, the `flex` parameter is interpreted as a weight or a priority instead of a percentage of the columns. Let's say, for instance, you'd like each of the columns to have equal widths. Set each column's `flex` to the same value, and they'll all have equal widths. If you wanted to have two of the columns expand to a total of one half of the width of the parent's container and the third to expand to the other half, make sure that the `flex` value for each of the first two columns is exactly half that of the third column. For instance:

```
defaults : {
    frame : true,
    width : 75
},
items    : [
    {
        title : 'Panel 1',
        flex  : 1
    },
    {
        title : 'Panel 2',
        flex  : 1
    },
    {
        title : 'Panel 3',
```

```
        flex  : 2
    }
]
```

Stacking items vertically is also possible with the VBox layout, which follows the same syntax as the HBox layout. To use the VBox layout, modify listing 5.8 by changing `layout` to `'vbox'`, and refresh the page. Next, you can apply the `flex` parameters described earlier to make each of the panels relative in height to the parent container. We like to think of the VBox layout as the Auto layout on steroids.

Contrasting the VBox layout with the HBox layout, there's one parameter change. Recall that the `align` parameter for the HBox layout accepts a value of `'top'`. For the VBox layout, though, you specify `'left'` instead of `'top'`.

Now that you've mastered HBox and VBox layouts, we'll switch gears to the Table layout, where you can position child components, such as a traditional HTML table.

5.10   *The Table layout*

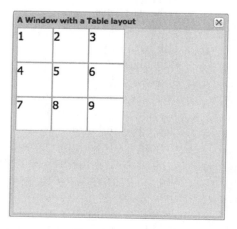

The Table layout gives you complete control over how you visually organize your components. Many of you are used to building HTML tables the traditional way, where you write the HTML code. Building a table of Ext JS components is different because you specify the content of the table cells in a single-dimension array, which can get a little confusing.

We're sure that once you've finished these exercises you'll be an expert in this layout. In the next listing you'll create a basic 3x3 Table layout like the one in figure 5.11.

Figure 5.11   The results of your first Table layout in listing 5.9

Listing 5.9   A vanilla Table layout

```
var myWin = Ext.create("Ext.Window", {
    height      : 300,
    width       : 300,
    border      : false,
    autoScroll  : true,
    title       : 'A Window with a Table layout',
    layout      : {
        type    : 'table',          ❶  Specifies layout
        columns : 3                     as 'table'
    },                              ❷  Sets number
    defaults    : {                     of columns
        height : 50,                ❸  Configures
        width  : 50                     default size
    },
```

```
    items       : [
       {
           html : '1'
       },
       {
           html : '2'
       },
       {
           html : '3'
       },
       {
           html : '4'
       },
       {
           html : '5'
       },
       {
           html : '6'
       },
       {
           html : '7'
       },
       {
           html : '8'
       },
       {
           html : '9'
       }
    ]
});
myWin.show();
```

The code in listing 5.9 creates a window container that has nine boxes stacked in a 3x3 formation like in figure 5.11. By now most of this should seem familiar to you, but we want to highlight a few items. The most obvious of these should be the layout `type` parameter ❶, set to `'table'`. Next, you set a layout `column` property ❷, which sets the number of columns. Always remember to set this property when using this layout. Last, you set `defaults` ❸ for all the child items to 50 pixels wide by 50 pixels high.

Often you need sections of the table to span multiple rows or multiple columns. To accomplish this you must specify either the `rowspan` or the `colspan` parameter explicitly on the child items. When you're done your layout will look like figure 5.12.

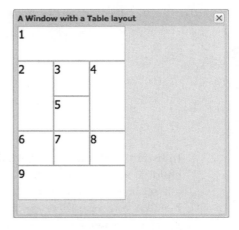

Figure 5.12   When using the Table layout you could specify `rowspan` **and** `colspan` **for a particular component, which will make it occupy more than one cell in the table.**

Let's modify your table so the child items can span multiple rows or columns, as shown in the following listing.

Listing 5.10   Exploring `rowspan` and `colspan`

```
items : [
    {
        html     : '1',
        colspan : 3,                    ①  Sets colspan to 3,
        width    : 150                       width to 150 px
    },
    {
        html     : '2',
        rowspan : 2,                    ②  Sets rowspan to 2,
        height   : 100                       height to 100 px
    },
    {
        html : '3'
    },
    {
        html     : '4',
        rowspan : 2,                    ③  Sets rowspan to 2,
        height   : 100                       height to 100 px
    },
    {
        html : '5'
    },
    {
        html : '6'
    },
    {
        html : '7'
    },
    {
        html : '8'
    },
    {
        html     : '9',
        colspan : 3,                    ④  Sets colspan to 3,
        width    : 150                       width to 150 px
    }
]
```

In listing 5.10 you reuse the existing `Container` code from listing 5.9 and replace the child `items` array. You set the `colspan` attribute for the first panel ① to 3 and manually set its width to fit the total known width of the table, which is 150 pixels. Remember that you have three columns of default 50x50 child containers. Next, you set the `rowspan` property of the second child item ② to 2 and its height to the total of two rows, which is 100 pixels. You do the same thing for panel 4 ③. The last change involves panel 9, which has the exact same attributes as panel 1 ④. The rendered table after the changes should look like figure 5.12.

When using the Table layout, keep a few things in mind. First, determine the total number of columns that'll be used and specify it in the layout `column` config property. Also, if you're going to have components span rows and/or columns, be sure to set their dimensions accordingly; otherwise the components laid out in the table won't seem to be aligned correctly. The Table layout is extremely versatile and can be used to create any type of box-based layout that your imagination conjures up, with the main limitation being that there's no parent-child size management.

Moving to our last stop on the Ext JS layout journey, we reach the ever-popular Border layout, which lets you divide any container into five collapsible regions that manage their children's size.

5.11   *The Border layout*

The Border layout made its debut in 2006, back when Ext was little more than a mere extension to the YUI library. It has since matured into an extremely flexible and easy-to-use layout that provides full control over its subparts, or regions. The Border layout has seen widespread use as an easy way to divide complex applications into manageable regions. These regions are aptly named by polar coordinates: North, South, East, West, and Center. Figure 5.13 illustrates a Border layout implementation from the Ext JS SDK.

Depending on the configuration options provided, the region can be resized or collapsed by the user. Options are also available to limit the resize of the region or prevent it from being resized altogether.

To explore the Border layout we'll use the `Viewport` class, shown in the next listing, which will make it easier for you to see the final result of this exercise.

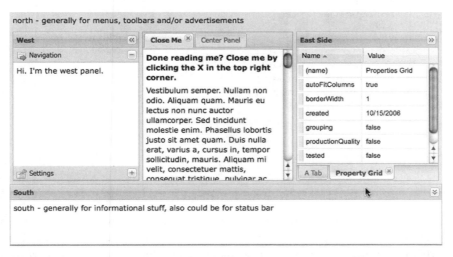

Figure 5.13   The Border layout is what attracts many new developers to the Ext JS framework and is widely used in many applications to divide the screen into task-specific functional areas.

Listing 5.11   Flexing the Border layout

```
Ext.create('Ext.Viewport', {
    layout    : 'border',                        ❶ Splits regions,
    defaults : {                                    allowing for resize
        frame   : true,
        split   : true
    },
    items : [                                    ❷ Adds north
        {                                           region
            title       : 'North Panel',
            region      : 'north',
            height      : 100,
            minHeight   : 100,
            maxHeight   : 150,
            collapsible : true
        },
        {                                        ❸ Sets resizable
            title       : 'South Panel',            south region
            region      : 'south',
            height      : 75,
            split       : false,
            margins     : {
                top : 5
            }
        },
        {                                        ❹ Configures the
            title       : 'East Panel',             east region
            region      : 'east',
            width       : 100,
            minWidth    : 75,
            maxWidth    : 150,
            collapsible : true
        },
        {                                        ❺ Adds west
            title        : 'West Panel',            region
            region       : 'west',
            collapsible  : true,
            collapseMode : 'mini',
            width        : 100
        },
        {
            title  : 'Center Panel',
            region : 'center'
        }
    ]
});
```

In listing 5.11 you accomplish a lot using Viewport in a few lines of code. You set layout to 'border' ❶ and set split to true in the default configuration object. There's a lot going on here at once, so feel free to reference figure 5.14, which depicts what the rendered code will look like.

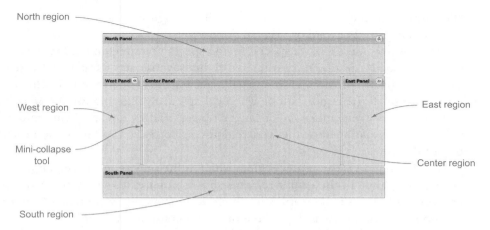

North region

West region

Mini-collapse tool

South region

East region

Center region

Figure 5.14   The Border layout's versatility and ease of use make it one of the most widely used in Ext JS–based RIAs.

Next, you begin to instantiate child items, which have Border layout region–specific parameters. To review many of them you'll make each region's behavior different from the other (see figure 5.14).

For the first child ❷, you set the region property to 'north' to ensure that it's at the top of the Border layout. You play a little game with the box component–specific parameter, height, and the region-specific parameters, minHeight and maxHeight. By specifying a height of 100, you're instructing the region to render the panel with an initial height of 100 pixels. minHeight instructs the region to not allow the split bar to be dragged beyond the coordinates that'd make the northern region the minimum height of 100. The same is true for the maxHeight parameter, except it applies to expanding the region's height. You also specify the panel-specific parameter collapsible as true, which instructs the region to allow it to be collapsed to a mere 30 pixels high.

Defining the south region, the viewport's second child ❸, you set some configuration items to prevent it from being resized but keeping the layout's 5-pixel split between the regions. By setting split to false you instruct the region to not allow it to be resized. Doing this also instructs the region to omit the 5-pixel split bar, which would make the layout somewhat visually incomplete. To achieve a façade split bar, you use a region-specific margins parameter, which specifies that you want the south region to have a 5-pixel buffer between itself and anything above it. One word of caution about this: although the layout now looks complete, end users may try to resize it, possibly causing frustration on their end.

The third child ❹ is defined as the east region. This region is configured much the same as the north panel, but it has sizing constraints that are a bit more flexible. Whereas the north region starts its life out at its minimum size, the east region starts its life between its minWidth and maxWidth. Specifying size parameters like these allows the UI to present a region in a default or suggested size while also allowing the panel to be resized beyond its original dimensions.

The west region ❺ has a special region-specific parameter, collapseMode, set to the string 'mini'. Setting the parameter in this way instructs Ext JS to collapse a panel to a mere 5 pixels, providing more visual space for the center region. Figure 5.15 illustrates how small the region will be when collapsed. By allowing the split parameter to remain true (remember the defaults object) and by not specifying minimum or maximum size parameters, the west region can be resized as far as the browser will physically allow.

The last region is the center region, which is the only required region for the Border layout. Although the center region seems a bit bare, it's special indeed. The center region is generally the canvas in which developers place the bulk of their RIA UI components, and its size is dependent on the dimensions of its sibling regions.

For all of its strengths, the Border layout has one huge disadvantage, which is that once a child in a region is defined or created it can't be changed. The fix for this is extremely simple. For each region where you wish to replace components, specify a container as a region. Let's try this by replacing the center region section for listing 5.11:

```
{
    xtype   : 'container',
    region  : 'center',
    layout  : 'fit',
    id      : 'centerRegion',
    items   : {
        title : 'Center Region',
        id    : 'centerPanel',
        html  : 'I am disposable',
        frame : true
    }
}
```

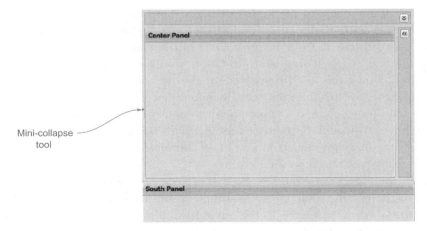

Figure 5.15 The Border layout, where two of the regions, north and east, are collapsed in regular mode and the west panel is collapsed in miniature mode

Remember that the viewport can be created only once, so a refresh of the page where the example code lies is required. The refreshed viewport should look nearly identical to figure 5.15 except that the center region now has HTML showing that it's disposable. In the previous example you define the container XType with a `layout` of `'fit'` and an `id` that you can use with Firebug's JavaScript console.

Think back to our previous discussion and exercises related to adding and removing child components to and from a container—can you recall how to get a reference to a component from its `id` and remove a child? If you can, excellent work! If you can't, we've already worked it out for you. But be sure to review the prior sections because they're extremely important to managing the Ext JS UI. Take a swipe at replacing the center region's child component, as shown in the next listing.

Listing 5.12   Replacing a component in the center region

```
var centerPanel  = Ext.getCmp('centerPanel'),
    centerRegion = Ext.getCmp('centerRegion');

centerRegion.remove(centerPanel, true);

centerRegion.add({
    xtype       : 'form',
    frame       : true,
    bodyStyle   : 'padding: 5px',
    defaultType : 'field',
    title       : 'Please enter some information',
    defaults    : {
        anchor : '-10'
    },
    items       : [
        {
            fieldLabel : 'First Name'
        },
        {
            fieldLabel : 'Last Name'
        },
        {
            xtype      : 'textarea',
            fieldLabel : 'Bio'
        }
    ]
});
```

Listing 5.12 uses everything you've learned so far regarding components, containers, and layouts, providing you with the flexibility to replace the center region's child, a panel, with a form panel, with relative ease. You can use this pattern in any of the regions to replace items at will.

5.12   Summary

This chapter explored the many and versatile Ext JS layout schemes. You learned about some of the strengths, weaknesses, and pitfalls associated with the various layouts. Remember that although many layouts can do similar things, each has its place in a UI. The correct layout to display components may not be immediately apparent and will take some practice to find if you're new to UI design.

If you aren't 100% comfortable with the material as you finish this chapter, we suggest moving forward and returning to it after some time has passed and the material has had some time to sink in. A good time to revisit this chapter is when you start part 3, "Building an application."

Now that we've covered many of the core topics, put your seatbelt on, because you're going to be in for a wild ride. Next, you'll learn more about Ext JS's UI widgets, starting with forms.

Forms in Ext JS

You just learned how to organize UI widgets with the various layout managers in the Ext JS framework. From here we'll spring into instantiating and managing Ext JS form elements. What's an application without user input?

It should be no surprise that developing and designing forms is a common task for web developers. Managing form validation is what JavaScript was mainly used for just a few years ago. Ext JS goes beyond typical form validation, building on the basic HTML input fields to both add features for the developer and enhance the user experience. For instance, let's say a user is required to enter HTML into a form. Using an out-of-the-box text area input field, the user would have to write the HTML content by hand. This isn't required with the Ext JS HTML Editor, where you get a full WYSIWYG input field, allowing the user to input and manipulate richly formatted HTML easily.

In this chapter we'll investigate the form panel, and you'll learn about many of the Ext JS form input classes. You'll also see how to build on what you know about layouts and the Container model to construct a complex form and use that implementation to submit and load the data via Ajax.

Because there are so many things to cover with input fields, this chapter will follow a cookbook style, where we walk you through the many Ext JS input fields such as the generic text field, text area, and number fields. We'll take a good look at the ComboBox, an input field that merges a simple text field with a custom drop-down list and that's arguably the most complex input field to implement in the framework. Once you get a solid grasp on these input fields, we'll tie things together by implementing and discussing the `FormPanel` class, where you'll learn the ins and outs of saving and loading data.

6.1   *Basic input fields*

The Ext JS form field and descendants add features to the existing HTML input field such as basic validations, a custom validation method, automatic resizing, and keyboard filtering. To use some of the more powerful features such as keyboard filters (masks) and automatic character stripping, you'll need to know about regular expressions.

> **Learn more about regex with JavaScript**
> If you're new to regular expressions, there's a plethora of information on the internet. One of our favorite sites to learn about this topic is www.regularexpressions.info/javascript.html.

6.1.1   *Input fields and validation*

We're going to explore quite a few features of fields at once. Please stay with us, because some of the example code can be lengthy.

Fields are built as children of a form panel to keep track of presentation issues. To start you'll create the `items` array, which will contain the XType definitions of the different text fields, as shown in the following listing.

Listing 6.1   Text fields

```
Ext.QuickTips.init();
var fpItems =[
    {
        fieldLabel : 'Alpha only',
        allowBlank : false,
        emptyText  : 'This field is empty!',          ❶ Specifies
        maskRe     : /[a-z]/i ,                           empty field
        msgTarget  : 'side'
    },                                                ❷ Specifies alpha-
    {                                                    only characters
        fieldLabel : 'Simple 3 to 7 Chars',
        allowBlank : false,
        msgTarget  : 'under',                         ❸ Allows min/max
        minLength  : 3,                                  number of characters
```

```
        maxLength   : 7
    },
    {
        fieldLabel    : 'Special Chars Only',
        msgTarget     : 'qtip',
        stripCharsRe  : /[a-zA-Z0-9]/ig
    },
    {
        fieldLabel : 'Web Only with VType',
        vtype        : 'url',
        msgTarget    : 'side'
    }
];
```

❹ Allows only special characters

❺ Uses url VType

In listing 6.1 you must work a lot of angles to demonstrate the capabilities of the simple text field. You create four text fields in the `fpItems` array. One of the redundant attributes that each child has is `fieldLabel`, which is the text to place in the `label` element for the `field` element.

For the first child you ensure that the field can't be blank by specifying `allowBlank` as `false`, which ensures that you use one of Ext JS's basic field validations. You also set a string value for `emptyText` ❶, which displays helper text and can be used as a default value. One important thing to be aware of is that it gets sent as the field's value during form submission. Next you set `maskRe` ❷, a regular expression mask, to filter keystrokes that resolve to anything other than alpha characters. The second text field is built so it can't be left blank and must contain from three to seven characters to be valid. You do this by setting the `minLength` ❸ and `maxLength` parameters. The third text field can be blank, but it has automatic alphanumeric character stripping. You enable automatic stripping by specifying a valid regular expression for the `stripCharsRe` property ❹. For the last child item ❺ you use the VType `url` to test whether the entered value is a URL. In the next listing you'll create a form panel to render your input fields.

Listing 6.2 Building the form panel for your text fields

```
var fp = Ext.create('Ext.form.Panel', {
    renderTo     : Ext.getBody(),
    width        : 400,
    height       : 240,
    title        : 'Exercising textfields',
    frame        : true,
    bodyStyle    : 'padding: 6px',
    labelWidth   : 126,
    defaultType  : 'textfield',
    defaults     : {
        msgTarget : 'side',
        anchor    : '-20'
    },
    items        : fpItems
});
```

❶ Sets default XType to textfield

❷ Sets validation message target

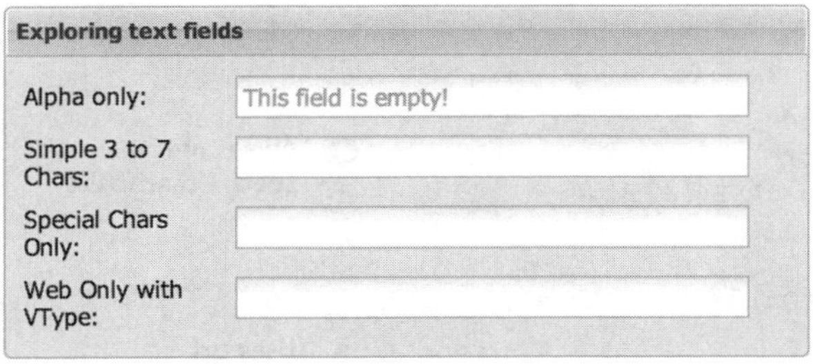

Figure 6.1   The rendered results of your form panel, which contains four text fields

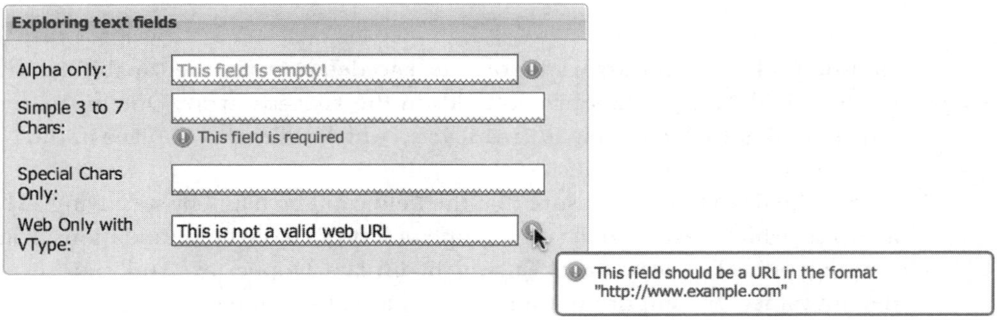

Figure 6.2   Validation error messages

Most of the code constructed in listing 6.2 should be familiar to you. But let's review a few key items relating to the Component model. You override the default component XType by setting the `defaultType` property ❶ to `'textfield'`, which, if you recall, will ensure your objects are resolved into text fields. You also set up some defaults ❷, which ensure your error message target is to the right side of the field and your `anchor` property is set. Last, you set the form panel's `items` config to the `fpItems` variable that you created earlier, which contains the four text fields. The rendered form panel should look like figure 6.1.

Notice in figure 6.1 that there's a little extra space to the right of the text fields. This is because you must ensure that validation error messages are displayed to the right of the fields. This is why you set `msgTarget` to `'side'` for your default object in your form panel definition. You can invoke validation one of two ways: focusing and blurring (losing focus) a field or invoking a form-wide `isValid` method call, `fp.getForm().isValid()`. Figure 6.2 shows what the fields look like after validation has occurred.

Each field can have its own `msgTarget` property, which can be any of five possible attributes:

- `qtip`—Displays an Ext JS quick tip on mouseover
- `title`—Shows the error in the default browser title area
- `under`—Positions the error message below the field

- side—Renders an exclamation icon to the right side of the field
- [element id]—Adds the text of the error message as the innerHTML of the target element

Note that the msgTarget property affects how the error message is displayed only when the field is inside a FieldContainer (typically a form panel). If the text field is rendered to some arbitrary element somewhere on the page (that is, using renderTo or applyTo), msgTarget will be set only to title. We encourage you to spend some time experimenting with the various msgTarget values; that way, when it comes down to building your first real-world form, you'll have a good understanding of the way they work. Let's see how to create password and file-upload fields using the text field.

6.1.2 Password and file-select fields

To create a password field, you select the password input type, and for a file input field, you set xtype to 'filefield'.

In Ext JS, to generate these, enter the following:

```
var fpItems =[
    {
        fieldLabel : 'Password',
        allowBlank : false,
        inputType       : 'password',
    },
    {
        fieldLabel : 'File',
        allowBlank : false,
        xtype      : 'filefield'
    }
];
```

Figure 6.3 shows a rendered version of the password and file input fields in a form panel.

We've covered a lot about text fields, field validations, and the password and file-upload fields. We'll now move on to looking at other input fields.

6.1.3 Building a text area

The TextArea class extends TextField. The text area field is a multiline input field. Constructing a text area is like constructing a text field, except you have to take the

Figure 6.3 Your password and file-upload fields with data filled in (left) and an example of the side validation error icons (right)

component's height into consideration. Here's an example text area with a fixed height but a relative width:

```
{
    xtype       : 'textarea',
    fieldLabel  : 'My TextArea',
    name        : 'myTextArea',
    anchor      : '100%',
    height      : 100
}
```

It's as easy as that. Let's take a quick look at how you can use the number field.

6.1.4   *The convenient number field*

Sometimes requirements dictate that you place an input field that allows only numbers to be entered. You could do this with the text field and apply your own validation, but why reinvent the wheel? The number field does pretty much all of the validation for you for integers and floating numbers. Let's create a number field that accepts floating-point numbers with precision to thousandths and allows only specific values:

```
{
    xtype            : 'numberfield',
    fieldLabel       : 'Numbers only',
    allowBlank       : false,
    emptyText        : 'This field is empty!',
    decimalPrecision : 3,
    minValue         : 0.001,
    maxValue         : 2
}
```

To apply your requirements for this number field, you specify the `decimalPrecision`, `minValue`, and `maxValue` properties. Doing so ensures that any floating number written with greater precision than 3 is rounded up. Likewise, the `minValue` and `maxValue` properties are applied to ensure that the valid range is 0.001 to 2. Any number outside of this range is considered invalid, and Ext JS will mark the field as such. The number field looks exactly like the text field when rendered, with the addition of triggers (buttons) that allow users to increment or decrement the value via mouse click. There are a few more properties that can assist with the configuration of the number field.

Now that we've looked at the text, text area, and number fields, let's look at their distant cousin, the ComboBox.

6.2   *Type-ahead with the ComboBox*

The cleverly named ComboBox field is like the Swiss Army knife of text input fields. It's a combination of a general text input field and a general drop-down box to give you a flexible and highly configurable combination input field. The ComboBox has the ability to automatically complete text entries (known as *type-ahead*) in the text input

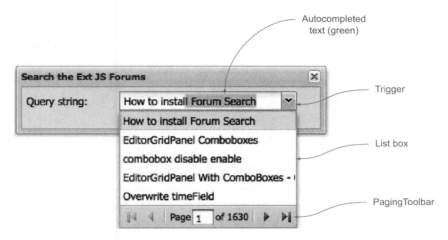

Figure 6.4   An example UI of a remote-loading and -paging ComboBox with type-ahead

area, and, coupled with a remote data store, it can work with the server side to filter results. If the ComboBox is performing a remote request against a large dataset, you can enable result paging by setting the `pageSize` property. Figure 6.4 illustrates the anatomy of a remote-loading and -paging ComboBox.

Before we look at how the ComboBox works, let's explore how to construct one. Because you're familiar with how to lay out child items, this is an excellent opportunity to use your new recently gained knowledge. So moving forward, when we discuss items that don't contain children, such as fields, we'll leave it up to you to build a container. You can use the form panel from listing 6.2.

6.2.1   Building a local ComboBox

Creating a text field is simple compared to building a ComboBox. This is because the ComboBox has a direct dependency on a class called data Store, which is the main tool to manage data in the framework. We'll just scratch the surface of this supporting class here and will go into much greater detail in chapter 7. In the following listing you'll build your first ComboBox using an XType configuration object.

Listing 6.3   Building your first ComboBox

```
var mySimpleStore = ({
    type   : 'array',
    fields : ['name'],
    data   : [
        ['Jack Slocum'],
        ['Abe Elias'],
        ['Aaron Conran'],
        ['Evan Trimboli']
    ]
});
```

**Builds
❶ ArrayStore**

```
var combo = {
    xtype        : 'combo',
    fieldLabel   : 'Select a name',
    store        : mySimpleStore,
    displayField : 'name',
    typeAhead    : true,
    mode         : 'local'
};
```

2 Specifies store in ComboBox

Sets display
3 field

Sets ComboBox
4 to local mode

In listing 6.3 you construct a simple store that reads array data, known as an *array store* **1** (a preconfigured extension of the Ext.data.Store class), which makes it easy for you to create a store that digests array data. You populate the consumable array data and set it as the data property for the configuration object. Next, you specify the fields property as an array of data points from which the data store will read and organize records. Because you have only one data point per array in your array, you specify only a single point and give it a name of 'name'. Again, we'll go into much greater detail on the data store in chapter 7, and you'll learn the entire gamut from records to connection proxies.

You specify your combo as a simple POJSO (Plain Old JavaScript Object), setting the xtype property as 'combo' to ensure that its parent container calls the correct class. You specify the reference of your previously created simple store as the store property **2**. Remember the fields property you set for the store? Well, displayField **3** is directly tied to the fields of the data store that the ComboBox is using. Because you have a single field, you'll specify your displayField with that single field, which is 'name'. Last, you

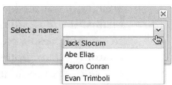

Figure 6.5   Your ComboBox from listing 6.3 rendered inside a window

set mode **4** to 'local', which ensures that the data store doesn't attempt to fetch data remotely. It's important to set this attribute correctly because the default value for mode is 'remote', which ensures that all data is fetched via remote requests. Forgetting to set it to 'local' will cause some problems. Figure 6.5 shows what the ComboBox looks like rendered.

To explore the filtering and type-ahead features, you can immediately start to type inside the text input field. Now your record set contains only four records, but you can begin to see how this works. Entering one or more letters into the text field allows type-ahead to occur the list. To try this, type A, and you'll see that the 'Abe Elias' value is auto-completed in the input field and that the record is preselected in the list. Likewise, entering 'Jac' results in the 'Jack Slocum' value being auto-completed and its corresponding record preselected. There you have it: a nice recipe for a local ComboBox.

Using a local ComboBox is great if you have a minimal amount of static data. It does have its advantages and disadvantages, though. Its main advantage is that the data doesn't have to be fetched remotely. This ends up being a major disadvantage when there's an extreme amount of data to parse through, which would make the

UI slow down, sputter, or even grind to a halt, showing that dreaded "This script is taking too long" error box. This is where the remote-loading ComboBox can be called into service.

6.2.2 *Implementing a remote ComboBox*

Using a remote ComboBox is somewhat more complicated than a static implementation. This is because you have server-side code to manage, which will include some type of server-side store like a database. To keep your focus on the ComboBox, you'll use the preconstructed PHP code at http://extjsinaction.com/dataQuery.php, which contains randomly generated names and addresses. Let's go ahead and implement your remote ComboBox, as shown in the next listing.

Listing 6.4 Implementing a remote-loading ComboBox

```
var remoteJsonStore = Ext.create(Ext.data.JsonStore, {
    storeId : 'people',
    fields      : [
        'fullName',
        'id'
    ],
    proxy    : {
        type    : 'jsonp',
        url     : 'http://extjsinaction.com/dataQuery.php',
        reader : {
            type            : 'json',
            root            : 'records',             ❶ Specifies root
            totalProperty : 'totalCount'                property
        }
    }
});

var combo = {
    xtype           : 'combo',
    queryMode       : 'remote',
    fieldLabel      : 'Search by name',
    width           : 320,
    forceSelection : true,
    displayField    : 'fullName',          ❷ Configures
    valueField      : 'id',                    autocomplete
    minChars        : 1,                       threshold
    triggerAction   : 'all',
    store           : remoteJsonStore
};
```

In listing 6.4 you change the data store type to `JsonStore` ❶, a preconfigured extension of the `Ext.data.Store` class, to allow you to easily create a store that can consume JSON data. You then specify `fields`, which is now an array containing a single object, `'fullName'`. You also create a mapping for the ID for each record, which you'll use for submission. Finally, for the store you specify a `proxy` property where you create a new instance of the JsonP proxy, a tool that's used to request data from across domains. You instruct the JsonP proxy to load data from a specific URL via the url property.

In creating your ComboBox you set forceSelection to true, which is useful for remote filtering (and type-ahead, for that matter), but it keeps users from entering arbitrary data. Next, you set displayField to 'fullName', which shows the full-name data point in the text field, and you set valueField to 'id', which ensures that the ID is used to send data when the ComboBox's data is being requested for submission. The hiddenName property is often overlooked, but it's important. Because you're displaying the name of the person but submitting the ID, you need an element in the DOM to store that value.

The minChars property ❷ defines the minimum number of characters that need to be entered into the text field before the Combo-Box executes a data store load and you override the default value of 4. Last, you specify trigger-Action as 'all', which instructs the ComboBox to perform a data store load querying for all the data. An example of your newly constructed ComboBox is shown in figure 6.6.

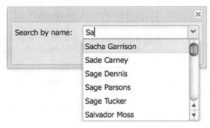

Figure 6.6   The remote-loading ComboBox from listing 6.4

Test out the rendered results, and you'll see how remote filtering can be a joy for a user to work with. Let's look at how the data coming back from the server is formatted (figure 6.7).

In examining this snippet of the resulting JSON, you can see the root that you specified in your remote ComboBox's JSON store and the fullName field you mapped to. The root contains an array of objects that the data store will translate. The data store will then remove any of the properties you map as "fields". Because you mapped

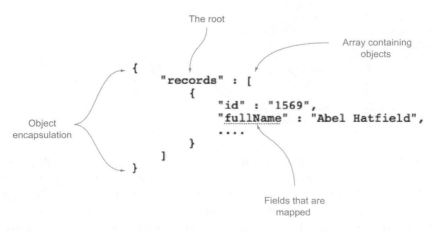

Figure 6.7   An exploded view of a slice of the served-up JSON

id and fullName, those fields will be ingested by the data store. All other properties will be ignored.

Following the format in figure 6.7 when implementing your server-side code will help ensure that your JSON is properly formatted. If you're unsure, you can use a free online tool at http://jsonlint.com, where you can paste in your JSON and have it parsed and verified.

When viewing the result of the example code in listing 6.4, you might notice that when you click the trigger, the UI's spinner stops for a brief moment. This is because all of the 2,000 records in the database are being sent to the browser and parsed, and DOM manipulation is taking place to clear the list box and create a node. The transfer and parsing of the data are relatively quick for this large dataset. DOM manipulation is one of the main reasons for JavaScript slowing down, and it's why you'd see the spinner animation stop. The amount of resources required to inject the 2,000 DOM elements is intense enough for the browser to halt all animation and focus its attention on the task at hand, not to mention that bombarding the user with that many records may present a usability issue. To mitigate these issues, you should enable paging.

To do so, your server-side code needs to be aware of the changes, which is the hardest part of this conversion. Luckily the PHP code that you're using already has the necessary code in place to adapt to the changes you're going to make. The first change you need to make is to add the following property to your JSON store:

```
totalProperty : 'totalCount'
```

Next you need to enable paging in your ComboBox. This can be done by adding a pageSize property:

```
pageSize : 20
```

That's it! Ext JS is now ready to enable pagination in your ComboBox. Refresh the code in your browser and either click the trigger or enter a few characters into the text input field, and you'll see the results of your changes, as shown in figure 6.8.

Thus far, we've explored the UI of the ComboBox and implemented both local and remote versions of Array and JSON stores. Although we've covered many aspects of the ComboBox, you've just been using it as an enhanced version of a drop-down box, and we haven't discussed how to customize the resulting data's appear-

Figure 6.8 Adding pagination to your remote ComboBox

ance. To show why we'll be changing some things, such as the inner template, we need to take a quick glance at the innards of the ComboBox.

6.2.3   *The ComboBox deconstructed*

At the nucleus of the ComboBox lie two helper classes. We've touched on the data store, which provides data fetching and loading, but we haven't discussed the data view, which is the component responsible for displaying the result data in the list box as well as providing the events necessary to allow users to select the data. Data views bind to data stores by subscribing to events such as `'beforeload'`, `'datachanged'`, and `'clear'`. They use the XTemplate, which provides the DOM manipulation to stamp out the HTML based on the HTML template you provide. Now that you've taken a quick look at the components of a ComboBox, you can continue creating your custom ComboBox.

6.2.4   *Customizing your ComboBox*

When you enabled pagination in your ComboBox, you saw only names. But what if you wanted to see the full address along with the names that you're searching? Your data store needs to know the fields you want to display. Modify listing 6.4; you'll need to add mappings for street, city, state, and zip. We'll wait here while you finish doing that.

Ready? Okay, before you can create a template, you must create some CSS that you'll need:

```
.combo-name {
    font-weight:      bold;
    font-size:        11px;
    background-color: #FFFF99;
}
.combo-full-address {
    font-size: 11px;
    color:     #666666;
}
```

This CSS code creates a class for each of the `div`s in your template. Now you need to create a new template so your list box can display the data that you want.

Enter the following code to create your ComboBox:

```
var combo = Ext.create('Ext.form.field.ComboBox', {
    fieldLabel      : 'Search by name',
    forceSelection  : true,
    displayField    : 'fullName',
    loadingText     : 'Querying....',
    pageSize        : 20,
    width           : 320,
    minChars        : 1,
    valueField      : 'id',
    triggerAction   : 'all',
    store           : remoteJsonStore,
    listConfig      : {
        getInnerTpl : function() {
            return ' <div data-qtip="{fullName}">' +
                '<div class="combo-name">{fullName}</div>' +
```

```
        '<div class="combo-full-address"> {street} </div>' +
        '<div class="combo-full-address">' +
            '{city} {state} {zip}</div>' +
      '</div>';
    }
  }
});
```

We won't cover the XTemplate in too much depth here because we covered it in chapter 2. It's important to note that by overriding `listConfig`, you specify `getInnerTpl`, which is a function that returns a string. This `getInnerTpl` function will be called by the `ListBox` class, and the string will be used to create an instance of XTemplate for you.

Your changes are now ready to be tested. If you did things correctly, your results should look similar to figure 6.9.

The way you customized your ComboBox is the tip of the iceberg! Because you have complete control over how the list box is rendered, you can even include images or QuickTips in the list box.

In this section you learned how to create a local and a remote ComboBox. You also learned about the `ArrayStore` and `JsonStore` data store classes. You had some fun adding pagination to your remote implementation, dissected the ComboBox, and customized the list box. Now let's move on to the time field.

6.3 The time field

`Time Field` is another convenience class that allows you to easily add a time-selection field to a form. To build a generic time field, you can create a configuration object with xtype set to `'timefield'`, and you'll get a list that has selectable items from 12:00 A.M. to 11:45 P.M. Here's an example of how to do that:

```
{
    xtype      : 'timefield',
    fieldLabel : 'Please select time',
    anchor     : '100%'
}
```

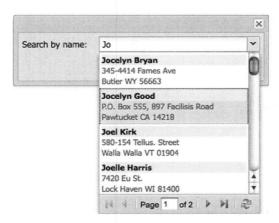

Figure 6.9 Your customized ComboBox

Figure 6.10 shows how this field would render onscreen. The time field is configurable, and you can set the range of time, increments, and even the format. Modify your time field by adding the following properties, which will allow you to use military time, set an increment of 30 minutes, and allow choices only from 9:00 A.M. to 6:00 P.M.:

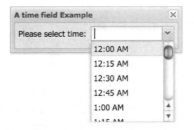

Figure 6.10   The generic time field

```
...
   minValue  : '09:00',
   maxValue  : '18:00',
   increment : 30,
   format    : 'H:i'
```

In this property list you set the `minValue` and `maxValue` properties, which set the range of time that you want your time field to have. You also set the `increment` property to 30 and format to `'H:i'`, or 24 hours and two-digit minutes. The `format` property must be valid per the `Date.parseDate` method. You should consult the full API documentation if you intend to use a custom format.

Now that you've seen how the ComboBox and time fields work, let's take a look at the HTML Editor.

6.4   The HTML Editor

The Ext JS HTML Editor is known as a WYSIWYG, or *what you see is what you get*, editor. It's a great way to allow users to enter rich HTML-formatted text without having to push them to master HTML and CSS. It allows you to configure buttons on toolbars to prevent certain interactions by users. Let's move on to building your first HTML Editor.

6.4.1   Constructing your first HTML Editor

Constructing a generic HTML Editor is simple:

```
var htmlEditor = {
   xtype      : 'htmleditor',
   fieldLabel : 'Enter in any text',
   anchor     : '100% 100%'
}
```

Your HTML Editor rendered to a form will look like figure 6.11.

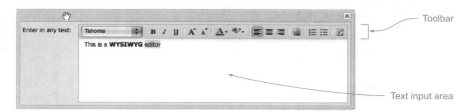

Figure 6.11   Your first HTML Editor in an Ext JS window

We discussed how the HTML Editor's toolbar could be configured to prevent some items from being displayed. This is easily done by setting the enable<someTool> properties to false. For instance, if you want to disable the font size and selection menu items, you set the following properties as false:

```
enableFontSize : false,
enableFont     : false
```

And that's all there is to it. After making the changes, refresh your page. You'll no longer see the text drop-down menu and the icons to change font sizes. To see a full list of the available options, be sure to visit the API. The HTML Editor is a great tool, but like many things, it has some limitations.

6.4.2 Dealing with lack of validation

The single biggest limitation to the HTML Editor is that it has no basic validation and no way to mark the field as invalid. When developing a form using the field, you'll have to create your own custom validation methods. A simple validate method looks like this:

```
var htmlEditor = Ext.create('Ext.form.HtmlEditor', {
    fieldLabel : "Enter in any text",
    anchor     : '100% 100%',
    allowBlank : false,
    validate   : function () {
        var val = this.getValue();
        return (this.allowBlank || val.length > 1);
    }
});
```

Although this validate method will return false if the message box is empty or contains a simple line-break element, it won't mark the field as invalid. We'll talk about how to test the form for validity before form submissions a little later in this chapter. For now, let's switch gears and look at the date field.

6.5 Selecting a date

The date field is a fun little form widget that's chock-full of UI goodness that allows a user to either enter a date via an input field or select one using the DatePicker widget. Let's build a date field:

```
var dateField = {
    xtype      : 'datefield',
    fieldLabel : 'Please select a date',
    anchor     : '100%'
}
```

Yes, it's that easy. Figure 6.12 shows how the date field renders.

This widget can be configured to prevent certain dates from being selected by setting a date property, which is an array of strings that match the format property. The

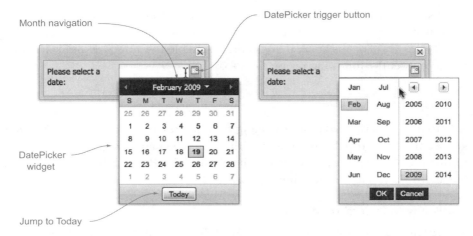

Figure 6.12   The date field exposed by the DatePicker widget (left), and the DatePicker's month and year selection tool (right)

`format` property defaults to m/d/Y, or 01/01/2001. Here are some recipes for disabling dates using the default format:

```
["01/16/2000", "01/31/2009"] disables these two exact dates
["01/16"] disables this date every year
["01/../2009"] disables every day in January for 2009
["^01"] disables every month of January
```

Now that you're comfortable with the date field, let's move on to explore the checkbox and radio fields and learn how you can use the `CheckboxGroup` and `RadioGroup` classes to create clusters of fields.

6.6   *Checkboxes and radio buttons*

This section focuses not only on instantiating checkboxes and radio buttons, but also on stacking them side by side and on top of one another. This knowledge will aid you in developing forms that allow for complex data selection.

The Ext JS checkbox field wraps Ext JS element management around the original HTML checkbox field, which also includes layout controls. As with the HTML checkbox, you can specify the value for the checkbox, overriding the default Boolean value. Next you'll create some checkboxes where you use custom values, as shown in the next listing.

Listing 6.5   Building checkboxes

```
var checkboxes = [
    {
        xtype      : 'checkbox',
        fieldLabel : 'Which do you own',
        boxLabel   : 'Cat',
        inputValue : 'cat'
    },
```

❶ Sets box label text

❷ Configures default value

```
    {
        xtype           : 'checkbox',
        fieldLabel      : ' ',
        labelSeparator  : ' ',
        boxLabel        : 'Dog',
        inputValue      : 'dog'
    },
    {
        xtype           : 'checkbox',
        fieldLabel      : ' ',
        labelSeparator  : ' ',
        boxLabel        : 'Fish',
        inputValue      : 'fish'
    },
    {
        xtype           : 'checkbox',
        fieldLabel      : ' ',
        labelSeparator  : ' ',
        boxLabel        : 'Bird',
        inputValue      : 'bird'
    }
];
```

The code in listing 6.5 builds four checkboxes, where you override the default input-Value for each node. The boxLabel property ❶ creates a field label to the right of the input field, and the inputValue property ❷ overrides the default Boolean value. An example rendering of this code is shown in figure 6.13.

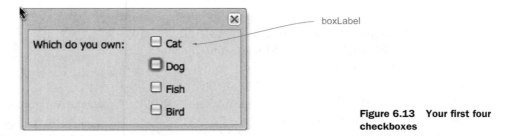

Figure 6.13 Your first four checkboxes

Although this approach will work for many forms, for some large forms it's a waste of screen space. In the next listing you'll use the checkbox group to automatically lay out your checkboxes.

Listing 6.6 Using a checkbox group

```
var checkboxes = {
    xtype       : 'checkboxgroup',
    fieldLabel  : 'Which do you own',
    anchor      : '100%',
    items       : [
        {
            boxLabel    : 'Cat',
            inputValue  : 'cat'
        },
```

```
    {
        boxLabel    : 'Dog',
        inputValue : 'dog'
    },
    {
        boxLabel    : 'Fish',
        inputValue : 'fish'
    },
    {
        boxLabel    : 'Bird',
        inputValue : 'bird'
    }
  ]
};
```

Using the checkbox group in this way will lay out your checkboxes in a single horizontal line, as shown in figure 6.14. Specifying the number of columns is as simple as setting the `columns` attribute to the number of desired columns.

Figure 6.14   Two implementations of the checkbox group: single horizontal line (left) and a two-column layout (right)

Figure 6.15   A single column of radio buttons

Your implementation of the checkbox group will depend on your requirements. Implementing the `Radio` and `Radio-Group` classes is nearly identical to using the `Checkbox` and `CheckboxGroup` classes. The biggest difference is that you can *group* radios by giving them the same name, which allows only one item to be selected at a time. Let's build a group of radio buttons, as shown in figure 6.15.

Because the `RadioGroup` class extends the `Checkbox-Group` class, the implementation is identical, so we'll save you from going over the same material. Now that we've explored the `Checkbox` and `Radio` classes and their respective `Group` classes, let's begin to tie these together by taking a more in-depth look at the form panel. You'll learn to perform form-wide checks and complex form layouts.

6.7   *The form panel*

With the Ext JS form panel, you can submit and load data using Ajax and provide live feedback to users if a field is deemed invalid. Because the `FormPanel` subclass is a descendant of the `Container` class, you can easily add and remove input fields to create a truly dynamic form.

> **File uploads aren't really Ajax**
> The XMLHttpRequest object in most browsers can't submit file data. To give the appearance of an Ajax-like submission, Ext JS uses an iFrame to submit forms that contain file input elements.

An added benefit is the form panel's ability to use other layouts or components, such as the tab panel with the Card layout, to create robust forms that take considerably less screen space than traditionally laid-out single-page forms. Because Form-Panel is a subclass of Panel you get all of Panel's features, including docked items such as toolbars.

6.7.1 Reviewing what you're building

Like the other Container subclasses, FormPanel can use any layout that's available from the framework to create exquisitely laid-out forms. To assist with the grouping fields, the form panel has a cousin called the fieldset. Before you build your components, take a sneak peek at what you're going to achieve (figure 6.16).

To construct your complex form you'll have to construct two fieldsets: one for the name information and another for the address information. In addition to the fieldsets, you'll set up a tab panel that has a place for some text fields and two HTML Editors. To complete this task you'll use all of what you've learned so far, which means we'll go over quite a bit of code.

6.7.2 Constructing the fieldsets

Now that you know what you'll be constructing, let's start by building the fieldset that'll contain the text fields for the name information, as shown in the following listing.

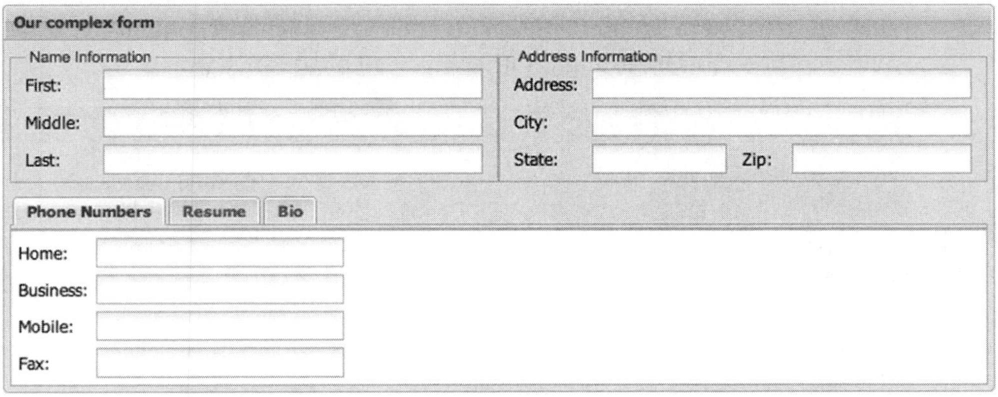

Figure 6.16   A sneak peek at the complex form panel you're going to build

Listing 6.7   Constructing your first fieldset

```
var fieldset1 = {
    xtype       : 'fieldset',                       ⟵┐  Sets xtype to
    title       : 'Name',                           ❶  'fieldset'
    flex        : 1,
    border      : false,
    labelWidth  : 60,
    defaultType : 'field',
    defaults    : {
       anchor    : '-10',
       allowBlank : false
    },
    items : [
       {
          fieldLabel : 'First',
          name       : 'firstName'
       },
       {
          fieldLabel : 'Middle',
          name       : 'middle'
       },
       {
          fieldLabel : 'Last',
          name       : 'lastName'
       }
    ]
};
```

In constructing your first fieldset XType ❶ you may think the parameters look like those of a panel or container. This is because the `FieldSet` class extends `Container` and adds some functionality for the collapse methods to allow you to include fields in a form. The reason you're using a fieldset in this instance is that it's giving you that neat little title up top, and in this way you get exposure to this component.

You'll skip rendering this first fieldset because you'll use it in a form panel a little later on. Let's go on to build the second fieldset, which will contain the address information. The following listing is rather large, so please stick with us.

Listing 6.8   Building your second fieldset

```
var fieldset2 = Ext.apply({}, {                    ⟵┐  Copies properties
    flex       : 1,                                 ❶  from first fieldset
    labelWidth : 30,
    title      : 'Address Information',
    defaults   : {
       layout : 'column',
       anchor : '100%'
    },
    items      : [
       {
          fieldLabel : 'Address',
          name       : 'address'
       },
```

```
    {
        fieldLabel : 'Street',
        name       : 'street'
    },
    {                                            ❷ Adds column
        xtype   : 'container',                      layout containers
        items   : [
            {
                xtype         : 'fieldcontainer',      ❸ Adds field
                columnWidth : .5,                         container
                items         : [
                    {
                        xtype       : 'textfield',       Configures
                        fieldLabel : 'State',           ❹ state text field
                        name        : 'state',
                        labelWidth : 100,
                        width       : 150
                    }
                ]
            },
            {                                          ❺ Adds field
                xtype         : 'fieldcontainer',          container
                columnWidth : .5,
                items         : [
                    {
                        xtype       : 'textfield',       Sets zip code
                        fieldLabel : 'Zip',            ❻ text field
                        name        : 'zip',
                        labelWidth : 30,
                        width       : 162
                    }
                ]
            }
        ]
    }
    ]
}, fieldset1);
```

In listing 6.8 you use Ext.apply ❶ to copy many of the properties from fieldset1 and apply them to fieldset2. This utility method is commonly used to copy or override properties from one object or another. We'll talk more about this method when we look into Ext JS's utility tool belt. To end up with the desired layout and have the state and zip code fields side by side, you must rely on a lot of nesting. The child ❷ of your second fieldset is a container that has its layout set to 'column'. The first child of that container is a field-container ❸, which contains the state text field ❹. The second child ❺ of your Column-Layout container is another fieldcontainer, which contains the zip code text field ❻.

You might be wondering why there are so many nested containers and why the code to get this done is so darn long. The container nesting is necessary in order to use different layouts within other layouts. This might not make sense to you immediately. We think the picture will be clearer to you when you render the form. For now, let's move on to building a place for these two fieldsets to live.

To achieve the side-by-side look of the form, you'll need to create a container for it that's set up to use the HBox layout. To have equal widths in the HBox layout, you must set the `stretch` property of each fieldset to 1. Let's build a home for the two fieldsets:

```
var fieldsetContainer = {
    xtype        : 'container',
    layout       : 'hbox',
    layoutConfig : {
        align : 'stretch'
    },
    items   : [
        fieldset1,
        fieldset2
    ]
};
```

In this code block you create a container that has a fixed height but no width set. This is because this container's width will be automatically set via the VBox layout, which your future form panel will use.

6.7.3   Creating the tab panel

Next you'll build a tab panel with three tabs, one for the phone number form elements and the other two for HTML Editors. This tab panel will use the bottom half of the form panel's available height. You'll configure all of the tabs in one shot, so the next listing is pretty lengthy.

Listing 6.9   Building a tab panel with form items

```
var tabs = [
    {
        xtype      : 'fieldcontainer',          ◁──┐   Adds container
        title      : 'Phone Numbers',              ❶  for the text fields
        layout     : 'form',
        bodyStyle  : 'padding:6px 6px 0',
        defaults   : {
            xtype : 'textfield',
            width : 230
        },
        items: [
            {
                fieldLabel : 'Home',
                name       : 'home'
            },
            {
                fieldLabel : 'Business',
                name       : 'business'
            },
            {
                fieldLabel : 'Mobile',
                name       : 'mobile'
            },
```

```
        {
            fieldLabel : 'Fax',
            name       : 'fax'
        }
    ]
},
{
    title  : 'Resume',
    xtype  : 'htmleditor',        ◁⌐┐
    name   : 'resume'              ❷   Adds two HTML
},                                     Editors as tabs
{
    title  : 'Bio',
    xtype  : 'htmleditor',
    name   : 'bio'
}
];
```

Listing 6.9 constructs an array consisting of three tabs that'll be children of your future tab panel. The first tab ❶ is a fieldcontainer that has four text fields. The second ❷ and third tabs are HTML Editors that will be used to enter a resume and a short biography. Let's move on to building the tab panel:

```
var tabPanel = {
    xtype             : 'tabpanel',
    activeTab         : 0,
    deferredRender    : false,
    layoutOnTabChange : true,
    border            : false,
    flex              : 1,
    plain             : true,
    items             : tabs
}
```

Your task in the next listing will be to construct the form panel itself, which is relatively trivial compared to all of its child items.

Listing 6.10 Piecing it all together

```
var myFormPanel   = Ext.create('Ext.form.Panel', {
    renderTo      : Ext.getBody(),
    width         : 700,
    title         : 'Our complex form',
    frame         : true,
    id            : 'myFormPanel',
    layout        : 'vbox',
    layoutConfig : {
        align : 'stretch'
    },
    items         : [
        fieldsetContainer,
        tabPanel
    ]
});
```

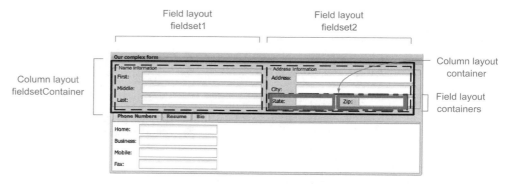

Figure 6.17   The results of your first complex layout form with the different containers used to compose the complex layouts

You finally get to create your form panel. You set `renderTo` to ensure that the form panel is automatically rendered. To have the `fieldsetContainer` and the tab panel properly sized, you use the VBox layout with `layoutConfig`'s `align` property set to `'stretch'`. Take a look at figure 6.17 to see how this beast of a form renders.

In the figure we highlighted the various containers that compose the first half of the form, which include the `fieldsetContainer`, two fieldsets, and their child components. By using this many containers you're ensuring complete control over how the UI is laid out. It's common practice to have these long code batches to create a UI with this type of complexity. When exploring your newly built form panel, flip through the three tabs and reveal the HTML Editors underneath.

By now you've seen how combining multiple components and layouts can result in something that's both usable and space saving. Now let's focus on learning to use forms for data submission and loading; otherwise your forms will be useless.

6.8   *Data submission and loading*

Submitting data via the basic form submit method is one of the areas new developers most commonly get tripped up on. This is because for so many years we were used to submitting a form and expecting a page refresh. With Ext JS, the form submission requires a bit of know-how. Likewise, loading a form with data can be a little confusing for some, so we'll explore a few ways you can do that as well.

6.8.1   *Submitting the good old way*

Submitting your form the good old way is extremely simple, but you need to configure the form panel's underlying form element with the `standardSubmit` property set to `true`. To perform the submission, you call

```
Ext.getCmp('myFormPanel').getForm().submit();
```

This code will call the generic DOM form `submit` method, which will submit the form the old-fashioned way. If you're going to use the form panel in this way, we suggest that you review submitting via Ajax, which will point out some of the features that you can't use when using the older form-submission technique.

6.8.2 Submitting via Ajax

To submit a form, you must access the form panel's `BasicForm` component. To do so you use the accessor method `getForm` or `formPanel.getForm()`. From there you have access to the `BasicForm`'s `submit` method, which you'll use to send data via Ajax. The code is shown in the next listing.

Listing 6.11 Submitting your form

```
var onSuccessOrFail = function(form, action) {
    var formPanel = Ext.getCmp('myFormPanel');
    formPanel.el.unmask();
    var result = action.result;
    if (result.success) {
        Ext.MessageBox.alert('Success',action.result.msg);
    }
    else {
        Ext.MessageBox.alert('Failure',action.result.msg);
    }
};

var submitHandler = function() {
    var formPanel = Ext.getCmp('myFormPanel');
    formPanel.el.mask('Please wait', 'x-mask-loading');
    formPanel.getForm().submit({
        url     : 'success.true.txt',
        success : onSuccessOrFail,
        failure : onSuccessOrFail
    });
};
```

❶ Displays message driven by JSON

❷ Performs form submission

In listing 6.11 you create a success and failure handler called `onSuccessOrFail`, which will be called if the form submission attempt succeeds or fails. It will display an alert message box ❶ depending on the status of the returning JSON from the web server. You then create the submission handler method, `submitHandler`, which performs the form submission ❷. You could have specified the URL at the `BasicForm` or form panel level, but you specify it here on the submit call because we wanted to point out that the target URL could be changed at runtime. Also, if you're providing any type of wait message, as you do here, you should have success and failure handlers.

At minimum, the returning JSON should contain a `'success'` Boolean with the value of `true`. Your success handler is expecting a `msg` property as well, which should contain a string with a message to return to the user:

```
{success: true, msg : 'Thank you for your submission.'}
```

Likewise, if your server-side code deems that the submission was unsuccessful for any reason, the server should return a JSON object with the `success` property set to `false`.

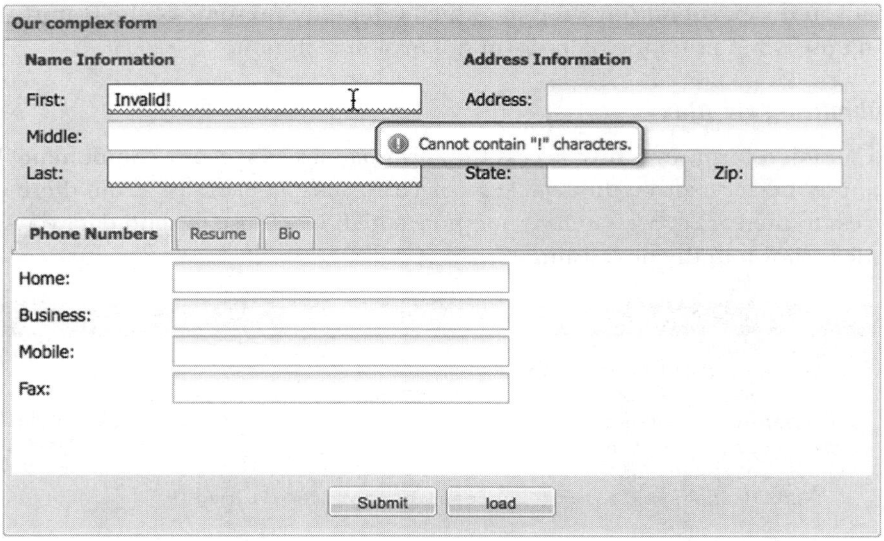

Figure 6.18   The results from our server-side `errors` object using the standard QuickTip error `msg`

If you want to perform server-side validation, which can return errors, your return JSON could include an `errors` object as well. Here's an example of a failure message with attached errors:

```
{
    success : false,
    msg     : 'This is an example error message',
    errors  : {
        firstName : 'Cannot contain "!" characters.',
        lastName  : 'Must not be blank.'
    }
}
```

If the returning JSON contains an `errors` object, the fields that are identified by that name will be marked invalid. Figure 6.18 shows the form with the JSON code served to it.

In this section you learned how to submit your form using the standard submit methods as well as the Ajax method. You also saw how to use the `errors` object to provide server-side validation with UI-level error notification. Next we'll look at loading data into the form using the `load` and `setValues` methods.

6.8.3   Loading data into your form

The use cycle of just about every form includes saving and loading data. With Ext JS you have a few ways to load data, but you must have data to load, so we'll dive right into creating some. Let's create some mock data and save it in a file called data.json:

```
{
    "success" : true,
    "data"    : {
        "firstName" : "Jack",
        "lastName"  : "Slocum",
        "middle"    : "",
        "address"   : "1 Ext JS Corporate Way",
        "city"      : "Orlando",
        "state"     : "Florida",
        "zip"       : "32801",
        "home"      : "123 345 8832",
        "business"  : "832 932 3828",
        "mobile"    : "123 332 2122",
        "fax"       : "392 322 9321",
        "resume"    : "Skills:<br><ul><li>Java Developer</li><li>Ext JS
Senior Core developer</li></ul>",
        "bio"       : " Jack is a stand-up kind of guy.<br>"
    }
}
```

Just like with form submission, the root JSON object must contain a success property with the value of true, which will trigger the setValues call. Also, the values for the form need to be in an object whose reference property is data. Likewise, it's great practice to keep your form element names in line with the data properties to load. Doing so will ensure that the right fields get filled in with the correct data. For the form to load the data via Ajax, you can call BasicForm's load method, whose syntax is just like submit:

```
var formPanel = Ext.getCmp('myFormPanel');
formPanel.el.mask('Please wait', 'x-mask-loading');
formPanel.getForm().load({
    url     : 'data.json',
    success : function() {
        formPanel.el.unmask();
    }
});
```

Executing this code will result in your form panel performing an Ajax request to fetch the data, and ultimately the form will be filled in with the values, as illustrated in figure 6.19.

If you have the data on hand, let's say from another component such as a data grid, you can set the values via myFormPanel.getForm().setValues(dataObj). Using this, dataObj would contain only the proper mapping to element names. Likewise, if you have an instance of Ext.data.Record you can use the form's loadRecord method to set the form's values.

> **TIP** To retrieve the values from any given form, call getValues from the FormPanel instance. For example, myFormPanel.getValues() would return an object containing keys representing the names of the fields and their values.

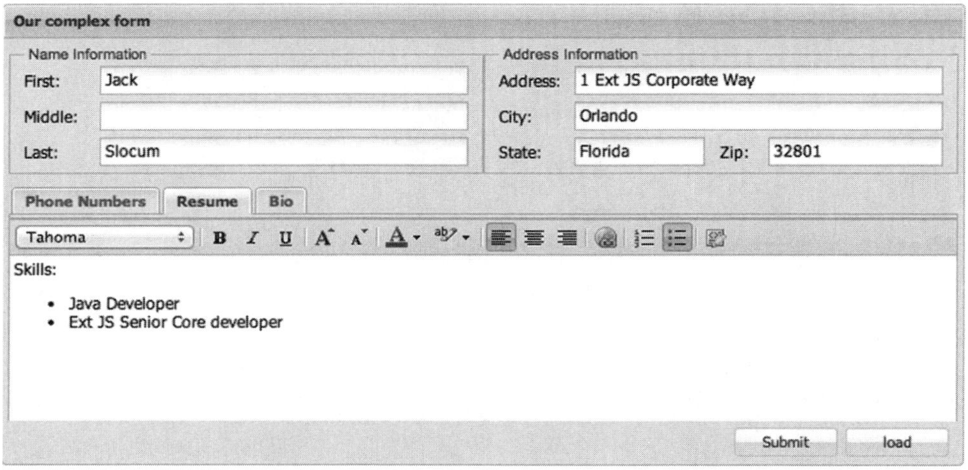

Figure 6.19   The results of loading your data via Ajax

Loading data can be as simple as that. Remember that if the server side wants to deny data loading, you can set the `success` value to `false`, which will trigger the `failure` method as referenced in the load's configuration object.

Congratulations! You've configured your first truly complex form panel and learned how to load and save its data.

6.9   *Summary*

In focusing on the `FormPanel` class, we covered quite a few topics, including many of the commonly used fields. You even got a chance to take an in-depth look at the ComboBox field, where you got your first exposure to its helper classes, `data Store` and `DataView`. Using that experience you saw how to customize the ComboBox's resulting list box. You also built a relatively complex layout form and used your new tool to submit and load data.

Moving forward, we're going to take an in-depth look at the data grid panel. You'll learn about its inner components and see how to customize the look and feel of a grid. You'll also see how to use the editor plug-ins for the grid panel that allow you to edit data in line. Along the way you'll learn more about the data store. Be sure to get some candy; this is going to be a fun ride!

The data store

7

This chapter covers
- Using the data store
- Understanding data proxies
- Exploring writers and validations

To create a real-world application, you need a way to persist data. Data persistence allows users of your application to access data between sessions, so the data should be stored on a medium that enables it to be accessed after your application has been stopped and started again.

Data persistence can happen by updating or retrieving the data from the components on screen using Ajax techniques if you're implementing simple applications. But if you're creating an Ext JS application that involves advanced interaction logic on the client side, you can use the functionality available in the Ext JS data store.

This chapter begins by taking a bird's-eye view of the data package. We'll introduce `Ext.data.Store` and its supporting classes, including `Ext.data.Model`. You'll learn how data flows and how it's consumed by the data store. We'll discuss the various data readers and explore data consumption with array, JSON, and XML data.

You'll become familiar with each of the data proxies and see how to load data from resident memory, Ajax, JSONP, and LocalStorage. At this end of the chapter we'll introduce advanced features of the data package in Ext JS 4 by demonstrating how to handle data validation and associations.

When you're done with this chapter, you'll have sufficient knowledge and confidence to create any data-driven view with the framework, beginning with grid panels in chapter 8.

7.1   Introducing the data store

The purpose of Ext.data.Store is to provide a foundation where you can store a local subset of the data available from the server and keep track of changes to this data before sending it back to the server (if your application allows editing of data).

The data store feeds quite a few widgets throughout the framework wherever data is needed. To put this in plain view, figure 7.1 enumerates the classes that depend on the data Store class.

As you can see, the data store supports quite a few widgets, including the data view, Combo Box, charts, grid panel, and tree panel. The data store also serves as the foundation for tree panels (we'll cover the tree store in chapter 10).

The data Store class plays an integral role in the framework and your applications, so it makes a lot of sense to cover this class in great detail. It's for this reason that we're going to spend the next few pages looking at data Store and how things work before you get your hands dirty with some code.

7.1.1   The supporting classes

You often load data using the data store, and rightfully so: data Store is sort of an interface class. The store itself is responsible for the marshaling of data but mainly manages other classes. These other classes support the data store in its effort to supply data to views to render onscreen.

To understand what supports the store, let's take a step back and look at a simplified view of the data package. Figure 7.2 shows that data Store is connected to many classes. Each class plays a role in how data is consumed by the framework. Table 7.1 contains a breakdown of what these classes do.

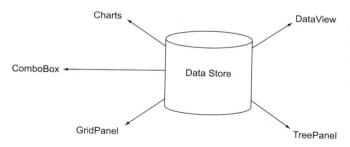

Figure 7.1 Data Store and the classes to which it feeds data. This illustration doesn't depict class hierarchy.

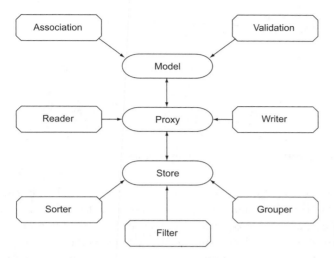

Figure 7.2 The data package at a glance

Table 7.1 Data Store **and its supporting classes**

Class	Purpose
Store	The interface class generally used for loading and saving data
Sorter	Responsible for sorting data
Filter	Manages the filtering of data
Grouper	Used to group data
Proxy	Manages how data typically is fed into the data store
Reader	Used to transform inbound data to be fed into instances of Model
Writer	Responsible for the marshaling of data to be sent to a data source for persistence
Model	Represents individual data rows for a particular data store
Association	Allows models to be associated to one another via preconfigured rules
Validation	Used as a means to prevent a model from becoming corrupt with incorrect or incomplete data

There's quite a bit of support for the data store in the framework. All of these parts are designed to make your job easier and help make your applications manage robust data in the browser easily.

You now know a little about how the data store uses supporting classes. Knowing how the data flows will be beneficial when you start working with the data store.

7.1.2 *How data flows*

Let's see how data flows from a data source to the store. We'll begin with a basic flow illustration, shown in figure 7.3.

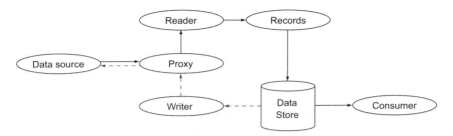

Figure 7.3   The data flow from a data source to a data store consumer

As you can see, the data always originates from a data source, and the loading and saving is managed by a data proxy. The data `Proxy` classes facilitate the retrieval of unformatted data objects from a multitude of sources and contain their own event models for communication with subscribed classes such as the data `Reader` class.

For example, changing the value of a model in a store that's bound to a consumer, like the grid panel, will result in the UI being updated when the model is committed. After the models are loaded into the data store, the bound consumer refreshes its view and the load cycle completes.

The specific data `Store` subclasses will have `load`, `remove`, and `sync` operations available. The `load` and `remove` operations manipulate the local list of models in the store, and the `sync` operation synchronizes the local content of the store with the data endpoint via the chosen proxy.

As you just learned, data proxies are crucial to the operation of data stores. Let's dive in and learn more about what data proxies are and what types of proxies are available to you to implement.

7.1.3   *All about data proxies*

In the framework is an abstract class aptly named `Ext.data.proxy.Proxy`, which serves as a base class for several subclasses responsible for retrieving data from and writing it to specific sources, as shown in figure 7.4.

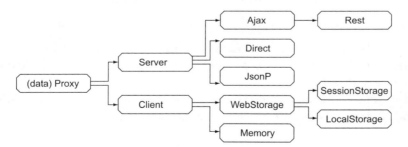

Figure 7.4   The data proxy and its seven specific implementations. Each is responsible for retrieving data from a specific data source.

Looking at all the different proxies can seem a bit overwhelming at first. If you're coming from Ext JS 3, it can look like the data package exploded! But you can relax when you discover that the Server, Client, and WebStorage proxies are base classes, leaving you with seven classes that you can use. We'll explore each of the seven classes in detail here.

The most common proxy is the Ajax proxy, which uses the browser's XHR object to perform generic Ajax requests. The Ajax proxy is limited to the same domain because of what's known as the *same-origin policy*. This policy dictates that XHR requests via XHR can't be performed outside of the domain from which a specific page is being loaded. This policy was meant to tighten security with XHRs but has been construed as more of an annoyance than a security measure. The Ext JS developers were quick to come up with a workaround for this "feature," which is where the JsonP proxy comes into the picture.

The JsonP proxy cleverly uses the script tag to retrieve data from another domain, and it works well, but it requires that the requesting domain return JavaScript instead of generic data snippets. This is important to know because you can't just use the JsonP proxy against any third-party website to retrieve data. The JsonP proxy requires the return data to be wrapped in a global method call, passing the data in as the only parameter. You'll learn more about the JsonP proxy in a bit because you'll use it with various APIs located on extjsinaction.com to retrieve data from our examples.

The `MemoryProxy` class offers Ext JS the ability to load data from a memory object. Although you can load data directly to an instance of `data Store` via its `loadData` method, use of the `MemoryProxy` class can be helpful in certain situations. One example is the task of reloading the data store. If you use `Store.loadData`, you need to pass in the reference to the data, which is to be parsed by the reader and loaded into the store. Using the Memory proxy makes things simple, because you only need to call the `Store.reload` method and let Ext JS take care of the dirty work.

The Direct proxy allows the data store to interact with the `Ext.direct` remoting providers, allowing for data retrievals via remote procedure calls (RPCs).

NOTE If you're interested in learning more about Ext Direct, feel free to take a peek at chapter 11, but come back right away. We're going to cover a lot of foundational material here that you'll need for chapter 11.

`RestProxy` is a subclass of `AjaxProxy` that specializes in talking to REST-style resources. For instance, if you want to retrieve employee data with ID 403, the Rest proxy automatically sends a GET request to /employee/403. This automatic URL creation can be handy in an environment that already uses this system.

When your application is offline or when you don't wish to talk to the server, you have the option of using the LocalStorage proxy or SessionStorage proxy to persist your data. These client-side proxies persist data in key/value mechanisms available via the HTML5 Web Storage API, so associated data structures will be automatically serialized to JSON. If the HTML5 Web Storage API isn't available on the browser, the proxy will throw an exception. Use the LocalStorage proxy if you want to persist data between sessions, and use the SessionStorage proxy if you only want the data to be stored while the browser session is active.

> **NOTE** Keep in mind that you need to provide a unique ID for each Web-Storage proxy.

All the proxies implement the same interface and in theory should be interchangeable. There are some things to note, though. Due to limitations in JavaScript, all parameters are passed using GET when issuing a write using a JsonP proxy. This makes sense, but it might come as a surprise when you have to reimplement the back-end for what started using an Ajax proxy if you choose to switch to a JsonP proxy. It should also be obvious that it doesn't make sense to keep a `url` setting when changing from an Ajax proxy to a LocalStorage proxy.

7.1.4   *Models and readers*

The cornerstone of the data store is the `Ext.data.Model`. It holds the data in a list of fields and describes associations to other models using `Ext.data.Association`, and it allows for validation using `Ext.data.validations`. You can read data into the store using `Ext.data.Reader` and write data back to the server using `Ext.data.Writer`.

If you're familiar with SQL databases, you may notice that `Ext.data.Model` somewhat resembles a table in a SQL database. Every time you instantiate a specific Ext JS data model, you could say that you mimic the content of an entry in the SQL database on the client side (remember that you aren't required to hold the entire dataset on the client).

Although the typical scenario for using a data store involves a SQL database on the server, the data store can also store data using LocalStorage or SessionStorage if it's available in the browser. Think of the Ext JS data store as an API, and your current choice of transportation (JSON, XML, or LocalStorage) as an implementation.

Let's start by defining the data-consumption options you have before peeking under the hood of the data store. After a proxy fetches the raw data, a reader then reads or parses it. A reader takes raw, unformatted data objects and abstracts the data points, known as *data indexes*, and arranges them into name data pairs, or generic objects. Figure 7.5 illustrates how this mapping works.

As you can see, the raw and unformatted data is organized and fed into instances of `Model` that the reader then creates. These instances of `Model` are then spooled into the data store and are ready to be consumed by a widget.

> **NOTE** `Ext.data.Record` from Ext JS 3 is known as `Ext.data.Model` in Ext JS 4. This name change more directly identifies the model part of the data store in the Model, View, Controller (MVC) pattern as described in part 3 of this book.

A `Model` is a fully Ext JS–managed JavaScript object. Much as Ext JS manages `Element`, the `Model` has getter and setter methods and a full event model for which the data

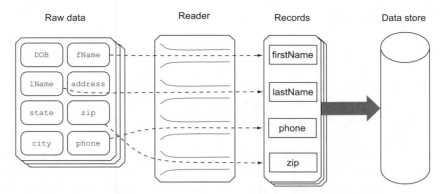

Figure 7.5 A reader maps raw or unformatted data so that it can be inserted into models, which then get spooled into a data store.

store is bound. This management of data adds usability and some cool automation to the framework.

In section 7.4 you'll see how to use the getters and setters to update model data via the data store, but first we'll build the foundation for data updates and describe how the data writer fits into the picture and how to validate your data before interacting with the store.

`Reader` is a class that's responsible for helping to translate the inbound data from your data source. It translates your inbound data and instantiates instances of your `Model` definition, which are collected by the data store. Many types of readers are available, and you're going to implement each of them in this chapter.

7.2 Loading and saving data

You have various options for consuming data. Each option has varying levels of complexity, so you should think carefully about your requirements before you start using a store. Your choice of data-transport mechanism will influence which subclasses of `Ext.data.Proxy`, `Ext.data.Reader`, and `Ext.data.Writer` you need to use.

When reading data, remember that the endpoint is the `Ext.data.model` that uses `Ext.data.Field` as an abstraction for storage. So when you finish reading the data, the steps taken to read data become irrelevant for the rest of your application code. This means that at a later stage you can choose JSON as a transport medium instead of XML, if your application started out using XML.

7.2.1 Reading array data

The simplest use of a store is to load inline data in a component. Imagine that you have a typical usage scenario of choosing a title for a person. You can implement this using a ComboBox approach, putting the list of titles in an inline data array like this:

```
{
    xtype    : 'combo',
    name     : 'title',
```

```
fieldLabel : 'Title',
queryMode  : 'local',
valueField : 'title',
store      : ['Mr.', 'Ms.', 'Dr.']
}
```

Note that the store declaration takes up only a single line here; the other lines are related to the ComboBox. If this is your first time around Ext JS, this example may seem a bit confusing. Ext JS provides a lot of shortcuts and convenience classes, and this is a prime example.

The ComboBox example doesn't have a model or fields definition. During the construction phase of the store, Ext JS will create Ext.data.ArrayStore, which uses Ext.data.reader.Array automatically for you and sets it up for use during runtime.

Let's explore the data array store and array reader a little more in depth to get better acquainted with the process of consuming array data, as shown in the next listing.

Listing 7.1   Creating a data store that loads local array data

```
var arrayData = [                                    ❶ Creates local
    ['Jay Garcia',    'MD'],                            array data
    ['Aaron Baker',   'VA'],
    ['Susan Smith',   'DC'],
    ['Mary Stein',    'DE'],
    ['Bryan Shanley', 'NJ'],
    ['Nyri Selgado',  'CA']
];
Ext.define('User', {                                 ❷ Creates user
    extend : 'Ext.data.Model',                          model
    fields : [
        {                                            ❸ Declares fields
            name    : 'name',
            mapping : 1
        },
        {
            name    : 'state',
            mapping : 2
        }
    ]
});
store = Ext.create('Ext.data.Store', {               ❹ Builds
    model : 'User',                                     store
    proxy : {
        type    : 'memory',
        reader : {
            model : 'User',
            type  : 'array'
        }
    }
});
store.loadData(arrayData);                           ❺ Loads data
console.log(store.first().data)                        into store
```

In listing 7.1 you implement the full gamut of data store configuration. You start by creating an array of arrays, which is referenced by the variable `arrayData` ❶. Please pay close attention to the format the array data is in, because this is the expected format for the `ArrayReader` class. The reason the data is an array of arrays is that each child array contained within the parent array is treated as a singular record.

You create a user model ❷, which will be used as the template to map your array data points to create records. You pass an array of object literals, which are known as *fields* ❸, to the configuration object, and detail each field name and its mapping. Each of these object literals is a configuration object for the `Ext.data.Field` class, which is the smallest unit of managed data within `Ext.data.Model`. In this case you map the field name to the first data point in each array record and the field state to the second data point.

Next, you create an instance of data `Store` with a Memory proxy, which is what will load your unformatted data from memory ❹.

You then add an instance of `ArrayReader` ❺, which is responsible for sorting out the data retrieved by the proxy and creating new instances of the new user model you just created. When the store loads the data, the array reader reads each record and creates a new instance of `User`, passing the parsed data to it, which is then loaded into the store.

This completes our end-to-end example of how to create a store that reads array data. With this pattern you can change the type of data the store is able to load. To do this you swap out the `ArrayReader` with either a `JsonReader` or an `XmlReader`. Likewise, if you wanted to change the data source, you could swap out `MemoryProxy` for another such as `Http Proxy`, `JsonP Proxy`, or `Direct Proxy`.

Recall that we mentioned something earlier about convenience classes to make our lives a little easier. If you were to re-create the store using the `ArrayStore` convenience class, this is what your code would look like using the previous `arrayData`:

```
var store = Ext.create('Ext.data.ArrayStore', {
  data   : arrayData,
  fields : ['personName', 'state']
});
```

As you can see in this example, you use shortcut notation for the fields to create an instance of `Ext.data.ArrayStore`. You achieve this by passing a reference of the data, which is your `arrayData`, and a list of fields, which provides the mapping. Notice how the `fields` property is a simple list of strings. This is a completely valid configuration of field mappings, because Ext JS is smart enough to create the name and index mapping based on string values passed in this manner. You could also have a mixture of objects and strings in a `fields` configuration array. For instance, the following configuration is completely valid:

```
fields : [
  'fullName',
  {
      name    : 'state',
```

```
        mapping : 2
    }
]
```

It can be really cool to use this flexibility. Just know that having a mixture of field configurations like this can make the code a bit hard to read.

Using this convenience class saved you from having to create a proxy, record template, and reader to configure the store. Use of the JSON or XML store is just as easy, which you'll learn more about soon. Moving forward, you'll use the convenience classes to save time.

7.2.2   *Reading JSON data*

A JSON store is a little more complex than an array store because it also lets you read associated data structures and retrieve data from the server. Many people choose to supply JSON data from their server-side stack because it's more easily digested by the browser.

Let's pretend that you have a listing of departments like this available in JSON from the server:

```
{
    "data" : [
        {
            "id"            : "1",
            "name"          : "Accounting",
            "active"        : null,
            "dateActive"    : "12/01/2001",
            "dateInactive"  : null,
            "description"   : null,
            "director"      : null,
            "numEmployees"  : "45"
        }
    ],
    "meta" : {
        "success" : true,
        "msg"     : ""
    }
}
```

When you're talking to the server, something could go wrong while you're retrieving the data (for example, the database could be down). So you send a "meta" part of the response to identify whether the response was successful and supply a custom error message if something went wrong. This approach allows you to easily exchange error messages without having to worry about specific setup details on the server (error handling is automated for you if you set the `successProperty` on the `proxy` as shown in listing 7.2).

The following listing shows how you can read the JSON using the `JsonStore` convenience class. You can find the data.json file detailed in this listing in examples/ch07.

Listing 7.2 Reading JSON data

```
var departmentStore = Ext.create('Ext.data.Store', {       ←———  Instantiates
    fields : [                                              1      JsonStore
        'name',
        'active',
        'dateActive',
        'dateInactive',
        'description',
        'director',
        'numEmployees',
        {
            name : 'id',
            type : 'int'
        }
    ],                                        2  Chooses
    proxy  : {                                   Ajax proxy
        type    : 'ajax',           ←———————                3  Sets URL
        url     : 'data.json',      ←——————————————————————
        reader : {                  ←———
            type              : 'json',
            root              : 'data',     Configures
            idProperty        : 'id',    4  JsonReader
            successProperty : 'meta.success'
        }
    }
});

departmentStore.load({
    callback : function(records, operation, successful) {
        if (successful) {
            console.log('department name:',
                              records[0].get('name'));    ←———  Prints out
        }                                                  5    first record
        else {
            console.log('the server reported an error');
        }
    }
});
```

First you set up a JsonStore **1** with the field definition; then you choose an Ajax proxy **2**, set the server url with which to communicate **3**, and configure the JsonReader (note that this example refers to a local installation; refer to the examples supplied with this book for an example listing running at http://extjsinaction.com/v4/examples/ch07). You set the reader type to json and root **4** to data. When configuring reader you set the idProperty and the successProperty to keep track of changes during updates on the server, as you'll see later. Ext JS needs the idProperty for internal bookkeeping before sending updates back to the server. Finally, you print out the first record in the list retrieved by the server **5**.

7.2.3   *Reading XML data*

You also have the option to read XML data into your store. Let's pretend the department listing was available in XML:

```xml
<?xml version="1.0" encoding="UTF-8" ?>
<Response>
  <data>
    <node>
      <id>1</id>
      <name>Accounting</name>
      <active>true</active>
      <dateActive>12/01/2001</dateActive>
      <dateInactive></dateInactive>
      <description>Accounting services</description>
      <director></director>
      <numEmployees>45</numEmployees>
    </node>
    ...
  </data>
  <meta>
    <success>true</success>
    <msg></msg>
  </meta>
</Response>
```

The next listing shows how to read data from XML into the same fields you used in the previous example. You can find the data.xml file in examples/ch07.

Listing 7.3   Reading XML data

```
var departmentStore = Ext.create('Ext.data.Store', {          ◁──┐  Uses
  fields : [                                           ◁───────┐  ❶ XmlStore
      'name',
      'active',
      'dateActive',                                            Declares
      'dateInactive',                                        ❷ fields
      'description',
      'director',
      'numEmployees',
      {
          name    : 'id',
          mapping : 'id'
      }
  ],
  proxy  : {
      type    : 'ajax',
      url     : 'data.xml',
      reader : {
          type             : 'xml',              ❸ Selects
          record           : 'node',                XmlReader
          idPath           : 'id',           ◁──┘
          successProperty  : 'meta/success'
      }
```

```
        }
    });
    departmentStore.load({
        callback : function(records, operation, successful) {
            console.log(operation)
            if (successful) {
                console.log("department:%o", records[0]);
            }
            else {
                console.log("the server reported an error");
            }
        }
    });
```

To read XML, you choose an XmlStore ❶ and declare fields ❷ similar to the way you did in the previous example. When reading XML, you need an XmlReader ❸ and you must declare where to find the record data in the XML using the record property. As in the previous example it can be helpful to set idPath and successProperty.

Now that you've learned how to read data into your store, it's time to reverse the flow and write data.

7.3 A store with Writer

Writer saves you time and effort by removing the need for you to code Ajax requests and exception handling, giving you more time to do the important stuff, like building the business logic for your application. Before you start coding your Writer implementation, you should review how Writer fits into the picture.

To use Writer you'll need to reconfigure your data store and the supporting proxy. Instead of configuring a url property for the proxy, you'll create a configuration object known as api. The proxy api is a new concept for you, and we'll discuss it in more detail in a bit when we review the example code.

You'll need to create an instance of Writer and plug it into your data store, as well as add some new configuration properties to the store's configuration object itself, as shown in the following listing.

Listing 7.4   The Employee store

```
var urlRoot = 'http://extjsinaction.com/crud.php?model=Employee&method=';
var employeeStore = Ext.create('Ext.data.Store', {
    model : 'Employee',              ◁──────    Refers to
    proxy : {                                    Employee
        type    : 'jsonp',           ◁──────  ❶ model
        api     : {
            create  : urlRoot + 'CREATE',   ◁──         Creates
            read    : urlRoot + 'READ',        Configures ❷ new proxy
            update  : urlRoot + 'UPDATE',   ❸ proxy api
            destroy : urlRoot + 'DESTROY'
        },
        reader : {                   ❹  Sets up
            type            : 'json',   ◁──   JSON reader
            root            : 'data',
```

```
        idProperty      : 'id',
        successProperty : 'meta.success'
    },
    writer : {                                          Configures
        type            : 'json',                    ⑤ writer
        encode          : true,
        writeAllFields  : true,
        root            : 'data',
        allowSingle     : true,
        batch           : false,
        writeRecords    : function(request, data) {
            request.jsonData = data;
            return request;
        }
    }
  }
});
employeeStore.load();
```

In listing 7.4 you create a data store that refers to the Employee model ❶ and uses an Ajax proxy ❷ with a configuration object as the property api ❸, which denotes URLs for each of the CRUD actions, with read as the request to load data. You'll use somewhat intelligent remote server-side code, where a controller exists for each CRUD action. Writer requires intelligent responses; thus, remote server-side code was developed. It's a good idea to use the same server-side technology for all of the CRUD actions (refer to the example application in part 3 of this book for an example of how it's done).

> **NOTE** In the examples accompanying this book, you'll find a version of this example that refers to extjsinaction.com (employee_store.html). This example will let you read but not update data. If you wish to explore the effect of executing the CRUD actions, we recommend that you follow the instructions in the accompanying readme.txt file for chapter 7. This file will walk you through how to set up the database in MySQL and how to configure the accompanying server-side code.

Next you create a subclass of Ext.data.Writer, known as Json Writer ❹, which potentially has the ability to save a request to modify a single record or batch (list) of records. By overriding updateRecords ❺, this example illustrates how to ensure that Writer writes only one record at a time. In the Json Writer configuration object, you set writeAllFields to true, which ensures that for each operation Writer returns all of the properties; this strategy is great for development and debugging. Naturally, you want to set this writeAllFields to false in production, which will reduce overhead over the wire and at the server-side and database stack.

> **NOTE** You can override Reader and Writer in the proxy as you can override most other functionality in Ext JS. If the supplied classes don't suit your needs, chances are that someone in the Ext JS community already implemented a custom class that might. Take a look at http://sencha.com/forum to see what you can find before you start implementing your own custom solution.

We suggest that when you develop with `Writer` you add a global exception event listener to your store. This listener is needed if you want something to occur upon any exception that the store raises. When developing our applications, we send all of the arguments to the Firebug console because it provides a wealth of information that's hard to find anywhere else during debugging. We strongly suggest you do the same. Trust us; doing so will save you time in the long run.

When implementing the server-side endpoint for the writer, you'll notice that all parameters are sent as GET parameters if you choose a JsonP proxy. Keep this in mind if you want to switch between using an Ajax and a JsonP proxy.

7.3.1 *Validating your model data*

In addition to identifying the expected type and format of the fields in your model, you can identify validations that can run before any attempt to update the store. In Ext JS 4 you can now validate fields directly using the model. Previously you had to perform validation using the form panel. Placing your validation code near your field type descriptions more clearly identifies the rules in your domain model.

As you might recall, `Ext.data.Field` can consist of

- A name
- A type (auto, string, int, float, Boolean, date)
- A `defaultValue`
- A convert function (used to convert from an incoming record)

When you use `Ext.data.Store`, all data passes `Ext.data.Model`, which makes it an obvious place to perform data validations. Let's explore this in the next listing by setting up a model to represent employees in a department.

Listing 7.5 The Employee model with validations

```
Ext.define("Employee", {
    extend     : 'Ext.data.Model',
    fields     : [
        'firstName',
        'lastName',
        'middle',
        'title',
        'street',
        'city',
        'state',
        'zip',
        'departmentName',
        'rate',
        'officePhone',
        'homePhone',
        'mobilePhone',
        'email',
        {
            name : 'id',
            type : 'int'
```

```
        },
        {
            name : 'departmentId',          ⊲──┐   Converts to
            type : 'int'                       ❶  integer
        },
        {
            name    : 'dateHired',
            type    : 'date',
            format  : 'Y-m-d'               ⊲──┐   Specifies
        },                                     ❷  dateHired
        {
            name    : 'dateFired',
            type    : 'date',
            format  : 'Y-m-d'
        },
        {
            name    : 'dob',
            type    : 'date',
            format  : 'Y-m-d'
        }
    ],
    validations : [
        {                                  ❸   Adds presence
            type  : 'presence',            ⊲   validation
            field : 'firstName'
        },
        {
            type  : 'presence',
            field : 'lastName'
        },
        {
            type  : 'presence',
            field : 'departmentId'
        },
        {                                  ❹   Configures format
            type    : 'format',            ⊲   validation
            field   : 'email',
            matcher : /@/
        }
    ]
});
```

A common usage scenario is to have an `id` and some foreign keys in type `int` ❶. You also identify `dateHired` ❷, `dateFired`, and `dob` as dates.

New to Ext JS 4 is the ability to perform validations directly on the model. In this example you can see how to use a presence validation ❸ and a format validation ❹.

Let's pretend that you want to add a very young new employee to department number 15:

```
var sofie = Ext.create('Employee', {
    firstName    : 'Sofie',
    lastName     : 'Andresen',
```

```
    dob           : Ext.util.Format.date('2007/12/15','Y-m-d'),
    email         : 'Sofie A'
});
```

If you run the following code

```
var errors = sofie.validate();
```

you'll get a list of two errors. The first error will indicate that Sofie isn't associated with a department yet, and the second pops up because she just learned how to type her name and doesn't know what an email is yet. So let's wait to add Sofie to the Employee store!

If you succeed in validating your model data with some other data with no errors, then you're ready to add the new employee to interact with the data store.

7.3.2   Syncing your data

As you'll recall from figure 7.1, the data store is intended to be used by consumer widgets. So for real applications, you'd respond to events from widgets and act according to the event in your code. For example, if you receive an `onClick` event on a save button, then it'd be fitting to update the appropriate model in the store using data present in the widget.

We'll cover the details of interacting with a store from a consumer widget in later chapters; for now, let's explore how to update employee data using commands available in the store and the model.

> **NOTE**   While learning how to interact with the data store, you can enter the JavaScript example snippets directly into your favorite browser's developer tools.

First you can update models using `set` and `get`. The data package is intelligent, so it knows when you have dirty data that needs to be updated when you sync:

```
var firstEmployee = employeeStore.first();
firstEmployee.set('firstName', 'Anita');
firstEmployee.set('lastName', 'Andresen');
employeeStore.sync();
```

Here you grab a reference to the first available Employee model in the Employee store, change the first name to Anita and the last name to Andresen, and sync the data store. This step activates the example custom writer supplied in listing 7.4.

If you want to add a new employee named Jacob to department 15, you can create the following Employee model:

```
var jacob = Ext.create('Employee', {
    firstname    : 'Jacob',
    lastName     : 'Andresen',
    departmentId : 15,
    email        : 'jacob.andresen@gmail.com'
});
```

Add it to the Employee store and then sync it:

```
employeeStore.add(jacob);
employeeStore.sync();
```

The sync operation on new records will fail if one of the validation operations on the model fails. For example, let's say that you forgot to assign a departmentId to the Jacob record. The record would then not be on the list of records to be created by calling sync.

> **NOTE** You can explore which records are to be created by calling getNew-Records on the store before you call sync. If you wish to explore the modified records, you can call getModifiedRecords, and getRemovedRecords shows you what records are to be removed when you sync.

If you want to remove the last record in the Employee store, you could do the following:

```
var lastEmployee = employeeStore.last();
employeeStore.remove(lastEmployee);
employeeStore.sync();
```

> **NOTE** In Ext JS 4 you can also perform a load, save, and destroy using proxy functionality directly from the model. Be sure to be consistent in your coding style throughout your program. The code can be hard to read if you mix the two programming styles.

If you've taken a look at the data URLs retrieved while loading data into the Employee store, you may have noticed the page, start, and limit parameters in a URL that looks like this:

```
http://extjsinaction.com/
    crud.php?model=Employee&method=READ&_dc=1359395332718&page=1&start=0&lim
    it=25&callback=Ext.data.JsonP.callback1
```

The page, start, and limit parameters are standard parameters supplied by the system and can be used to perform paging operations (splitting up the data display into smaller chunks rather than displaying the entire dataset at once). We'll explore paging in detail in chapter 8 when we cover pagination.

By now you should have a working knowledge of what the data store is and how it works. So let's wrap up this chapter with one of the more advanced features introduced in Ext JS 4: the ability to nest data by using Ext.data.Association between your models.

7.4   *Associating data*

By nesting data, you can meet additional requirements to spare bandwidth while running highly interactive applications. It also gives you the ability to express business logic in a more concise way than was possible with Ext JS 3.

Let's imagine that the HR department has given you the task of optimizing your application so that it allows rapid modifications of employee data in all of the departments of your company. The head of the HR department is growing tired of your application, which she calls "a traditional internet application." "It's just too slow," she says. "All it does is talk to the server when I browse my data. I just want the application to instantly update the employee data when I browse through a list of employees in all the departments. Can you please load all the data upon start-up? I don't care that the application takes a bit longer to start, and I only expect to be using it on our gigabit intranet."

After resisting the urge to point out that you had the good idea to split up the employee list by department so the application would render faster and that your application is pretty fast already, you start looking for options. Luckily, it doesn't take you long to find a description of Ext.data.Model in the documentation and see that it contains associations in Ext JS 4. It looks like you just have to make some minor adjustments to your existing code to use an associated data load. This way, you can load the description of all departments and all employees at once.

You start by adding a hasMany association from the department model to the Employee model, as shown in the next listing.

Listing 7.6 Department model with associations

```
Ext.define('Department', {
    extend: 'Ext.data.Model',
    fields: [
        'id',
        'name',
        'active',
        'dateActive',
        'dateInactive',
        'description',
        'director',
        'numEmployees'
    ],
    sortInfo: {
        field : 'name',
        dir   : 'ASC'
    },
    associations: [{                    ❶ Contains hasMany
        type    : 'hasMany',              relation
        model   : 'Employee',
        name    : 'employees'
    }]
});
```

In the Department model, you identify that a department has many employees ❶. You set the association key to employees. Similarly, you need to set up a belongsTo association in the employeeModel from listing 7.5:

```
Ext.define("Employee", {
    extend: 'Ext.data.Model',
    fields: [ ... ],
    associations: [{
```

```
        type          : 'belongsTo',
        model         : 'Department',
        associationKey: 'departmentId'
    }]
});
```

Doing so allows you to access the employee data associated with the current department. The next listing uses the Department and Employee models from listings 7.5 and 7.6.

Listing 7.7   Reading associated employee data for departments

```
var urlRoot = 'http://extjsinaction.com/crud.php?model=Department&method=';

var departmentStore = Ext.create('Ext.data.Store', {
    model : 'Department',
    proxy : {
        type    : 'jsonp',
        api     : {
            create  : urlRoot + 'CREATE',
            read    : urlRoot + 'READ',
            update  : urlRoot + 'UPDATE',
            destroy : urlRoot + 'DESTROY'
        },
        reader : {
            type            : 'json',
            root            : 'data',
            idProperty      : 'id',
            successProperty : 'meta.success'
        }
    }
});

departmentStore.load({
    params    : {
        detail : true,                          ❶ Asks for
        limit  : 5                                 details
    },
    callback : function() {                     ❷ Reads
        departmentStore.each(function(department) {  associated data
            department.employees().each(function(employee) {
                var departmentId   = department.get('id'),
                    departmentName = department.get('name'),
                    employeeId     = employee.get('id'),
                    employeeName   = employee.get('firstName');

                console.log(departmentId, departmentName,
                            employeeId, employeeName);
            });
        });
    }
});
```

In this example you ask the example server-side code to supply the associated details for the departments (in the same data model format as for the employees, just filtered for departments). The parameter detail ❶ is set to true to indicate that server-side code should supply the associated employees for the department.

You can then consume the associated employee data using the name property as a function, in this example, department.employees() ❷. Recall that you supplied the name property in the hasMany association for the Department model in listing 7.6. By calling department.employees() you obtain a reference to the Employee store that you can use to traverse the employees associated with the department. In this example we've chosen to print out the department name and the first name of the employee; this should show that you can reach the associated employee data.

There you have it: nested data with Ext JS data stores.

7.5 Summary

In this chapter you learned about the data store, beginning with an overview of the many classes that support it. You saw a breakdown of the various supporting classes and learned that proxies are responsible for fetching data and that readers are responsible for translating data and creating instances of Model to stuff into the data store itself.

After your introduction into the world of the data store, you dove into loading and using Array, XML, and JSON data. You then learned how to persist data using data writers and the store's sync method. Finally, you explored the data-association capabilities with the data package, where you loaded department data with associated employees.

In the next chapter you're going to take a deep dive into your first complex data-driven view: the grid panel.

The grid panel

Since the early days of Ext JS the grid panel has been the centerpiece of the framework. In many respects this holds true today, and the grid panel is arguably one of the widgets with the most advanced functionality available in Ext JS, allowing for rapid data entry in a tabular form. When you use the grid panel, you gain the ability to visualize and manipulate large datasets in an intuitive way, so this class should fit into most enterprise and office applications. Note that the grid has seen a major overhaul of performance in Ext JS 4.1, and it's now so fast that the list view from previous releases of Ext JS is no longer needed.

This chapter focuses on the grid panel and builds on what you learned about data stores in the previous chapter. You'll start by constructing a grid panel that feeds from a store that reads local in-memory array data. After exploring the basics, you'll move on to advanced features like paging and scrolling. Finally, you'll learn how to edit and interact with data using the data store from the grid panel and the CRUD actions covered in the last chapter.

At each step of the process you'll learn more about the grid panel and its supporting classes. But before we start, we'll introduce you to the grid panel.

8.1 Introducing the grid panel

At first glance, the grid panel may look like a glorified HTML table, which has been used for ages to display data. If you take a moment to look at one of the Ext JS grid examples, you'll realize that this is no ordinary HTML table. You can see one example implementation of the grid panel that uses an array store at http://mng.bz/HAcK (see figure 8.1).

In the array grid example, you can see that the features provided by this widget extend beyond those of a typical HTML table. These include column-management features such as sorting, resizing, reordering, showing, and hiding. Mouse events are also tracked out of the box to allow you to highlight a row by hovering over it and even select it by clicking it.

The example also demonstrates how the grid panel's view (known as the *grid view*) can be customized with what are known as *custom renderers*, which are applied to the Change and % Change columns. These custom renderers color the text based on negative and positive values.

This example merely skims the surface when it comes to how the grid panel can be configured or extended. To fully understand the grid panel and why it's so extensible, you need to know more about its supporting classes.

8.1.1 Looking under the hood

The key supporting classes driving the grid panel are `grid.View`, `SelectionModel`, and `Store`. Let's take a quick glance at an implementation of a grid panel and see how each class plays a role in making the grid panel work (figure 8.2).

Array Grid

Company	Price	Change	% Change	Last Updated
3m Co	$71.72	0.02	0.03%	09/01/2009
Alcoa Inc	$29.01	0.42	1.47%	09/01/2009
Altria Group Inc	$83.81	0.28	0.34%	09/01/2009
American Express Company	$52.55	0.01	0.02%	09/01/2009
American International Group, Inc.	$64.13	0.31	0.49%	09/01/2009
AT&T Inc.	$31.61	-0.48	-1.54%	09/01/2009
Boeing Co.	$75.43	0.53	0.71%	09/01/2009
General Electric Company	$34.14	-0.08	-0.23%	09/01/2009
General Motors Corporation	$30.27	1.09	3.74%	09/01/2009
Hewlett-Packard Co.	$36.53	-0.03	-0.08%	09/01/2009

Figure 8.1　The array grid example found in the examples folder of the downloadable SDK

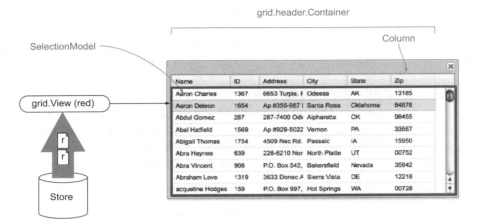

Figure 8.2   The grid panel's supporting classes: `grid.View`, `SelectionModel`, and `Store`

In figure 8.2, you see a grid panel with its supporting classes highlighted. Starting from the beginning, the data source, you see the `Store` class. Data stores work by using a reader, which is used to "map" data points from a data source and populate the data store. They can be used to read array, XML, or JSON data via the array, XML, and JSON readers. When the reader parses data, it's organized into records, which are organized and stored inside the data store.

The `grid.View` class is the UI component of the grid view. It's responsible for reading the data and controlling the painting of data onscreen.

Columns are classes that map the data fields from each individual record for placement on screen. They do this by means of a `dataIndex` property, which is set for each column and is responsible for displaying the data it obtains from the field it's mapped to.

Finally, `SelectionModel` is a supporting class that works with a view to allow users to select one or more items onscreen. Out of the box, Ext JS supports Row, Cell, Checkbox, and Tree selection models. `SelectionModel` is what keeps track of what you've selected onscreen.

Now that we've covered the fundamentals, you'll build a simple grid panel.

8.2   *Building a simple grid panel*

When implementing grid panels, you typically start by configuring the data store. This is because configuring the columns is directly related to configuring fields in the data store. Let's continue to use the Employee store you constructed in the previous chapter and hook it up to a grid panel by declaring the columns needed to render the grid panel, as shown in the next listing.

Listing 8.1 Creating an `ArrayStore` and binding it to a grid panel

```
var arrayData = [
    ['Jay Garcia',    'MD'],
    ['Aaron Baker',   'VA'],
    ['Susan Smith',   'DC'],
    ['Mary Stein',    'DE'],
    ['Bryan Shanley', 'NJ'],
    ['Nyri Selgado',  'CA']
];

var store = Ext.create('Ext.data.ArrayStore', {
    data        : arrayData,
    fields      : ['fullName', 'state']
});

var grid = Ext.create('Ext.grid.Panel', {
    title         : 'Our first grid',
    renderTo      : Ext.getBody(),
    autoHeight    : true,
    width         : 250,
    store         : store,                    ❶ Refers to store
    selType       : 'rowmodel',               ❷ Sets selection model
    singleSelect  : true,
    columns       : [                         ❸ Maps dataIndexes to columns
        {
            header    : 'Full Name',
            sortable  : true,
            dataIndex : 'fullName'
        },
        {
            header    : 'State',
            dataIndex : 'state'
        }
    ]
});
```

The first thing you do is reference the associated store with name and state values ❶. The values from the store are mapped to the column values ❸. For each column you set the corresponding `dataIndex` in the store. You declare the Full Name column to be sortable. Finally, you specify `'rowModel'` as the selection type ❷. Figure 8.3 shows how the grid will look onscreen.

You can see that the data isn't in the order specified. This is because before we took the snapshot, we clicked the Full Name column, which invoked the click handler for that column. The click handler checks to see if this column is sortable (which it is) and invokes a data store `sort` method call, passing in the data field (`dataIndex`), which is `fullName`. The `sort` method call then sorts all of the records in the store based on the field that was just passed. It first sorts in ascending order, then toggles to descending. A click on the State column wouldn't result in any sorting, because you didn't specify `sortable: true` as you did for the Full Name column.

Figure 8.3 Your first grid rendered onscreen demonstrating the configured row `SelectionModel` and the sortable Full Name column

The grid panel has other features that you can use. You can drag and drop the columns to reorder them, resize them by dragging the resize handle, or click the Columns menu icon, which appears whenever the mouse hovers over a particular column.

To use the selection model, select a row by clicking it. Once you've done that, you can use the keyboard to navigate rows by pressing the up- and down-arrow keys. You can modify the selection model by removing the `singleSelect: true` property and enabling `multiSelect: true`. Reloading the page will allow you to select many items by using typical operating system multiselect gestures such as Shift-click or Ctrl-click.

Creating your first grid was a cinch, wasn't it? Obviously, there's much more to grid panels than displaying data and sorting it. Features like pagination and setting up event handlers for gestures like right-clicks are used frequently. These advanced uses are exactly where we're heading next.

8.3 *Advanced grid panel construction*

In the previous section you built a grid panel that used static in-memory data. You instantiated every instance of the supporting classes, which helped you get some exposure to them. Like many of the components in the framework, the grid panel and its supporting classes have alternate configuration patterns. In building your advanced grid panel, you'll explore some of these alternate patterns in a couple of the supporting classes.

8.3.1 *What you're building*

The grid panel you'll construct will use some advanced concepts, the first of which is using a data store to query against a large dataset of randomly generated data, giving you the opportunity to use a paging toolbar. You'll then learn how to use the

`TemplateColumn` class to set up custom renders for two columns. One of these will apply color to the ID column, and the other will be more advanced, concatenating the address data into one column.

After you build this grid panel, you're going to circle around and set up a `rowdbl-click` handler. You'll be introduced to context menus as you learn to use the grid panel's `rowcontextmenu` event. Put on your propeller hat if you have one; we'll cover a lot of material here!

8.3.2 The required data store and model

First you have to configure the supporting data store. You'll use Employee model data store definitions similar to what you did in chapter 7. We'll include them in this section to refresh your memory. You can find the contents of the following listing in examples/ch08/datastores.js.

Listing 8.2 Configuring the model and store

```
Ext.define('Employee', {
    extend     : 'Ext.data.Model',
    idProperty : 'id',
    fields     : [                                    ❶ Forces data
        {name : 'id', type : 'int'},                     types
        {name : 'departmentId', type : 'int' },
        {name : 'dateHired', type : 'date', format : 'Y-m-d'},
        {name : 'dateFired', type : 'date', format : 'Y-m-d'},
        {name : 'dob', type : 'date', format : 'Y-m-d'},
        'firstName',
        'lastName',
        'title',
        'street',
        'city',
        'state',
        'zip'
    ]
});

var urlRoot = 'http://extjsinaction.com/crud.php'
                  + '?model=Employee&method=';

var employeeStore = Ext.create('Ext.data.Store', {
    model    : 'Employee',
    pageSize : 50,
    proxy    : {                                       ❷ Prepares for grid
        type : 'jsonp',                                   panel pagination
        api  : {
            create  : urlRoot + 'CREATE',
            read    : urlRoot + 'READ',
            update  : urlRoot + 'UPDATE',
            destroy : urlRoot + 'DESTROY'
        },
        reader : {
            type               : 'json',
            metaProperty       : 'meta',
```

```
            root             : 'data',
            idProperty       : 'id',
            totalProperty    : 'meta.total',
            successProperty  : 'meta.success'
        },
        writer : {
            type             : 'json',
            encode           : true,
            writeAllFields   : true,
            root             : 'data',
            allowSingle      : true,
            batch            : false,
            writeRecords     : function(request, data) {
                request.jsonData = data;
                return request;
            }
        }
    }
});
```

The contents of listing 8.2 should seem familiar to you. The difference is that you force the data types for the models ❶ and inject a pageSize property ❷ to the store configuration. The pageSize property allows for easy integration with the paging toolbar, as you'll see later in this chapter.

Before we move on, notice that you're using the reference employeeStore to point to an instance of a data store. You'll use that reference when you configure the grid.

8.3.3 *Setting up columns*

The columns you used for your first grid panel were pretty boring. All they did was map the column to the record data field. In this example, you'll use two template columns, shown in the next listing, one of which will allow you to use the address data fields to build composite and stylized cells. The template column is just one of the options available (you can also use action, Boolean, and number columns).

Listing 8.3 Setting up the columns

```
var columns = [
    {
        xtype     : 'templatecolumn',            ❶ Uses template
        header    : 'ID',                             column
        dataIndex : 'id',
        sortable  : true,
        width     : 50,
        resizable : false,                       ❷ Hides ID
        hidden    : true,                            column
        tpl       : '<span style="color: #0000FF;">{id}</span>'
    },                                           ❸ Renders
    {                                                IDs blue
        header    : 'Last Name',
        dataIndex : 'lastName',
        sortable  : true,
        hideable  : false,
```

```
        width      : 100
    },
    {
        header     : 'First Name',
        dataIndex  : 'firstName',
        sortable   : true,
        hideable   : false,
        width      : 100
    },
    {
        header     : 'Address',
        dataIndex  : 'street',
        sortable   : false,
        flex       : 1,
        tpl        : '{street}<br />{city} {state}, {zip}'
    }
];
```

❹ Sets up template for address

Configuring these columns is much like configuring the columns for your previous grid. There are some notable differences, though. First, you use a template column ❶ to render the ID column blue ❸. Note that the ID column is hidden by default ❷. You also set the `hideable` property for both the Last Name and First Name columns to `false`, which will prevent them from being hidden via the Columns menu. You'll get a chance to see this in action after you render the grid panel.

The Address column is a bit special: you've disabled sorting. You do so because you're rendering the column with content based on a composite of other fields in the record, such as city, state, and zip; this is done using the template for address ❹. You do enable sorting on each column.

Now that you've constructed the array of column configuration objects, let's move on to piecing together your paging grid panel.

8.3.4 Configuring your advanced grid panel

You now have just about all the pieces required to configure your paging grid panel. To do so you'll need to configure the paging toolbar, which will be used as the bottom toolbar in the grid panel, as shown in the next listing.

Listing 8.4 Configuring your advanced grid panel

```
var pagingToolbar = {
    xtype       : 'pagingtoolbar',
    store       : employeeStore,
    dock        : 'bottom',
    displayInfo : true
};
var grid = Ext.create('Ext.grid.Panel', {
    xtype       : 'grid',
    columns     : columns,
    store       : employeeStore,
    loadMask    : true,
    selType     : 'rowmodel',
```

❶ Configures paging toolbar

❷ Creates grid panel

```
    singleSelect : true,
    stripeRows   : true,
    dockedItems  : [
        pagingToolbar
    ]
};
```

In listing 8.4 you use the XType as a shortcut to configure both the paging toolbar and the grid panel. For the paging toolbar configuration ❶ you bind the Employee data store configured earlier and set the `pageSize` property to 50. Doing so enables the paging toolbar to bind to the data store, allowing it to control requests. The `pageSize` property will be sent to the remote server as the `limit` property, and it'll ensure that the data store receives bundles of 50 (or fewer) records per request. The paging toolbar will use the `limit` property along with the server's returning `totalCount` property to calculate how many "pages" there are for the dataset. The last configuration property, `displayInfo`, instructs the paging toolbar to display a small block of text, which displays the current page position and how many records are available to be flipped through (remember `totalCount`). We'll point this out when you render the grid panel.

You then configure a grid panel instance ❷. In this instance you bind the configuration variables `columns`, `employeeStore`, and `pagingToolbar`. The `loadMask` property is set to `true`, which will instruct the grid panel to create an instance of `Ext.LoadMask` and bind it to the `bwrap` (body wrap) element, the tag that ultimately wraps or contains all of the elements below the title bar of a panel. These elements include the top toolbar, content body, bottom toolbar, and `fbar` (the bottom button footer bar). The `LoadMask` class binds to various events that the store publishes to show and hide itself based on the situation the store is in. For instance, when the store initiates a request, it'll mask the `bwrap` element; and when the request completes, it will unmask that element.

You set the `dockedItems` property to your `pagingToolbar` XType configuration object, which will render an instance of the paging toolbar widget with that configuration data as the bottom toolbar in the grid panel.

Your grid panel is now configured and ready to be placed in a container and rendered. You could render this grid panel to the document body element, but let's place it as a child of an instance of `Ext.Window`; this way, you can easily resize the grid panel and see how features like the automatic sizing of the Address column work.

8.3.5   *Configuring a container for your grid panel*

Let's create the container for your advanced grid panel. Once you render the container, you'll initiate the first query for the remote data store you created a while ago:

```
Ext.create('Ext.Window', {
    height : 350,
    width  : 550,
    border : false,
```

```
    layout : 'fit',
    items  : grid
}).show();

employeeStore.load();
```

Here you perform two tasks. The first is creating `Ext.Window`, which uses the Fit layout and has the grid panel as its only item. You use method chaining to call the `show` method directly from the result of the constructor call. Then you execute `load` on `employeeStore`. Your rendered grid panel should look like the one in figure 8.4. As you can see from the fruits of your labor, your grid panel's Address column displays a composite of the address fields in one neat column that's dynamically sized and can't be sorted, whereas all the other columns start life with a fixed size and can be sorted.

A quick look at the communication from the first request via Firebug will show you the parameters sent to the server. Figure 8.5 illustrates those parameters.

We covered the `callback`, `limit`, and `start` parameters a short while ago when we discussed the paging toolbar, but you haven't seen the _dc parameter yet. The dc

Composite column

Last Name	First Name	Address
Andresen	Louis	147-8927 Nonummy Ave
Fry	Gillian	P.O. Box 773, 1323 Leo. Road
Chaney	Shoshana	2511 Morbi Avenue
Gilbert	Bernard	Ap #618-1126 Egestas, Av.
Santiago	Ingrid	7522 At, St.
Clarke	Quon	1561 Sem Rd.
Barker	Bert	541-7646 Pede. Rd.
Dunn	Jordan	484-4101 Sed Av.
Wilkerson	Maris	6316 Nisl. Avenue
Gilmore	Vernon	P.O. Box 864, 4093 Consequat Av.
Patrick	Daria	Ap #238-225 Metus St.
Reed	Scarlet	P.O. Box 594, 5659 At, Road
Mason	Leo	3083 Etiam St.

Page 1 of 12   Displaying 1 - 50 of 599

displayInfo

Figure 8.4   The results of your advanced paging grid panel implementation

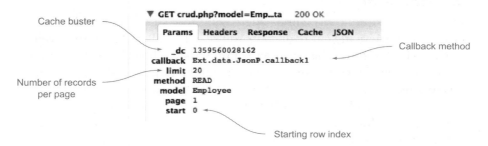

Cache buster

Number of records per page

Callback method

Starting row index

```
▼ GET crud.php?model=Emp...ta   200 OK
   Params  Headers  Response  Cache  JSON

       _dc  1359560028162
   callback  Ext.data.JsonP.callback1
      limit  20
    method  READ
     model  Employee
      page  1
     start  0
```

Figure 8.5   Parameters sent to the remote server to request paged data

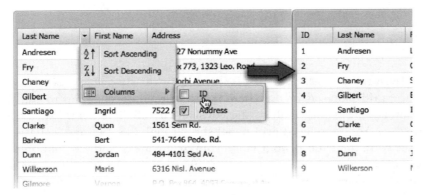

Figure 8.6   Enabling the ID column via the Columns menu

parameter is what's known as a *cache buster* parameter that's unique for every request and contains the timestamp for which the request was made in the Unix epoch format (the number of seconds since the beginning of computer time, or 12 a.m. on January 1, 1970). Because the value for each request is unique, the request bypasses proxies and prevents them from intercepting the request and returning cached data.

You haven't seen your ID column in action because you configured it as a hidden column. To enable it, you can use the Columns menu and check the ID column, as shown in figure 8.6.

After checking the ID column in the Columns menu, you'll see it appear in the grid view. In this menu you can also specify the direction in which a column is to be sorted. One thing you may notice right away by looking at the Columns menu is that the menu options for the First Name and Last Name columns are missing. This is because you set the `hideable` flag to `false`, which prevents their respective menu options from being rendered. The Columns menu is also a great way to sort a column directly in the order you desire.

You now have your grid panel constructed. You can configure some event handlers for the grid panel that'll allow you to interact with it more. Before that, let's explore buffered paginated scrolling, an alternative to using the paging toolbar.

8.3.6   *Buffered paginated scrolling*

Do you want to avoid presenting the paging toolbar without having to wait for the browser to retrieve the entire dataset? You're in luck! Ext JS 4.1 introduced the paging grid scroller for grids. The new paging grid scroller allows Ext JS to paginate the dataset behind the scenes and retrieve the data to be displayed ahead of time. We realize this sounds a bit complicated, so let's explore it in action.

The main idea behind buffered paginated scrolling is still to split up the dataset into pages. In this system you prefetch data before the user scrolls to the bottom or the top. For example, if the user is scrolling near the bottom of the grid, you retrieve a certain amount of data before the user scrolls to the end of the grid. This way, you can avoid making the user wait while the application communicates with the server and renders results. To kick things off, you'll need to configure a buffering data store, as shown in the following listing.

Listing 8.5 Buffered employee data store

```
var url = 'http://extjsinaction.com/crud.php?model=Employee&method=READ';
var bufferedEmployeeStore = Ext.create("Ext.data.Store", {
    model      : 'Employee',
    pageSize   : 50,
    buffered   : true,
    remoteSort : true,
    sorters    : {
        property  : 'lastName',
        direction : 'ASC'
    },
    proxy      : {
        type   : 'jsonp',
        url    : url,
        reader : {
            type            : 'json',
            root            : 'data',
            idProperty      : 'id',
            successProperty : 'meta.success',
            totalProperty   : 'meta.total'
        }
    }
});
```

❶ Identifies pageSize

❷ Sets buffered to true

❸ Reads total number of results

First you need to identify the page size ❶. You should adjust this size to get the best performance from your back-end services and the least amount of latency for the UI. Keep in mind that network speed and the number of bytes being transferred matter as well.

Also remember to set `buffered` to `true` for your store ❷. Doing so will enable buffering and allow buffered paginated scrolling to work. You should sort on a property so that it's easy to follow the scroll progress on the screen. In this example we enabled sorting on `lastName`. A good rule of thumb is to sort on the property that you enable as the first column when you render the grid onscreen.

Finally, remember to read the total number of results for the query from the server ❸. Without this setting, the data store won't be able to calculate how to configure the grid panel's scroller.

For buffered paginated scrolling, you need to configure a vertical scroller for the grid. To accomplish this, use your previously defined columns and `Window` instance to render the grid panel. As you'll see, the biggest difference is that you're adding a `verticalScroller` configuration object to the grid panel:

```
var grid = Ext.create('Ext.grid.Panel', {
    xtype           : 'grid',
    columns         : columns,
    store           : bufferedEmployeeStore,
    loadMask        : true,
```

```
    verticalScroller : {
        trailingBufferZone : 10,
        leadingBufferZone  : 10
    }
});
```

trailingBufferZone lets you configure how many rows should be stored in memory "on top" (after it has left the visible screen, after the user has scrolled down). leading-BufferZone lets you configure how many rows should be retrieved ahead of time.

Take a look at the results of your code changes in the browser. Are you as impressed as we are? Remember to use this feature only when it makes sense. If you plan to enable editing in your grids, be aware that multi-item editing is easier to implement using paging with a toolbar. Static paging makes it easier to keep track of the user interaction with the grid. Plan carefully before enabling this awesome feature.

Let's explore how to apply event handlers allowing the user to interact with the grid.

8.3.7   *Applying event handlers for interaction*

To create row-based user interaction, you need to bind event handlers to events that are published by the grid panel. Here you'll learn how to use the rowdblclick event to display a dialog box when a double-click is detected on a row. Likewise, you'll listen for a contextmenu (right-click) event to create and show a single-item context menu using the mouse coordinates.

You'll begin by creating a method to format a message for the Ext JS alert message box and then move on to create the specific event handlers, as shown in the next listing. You can insert this code anywhere before your grid panel configuration.

Listing 8.6   Creating event handlers for your data grid

```
var doMsgBoxAlert = function() {                                           ◀─┐   Shows alert
    var record    = grid.selModel.getSelection()[0];                        ❶   message box
    var firstName = record.get('firstName');
    var lastName  = record.get('lastName');
    var msg = String.format('The record you chose:<br /> {0}, {1}',
            lastName , firstName);
    Ext.MessageBox.alert('', msg);
};                                              ❷  Adds rowdblclick
var doRowDblClick = function()  {        ◀─┘      handler                       ❸  Adds
    doMsgBoxAlert();                                                               itemcontextmenu
};                                                                                handler
var doRowCtxMenu = function(view, record, item, index, e) {   ◀─
    e.stopEvent();                                            ◀──────────────  Hides browser's
    if (!view.rowCtxMenu) {                                   ◀──────┐  ❹      context menu
        view.rowCtxMenu = Ext.create('Ext.menu.Menu', {              
            items : {                                           Creates static
                text    : 'View Record',                        instance of
                handler : function() {                      ❺   menu
                    doMsgBoxAlert();
                }
            }
        });
```

```
    }
    view.rowCtxMenu.showAt(evtObj.getXY());
};
```

In listing 8.6 you create three methods. The first of these, doMsgBoxAlert ❶, is a utility method that's a pointer to the grid panel generating the event. It uses Selection-Model's getSelection method to obtain a reference to the selected record and the record.get method to extract the first and last name fields. It uses those fields to display an alert message box that contains a message with those two properties.

> **Context menus typically select items**
>
> Most desktop applications select an item when the user right-clicks it. Because Ext JS doesn't provide this functionality out of the box in the grid panel, you can force the selection of the item that the user is right-clicking. Doing so will give your application more of a desktop feel.

Next you create the first handler, doRowDblClick ❷. All this method does is execute the doMsgBoxAlert method that we discussed earlier.

The last method, doRowCtxMenu ❸, is much more complicated and accepts five parameters. The first is the reference to grid view, the second is the record being manipulated in the data store, the third is the items element, the fourth is the items index, and the fifth is an instance of Ext.EventObject. Knowing this is important because on some browsers, such as Firefox for Mac OS X, you need to prevent the browser's own context menu from displaying. This is why you call e.stopEvent ❹ as the first task. Calling stopEvent stops the native browser context menu from showing.

Next, this handler uses the record parameter to force the selection of the row for which the event was generated by calling SelectionModel's select method, passing in the record parameter.

You then test to see whether the grid has a rowCtxMenu property, which on the first execution of this method will be false, so the interpreter will dive into this branch of code. You do this because you want to create the menu once if it doesn't exist. Without this fork in the logic, you'd be creating menus every time the context menu is called, which would be wasteful.

You then assign the rowCtxMenu property ❺ to grid as the result of a new instance of Ext.menu.Menu. The first property of the menu item is the text that'll be displayed when the menu item is shown. The other is a handler method that's defined inline and causes doMsgBoxAlert to be called with the referenced record.

The last bit of code calls on the newly created rowCtxMenu's showAt method, which requires the X and Y coordinates to display the menu. You do this by directly passing the results of evtObj.getXY() to the showAt method. evtObj.getXY will return the exact coordinates where the event was generated.

Your event handlers are now armed and ready to be called on. Before you can use them in the grid, you need to configure them as listeners, as shown here:

```
listeners : {
    itemcontextmenu :  doRowCtxMenu,
    itemdblclick     :  doMsgBoxAlert
}
```

To configure the event handlers to the grid, you add a `listeners` configuration object, with the event to handle mapping. Because your event handlers can handle only one selected record, you have to enforce single selection. To do so you add a `selType` of `rowmodel` with the `singleSelect` option set to `true`.

Refresh the page and generate some double-click and right-click gestures on the grid. What happens? See figure 8.7.

Now double-clicking any record will cause the Ext JS alert message box to appear. Likewise, right-clicking a row will cause your custom context menu to appear. If you click the View Record menu item, the alert box will appear.

Adding user interaction to a grid can be as simple as that. One key to effective development of UI interactions is not to instantiate and render widgets only once and when needed, as you did with the context menu. Although this technique works to prevent duplicate items, it falls short when it comes to cleanup. Remember the destruction portion of the component life cycle? You can attach a method to destroy the context menu when the grid panel is destroyed by adding a `destroy` handler method to the list of listeners:

```
listeners        : {
    itemdblclick     : doRowDblClick,
    itemcontextmenu : doRowCtxMenu,
    destroy          : function(grid) {
        if (grid.rowCtxMenu) {
            grid.rowCtxMenu.destroy();
        }
    }
}
```

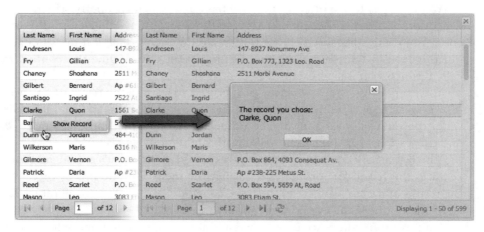

Figure 8.7   The results of adding the context menu handler to your advanced grid

In this code snippet you add the destroy event handler inline instead of creating a separate referenced method for it. The destroy event always passes the component that's publishing the event, which is labeled grid. In that method you test for the existence of the rowCtxMenu variable. If this item exists, you call its destroy method.

Context menu cleanup is one of those areas that developers often miss and that can lead to lots of leftover DOM node garbage, which chews up memory and can contribute to application performance degradation over time. If you're attaching context menus to any component, always be sure to register a destroy event handler for that component that destroys any existing context menus.

So there you have it! Now you know how to operate a grid panel. Next we'll explore how to build a working editable grid panel, which will allow you to modify data inline much as you can in popular desktop spreadsheet applications like Microsoft Excel. You'll do so by using the grid panel edit plug-ins new to Ext JS 4.

8.4   *Editing data in the grid panel*

In earlier versions of Ext JS, you had to implement a separate editor grid panel to be able to edit content available in your grid. With Ext JS 4, you can now reuse your existing grid panel and enable editing using plug-ins. The editing plug-ins inject editing capabilities into the grid panel so that you can reuse the data store attached to your grid for persisting data. You can now choose the RowEditing or CellEditing plug-in, depending on whether you want to enable editing on a row or a cell level.

Using the grid panel editing plug-ins should streamline your development considerably, but you still need to wire event handlers to perform the CRUD actions using your data store. We'll explore this by expanding the complex grid panel you've constructed, but with some changes to allow you to edit data using the RowEditing plug-in.

Excited yet? Let's take a sneak peek at what the grid panel looks like with the RowEditing plug-in enabled before we continue (figure 8.8).

You'll start by enabling the editing plug-in so you can get an introduction into how edits are possible. Then we'll discuss the ins and outs of setting up UI widgets for interaction to support insert and delete CRUD operations, as well as how to get modified records from the store or even reject changes using the data store we described in the previous chapter. Building an editable grid panel without saving the data is useless, so we'll take advantage of this opportunity to show you how to code for CRUD operations. This will be the most complex code you've seen so far, and you'll create it in phases.

The first phase is to enable the RowEditing plug-in and get the editors to work. You'll then circle back and add slices of each CRUD action, one at a time.

8.4.1   *Enabling the editing plug-in*

Because you're expanding the complex grid panel created earlier, you'll see some of the same code and patterns. We're doing it this way so the flow of the code is as

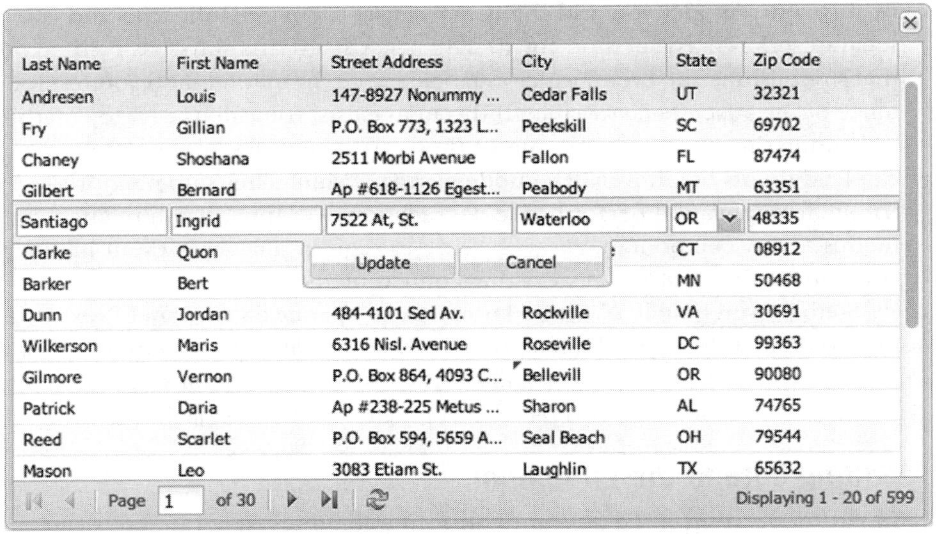

Figure 8.8   A quick peek at what you'll be constructing in this section

smooth as possible. In most cases there'll be changes, so please take the time to read through every bit. We'll point out all of the pertinent modifications.

This section will build on what you learned about data stores in chapter 7. You'll begin in the next listing by creating the instances of the supporting classes for this editable grid, such as the data store, the RowEditing plug-in, and column editor configurations.

Listing 8.7   Creating the supporting class instance for grid panel editing

```
Ext.define('State', {
    extend : 'Ext.data.Model',
    fields : ['id', 'state']
});

var url = 'http://extjsinaction.com/crud.php??model=State&method=READ';
var stateStore = Ext.create("Ext.data.Store", {          ◁───┐
    model : 'State',                                          │ Creates
    proxy : {                                              ❶  data store
        type    : 'jsonp',
        url     : url,
        reader : {
            type            : 'json',
            root            : 'data',
            idProperty      : 'id',
            successProperty : 'meta.success'
        }
    }
});
```

```
var rowEditing = Ext.create('Ext.grid.plugin.RowEditing', {
    clicksToEdit : 2,
    autoCancel   : false
});
var textField = {
    xtype : 'textfield'
};
var stateEditor = {
    xtype         : 'combo',
    triggerAction : 'all',
    displayField  : 'state',
    valueField    : 'state',
    store         : stateStore
};
```

Sets up new
RowEditing
② instance

③ Adds text editor
config object

Sets up ComboBox
④ config object

You kick things off by creating a data store **①** to support the ComboBox editor **④** used to modify the State field of each record. Next you create an instance of the RowEditing **②** grid plug-in class. You set clicksToEdit to 2, so that a double-click event will bring up the editor, a common workflow in most user interfaces. autoCancel is set to false to persist changes if the user decides to edit another row. We like to set this as false because the user can always cancel changes via the RowEditing plug-in's built-in Cancel button.

Next you set up a reusable text field configuration object that'll be used in just about every column in the editable grid panel **③**. Finally you declare a ComboBox configuration object **④**. This one will be used in the State column of the grid panel.

Now you can declare your columns and assign the editors, as shown in the next listing.

Listing 8.8 Creating the columns with editors

```
var columns = [
    {
        header    : 'Last Name',
        dataIndex : 'lastName',
        sortable  : true,
        editor    : textField
    },
    {
        header    : 'First Name',
        dataIndex : 'firstName',
        sortable  : true,
        editor    : textField
    },
    {
        header    : 'Street Address',
        dataIndex : 'street',
        flex      : 1,
        sortable  : true,
        editor    : textField
    },
    {
        header    : 'City',
        dataIndex : 'city',
```

Uses text
① field editor

```
            sortable  : true,
            editor    : textField
    },
    {
            header    : 'State',
            dataIndex : 'state',
            sortable  : true,
            width     : 50,                          ❷ Specifies
            editor    : stateEditor        ◄──┐         stateEditor
    },
    {
            header    : 'Zip Code',
            dataIndex : 'zip',
            sortable  : true,
            editor    : textField
    }
];
```

As you review the columns configuration array, you'll see familiar properties such as header, dataIndex, and sortable. You'll also see a new kid on the block, editor ❶, which allows you to specify an editor for each of the columns. You'll also notice the stateEditor ❷ used for the State column.

You now have your store, editors, and columns configured. You can move on to creating your paging toolbar in the following listing. For this task, you'll reuse the employeeStore instance you created earlier.

Listing 8.9 Creating the paging toolbar, grid panel, and window

```
var pagingToolbar = {
    xtype        : 'pagingtoolbar',
    store        : employeeStore,
    displayInfo  : true
};

var grid = Ext.create('Ext.grid.Panel', {
    columns      : columns,
    store        : employeeStore,
    loadMask     : true,
    bbar         : pagingToolbar,                 ❶ Enables RowEditing
    plugins      : [ rowEditing ],      ◄──┐         plug-in
    stripeRows   : true,
    selType      : 'rowmodel',
    viewConfig   : {
        forceFit : true
    },
    listeners    : {
        itemcontextmenu : doRowCtxMenu,
        destroy         : function(thisGrid) {
            if (thisGrid.rowCtxMenu) {
                thisGrid.rowCtxMenu.destroy();
            }
        }
    }
});
```

```
Ext.create('Ext.Window', {
    height    : 350,
    width     : 600,
    border    : false,
    layout    : 'fit',
    items     : grid
}).show();

employeeStore.load();
```

In listing 8.9 you create the rest of your grid panel, starting with the paging toolbar, which uses your Employee store. Next you create your grid panel ❶, using `columns`, `employeeStore`, and `pagingToolbar`.

You then create the container for your grid panel, which is an instance of `Ext.Window`, and set its layout to `'fit'`. You use chaining to show the window immediately after it's instantiated.

Last, you call `employeeStore.load` ❷ and pass a configuration object that specifies the parameters to send to the server. This ensures you start at record 0 and limits the number of returning records to 50.

All of the pieces of the puzzle are in place for this phase. You can now render your grid panel and begin to edit data. Figure 8.9 shows the grid panel with the RowEditing plug-in engaged.

You can see that your editable grid panel and paging toolbar have rendered with data just waiting to be modified. Initially this seems like a normal grid panel. But under the covers lies a whole new level of functionality just waiting to be unleashed. We'll take a moment to discuss how you can use it.

Last Name	First Name	Street Address	City	State	Zip Code
Andresen	Louis	147-8927 Nonummy ...	Cedar Falls	UT	32321
Fry	Gillian	P.O. Box 773, 1323 L...	Peekskill	SC	69702
Chaney	Shoshana	2511 Morbi Avenue	Fallon	FL	87474
Gilbert	Bernard	Ap #618-1126 Egest...	Peabody	MT	63351
Santiago	Ingrid	7522 At, St.	Waterloo	OR	48335
Clarke	Quon	1561 Sem Rd.	Steubenville	CT	08912
Barker	Bert	541-7646 Pede. Rd.	Aberdeen	MN	50468
Dunn	Jordan	484-4101 Sed Av.	Rockville	VA	30691
Wilkerson	Maris	6316 Nisl. Avenue	Roseville	DC	99363
Gilmore	Vernon	P.O. Box 864, 4093 C...	Belleville	OR	90080
Patrick	Daria	Ap #238-225 Metus ...	Sharon	AL	74765
Reed	Scarlet	P.O. Box 594, 5659 A...	Seal Beach	OH	79544
Mason	Leo	3083 Etiam St.	Laughlin	TX	65632

Page 1 of 12   Displaying 1 - 50 of 599

Figure 8.9   The editable grid panel

8.4.2   *Navigating your editable grid panel*

You can use mouse or keyboard gestures to navigate through the cells and enter or leave editing mode. To initiate editing mode via the mouse, double-click a cell and the editor will appear, as shown earlier in figure 8.8. You can then modify the data and click or double-click another cell, or anywhere else on the page, to cause the blur of the editor to occur. Repeat this process to update as many cells as you wish.

You can modify how many clicks it takes to edit a cell by adding a `clicksToEdit` property to the RowEditing plug-in and specifying an integer value. Some applications allow editing via a single click of a cell; if that's what you want, you can set `clicks-ToEdit` to 1 and be done.

As command-line junkies, we feel that keyboard navigation offers you much more power than the mouse. If you're a power user of Excel or a similar spreadsheet application, you know what we're talking about. To initiate keyboard navigation, you can use the mouse to focus on the first cell you want to edit. This immediately places focus exactly where you need it. You can use the Tab key, or Shift-Tab key combination, to move left or right. You can also use the arrow keys to focus on any cell.

To enter edit mode using the keyboard, press Enter, which displays the editor for that cell. While in edit mode you can modify adjacent cells by pressing Tab to move one cell to the right or Shift-Tab to move one cell to the left.

To exit edit mode, you can press Enter again or press Esc. If the data you entered or modified validates properly, the record will be modified and the field will be marked as dirty (changed). You can see quite a few fields being modified in figure 8.10.

When you exit an editor, depending on whether the field has a validator and on the results of the validation, the data will be discarded. To test this, edit a Zip Code

Last Name	First Name	Street Address	City	State	Zip Code
Andresen	Louis	147-8927 Nonummy ...	Cedar Falls	UT	32321
Fry	Gillian	P.O. Box 773, 1323 L...	Peekskill	SC	69702
Chaney	Shoshana	2511 Morbi Avenue	Fallon	FL	87474
Gilbert	Bernard	Ap #618-1126 Egest...	Peabody	MT	63351
Santiago	Ingrid	7522 At, St.	Waterloo	OR	48335
Clarke	Quon		ville	CT	08912
Barker	Bert			MN	50468
Dunn	Jordan	484-4101 Sed Av.	Rockville	VA	30691
Wilkerson	Maris	6316 Nisl. Avenue	Roseville	DC	99363
Gilmore	Vernon	P.O. Box 864, 4093 C...	Belleville	OR	90080
Patrick	Daria	Ap #238-225 Metus ...	Sharon	AL	74765
Reed	Scarlet	P.O. Box 594, 5659 A...	Seal Beach	OH	79544
Mason	Leo	3083 Etiam St.	Laughlin	TX	65632

Update   Cancel

Page 1 of 12   Displaying 1 - 50 of 599

Figure 8.10   The grid panel with an editor and dirty field markers

cell and enter more or fewer than five integers. Then exit edit mode by pressing Enter or Esc.

You can now edit data, but the edits are useless unless you save your changes. This is where you enter the next building phase: adding the CRUD layers.

8.5 *Getting the CRUD in*

With the grid panel, CRUD server requests can be fired either automatically or manually. Automatic requests take place whenever a record is modified or when modifications occur and a preset timer expires in the client-side logic, firing off a request to the server. To set up automatic CRUD, you can create your own logic to send the requests, or you can do things the easy way and use the Employee store you created in the previous chapter, which is exactly what you'll do later in this chapter.

8.5.1 *Adding save and reject logic*

You'll begin by creating the save and change rejection methods, which you'll tie into buttons that will live in your paging toolbar, as shown in the following listing. The buttons Save Changes and Reject Changes can be implemented directly using the paging toolbar.

Listing 8.10 Reconfiguring the paging toolbar to include Save and Reject buttons

```
var pagingToolbar = {
    xtype       : 'pagingtoolbar',
    store       : employeeStore,
    pageSize    : 50,
    displayInfo : true,
    items       : [                         ❶ Adds
        '-',                                   spacer
        {
            text    : 'Save Changes',
            handler : function () {
                employeeStore.sync();       ❷ Saves
            }                                  data
        },
        {
            text    : 'Reject Changes',
            handler : function () {
                employeeStore.rejectChanges();  ❸ Rejects
            }                                      changes
        },
        '-'
    ]
};
```

In listing 8.10 you reconfigure the `pagingtoolbar` XType configuration object to include `items` ❶. The string entities that you see with the hyphens (-) are shorthand for the `Ext.Toolbar.Separator`, which will place a tiny vertical bar between toolbar child items. You're doing this because you want to show some separation between the buttons and the generic paging toolbar navigational items. You implement Save

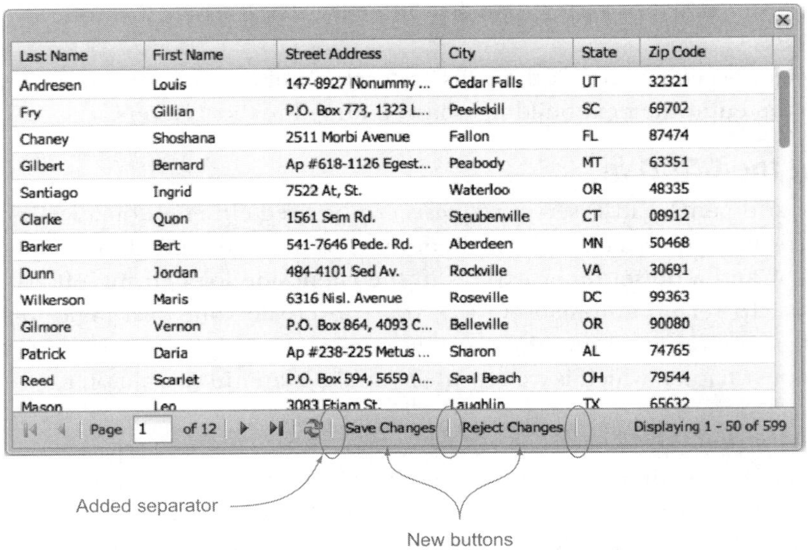

Figure 8.11   Your grid panel with Save Changes and Reject Changes buttons added

Changes using the `sync` operation on the `employeeStore` ❷ and use the `rejectChanges` operation on the `employeeStore` to implement Reject Changes ❸.

Also in the list are generic objects, which are translated to instances of `Ext.Toolbar` `.Button`. Figure 8.11 shows the Save Changes and Reject Changes buttons, which have their respective handlers set. As you can see in the figure, the buttons are placed neatly inside the paging toolbar's center, which is normally empty space, and they're separated by neat button separators. You can now begin to edit data and use your modified paging toolbar functionality and newly created CRUD methods.

8.5.2   *Saving or rejecting your changes*

To use your Save and Reject buttons, you need to first modify data. Using what you know about the grid panel, change some data and click Save Changes. You should see the grid panel's element mask appear briefly and then disappear once the save completes and the cells that are marked as dirty are marked clean or committed. Figure 8.12 shows the masking in action.

Now that you've seen what it takes to perform remote saves to modified records, you'll add create and delete functionality to your grid panel, which will complete your CRUD actions.

8.5.3   *Adding create and delete*

When configuring the UI for your save and reject functionality, you added buttons to the paging toolbar. Although you could add create and delete functionality the same way, it's best to use a context menu because doing so makes it much smoother to

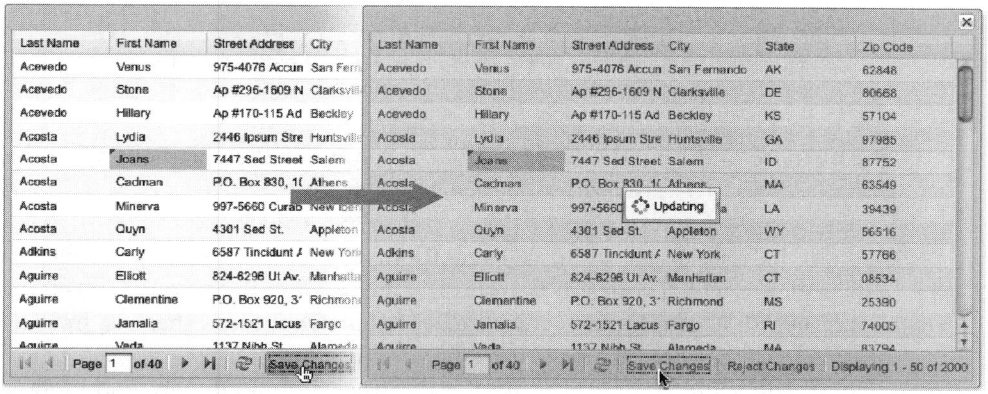

Figure 8.12 The load mask shows when save requests are being sent to the server.

delete and add. Think about it for a second; if you've ever used a spreadsheet application, you know that right-clicking a cell brings up a context menu that, among other things, has Insert and Delete menu items. We're going to introduce the same paradigm here.

As you did with the previously added functionality, you'll develop the supporting methods in the next listing before you construct and configure the UI components. We're going to ratchet up the complexity.

Listing 8.11 Constructing your delete and insert record methods

```
var onDelete = function() {                                    ┌─◁ Adds delete
    var selected = grid.selModel.getSelection();           ❶    operation method
    Ext.MessageBox.confirm(
        'Confirm delete',
        'Are you sure?',
        function(btn) {
            if (btn == 'yes') {
                grid.store.remove(selected);              ┌─◁ Deletes selected
                grid.store.sync();                     ❷    item from store
            }
        }
    );
};
```

Here you start by declaring the `onDelete` function to delete records ❶. After finding the record to delete by asking the selection model, you then ask your user for confirmation to delete the record with a call to `Ext.MessageBox.confirm`. If you get a confirmation, you move on to delete the selected record with a call to the `remove` method on the store ❷ with the selected record.

Before you move on to deploy `delete`, you should add the `insert` handler. This one is relatively small:

```
var onInsertRecord = function() {
    var selected = grid.selModel.getSelection();
```

```
    rowEditing.cancelEdit();
    var newEmployee      = Ext.create("Employee");
    employeeStore.insert(selected[0].index, newEmployee);
    rowEditing.startEdit(selected[0].index,0);
};
```

The purpose of this method is to locate the row index that was right-clicked and insert a phantom record at the index. Here's how it works.

First you create a new record via a call to `Ext.create("Employee")`. A call is then made to the `employeeStore`'s `insert` method, which requires two parameters. The first is the index at which you wish to insert the record, and the second is a reference to an actual record. This effectively inserts a record above the row that's right-clicked, emulating one of the spreadsheet features we discussed earlier.

Last, you want to initiate editing of that record immediately. You accomplish this by a call to the RowEditing plug-in's `startEdit` method, passing it the row for which you inserted the new record, and 0, which means the first column.

This concludes the supporting methods for the `create` and `delete` functions. You can now move on to create the context menu handler and reconfigure the grid to listen to the `itemcontextmenu` event, as shown in the next listing.

Listing 8.12 Setting up your context menu handler for the grid panel

```
var doRowCtxMenu = function(view, record, item, index, e) {            Adds
  e.stopEvent();                                                    ❶ listener

  if (!grid.rowCtxMenu) {
    grid.rowCtxMenu = Ext.create('Ext.menu.Menu', {                    Tests if
        items : [                                                      rowCtxMenu
                {                                                    ❷ exists
                    text     : 'Insert Record',
                    handler : onInsertRecord
                },
                {
                    text     : 'Delete Record',
                    handler : onDelete
                }
            ]
        });
  }
  grid.selModel.select(record);                                  ❸ Selects right-
  grid.rowCtxMenu.showAt(e.getXY());                                 clicked cell
};
```

Listing 8.12 contains `doRowCtxMenu` ❶, a method for handling the `itemcontextmenu` event from the grid panel, which is responsible for creating and showing the context menu for the `insert` and `delete` operations. Here's how it works.

`doRowCtxMenu` accepts five arguments, which are passed by the `itemcontextmenu` handler:

- `view`, a reference to the view from the grid panel that fired the event
- `record`

- `item` and `index`, which identify the record being edited
- `e`, an instance of `Ext.EventObject`

The first function that this method performs is to prevent the right-click event from bubbling upward by calling `e.stopEvent`, preventing the browser from displaying its own context menu. If you didn't prevent the event from bubbling, you'd see the browser context menu on top of yours, which would be silly and unusable.

`doRowCtxMenu` then tests ❷ to see if the grid panel has a `rowCtxMenu` property and creates an instance of `Ext.menu.Menu` and stores the reference as the `rowCtxMenu` property on the grid panel. This effectively allows for the creation of a single menu, which is more efficient than creating a new instance of `Ext.menu.Menu` every time the event is fired. It'll last until the grid panel is destroyed, as you'll see later.

You pass a configuration object to the `Ext.menu.Menu` constructor, which has a single property, `items`, which is an array of configuration objects that are translated to an instance of `Ext.menu.MenuItem`. The `MenuItem` configuration objects both reference the respective handlers to match the item text.

The last two functions that this method performs are selecting the cell that was right-clicked and showing the context menu at the correct X and Y coordinates onscreen. It does this by calling the `select` ❸ method of the grid panel's row `SelectionModel` and passing it the selected record. Last, you display the context menu using the coordinates where the right-click event occurred.

Before you execute your code, you'll have to reconfigure the grid to register the context menu handler. Add the following to your grid configuration object:

```
listeners : {
    itemcontextmenu : doRowCtxMenu
}
```

You now have everything you need to start using your new UI features. Let's see this thing in action.

8.5.4 Using create and delete

At this point you have your insert and delete handlers developed and ready to be used. You just finished creating the context menu handler and reconfigured your grid to call it when the `rowcontextmenu` event is fired. You'll start your exploration by creating and inserting a new record, as shown in figure 8.13.

As illustrated in figure 8.13, you can display the context menu by right-clicking any cell, which calls the `doRowCtxMenu` handler. This causes the selection to occur and displays the custom Ext JS menu at the mouse pointer's coordinates. Clicking the Insert Record menu item forces the call to the registered handler, `onInsertRecord`, which inserts a new record at the index of the selected row and begins editing on the first column. Cool!

In order to save changes, you need to modify the newly inserted record and then click the Save Changes button that you created earlier. Figure 8.14 shows this screen.

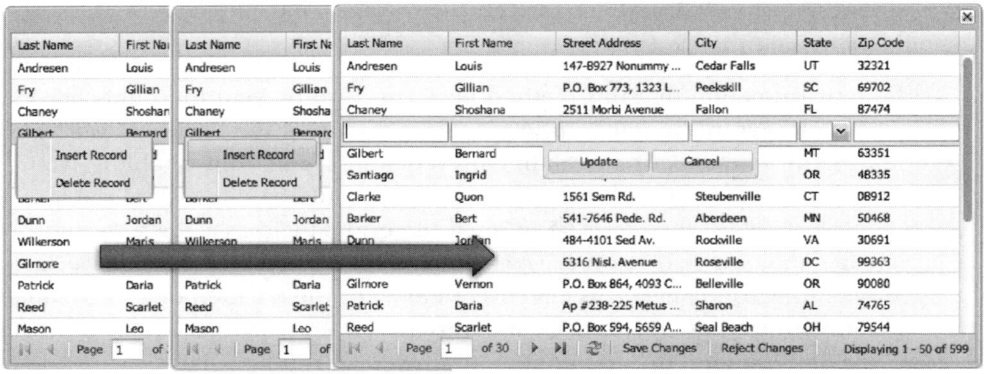

Figure 8.13   Adding a new record with your newly configured Insert Record menu item

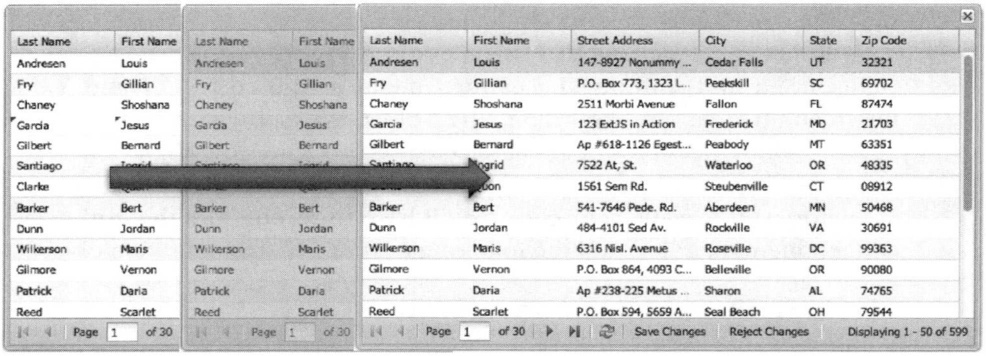

Figure 8.14   The UI transitions when saving your newly inserted record.

Whoa, that's a lot of material just for the creation of records. What about deleting? Surely that's simpler, right?

Absolutely! Before we discuss the process of deleting records, we'll examine how the UI works.

When you right-click a record, an `Ext.MessageBox` displays to confirm the delete operation, as shown in figure 8.15. You click Yes, and an Ajax request is made to the controller to delete the record.

This works because your `onDelete` handler called `MessageBox.confirm` and will call your `onDelete` method. The `onDelete` function looks like this:

```
var onDelete = function() {
    var selected = grid.selModel.getSelection();
    Ext.MessageBox.confirm(
        'Confirm delete',
        'Are you sure?',
        function(btn) {
```

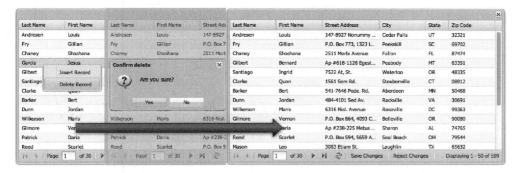

Figure 8.15 The UI workflow for deleting a record

```
if (btn == 'yes') {
    grid.store.remove(selected);
    grid.store.sync();
}
}
);
};
```

Here you use the Employee Store on the grid to remove the selected record and then sync.

You've now implemented all of the CRUD operations for your first editable grid panel. In doing so, you learned more about stores and records and how to detect changes and save them. Along the way, you got a chance to see a real-life case of an Ext JS confirmation message box in action.

8.6   Summary

In this chapter, you learned quite a bit about the grid panel and how to use the data store from a grid panel. While building your first grid panel, you got to see how the data store is used to read data and how to paginate data and perform buffered paginated scrolling. You also added grid interactions to the grid panel, where mouse double-click and right-click gestures were captured and the UI responded. In doing so, you got a quick glance at menus and learned the importance of cleaning up menu items after their parent component is destroyed.

Finally, you got your first exposure to the `Grid` class and learned how it uses the RowEditing plug-in to allow for editing of data on the fly. This gave you an opportunity to learn about the row `SelectionModel` and some of its methods, such as `get-Selection`. You also learned how you could use keyboard and mouse gestures to navigate the grid panel and edit data relatively rapidly.

Now that we've covered the basics of how to display and interact with data, the next chapter dives into how to visualize data using charts.

Taking root with trees

9

This chapter covers

- Dissecting the tree panel widget
- Rendering in-memory data
- Using a remote-loading data tree panel
- Creating a custom context menu
- Editing node data

In this chapter you'll learn about the Ext JS tree panel, which is used to display hierarchical data, much like a typical filesystem. You'll learn how to set up both static and dynamic implementations of this widget. After getting comfortable with this component, you'll set up CRUD operations by using a data store and a dynamically updating context menu.

9.1 Tree panel theory

To understand trees you first need to understand *hierarchy*. Hierarchy is an arrangement of relationships where items belong above, under, or at the same level as one another. In simple implementations it's a one-to-one relationship, but it can also be a complex many-to-many ordered set. Hierarchies exist in societies, corporations, the military, social networks, education and learning, psychology, and, of course, computer science.

9.1.1 Tree panel keywords

You also need to understand the special vocabulary tied to hierarchy and trees. Certain concepts are represented by various names, which is why it's a good idea to define the terminology before getting any deeper into the subject. Table 9.1 explains Sencha's terminology.

Table 9.1 Tree terminology

Name	Meaning
Tree panel	A container with the superpowers of `Ext.panel.Panel` that renders hierarchical data in a treelike format.
Tree view	A component that's responsible for rendering and manipulating a tree's DOM.
Tree	Represents a hierarchy of items (nodes).
Node	A single item in a hierarchy. In Ext JS 4, a node is configured via `Ext.data.NodeInterface`.
Parent	A node to which an observed node belongs. Root is the topmost parent.
Child	A direct descendant of another node. All nodes are root's children.
Root	A single node that contains (parents) all other nodes (children) in the first or any subsequent level. Only one node can be a root.
Leaf	A node without any children.
Branch	A collection of nodes sharing a direct parent.
Depth	The distance of a node's branch from the root level. Root's direct children are one level deep, their children are two levels deep, and so on.

In the UI world, the word *tree* is meant to describe a widget or control that displays hierarchical data, which generally begins at some central point, known as a *root*. And like the botanical tree, trees in UIs have branches, which means that they contain other branches or leaves. Unlike botanical trees, computer trees have only one root.

In the computer world, this paradigm is ubiquitous and lives under our noses without much thought. Ever browse your computer's hard disk? The directory structure is a tree structure. It has a root (any drive letter in Windows), branches (directories), and leaves (files). Trees are used in application UIs as well and are known by a few other monikers.

In other UI libraries, other names for this type of widget include the tree view, tree UI, or simply tree, whereas in Ext JS it's known as the tree panel. The reason it's called the tree panel is that it's a direct descendant of the `Panel` class. And much like the grid panel, it isn't used to contain any children except those for which it was designed.

The reason the `TreePanel` class extends from `Panel` is simple: convenience. This allows you to use all of the panel's UI goodness, which includes the top and bottom toolbars and the footer button bar.

The tree panel shares prototypal inheritance with the grid panel. Not only does this much-desired upgrade introduced in Ext JS 4 mean tree panels are now easier to extend, it also means that tree panels are now able to use the data package to its full potential: stores, readers, proxies, and writers. A specially designed `TreeStore` class manages hierarchical relationships for you, making CRUD operations easier than ever.

9.1.2   *Looking under the roots*

To get a tree panel to work, you first need to have some data. Loading data through a `TreeStore` instance will internally parse relationships and apply all tree-related methods to the `Model` instance, such as expand/collapse, `findChild`, and `getPath`, along with extra fields that maintain the tree state, like `checked`, `allowDrop`, and `parentId`. The magic happens automatically, employing the `Ext.data.NodeInterface` class.

This is where tree panels take over, laying out a panel as a tree container and distributing the rest of the work to the view. `Ext.tree.View` is responsible for the hard work of outputting the UI for each node.

Here comes the tricky part. As mentioned in chapter 1, tree panels and grid panels share the same core logic. It sounds unbelievable at first, but in reality it makes a lot of sense. They both exist on top of the `Ext.panel.Table` and `Ext.view.Table` classes. That's right—a tree is encapsulated in a table, both in logic and as rendered.

This manifests as a whole tree being represented by a table, with each node belonging to a column in a respective row. A node is, by default, a representation of a text and an icon, but it can be extended for a more advanced usage. Nodes that belong to a `Model` instance can be assigned any additional data. This extra information can be used to add new columns to the left or right of the core tree, implementing an often-needed `TreeGrid` functionality. The whole process is laid out in figure 9.1.

Up to a certain level, a rendered tree panel will share `GridPanel`'s CSS properties such as `x-grid-table`, `x-grid-row`, `x-grid-cell`, and many more. But additional tree features are specified in dedicated styles, all dictated in the `Ext.tree.View` class that extends `Ext.view.Table`. So if you want to add a custom look and feel to the tree nodes, this is where you'll want to start.

You now have a high-level understanding of what a tree panel is and how it works. You can start constructing your first tree panel, which will load data from memory.

9.2   *Planting your first tree panel*

Coding a tree panel, a relative of the grid panel, is simple. You'll start out by constructing the tree panel, which loads its data from memory. This will give you more insight into what you learned some time ago. The following listing shows how to construct a static tree panel.

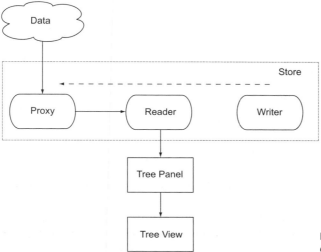

Figure 9.1 The tree panel data flow and render cycle

Listing 9.1 Building a static tree panel

```
var store = Ext.create('Ext.data.TreeStore', {        ① Sets up
    root : {                                              root node      ② Expands
        text     : 'Root Node',                                            true node on
        expanded : true,                                                   initialization
        children : [
            {                                            ③ Specifies
                text : 'Child 1',                          child nodes
                leaf : true
            },                                           ④ Specifies
            {                                              node as leaf
                text : 'Child 2',
                leaf : true
            },
            {
                text    : 'Child 3',
                children : [
                    {
                        text    : 'Grand Child 1',
                        children : [
                            {
                                text : 'Grand... you get the point',
                                leaf : true
                            }
                        ]
                    }
                ]
            }
        ]
    }
});
```

```
Ext.create('Ext.window.Window',{
    title      : 'Our first tree',
    layout     : 'fit',
    autoShow   : true,
    height     : 180,
    width      : 220,
    items      : {
        xtype       : 'treepanel',
        border      : false,
        store       : store,
        rootVisible : true
    }
});
```

⑤ Configures tree panel

Most of the code in listing 9.1 is the data to support the tree panel. In walking through the root ❶ you see that the Root Node object has a text attribute. This is important because the text property is what Ext.view.Tree uses to display the node's label. When writing the server-side code to support this widget, be sure to keep this property in mind. If you don't set it, the nodes may appear in the tree panel, but they won't have labels.

You also see an expanded property ❷, which is set to true. This setting ensures that when rendered, the node is expanded immediately, displaying its contents. You set it here so that you can see the root's children immediately upon the rendering of the tree panel. This parameter is optional; leave it out to have the node render initially collapsed.

A children property is set on the Root Node object ❸, which is an array of objects. Note that Ext.data.NodeInterface takes care of children and parses them as soon as child data is available. When a node has a children array, the objects in that array will be converted to records (Model) and populated in the parent node's childNodes array. A similar paradigm can be found in the container hierarchy, where a container has children in its item's MixedCollection.

If you walk through the Root Node object's children, you see that the first and second children don't have a children property but do have a leaf property ❹, which is set to true. Setting a node's leaf property to true ensures that the node will never contain other child nodes, thus making it a leaf and not a branch. In this case, 'Child 1' and 'Child 2' are leaf nodes, whereas 'Child 3' is a branch, because it doesn't have a leaf property set to true.

The 'Child 3' node contains one child node. This node has a single child, which also has a single child. The last child node is a leaf node because its leaf property is set to true.

After configuring the supporting data, you move on to configure the tree panel using an XType ❺ configuration object. This is where you see the simplistic nature of the configuration of this widget. All of these properties should make sense to you except root, which is what you use to configure the root node. In this case, the topmost object of the root node JSON will be treated as the tree panel's root.

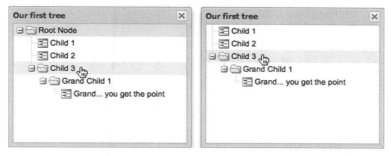

Figure 9.2   Your first (expanded) tree panel with the root node visible (left) and the root node hidden (right)

You can change your node icons by adding either an `icon` or `iconCls` property to the node's configuration object, where `icon` specifies a direct location for an image and `iconCls` is the name of a CSS class for an icon style. The `iconCls` property for the node works like the panel's `iconCls` configuration object and is the preferred method for changing the icon.

The last thing you do in this listing is create an instance of `Ext.window.Window` to display your tree panel. Figure 9.2 shows what your rendered tree panel looks like.

After rendering your tree panel, you can see the nodes displayed as you laid them out in the JSON. You can expand `'Child 3'` and its child node to display the rest of the hierarchy. It's easy to use the Selection model by clicking a node. If you want to hide the root node, set `rootVisible` in the `TreePanel` configuration object to `false`. You can see the results in figure 9.2 (right).

And there you have it, a static tree panel in action. Simple stuff, huh? Now that we have this out of the way, let's move on to creating a remote tree panel.

9.3   Growing dynamic tree panels

Because your first tree panel was static, there was no need to directly create a full-blown store instance with a proxy and a reader. All that changes with a remote-loading tree panel. You're going to develop a tree panel that'll use the same data that you used for your grid panels in chapter 7, where you displayed data identifying people. It just so happens that those people are employees of My Company and belong to different departments.

9.3.1   Creating a remote-loading panel

The next listing shows how to configure the tree panel to use the server-side component to list employees by department.

> **Listing 9.2   Building a dynamic tree panel**

```
var store = Ext.create('Ext.data.TreeStore', {        ❶ Syncs data
    autoSync: true,                                      automatically
    proxy   : {
```

```
        type : 'jsonp',
        url  : 'http://extjsinaction.com/treeData.php'
    },
    root     : {
        text        : 'My Company',
        id          : 'mycompany',
        expanded    : true
    }
});

Ext.create('Ext.window.Window', {
    title       : 'Our first remote tree',
    layout      : 'fit',
    autoShow    : true,
    height      : 360,
    width       : 280,
    items       : {
        xtype       : 'treepanel',
        store       : store
    }
});
```

Remotes
❷ data URL

Configures root
❸ node inline

Sets ID of
❹ root node

As you can see in listing 9.2, you let the store know that it's responsible for syncing ❶ changed data as soon as a change happens. Then you configure an Ext.data.proxy ❷, in this case a JsonP proxy with a configuration object passed that contains a url property set to treeData.php, which is hosted at http://extjsinaction.com. When configuring your tree panel, replace this PHP file with your controller of choice as well as the proxy type to Ajax if the controller is in the same domain. Before you start coding your controller, though, let's finish walking through the request-and-response cycle, which follows shortly after we look at the rendered version of this tree panel implementation.

The next step when configuring your tree panel is to configure the root ❸ inline. It's extremely important to note the addition of an id property ❹ to this node. As you'll see, this property will be used to request the child data from the server. Also notice that you set expanded to true. Doing so ensures that the root node expands and loads its children as soon as it's rendered.

Interestingly, a root node configuration isn't a necessity in an Ext.data.Tree-Store. If you choose not to include it, make sure the root is included in the initial data load. This feature can be useful in certain setups.

Finally, you configure a bigger instance of Ext.Window to contain your tree panel. Configuring the window a bit bigger for this demonstration will both increase the tree panel's viewing space and eliminate potential invocation of the Ext.util.Format .ellipsis method because of long names.

After rendering the tree panel, you see the root node (My Company) load immediately, as shown in figure 9.3 (left), displaying all of the departments in My Company. To view the employees in a particular department, click the expand icon (+) or double-click the label, and you'll see the remote-loading indicator appear in place of the folder icon, as shown in the center of figure 9.3. Once the employee nodes are

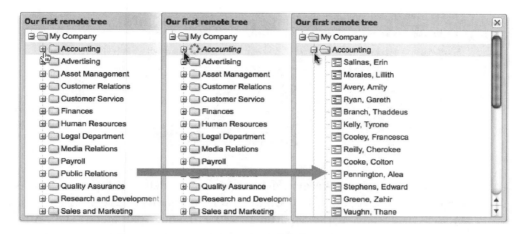

Figure 9.3 Your remote tree panel displaying its ability to load data remotely

loaded successfully, they'll appear below the department node, as shown in figure 9.3 on the right.

We went through this pretty fast. Let's recap a bit and look at the requests being fired. We'll discuss what the server-side controller is doing to support this implementation of the tree panel.

9.3.2 *Fertilizing the tree panel*

To analyze the client/server interaction model with the tree panel, let's start with the load request fired off by the automatic expansion of the root node, as shown in figure 9.4. Remember that you set the root's `expanded` property to `true` and that this expands a node when it's rendered, thus either rendering the children if they're in memory or firing a load request.

As you can see, the first request to the getCompany.php controller was made with a single parameter, `node`, which has a value of `myCompany`. Can you remember where you set that value and which property you set it to? If you said "the id property of the root node," you're correct! When an asynchronously loading node is being expanded for the first time, the store will use its `id` property to pass the child data to the controller.

The controller will accept this parameter and query the database for all nodes associated with that `id` and return a list of objects, as illustrated in figure 9.5. In this figure you see an array of objects that defines a list of departments. Each object has both `text` and `id` properties. The text applies to the label of the node. Notice that the departments lack the `leaf` and `children` properties. Are these leaf or branch nodes?

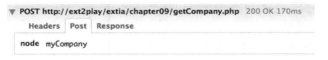

▼ POST http://ext2play/extia/chapter09/getCompany.php 200 OK 170ms

Headers	Post	Response

node myCompany

Figure 9.4 The POST parameter of the initial node request

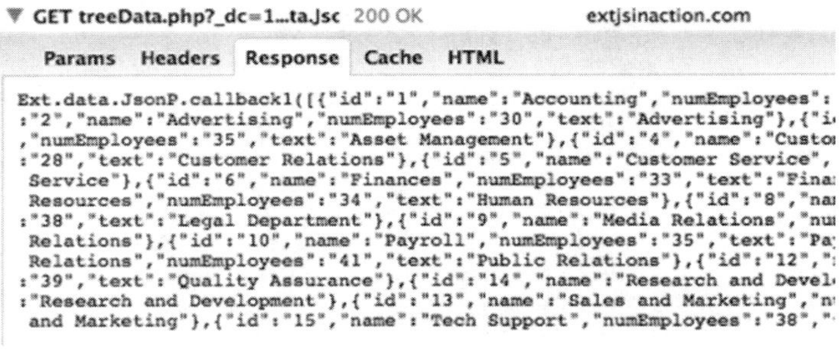

▼ GET treeData.php?_dc=1...ta.Jsc 200 OK   extjsinaction.com

| Params | Headers | **Response** | Cache | HTML |

Ext.data.JsonP.callback1([{"id":"1","name":"Accounting","numEmployees":
:"2","name":"Advertising","numEmployees":"30","text":"Advertising"},{"i
,"numEmployees":"35","text":"Asset Management"},{"id":"4","name":"Custo
:"28","text":"Customer Relations"},{"id":"5","name":"Customer Service",
Service"},{"id":"6","name":"Finances","numEmployees":"33","text":"Fina
Resources"},"numEmployees":"34","text":"Human Resources"},{"id":"8","na
:"38","text":"Legal Department"},{"id":"9","name":"Media Relations","nu
Relations"},{"id":"10","name":"Payroll","numEmployees":"35","text":"Pa
Relations"},"numEmployees":"41","text":"Public Relations"},{"id":"12","
:"39","text":"Quality Assurance"},{"id":"14","name":"Research and Devel
:"Research and Development"},{"id":"13","name":"Sales and Marketing","n
and Marketing"},{"id":"15","name":"Tech Support","numEmployees":"38","

Figure 9.5   The results of the initial request to the getCompany.php controller

They're branch nodes. Because neither property is defined, they're treated as branch nodes. This means that when they're initially expanded, `TreeStore` will invoke an `Ajax.request`, passing the department's ID as the `node` parameter. The controller will accept the `node` parameter and return a list of employees for that department.

Using what you just learned, you can safely predict that when you expand the Accounting department node a request to the getCompany.php controller will be made with a single parameter, `node`, passed with a value of `'Accounting'`. Let's take a quick look at the results from the controller request, shown in figure 9.6.

As you look at the JSON results, you see that a list of objects is returned, each with `id`, `text`, and `leaf` properties. Remember, because the `leaf` property is set, the nodes appear as nonexpanding leaf nodes.

Congratulations! You've successfully constructed static and dynamic tree panels to display hierarchical data. You also now have a basic understanding of the client/server interaction model between the tree panel and the web service feeding the tree panel data.

▼ GET treeData.php?_dc=1...ta.J: 200 OK   extjsinaction.com   5.7 k

| Params | Headers | **Response** | Cache | HTML |

Ext.data.JsonP.callback2([{"id":"employee-24","firstName":"Sawyer","lastNam
,"title":"Mrs.","street":"Ap #880-4070 Faucibus St.","city":"Peru","state":
:"1","dateHired":"08\/14\/2005","dateFired":null,"dob":"04\/16\/1983","rate
,"homePhone":"498-430-3331","mobilePhone":"698-130-3775","email":"Phasellus.
:true,"text":"Kemp,Sawyer","name":"Kemp,Sawyer"},{"id":"employee-28","first
:"Hamilton","middle":"Nash","title":"Mrs.","street":"P.O. Box 889, 4804 Vel
,"state":"ID","zip":"81062","departmentId":"1","dateHired":"09\/18\/2001","
\/29\/1942","rate":"74","officePhone":"764-942-8728","homePhone":"399-620-5
,"email":"enim@augueporttitor.org","leaf":true,"text":"Hamilton,Skyler","na
:"employee-34","firstName":"Shelly","lastName":"Levy","middle":"John","title
Rd.","city":"Fitchburg","state":"NE","zip":"15919","departmentId":"1","date
:null,"dob":"07\/26\/1972","rate":"67","officePhone":"432-162-9403","homePho
:"551-193-6220","email":"mauris.erat@Cras.edu","leaf":true,"text":"Levy,She
},{"id":"employee-41","firstName":"Oleg","lastName":"Alford","middle":"Oren
Euismod Rd.","city":"Mesquite","state":"FL","zip":"22275","departmentId":"
,"dateFired":null,"dob":"02\/07\/1945","rate":"24","officePhone":"177-258-7
,"mobilePhone":"313-772-8486","email":"per@eueuismodac.ca","leaf":true,"tex
,Oleg"},{"id":"employee-52","firstName":"Forrest","lastName":"Peterson","mi
:"P.O. Box 842, 5874 Consectetuer, Rd.","city":"Oshkosh","state":"SD","zip"
,"dateHired":"12\/09\/2002","dateFired":null,"dob":"05\/16\/1981","rate":"4
,"homePhone":"393-330-3016","mobilePhone":"349-481-3311","email":"Cras@etpe
:"Peterson,Forrest","name":"Peterson,Forrest"},{"id":"employee-58","firstNa
,"middle":"Armand","title":"","street":"Ap #288-4247 Massa. St.","city":"Bo
,"departmentId":"1","dateHired":"07\/15\/2007","dateFired":null,"dob":"11\/
:"197-550-2538","homePhone":"267-701-1670","mobilePhone":"797-814-3265","em

Figure 9.6   The results from the Accounting department node request

Configuring a tree panel for loading is just a small part of the job if you're tasked to build a UI that offers CRUD functionality for this type of widget. Next we'll look at how to construct a tree panel for these types of interactions.

9.4 Implementing CRUD on a tree panel

To configure CRUD UI functionality, you'll need to add much more code to the mix. After all, the tree panel doesn't support these features natively. Here's what you're going to do.

To enable CRUD actions, you'll modify your tree panel by adding an `itemcontext-menu` listener to it, which will call a method to select the node that was right-clicked and create an instance of `Ext.menu.Menu` to be displayed at the mouse cursor's X and Y coordinates. This process will be similar to how you coded the editor grid panel's context menu handler in the previous chapter.

You'll create three menu items: add, edit, and delete. Because you can only add employees to a department, you'll dynamically change text for the menu items and enable and disable the various menu items based on the type of node that was clicked: root, branch, or leaf.

Each of the handlers will perform an appropriate store's CRUD API method to mock controllers for each CRUD action. Because the store is performing much of the CRUD work automatically, the whole data-creation and -destruction process will look much like the examples previously covered in this book.

Get ready—this will be the most complicated tree code yet. You'll start by creating the context menu handler and the context menu factory method.

9.4.1 Displaying context menus

To add a context menu to the tree panel, you must register a listener for the `item-contextmenu` event. This is super simple. Add a `listeners` configuration option to the `Window` creation under `items` in listing 9.2 as follows:

```
listeners    : {
    itemcontextmenu : onCtxMenu
}
```

Adding this code will ensure that the `onCtxMenu` handler will be called when the `item-contextmenu` (or right-click) event is fired.

Cool! Your tree panel is now set up to call the `onCtxMenu` handler. Before you code it, you should construct a factory method to generate an instance of `Ext.menu.Menu`. This will help simplify `onCtxMenu` quite a bit. You'll see what we mean once you've finished with the factory method. The next listing walks you through constructing a context menu factory method.

Listing 9.3 Configuring a context menu factory method

```
var onConfirmDelete = Ext.emptyFn;
var onDelete        = Ext.emptyFn;
var onEdit          = Ext.emptyFn;
var onAdd           = Ext.emptyFn;
```

```
var buildCtxMenu = function() {
    return Ext.create('Ext.menu.Menu',{
        items: [
            {
                itemId  : 'add',
                handler : onAdd
            },
            {
                itemId  : 'edit',
                handler : onEdit
            },
            {
                itemId  : 'delete',
                handler : onDelete
            }
        ]
    });
}
```

In listing 9.3 you first set up several placeholder methods that point to Ext.emptyFn, which is the same thing as instantiating a new instance of a function but easier on the eyes. You're adding them now so that when you circle back and fill in these methods you'll know exactly where to place them.

Next, you generate the buildCtxMenu factory method, which returns an instance of Ext.menu.Menu and will be used by the onCtxMenu handler that you'll generate next. In case you've never seen or heard of a factory method, from a high level it's a method that constructs (hence the name *factory*) something and returns what it constructed. That's all there is to it.

Notice that none of the menu items has a text property but each has itemId specified. This is because the onCtxMenu will dynamically set the text for each menu item to provide feedback to the user that something may or may not be allowed. It'll use the itemId property to locate a specific item in the menu item's MixedCollection instance.

The itemId configuration property is similar to the id property of the component, except that it's local to a child component's container. This means that unlike the component's id property, itemId isn't registered with ComponentMgr. Thus, only the parent component has the ability to look into its item's MixedCollection to find a child component with a specific itemId. Moreover, components can be just as easily located by executing an Ext.ComponentQuery where both ids and itemIds are prefixed with a #, such as #myComponent.

Each MenuItem currently has a hardcoded handler to Ext.emptyFn as a placeholder so you can see your menu display in the UI without having to code the real handler. You'll go on to create each handler after you develop and review the onCtx-Menu handler, which is shown in the next listing.

> **Listing 9.4   Configuring a context menu factory method**

```
var onCtxMenu = function(view, record, element, index, evtObj) {
    view.select(record);
    evtObj.stopEvent();
```

```
if (! this.ctxMenu) {
    this.ctxMenu = buildCtxMenu();
}
this.ctxMenu.treeNode = record;
this.ctxMenu.treeView = view;

var ctxMenu    = this.ctxMenu;
var addItem    = ctxMenu.getComponent('add');
var editItem   = ctxMenu.getComponent('edit');
var deleteItem = ctxMenu.getComponent('delete');

if (record.getId() =='mycompany') {
    addItem.setText('Add Department');
    editItem.setText('Nope, not changing the name');
    deleteItem.setText('Can\'t delete a company, silly');

    addItem.enable();
    deleteItem.disable();
    editItem.disable();
}
else if (!record.isLeaf()) {
    addItem.setText('Add Employee');
    deleteItem.setText('Delete Department');
    editItem.setText('Edit Department');

    addItem.enable();
    editItem.enable();
    deleteItem.enable();
}
else {
    addItem.setText('Can\'t Add Employee');
    editItem.setText('Edit Employee');
    deleteItem.setText('Delete Employee');

    addItem.disable();
    editItem.enable();
    deleteItem.enable();
}

ctxMenu.showAt(evtObj.getXY()) ;
}
```

❶ Adds factory method

❷ Configures each type of node

In listing 9.4 you construct your onCtxMenu handler, which helps to enable your context menu to be dynamic. The first task that this handler accomplishes is to select the node in the UI by firing the view's select method. The select method is shared with all other components inheriting from Ext.view.AbstractView, such as Ext.grid.GridPanel and Ext.picker.Time. You select the node because you're going to need to query the tree panel for the selected node further on, after Ajax calls are made through a TreeStore proxy.

Every time the tree panel's itemcontextmenu event fires, it passes six arguments:

- The view in which the event was captured
- A Model instance representing a Ext.data.NodeInterface record
- The Ext.Element reference to the node that was right-clicked

- The node's numerical index
- The instance of Ext.EventObject that was generated
- The options object passed to Ext.util.Observable.addListener

Going back to the source code, you'll notice that you aren't using that last reference because you don't really need it. That's a wealth of references to work with, isn't it? If bells are ringing in your ears, it's probably because this is similar to the grid panel's itemcontextmenu event.

Next, you stop the browser's default context menu from showing up by calling evtObj.stopEvent. You'll see this pattern repeat any time you need to display your own context menu in place of the browser's.

The handler then constructs the context menu by calling the buildCtxMenu factory method you created a bit ago ❶. It stores the reference locally as this.ctxMenu so it doesn't have to reconstruct a menu for each subsequent handler call.

At this point you want to reference the view and the node selected so that you can use them later on. You do so to avoid future component querying and to avoid calling the dangerous Ext.getCmp method.

You then create a local reference to the context menu, ctxMenu, and each of the menu items. You're doing this for readability further on when you need to manage the menu items.

After you create the local references you move on to an if control block ❷, where you detect the type of node and modify the menu items accordingly. This is the bulk of the code for this handler. Here's how the logic breaks down.

If the node that was right-clicked is the root (record.getId() == 'myCompany'), you configure the menu items to allow the addition of departments but disallow the deletion and editing of the company text. You also disable those menu items so they can't be clicked. After all, you don't want anyone to destroy the entire company's data with a single mouse click, do you?

Moving on, you detect whether the node is not a leaf (department). You then modify the text to allow the addition of employees and deletion of the entire department. Remember, the company needs to be able to downsize by removing an entire department if need be. You also enable all menu items.

The code will encounter the else block if the node that was right-clicked is a leaf item. In this case, the text for the add item is modified and disabled to reflect the inability to add an employee to an employee, which would be nonsensical. Then you modify and enable the edit and delete menu item texts.

Last, you show the context menu at the coordinates of the mouse by calling EventObject's getXY method. Figure 9.7 shows what the menu looks like customized for each node.

As illustrated in figure 9.7, the context menu display changes for each type of node that's right-clicked, which demonstrates how you can use the same menu to perform similar tasks with some modifications. If you wanted to not show or hide the menu items instead of enabling and disabling them, you'd swap the menu button enable

Figure 9.7 Displaying your dynamic context menu for the company (left), department (center), and employee (right) nodes

calls for `show` and `disable` for `hide`. You can now begin to wire up handlers for your context menus. You'll start with the easiest, `edit`.

9.4.2 Wiring up the edit logic

You probably noticed that clicking a menu item resulted in nothing more than the menu disappearing. This is because you have your context menu set but no real handlers for it to call. Now you'll create the `edit` handler, which is by far the easiest handler to code.

In case you're familiar with Ext JS 3 or, even more so, if you're migrating an editable tree to Ext JS 4, at this step you might notice a certain peculiarity in the higher-version framework. It's lacking editing features!

You can always use an external field bound to a form and/or a window, but let's think again. `Ext.tree.Panel` uses many of the `Ext.grid.Panel` features, and grids have that cool `Ext.grid.plugin.CellEditing` plug-in we discussed in chapter 8. Let's try applying it to your tree. You need to override a method inherited from the `Ext.grid.plugin.Editing` class, and you're good to go. Let's look at your plug-in code in the next listing. You'll call the plug-in TreeCellEditing.

Listing 9.5 Extending the CellEditing plug-in

```
Ext.define('TreeCellEditing', {
    alias: 'plugin.treecellediting',
    extend: 'Ext.grid.plugin.CellEditing',

    init: function(tree) {
        var treecolumn = tree.headerCt.down('treecolumn');
        treecolumn.editor = treecolumn.editor
                        || {xtype: 'textfield'};

        this.callParent(arguments);
    },
```

1 Extends
Ext.grid.plugin.CellEditing

2 Assigns
editor

```
getEditingContext: function(record, columnHeader) {
    var me = this,
        grid = me.grid,
        store = grid.store,
        rowIdx,
        colIdx,
        view = grid.getView(),
        root = grid.getRootNode(),
        value;

    if (Ext.isNumber(record)) {
        rowIdx = record;
        //record = store.getAt(rowIdx);
        record = root.getChildAt(rowIdx);
    } else {
        //rowIdx = store.indexOf(record);
        rowIdx = root.indexOf(record);
    }
    if (Ext.isNumber(columnHeader)) {
        colIdx = columnHeader;
        columnHeader = grid.headerCt.getHeaderAtIndex(colIdx);
    } else {
        colIdx = columnHeader.getIndex();
    }

    value = record.get(columnHeader.dataIndex);
    return {
        grid: grid,
        record: record,
        field: columnHeader.dataIndex,
        value: value,
        row: view.getNode(rowIdx),
        column: columnHeader,
        rowIdx: rowIdx,
        colIdx: colIdx
    };
}
});
```

❸ **Finds selected node at specified index**

❹ **Finds selected node via record reference**

This extension code is more straightforward than it looks. You're doing things that will be further explained in chapter 13, so please bear with us. You accomplished two goals here. In your extended class that you now call `TreeCellEditing` ❶, you used `AbstractPlugin`'s `init` method to check if the tree already had an editor and assign one if the test was unsuccessful ❷. The only way the editor would've been there is if you wanted to define the tree panel's `columns` property yourself and set up a tree column with a custom editor right there. Because tree panels automatically create a tree column, you just needed to add an editor to it. Voilà, first goal accomplished.

The second goal is a bit harder to see. As we mentioned earlier, the piece of code that you needed to change lies one level down the prototype chain, in `Ext.grid.plugin .Editing`. The entire `getEditingContext` method is copied from the source with two simple overrides. This method needs to return the exact node you selected, so you could find it either through its index ❸ or through its record reference ❹, whichever was passed as the first argument in a function call. Right above the two overrides, you can see the original code used for grids. You now have your plug-in ready.

It's time to put your new plug-in to work. Ext JS 4 makes it easy for you to add this new feature to your tree panel in the following listing.

Listing 9.6　Finalizing tree configuration

```
var treeEditor = Ext.create('TreeCellEditing', {clicksToEdit: 2});        ◁─┐

Ext.create('Ext.window.Window',{
        title      : 'Our first remote tree',          Instantiates
        layout     : 'fit',                            TreeCellEditing  ❶
        autoShow   : true,
        height     : 360,
        width      : 280,
        items      : {
            xtype         : 'treepanel',
            store         : store,
            rootVisible   : true,
            listeners: {
                itemcontextmenu: onCtxMenu      ◁──┐   Assigns context
            },                                      ❷  menu listener
            plugins: [
                treeEditor
            ]
        }
    }
});
```

In listing 9.6 you start with the TreeCellEditing plug-in instantiation. You use the `treeEditor` variable so that you can reference this instance in your tree panel. You could've just used a `ptype` configuration for lazy instantiation, but you can benefit from referencing the plug-in directly later in your editing logic. To complete the listing you configure the `itemcontextmenu` listener ❷, as mentioned earlier.

You're ready to build your editing logic now. One thing we want to mention at this point is the `clicksToEdit` config option in listing 9.6 ❶. Just as with editable grid panels, you could leave the whole context menu editing hassle out of the picture and use the already-registered `dblclick` event to enter editing mode. But it's a good opportunity to show how a tree panel's internals interact. That's why you'll initiate the editor from your new context menu in the next listing.

Listing 9.7　Configuring the context menu editing trigger

```
var onEdit = function(button, node) {              ❶  Finds menu
    var menu     = button.up(),              ◁──┐
        node     = node || menu.treeNode,    ◁──┐   Accesses
        view     = menu.treeView,                ❷  refs
        tree     = view.ownerCt,
        selMdl   = view.getSelectionModel(),
        colHdr   = tree.headerCt.getHeaderAtIndex(0);    ❸  Gets column
                                                 ◁──┐       index
    if (selMdl.getCurrentPosition) {
        pos = selMdl.getCurrentPosition();
```

```
            colHdr = tree.headerCt.getHeaderAtIndex(pos.column);
        }
        treeEditor.startEdit(node, colHdr);
};
```

4 Shows editor

You've see larger chunks of code in this chapter, but the piece in listing 9.7 may look like the most complicated of all. There are several variables that you need to register first: menu, which you get from retrieving the clicked button's parent ❶; node ❷ and view, which you capture from the menu's properties you defined earlier (in listing 9.4); the tree panel itself (tree); the selection model (selMdl); and the column header (colHdr). The selection model will give you the column index of your tree (remember, tree panels are tables, and tree views are rendered in columns, similar to a grid's behavior), whereas the column header is needed to identify the editor field assigned to the tree. Going back to node ❷, make sure you noticed that node can be an argument as well. You'll use that later when you start adding nodes.

In case your tree was configured to use the cell collection model (cellmodel), you can get the position of your tree column automatically ❸ to make sure you're editing the right field in the grid. Finally, you execute the startEdit method ❹ that lives in the treeEditor plug-in instance. See how you got to reuse the treeEditor reference?

Right now you have a fully functional tree panel with the ability to show the editor for each node. What do you think happens when a user presses the Enter key? You got it: the record is updated, and the store will sync the changes through the proxy over to the server. The store handles that much work on its own.

Refresh your page, right-click a node, and click the Edit button. In figure 9.8 we've changed the Accounting department's name to Legal by right-clicking it, which selects the node. We then clicked the Edit menu button, which rendered the text field as an editor at the node's physical location. Next we changed the name from Accounting to Legal and pressed Enter. This caused the Node value to change and the store's datachanged event to fire, triggering the sync method. Because the server accepted the value, the new value persisted in the UI. Remember that if the server had

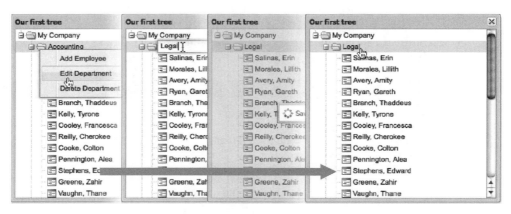

Figure 9.8 The results of editing a node in the tree panel using the tree editor

returned { success : false } or if the request had failed, the text value of Node would've been reverted.

This wraps up the easiest of the CRUD functionality for your tree panel. Editing names in this widget is a common task in web applications. Naturally, how you implement it depends on business requirements. Using the newly created TreeCellEditing plug-in results in a cleaner application flow by saving you from having to use an input dialog box, such as a message prompt.

Next you're going to tackle the deletion of nodes. Even though it'll require an additional confirmation step, deletion will be easier than what you've done so far in this chapter.

9.4.3 *Tackling delete*

To set up the delete functionality of your tree panel, you'll create a handler for the Delete menu button. Naturally, requirements usually dictate that a confirmation dialog box be presented to the user, so you'll have to code for user confirmation. To make things a bit easier, you'll use the out-of-the-box Ext.Msg.confirm method to show the dialog box. This means that you'll have to construct a callback method for the confirmation dialog box. The dialog box callback will trigger the store's sync method and ultimately delete the node.

Now that you have an idea of what you need to do, you can get on with coding the handler methods, as shown in the following listing.

> **Listing 9.8   Adding deletion functionality to your tree panel**

```
var onConfirmDelete = function(answer, value, cfg, button) {      ❶ Returns if
    if (answer != 'yes') return;                                       Yes clicked

    var menu    = button.up(),
        node    = menu.treeNode;               ❷ Removes,
    node.remove(true);                            destroys node
};
var onDelete = function(button) {
    var callback = Ext.bind(onConfirmDelete, undefined, [button],    Creates
    ➥ true);                                                        callback
                                                               ❸ function
    Ext.Msg.confirm(
            'Approve deletion',
            'Are you sure you want to delete this node?',
            callback
    );
};
```

In listing 9.8 you create the two methods that take care of the delete operations of your CRUD functionality. The first method, onConfirmDelete, is the handler for the confirmation dialog box that you'll create a little later. If the Yes button is clicked ❶ in the confirmation dialog box, it'll look up the NodeInterface reference and delete it. You set the deletion argument to true ❸, meaning it'll also destroy the node ❷. This action will again trigger the store's datachanged event, forcing the store to sync.

In this fictitious mini-application, the server would take the value of the node ID and perform a delete operation in the database or filesystem and return something like {success:true}, which confirms the deletion.

The second method you create, onDelete, is the handler for the Delete button. When this method is called, it presents a confirmation dialog box by using the out-of-the-box Ext.Msg.confirm method and passing in three arguments: the title, message body, and callback.

The callback was created with the utility function Ext.bind (short for Ext.Function .bind). This useful function creates a new method that'll essentially create a closure that calls your targeted function onConfirmDelete in a default scope, also appending the button argument to the passed arguments. Therefore, Ext.bind will receive four arguments: the function to be called, the scope, the array of arguments, and the Boolean value that tells whether to append those arguments (true) or override the arguments passed by the function caller (false). The default arguments are dictated by Ext.Msg.confirm, and they're the answer string ("yes" or "no"), input value (undefined, used only with Ext.Msg.prompt), and confirm's config object. You want to use the answer argument, so keep them all.

Your application now presents the user with a message and two options to proceed. Either button will trigger the callback, but remember that to perform the deletion of the node, the Yes button has to be clicked.

Refresh your UI, and delete a node. Figure 9.9 illustrates what happened when we refreshed our UI and deleted the Accounting department node.

After we right-clicked the Accounting department node, our customized context menu appeared. We then clicked the Delete button, which triggered the onDelete handler. This immediately displayed the confirmation dialog box. We clicked Yes, which caused the onConfirmDelete method to fully execute, looking up the node reference stored in the context menu and deleting (and destroying) the node itself.

In a real-world application, deleting a branch node would generally require the server to recursively gather a list of all of the child nodes and remove them from

Figure 9.9 Deleting a node with a confirmation box

the database before removing the branch node itself. One clever way to do this would be to set up a trigger in the database to call a stored procedure to delete all associated child nodes when a delete operation is performed on a container node.

Deleting nodes from your tree panel takes a bit of effort because of the typically required confirmation dialog box. Adding a node, though, is equally difficult, because the UI code needs to know what type of node is being added. Is it a branch or a leaf node? Next you'll see how to code for this type of action and have the UI react accordingly.

9.4.4 Creating nodes for your tree panel

To create a node interface, you're going to have to recycle some of the work already done, while still using some of the cool JavaScript features, like closures. Because the tree editor needs to bind and display on top of a node, you'll need to inject a node interface into the tree panel and trigger an edit operation on the new node. As soon as you create the node, the store will sync the new data to the server. Because you'll get a chance to edit the name of the node immediately on creation, the store will once again sync the data once you update the text. This works similarly to the way rows are added to the editor grid you created in the previous chapter. The next listing contains the code for the create-node functionality.

> **Listing 9.9 Adding create functionality to your tree panel**

```
var onAdd = function(button) {
    var menu     = button.up(),
        node     = menu.treeNode,
        view     = menu.treeView,
        delay    = view.expandDuration + 50,      ①  Determines
        newNode,                                       animation length
        doCreate;
                                                   ②  Creates closure
    doCreate = function() {
        newNode = node.appendChild({text: 'New employee', leaf: true});
        onEdit(button, newNode);
    };

    if (!node.isExpanded()) {
        node.expand(false,
            Ext.callback(doCreate, this, [], delay));    ③  Delays collapse
    }                                                        of node
    else {
        doCreate();
    }
};
```

You're doing an interesting bit of work in listing 9.9 to get the create functionality to proceed smoothly. Here's how it all works.

Just as with the `onEdit` method, you need to retrieve a couple of references stored for you in the menu: `NodeInterface` and `View`. The latter one you use to find out how long the expand animation will last ①. Yes, user interface animations have little in common with data processing, but this time you need to count them in. Should the parent node be collapsed, you need to expand it first, wait for the animation to finish, and only then continue with the editing process.

The duration itself is hidden in the view configuration, to which you add an extra 50 milliseconds to let the UI settle nicely. Unfortunately, the framework doesn't take care of waiting for the node to be expanded, so you need to add an adequate delay to the callback.

During the process of planning the onAdd handler, you anticipated two possible scenarios in regard to the target parent node being expanded or collapsed. The first case is straightforward, and you could continue by creating the node followed by the editing process, but what if the node is collapsed? In such a case you'll have to expand it and pass the very same process of creation and editing to the expand method's callback argument ❸. Because repeating such a block of code wouldn't make much sense, you've created a nice little closure, doCreate ❷. Closures are quite useful here; you get to access all the previously assigned variables in the parent function, yet they make it possible to reuse the underlying code.

The doCreate closure encapsulates two commands. First, you append the child to the selected node and set its name to "New employee" and leaf to true. Remember, you're creating an employee, so use leaf: true. As soon as you create the employee, you'll want to edit it and assign an adequate name. Here you're reusing the onEdit method, passing the same menu button instance to it along with the newly created node so that TreeCellEditing knows where to show the edit field.

Wow, that was a fun one! Let's refresh the UI and see the code in action, as shown in figure 9.10. Here you can see how you use TreeCellEditing to add nodes to the tree panel in a way that mimics operating system behavior.

When we right-clicked the Accounting department node, the dynamic context menu appeared as expected. We clicked the Add menu button, which triggered the onAdd handler. This caused the Accounting node to expand. After the child nodes were loaded, a new node was inserted, firing TreeStore's sync method, and an edit

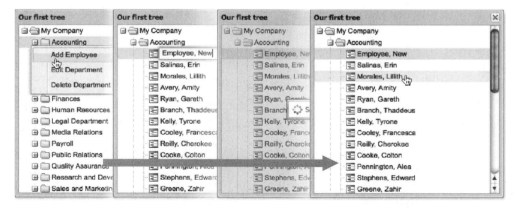

Figure 9.10   Adding a new node to your tree panel using TreeCellEditing

operation was immediately triggered on that node using TreeCellEditing. We typed in a new employee name and pressed Enter. This caused the `complete` event to be fired by the tree store, thus invoking the `sync` handler, which performed yet another XHR (`XMLHttpRequest`). You can also implement this code to add department nodes to the tree, and add employees to those.

Great work! You now know how to construct tree panels, feed them data from the server, and apply CRUD workflows to them. You can now add these widgets to your applications.

9.5 Summary

In this chapter we covered quite a bit of code when discussing tree panels and how to set up really cool CRUD interactions for nodes. We began by talking about `Ext.tree.Panel` and discussed supporting classes such as `Ext.tree.View`, `Ext.data.TreeStore`, and `Ext.data.NodeInterface`. You learned how `TreePanel` shares `GridPanel`'s infrastructure, making it more powerful than ever. You constructed a static tree panel, where the nodes were read from memory, and you saw how the JSON should be formatted.

You then moved on to build a dynamic tree panel that loaded data from a remote data source, and you spent a lot of time enabling full CRUD operations. To enable CRUD, you learned how to dynamically modify, enable, and disable the reusable context menu. You saw what it took to set up adding and editing using your very own Tree-CellEditing plug-in, which gives the tree panel the ability to edit node names inline.

So far you've only scratched the surface of some of the framework's widgets responsible for data administration. In the next chapter you'll dive deep into visual data representation using drawings and charts, and you'll learn more about how they work and how to better put them to work in your applications.

Drawing and charting

This chapter covers

- Drawing in the browser with Ext.draw
- Understanding shapes and surface
- Creating sample drawings
- Using Ext charts and charting themes
- Configuring legends

Visual data representation is considered to be one of the most effective user experience mechanisms. Charts in particular are valuable eye candy for any decision maker, which is why chart-rich dashboards are often the front-facing features of software presentations.

Web applications are also prone to the same trends. But plug-in-less charting support has only just begun to see the day of light, with Sencha acting as a trendsetter in the movement.

Compared to its predecessor, Ext JS 4 has a vast number of upgraded components. The charting package has not only been upgraded but also completely rewritten. No longer does it require Flash or any other external dependencies to render awesome charts. Powered by the Ext.draw package, Ext JS 4 features new chart types, such as Scatter, Gauge, and Radar. In this chapter you'll learn how to implement the available chart types.

Because the goal of Ext JS charts is to no longer rely on Flash to display awesome graphics, the Sencha team has come up with an API dedicated to drawing that enables lines and shapes to be drawn directly within a browser. For you to understand how charts work, we'll first take a deep dive into the new Ext.draw package and learn how charts are drawn. Be sure to read the chapter text that goes with the examples; this is a complex topic.

10.1 Drawing shapes

Visualization has been a hot topic in the browser world for a long time. Technologies have emerged with support for exciting new features, thus deprecating previous standards. A critical mission for an enterprise-level framework is to provide support for browsers as old as Microsoft Internet Explorer (IE) 6. This means supporting stable but unexciting JavaScript, or should we say JScript, standards and visualization technologies.

The Ext JS drawing package supports Scalable Vector Graphics (SVG) and Vector Markup Language (VML). Both are well supported in popular browsers and are capable of delivering vector graphics to a user's screen. Although VML is supported in even older browsers than those supported by the framework, it lacks the flexibility of SVG. That's why SVG is the default drawing engine in Ext.draw. Note that most IE browsers will require VML instead.

If you take a good look at Ext.draw's internals, you'll notice that it almost acts as a middleware to the drawing engine. The goal is to provide uniform configuration options and then forward commands to each of the drawing engines in order for them to render identical outputs. On a side note, Ext.draw relays configurations so precisely that, on occasion, it breaks the consistency of other Ext JS components. Specifically, you'll have to quote certain config properties when drawing:

- `fill-opacity`
- `font-size`
- `stroke-opacity`
- `stroke-width`

Notice that all of these properties include a hyphen, and hyphens are only allowed in JavaScript object properties if properly quoted.

Before you put these properties into action, let's go over the basics of in-browser vector drawing. The following section discusses the most important concepts.

10.2 Drawing concepts

A prerequisite for drawing is a surface. It's intentionally not named a canvas to avoid confusion with the HTML canvas tag. A surface is an interface, usually inside an `Ext.draw.Component` instance. It provides an abstraction layer between JavaScript and the VML or SVG engine.

Canvas in Ext JS charts

Ext JS 4.1 charts use SVG and VML as the only drawing engines. Sencha Touch charts provide a similar interface, but they use the HTML5 canvas tag, which yields better performance on mobile devices.

The surface, as an instance, exists as a property of an `Ext.draw.Component` instance. As such, the surface can be used to draw sprites. *Sprites* are regular or irregular paths that make up a shape. You're about to see how a surface interacts with sprites.

10.3 *Surfacing sprites*

Because drawing can't take place without a surface, and the surface is used through an `Ext.draw.Component`, let's examine how the latter handles the artistic strokes.

`Ext.draw.Component` directly inherits from `Ext.Component`. Thus, it shares the ability to manage all of the component life-cycle plumbing. Its single most distinctive feature, the surface, can fit as many shapes as you like. With that in mind, the children of `Ext.draw.Component` are meant to be shapes.

There are only a few configuration options for customizing an Ext.draw component. Each can make a terrific impact on the outcome of your drawing:

- `autoSize`—Positions the sprite to the top left of the surface. Although it doesn't obey the X and Y coordinates of a sprite, they need to be set.
- `viewBox`—Sets as true to scale and positions items to fill the component. Overrides sizing and positioning settings (X, Y, radius, and so on).
- `gradients`—A set of gradients you can use with sprites based on `gradientId`.
- `enginePriority`—Specifies the first drawing engine you want to use, if it's supported by the client's browser.

Some options directly influence the behavior of the underlying sprites. The shapes supported by Ext.draw sprites resemble the shapes natively supported by the drawing engines:

- `circle`
- `ellipse`
- `rect` (rectangle)
- `text`
- `path`
- `image`

Of course, `path` is the Jack of all trades here. All other shapes that you may want to draw can be made using paths. We'll cover `path` syntax basics later in this chapter.

Sprites can be further customized with these useful properties:

- `width`— Specifies the rectangle width
- `height`—Specifies the rectangle height

- size—Specifies the length of a square's side
- radius—Specifies the radius of a circle
- x—Specifies the top-left position on the X-axis
- y—Specifies the top-left position on the Y-axis
- cx—Indicates a circle's or an ellipse's center position on the X-axis
- cy—Indicates a circle's or an ellipse's center position on the Y-axis
- stroke—Specifies the stroke color
- stroke-width—Specifies the width of a stroke
- fill—Specifies the color of a sprite's body
- opacity—Specifies the transparency level of a sprite
- text—Contains the text string to render
- font—Provides a CSS-style font description for text
- path—Provides an SVG-syntax interface for drawing paths

Configuration options are selective, based on the exact shape used for the sprite. For example, size is only used with squares, whereas radius is used with circles and no other shape. The exact mappings are well described in the framework's documentation.

10.3.1 Drawing a sprite

It's about time you created your first work of art. The following listing shows you how to create a simple circle and maximize its view size while maintaining the aspect ratio.

Listing 10.1   Drawing a circle

```
Ext.onReady(function() {
    var dc = Ext.create('Ext.draw.Component', {
        items   : [{
            type    : 'circle',          Draws
            fill    : '#79BB3F',     ❶  circle
            radius  : 100,
            x       : 200,
            y       : 200
        }]
    });

    Ext.create('Ext.window.Window', {    Creates parent
        width       : 600,           ❷  container
        height      : 400,
        autoShow    : true,
        title       : 'Simple Circle',
        maximizable : true,
        layout      : 'fit',
        items       : dc,
        resizable   : {
            dynamic: true
        }
```

```
    });
});
```

Listing 10.1 creates the most basic drawing. Essentially, you've just created a default surface inside an Ext.draw component and placed a circle-shaped sprite onto it ❶. The circle's radius is 100px, and the X- and Y-axis coordinates are set to 200px each. The image is rendered inside `Ext.window.Window` ❷. If you render this example in a browser, you'll see an image resembling figure 10.1.

Nice going! You've just created your first drawing with Ext JS. In the next section you'll learn how to mix the settings of a surface with the settings of a sprite. The example will refer to the code in listing 10.1 and further extend it to prove essential concepts.

10.3.2 *Managing positioning and sizing*

You've successfully created your first drawing, a gorgeous green circle. Your trained eye will immediately tell you that this circle's radius goes well beyond the configured 100 pixels. The reason is hidden from your configuration. It lies in the default `view-Box` configuration option, set to `true`. It means that the circle will be maximized to the surface's size, ignoring the `radius` setting.

There's more to the interaction of configuration options. Notice the x and y settings again. The `viewBox` setting doesn't care about them, as long as they're set. This sounds peculiar, so we'll use it in a few examples.

First, set x and y each to 1:

```
x: 1,
y: 1
```

The circle is rendered in the same fashion, even though x and y have been changed. This proves that `viewBox: true` overrides coordinates.

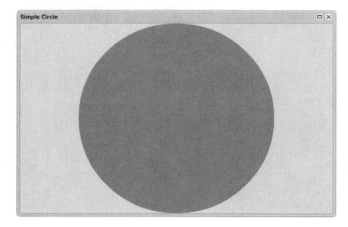

Figure 10.1 Your first circle, rendered

Figure 10.2 With X- and Y-axis coordinates unset, the circle's center is set to 0,0 and the `radius` setting is no longer ignored.

Now try it without x and y settings:

```
{
    type    : 'circle',
    fill    : '#79BB3F',
    radius  : 100
}
```

Talk about peculiar. It takes just one of the coordinates to be undefined, and the `viewBox` property is no longer taken into account (see figure 10.2). But the question remains, how do you explicitly set the circle's radius and position?

There are two ways. The first approach is setting `viewBox` to `false`, as shown in the next listing.

Listing 10.2   Disabling `viewBox`

```
var dc = Ext.create('Ext.draw.Component', {
    viewBox : false,                              ◁⎯┐   Sets viewBox
    items   : [{                                   ❶   to false
        type    : 'circle',
        fill    : '#79BB3F',
        radius  : 100,
        x       : 200,
        y       : 200
    }]
});
```

Now that `viewBox` is disabled ❶, let's see what you get in your example image (figure 10.3).

You've disabled the automatic size and position calculations in favor of fixed settings. Circles logically shouldn't care about x and y properties, because a circle doesn't have a top-left corner (or any other corner for that matter). Ext JS will instead translate the coordinates to match the center of the circle.

The second method would be to set center X (cx) and center Y (cy) properties instead of x and y, as shown in the following listing.

Figure 10.3   The circle is now positioned and sized exactly as you wanted it.

Listing 10.3   Forceful circle positioning with `cx` and `cy`

```
items   : [{
    type    : 'circle',
    fill    : '#79BB3F',
    radius  : 100,
    cx      : 200,
    cy      : 200
}]
```

❶ Sets center X and Y coordinates

You've achieved the same effect with less coding. Explicitly setting the center X and Y coordinates ❶ will render the same effect as disabling `viewBox`.

So far you've only played with a single Ext.draw component's behavior-controlling configuration, `viewBox`. In the examples to come, we'll show you how `autoSize` interacts with your sprite.

10.3.3   *Automatically sizing sprites*

The `autoSize` property (see listing 10.4) obeys sizing of the child sprite or sprites but makes sure the entire rendered drawing takes the minimum possible size in terms of its width and height. Naturally, it rules out the `viewBox` setting, but it keeps its x and y setting requirements. That means that you have to set x and y to positive integers, but it doesn't matter how big those integers are.

Listing 10.4   Enabling `autoSize`

```
var dc = Ext.create('Ext.draw.Component', {
    autoSize: true,
    items   : [{
        type    : 'circle',
        fill    : '#79BB3F',
        radius  : 100,
        x       : 1,
        y       : 1000
    }]
});
```

❶ Sets autoSize to true

❷ Sets minimum positive integer

❸ Assigns exceptionally large integer

Figure 10.4   The circle is drawn respecting the `radius` setting but placed in the top-left corner of the surface.

With `autoSize` set to `true` ❶, the surface will automatically position sprites inside it to make sure they take the least amount of space possible, relative to the top left (0,0). To show how a sprite manages the circle when so configured, you're setting x to the minimal positive integer ❷ and y to an exceptionally large integer ❸. You'd certainly notice if the circle was positioned at (1,1000). As you can see in figure 10.4, X and Y coordinates are totally ignored, but they needed to be set. Otherwise the effect would've been the same as in figure 10.2.

So far you've only created a simple circle, yet you've seen numerous implications of mixing various sprite and `Ext.draw.Component` (surface) settings. Next to come are somewhat more exciting demonstrations of how to dynamically add sprites, animation, and event binding to the mix.

10.4 *Sprite interactions*

It's likely that you'll want to use Ext.draw for something more complex than to lay out a circle. Let's add a pinch of fun to the existing recipe in order to create an interactive example.

In the next example (listing 10.5), you'll reuse the circle from the previous example and place it at a fixed position, disabling `viewBox`. You'll dynamically add another circle with a fade-in animation for a prettier entrance. Finally, you'll assign event listeners to the newly added circle in order to make it move on mouseover and then go back to its initial position on mouseout.

Listing 10.5   Dynamically appending a shape

```
var dc = Ext.create('Ext.draw.Component', {          Instantiates
    viewBox : false,                              ❶ Ext.draw.Component
    items   : [{
        type   : 'circle',
        fill   : '#79BB3F',
        radius : 100,
        x      : 200,
        y      : 200
```

```
        }]
});

Ext.create('Ext.window.Window', {
    width        : 600,
    height       : 400,
    autoShow     : true,
    title        : 'Dynamically adding a new sprite to '
                   +'surface with a 2-sec delay',
    maximizable : true,
    layout       : 'fit',
    items        : [dc],
    resizable    : {
        dynamic: true
    },

    listeners: {
        show: function() {
            var sprite = dc.surface.add({
                type             : 'circle',
                fill             : '#846393',
                stroke           : '#a54222',
                'stroke-width'   : 5,
                opacity          : .8,
                radius           : 100,
                x                : 300,
                y                : 200
            });

            sprite.show();
        }
    }
});
```

❷ Accesses surface to add new sprite

❸ Configures stroke

❹ Adds stroke-width

❺ Controls stroke and fill

❻ Shows sprite on surface

First you create an Ext.window.Window with a single child, Ext.draw.Component ❶, thus creating a surface for your drawing (hidden in dc.surface). The Ext.draw.Component is configured to disable both viewBox and autoSize, because you want to take control of sizing and placement of your sprites. The first sprite is configured right within the items property, and it's the first circle, just as in the previous examples.

Immediately following the Ext.window.Window instantiation, you're adding a new sprite ❷. You'll be waiting for the window to render and show, because only when Ext.draw.Component is rendered will the surface be created. You guessed it; you can't add sprites without a created surface.

Alternatively, you could've created a surface manually. Ext.draw.Component has a createSurface() method that does the job of creating a surface. Now that you know this trick, you can create drawings before they're presented to the end user.

Back to our example. Your newly added circle is of the same size as the original, but it's placed 100px to the left, it's colored differently, and its opacity is set to 0. The stroke can be configured separately from the fill, specifying its color ❸ and width ❹. The opacity setting affects both fill (body) and stroke (border) colors ❺. Should you need to set the opacity of just one of these, or set each property differently, you can

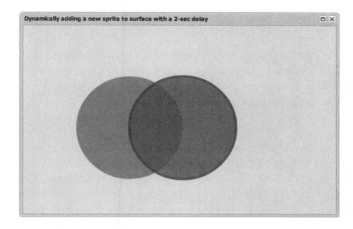

Figure 10.5 The second circle dynamically added

always reach out for the power of CSS and use an RGBA color setting for the fill and/or stroke (such as `rgba(012, 123, 230, 0.4)`).

It's time to look at your sprite (figure 10.5). The sprite's `show()` method **6** offers an optional but convenient `redraw` argument. It tells the surface to render the sprite all over again. You won't enjoy any of the benefits of redrawing right now, so you can safely leave it off.

Because the sprite's opacity was initially configured to be 0, you'll need to make the circle visible by increasing the number. To make this process cooler, you'll animate the transition with the following code block, which you place after `sprite.show();`:

```
sprite.animate({
    duration: 1000,
    easing: 'easeOut',
    to: {
        opacity: .9
    }
});
```

Opacity ranges from 0 to 1. A setting of 0.9 will make the sprite almost fully visible. The animation will last 1 second (1000 ms) and will slow down (ease out) as it gets closer to the last milliseconds.

You now have a nice entrance. Let's add a couple of events to make your drawing responsive to mouse pointer movement. Add the following code block after the `sprite.animate()` code block you just added:

```
sprite.on('mouseover', Ext.bind(
    sprite.animate,
    sprite,
    [{
        duration: 500,
        easing: 'easeOut',
        to: {
            opacity: .6,
            translate: {
```

```
                x: -100
            }
        }
    }]
));

sprite.on('mouseout', Ext.bind(
    sprite.animate,
    sprite,
    [{
        duration: 300,
        easing: 'easeIn',
        to: {
            opacity: .9,
            translate: {
                x: 0
            }
        }
    }]
));
```

The second circle will react when the mouse pointer is moved over it by moving to a position further left, as seen in figure 10.6. Moving the mouse out of the circle will animate the sprite to reset its position. Both events' callbacks animate movement of the desired sprite.

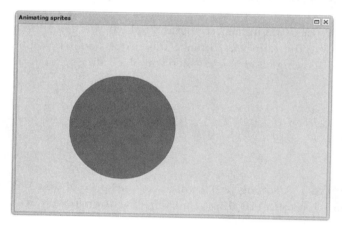

Figure 10.6   With mouseover, the second circle moves on top of the first one.

You've just learned how to dynamically add sprites to a surface as well as how to animate and register events on them. You've probably noticed patterns shared with predefined chart types. In the next section you'll see how charts are drawn and create a custom shape using a path sprite.

10.5   *Mastering the path*

SVG and VML are engines with syntax of their own. So far in this chapter you've successfully used both engines without directly talking to either in its own language. It's time to touch on the basics of creating custom paths. It'll be a fun adventure outside the JavaScript world.

Drawing a path is essentially drawing a line from point A to point Z, with N points in between. Their coordinates relative to the X- and Y-axis specify points. The area surrounded by the path can be defined by separate styling as well. Furthermore, two points can connect in a straight line or a curved line in numerous ways. Such behavior is directed through the following commands:

- M = Move to
- L = Line to
- H = Horizontal line to
- V = Vertical line to
- C = Curve to
- S = Smooth curve to
- Q = Quadratic Bézier curve to
- T = Smooth quadratic Bézier curve to
- A = Elliptical arc
- Z = Close path

All of these commands can also be expressed with lowercase letters. Capital letters indicate absolutely positioned points, whereas lowercase letters indicate relatively positioned points.

> **TIP** For a more comprehensive explanation of vector drawing please refer to *HTML5 in Action* (Manning, 2013).

An example will explain the usage best. Take a sheet of paper and a pen. Now draw a five-pointed star (figure 10.7).

How many strokes did it take? Let's count with the help of the figure. There's the starting position, four points, and back to the starting point: that's five strokes.

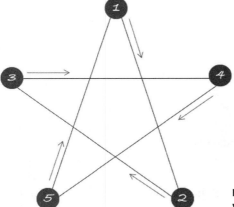

Figure 10.7   A hand-drawn star with a step-by-step point workflow

Translate the image to a Cartesian coordinate system. Each point is a pair of coordinates expressed in pixel distance from the origin (middle of the plane). Let's start from 0,–100 and work from there:

```
M 0 -100 L 58 81 -95 -31 95 -31 -59 81 Z
```

It may look like magic on first sight, but in fact it's only geometry. In plain English, this says

1 (M) Move to 0,–100.
2 (L) Line from 0,–100 to 58,81.
3 (Repeat L) Line from 58,81 to –95,–31.
4 (Repeat L) Line from –95,–31 to 95,–31.
5 (Repeat L) Line from 95,–31 to –59 81.
6 (Z) Finish the path and draw a line back to the starting position.

Now that we've covered theory, it's time to plug the path code into an Ext JS 4 application, as shown in the next listing.

Listing 10.6   Drawing a star

```
var dc = Ext.create('Ext.draw.Component', {
    items   : [{
        type    : 'path',
        fill    : '#ca433F',
        path    : 'M 0 -100 L 58 81 -95 -31 95 -31 -59 81 Z'
    }]
});

Ext.create('Ext.window.Window', {
    width       : 600,
    height      : 400,
    autoShow    : true,
    title       : 'Star (path)',
    maximizable : true,
    layout      : 'fit',
    items       : dc,
    resizable   : {
        dynamic : true
    }
});
```

As you can see, the pattern is consistent with other sprite types. Inside the draw component you added a path, but it'll take an extra step to actually draw the path. Paths aren't preconfigured like circles or squares, meaning you'll need to feed it with point instructions. You assign instructions to the path property. Figure 10.8 shows what the output looks like.

The shape of the star looks just like the one you drew by hand. In addition, we painted its body, which made it look more compact. At this point in the book you're familiar with creating and configuring components, so the only new thing you had to

Figure 10.8 Star-shaped path drawn with Ext.draw

apply in this example is the path data. It comes in the form of a string, exactly as it's passed on to the drawing engine.

You now understand how drawing works in Ext JS 4. With the information in this chapter so far you can understand how the Ext.chart package draws charts on a Cartesian coordinate system plane, and you can even create your own chart types.

You'll create various types of charts in the rest of this chapter. It's going to be an interesting journey, drawing animated, event-powered shapes, lines, and areas with Ext JS 4.

10.6 *A deep dive into charts*

Before drawing your first chart, let's dissect the main components of a chart. A chart provides a graphical representation of data stored in a store. Furthermore, a chart component directly inherits from `Ext.draw.Component`, meaning you can spice up your charts with custom drawings.

As shown in figure 10.9, the three main components of a chart are

- *Axes* (`Ext.chart.axis.*`)—Defines data dimensions
- *Series* (`Ext.chart.series.*`)—Represents a data item visually: a line (dot), bar, pie (slice), and so on
- *Legend* (`Ext.chart.Legend`)—Provides an optional list of variables appearing in the chart, each representing the sprite that's assigned for the data points

In Cartesian plane–based charts (line, bar, scatter, column, or area), axes are referred to as X-axis and Y-axis, representing horizontal and vertical axes, respectively. Each axis is accompanied by numerical or categorical indications, easily extracted from `Ext.data.Store` records. Records feed series with data to provide the means for graphical comparison.

Series represent what a viewer is interested in. They're the actual drawings that represent specific values. In the world of Ext JS charts, eight types of series are available (figure 10.10):

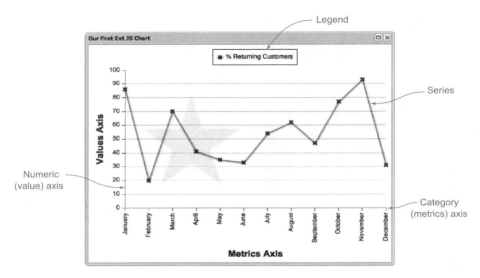

Figure 10.9   Your first chart

- Line
- Bar
- Column
- Area
- Scatter
- Pie
- Gauge
- Radar

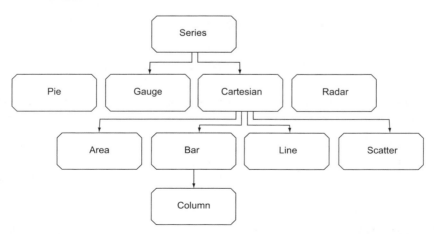

Figure 10.10   Series inheritance model illustrated. The Cartesian series is displayed here because it's a superclass to the Area, Bar, Line, and Scatter classes, but we don't configure instances of the Cartesian class itself.

Let's examine the list of available series and the series inheritance model. If it looks complicated to you, don't worry. You can easily put each type in one of two groups: those that require axes (pie, gauge, and radar) and those that don't (all Cartesian types).

Most of us at one point face a decision of which chart type (series) is the most appropriate option for a display result. Here are some general rules of thumb for which series to use:

- *Line*—Shows trends of value changes in short or long spans; useful with smaller deltas
- *Bar*—Compares values one to another, stacked vertically
- *Column*—Same as Bar, but stacked horizontally
- *Area*—Similar to Line; especially useful when tracking changes in two or more groups that make up a whole
- *Scatter*—Used to determine the relationship between two different variables; useful for visualizing densities
- *Pie*—Unlike the Cartesian types, shows proportion of a slice relative to a whole or total (%)
- *Gauge*—Shows values relative to given minimum and maximum counterparts
- *Radar*—Compares options across several parameters in parallel

Because a chart is yet another surface, you can easily append custom shapes or even images. But be sure to properly lay them out on the plane, because `viewBox` is false in the charts. You've already learned that `viewBox` implements automatic shape-positioning calculations.

Now that we've covered the basics, you'll learn how to construct a chart just like the one in figure 10.9, step by step.

10.7 *Implementing Cartesian charts*

Earlier in this chapter you accessed the surface with an instance of `Ext.draw.Component`. When drawing a chart, you'll make use of the `Ext.chart.Chart` class that directly inherits from `Ext.draw.Component`, with one important difference: the `items` property will rarely be used. You'll see why in a moment.

10.7.1 *Configuring the axes*

Again, let's look at the case from a more elementary perspective: hand drawing. When sketching diagrams, what do you draw first? That's right: the axes. But even before you start drawing the axes, you think about what kind of data to expect: minimum to maximum range, what to compare on each axis, and how to space out the metrics. Without further ado, let's lay out the axes in the following listing.

Listing 10.7 Laying out the axes

```
Ext.onReady(function () {
    var generateData = function (n, floor){
```

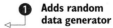 **1** Adds random data generator

```
        var data = [],
            i;

        floor = (!floor && floor !== 0)? 20 : floor;

        for (i = 0; i < (n || 12); i++) {
            data.push({
                name: Ext.Date.monthNames[i % 12],
                data1: Math.floor(Math.max((Math.random() * 100), floor)),
                data2: Math.floor(Math.max((Math.random() * 100), floor)),
                data3: Math.floor(Math.max((Math.random() * 100), floor)),
                data4: Math.floor(Math.max((Math.random() * 100), floor)),
                data5: Math.floor(Math.max((Math.random() * 100), floor)),
                data6: Math.floor(Math.max((Math.random() * 100), floor)),
                data7: Math.floor(Math.max((Math.random() * 100), floor)),
                data8: Math.floor(Math.max((Math.random() * 100), floor)),
                data9: Math.floor(Math.max((Math.random() * 100), floor))
            });
        }
        return data;
    };
var store = Ext.create('Ext.data.JsonStore', {                      ❷ Adds data
    fields: ['name', 'data1', 'data2', 'data3', 'data4', 'data5'],     store
    data: generateData()
}),

chart = Ext.create('Ext.chart.Chart', {
    store: store,
    background: {
        fill: '#fff'
    },                                           ❸ Defines
    axes: [                                         axes        ❹ Sets axis
        {                                                          type
            type: 'Numeric',
            position: 'left',
            title: 'Values Axis'                 ❺ Specifies axis
        },                                          location
        {
            type: 'Category',                    ❻ Configures
            position: 'bottom',                     category axis
            fields: 'name',
            title: 'Metrics Axis'
        }
    ]
});

Ext.create('Ext.window.Window', {
    width       : 600,
    height      : 470,
    autoShow    : true,
    title       : 'Our Very First Ext JS Chart',
    maximizable : true,
    layout      : 'fit',
    items       : [chart],
    resizable   : {
```

```
        dynamic: true
    }
    });
});
```

Listing 10.7 is lengthy, because it contains bits that you'll reuse in other examples. The reusable parts are the random data generator ❶ and the data store ❷. Instead of items, you need to specify the axes ❸. Axes are a special kind of item in which children are always instances of `Ext.chart.axis.Axis`. Preconfigured axis types ❹ are numeric (numbers), category (text), time (date object), and gauge.

Each axis needs to be placed somewhere on a Cartesian plane. In most charts, Ext JS charts being no exception, you observe a single quarter of a full Cartesian plane. That's why you have to specify which side of the quarter you want an axis to border ❺. Possible values are `left`, `right`, `top`, and `bottom`.

Finally, each axis should be assigned some data. To do that you must reference a field from the store, as in ❻. Note that in the left axis you didn't assign a field. Ext JS will automatically assign a range from 0 to max, equally spaced out in equal step increments. The maximum number is calculated from the maximum used in the series. If no series are specified—and this should never be the case in an application—max equals 1. You'll fix this in the next step, when you configure the series.

As you can see in figure 10.11, the axes are laid out as intended. The numeric axis, Values, is drawn exactly as expected, given the lack of a specified series. The Metrics axis, on the other hand, misses a few labels. February, September, and November—the names with the highest number of characters in them—have fallen out of the picture. Ext JS does this automatically to make room for as many labels as possible.

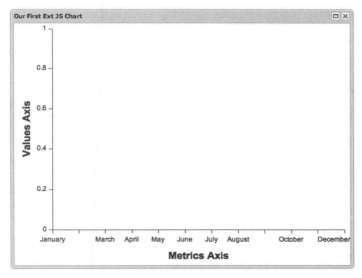

Figure 10.11 Axes drawn on a surface

To show all the labels, you must rotate them to display vertically. Specify the label configuration as follows:

```
{
    type: 'Category',
    position: 'bottom',
    fields: 'name',
    title: 'Metrics Axis',
    label: {
        rotate: {
            degrees: 270
        }
    }
}
```

Voilà, exactly as demonstrated in figure 10.9! In addition to rotation, labels can be customized to show in a specific color or font. You can even custom-format the values using a renderer. Remember how you used renderers for columns in panels?

10.7.2 Adding series

Axes are worthless unless you add series to the chart. From the randomly generated data set, you'll pick the data1 field and show how it changes as months go by (the name field). Next you'll append an array of series to the axes configuration where the Chart is created in listing 10.7.

Listing 10.8 Configuring series

```
series: [
    {                          ➊ Configures
                                 line series
        type: 'line',   ◁──         ➋ Sets left
        axis: 'left',   ◁──            position
        xField: 'name',   ◁──        Sets field for
        yField: 'data1'   ◁──     ➌ horizontal values
    }             Sets field for
]        ➍ vertical values
```

First you need to determine the type of chart ➊. The series of choice is line, and you'll bind it to the left axis ➋. Now you only need to configure the names of store fields corresponding to the X- ➌ and Y-axis ➍ progression. In most cases, the latter two will equal the X- and Y-axis settings. Figure 10.12 shows the result.

Looks nice, doesn't it? Also note the month labels rotated vertically to give more space. Your chart still needs some work, though. This way it's hard to compare May and October. It'd be easier with some grid lines, which is a feature that belongs to axes. You'll add them to the Y-axis (values). You'll also decorate the Y-axis with tick marks for minor and major steps. In total, you want 10 major tick steps, with 5 small steps between each of the major pairs.

Look at figure 10.12 more closely and notice where the Y-axis starts: number 20. This is automatic because it's the smallest value in all data records. You can also force this number, which is exactly what you're about to do.

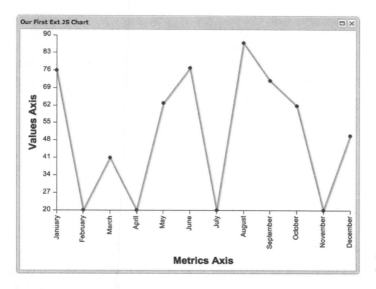

Figure 10.12 Series are drawn as configured.

10.7.3 *Improving visual aids*

And that's not all, folks. Let's say you feel especially adventurous, so you make sure that the Y-axis shows numbers rounded to the first decimal point. All right, let's see what you just cooked in the next listing.

Listing 10.9 Improved visual aids in the Y-axis

```
{
    type         : 'Numeric',
    position     : 'left',
    fields       : ['data1'],
    title        : 'Values Axis',
    grid         : true,
    minimum      : 0,
    minorTickSteps: 5,
    majorTickSteps: 10,
    label        : {
        renderer: Ext.util.Format.numberRenderer('0,0.0')
    }
}
```

This was fairly straightforward, but you're not quite done with visual aids. Let's add some interaction to the chart. As the first step, instead of the dots, you'll configure the series to display a cross for each value, as shown in the following listing.

Listing 10.10 Defining marker configuration

```
markerConfig: {
    type         : 'cross',
    size         : 4,
    radius       : 4,
```

```
'stroke-width': 0
}
```

Inside the series configuration object, in listing 10.8 after yField : 'data1', you create a new member, markerConfig. It accepts a configuration almost exactly the same way as Ext.draw.Sprite. The sole difference is the type property that is predefined in the Ext.chart.Shape singleton. The available types are

- Circle
- Line
- Square
- Triangle
- Diamond
- Cross
- Plus
- Arrow

Each cross will be somewhat larger than the dots you used previously, which makes it easier for a user to mouse over it. Let's also make it highlighted by adding the following block to the numeric line series configuration (listing 10.8):

```
highlight: {
    size: 7,
    radius: 7
}
```

You could also set the highlight object to true to show the default highlight resolution, but in the spirit of recent customization you instead specify the amount of highlight.

Mouseover highlighting will make even more sense if you add a nice tooltip to display the selected value:

```
tips: {
    trackMouse: true,
    width     : 150,
    height    : 28,
    renderer  : function(record, item) {
        this.setTitle(record.get('name') + ': '
            + record.get('data1') + ' customers');
    }
}
```

Now run the chart in a browser, and you'll get something similar to figure 10.13.

It's looking good. The tick marks and grid lines are here, and the Values axis labels start from 0 and show in the precision of the first decimal spot. Crosses have replaced circles, and in the screen shown in figure 10.13 the line is highlighted, emphasizing the selected cross, too. Finally, pointing the cursor over a cross will show its recorded value.

Let's put all the pieces together in the next listing and revise the entire code used to display the chart in the figure.

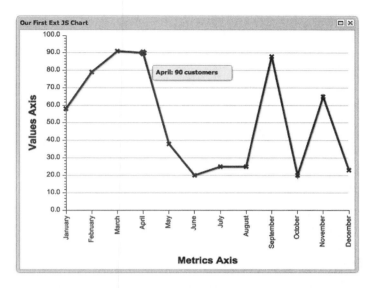

Figure 10.13 Visual improvements for the Y-axis and the series

Listing 10.11 The full line chart configuration

```
Ext.create('Ext.chart.Chart', {
    store: store,
    background: {
        fill: '#fff'
    },
    items   : [{
        type   : 'path',
        fill   : '#fff2cc',
        path   : 'M 200 100 L 258 281 105 169 295 169 141 281 Z'
    }],
    axes: [
        {
            type           : 'Numeric',
            position       : 'left',
            fields         : ['data1'],
            title          : 'Values Axis',
            grid           : true,
            minimum        : 0,
            minorTickSteps: 5,
            majorTickSteps: 10,
            label         : {
                renderer: Ext.util.Format.numberRenderer('0,0.0')
            },
        },
        {
            type: 'Category',
            position: 'bottom',
            fields: 'name',
            title: 'Metrics Axis',
            label: {
                rotate: {
```

```
                    degrees: 270
                }
            }
        }
    ],
    series: [
        {
            type: 'line',
            highlight: {
                size: 7,
                radius: 7
            },
            axis: 'left',
            xField: 'name',
            yField: 'data1',
            title: '% Returning Customers',
            markerConfig: {
                type: 'cross',
                size: 4,
                radius: 4,
                'stroke-width': 0
            },
            tips: {
                trackMouse: true,
                width    : 150,
                height   : 28,
                renderer : function(record, item) {
                    this.setTitle(record.get('name') + ': ' +
                record.get('data1') + ' customers');
                }
            }
        }
    ]
});
```

In the next section you'll enhance the chart with custom shapes derived from the lessons you've learned with Ext.draw.

10.7.4 *Adding custom shapes*

The chart you've created is a surface full of sprites. In various ways, you've accessed the sprite configuration, not through the usual `items` configuration property, but through `axis`, `series`, and even `markerConfig`. That doesn't mean that the `items` property is inaccessible; quite the opposite. In the following listing, you'll use it to add a custom shape to the chart.

Listing 10.12 Adding a custom sprite

```
items    : [{
    type    : 'path',
    fill    : '#fff2cc',
    path    : 'M 200 100 L 258 281 105 169 295 169 141 281 Z'
}]
```

The `items` property can be used in the same manner as you would've done with an `Ext.draw.Component`. After all, charts inherit from it. Here you use the same star-shaped sprite created in listing 10.6. Compare the two listings, and you'll notice different point values in the `path` properties. Why do you think that is? Pause here if you want to figure it out yourself.

When `Ext.chart.Chart` extends `Ext.draw.Component`, the default for the `viewBox` configuration option is `false`. This implies no positioning automation on the X- and Y-axis plane. Instead, every coordinate is absolute, and you have to treat your sprite accordingly. Figure 10.14 shows what the star looks like in the chart.

Let's go even further with custom shapes and replace the crosses with stars (listing 10.13). This time a simple configuration won't suffice. You'll have to register a new shape in the `Ext.chart.Shape` singleton, which will be good practice for using the new Ext JS class system.

Listing 10.13   Custom marker installation

```
Ext.chart.Shape.self.override({
    star: function (surface, opts) {
        return surface.add(Ext.applyIf({
            type             : 'path',
            path             : 'M 0 -10 L 6 8 -9 -3 10 -3 -6 8 Z',
            'stroke-width' : 0,
        }, opts));
    }
});
```

To access a singleton's `override` property—which is a goodie coming from the new Ext JS class system—you have to access its `self` property first. In listing 10.13, you're adding a new method, `star`, that will represent a new marker configuration type.

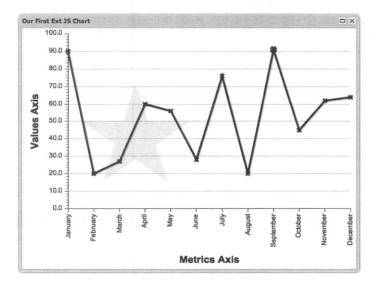

Figure 10.14   Custom shape rendered on a chart

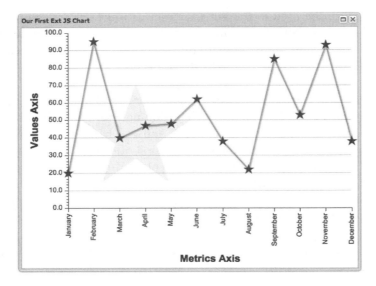

Figure 10.15   Star points

The path needs to be adjusted again. This time each star should be placed in the middle of each point, hence the pixel point adjustments. Finally, you don't stop the stroke when each star is drawn. You can access all of the sprite defaults through the `opts` argument in the `star` method. Let's plug the star into the marker configuration:

```
markerConfig: {
  type: 'star'
}
```

No further configuration is necessary. That's all there is to it. Now run the new code, and you should see something like figure 10.15.

Many times you want to compare two or more different data sets relative to a common value, such as months. Our next discussion focuses on that.

10.7.5 *Multiple series on the same chart*

The series property in an `Ext.chart.Chart` configuration is an array of `Ext.chart .series.Series` instances. In other words, a chart can take on a reasonable number of series. This makes sense particularly in Cartesian-type charts that share the same X and Y plane.

Reusing the same code you've been working on, add a new series configuration in the following listing to present the number of new customers compared to the number of returning customers.

Listing 10.14   Adding series

```
,{
    type: 'line',
    highlight: {
```

```
        size: 7,
        radius: 7
    },
    axis: 'left',
    xField: 'name',
    yField: 'data2',
      markerConfig: {
        type: 'diamond'
      }
}
```

❶ Configures different data resource

❷ Adds new marker type

As simple as that, you've added a new configuration object that accounts for a new series. You're already familiar with the configuration. The only major change is a different `yField` data resource ❶. To make points easier to track, this series will draw diamonds ❷ in place of values (see figure 10.16).

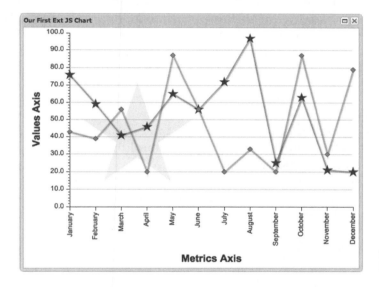

Figure 10.16   Multiple line-type series

Looks good but chaotic. In the first place, which line represents which data? Calling legends to the rescue!

```
legend: {
    position: 'top'
}
```

Turning on the legend, and placing it at the top, required allocating a bit of vertical space for a much-needed legend. The legend will display an example of a marker with its color and the title of the series. If a title isn't supplied, the corresponding field name will be shown, as specified in the `Ext.data.Model` configuration. Make both changes:

```
{
...
    title: '% Returning Customers',
...
```

```
},
{
...
    title: '% New Customers',
...
}
```

Each title goes to the respective series configuration. This change might not be satisfying in terms of graphical clarity, which is why you're about to turn the second series, the % New Customers, into an area chart:

```
type: 'area'
```

Is that all that's needed for such a conversion? You bet! See the proof in figure 10.17.

Much more readable, isn't it? The legend properly shows each series' title, and you made the difference between the two data sets clear by using a new series type. Area charts have a different kind of highlighting mechanism, displaying a thin, slightly darker column to show the position on the horizontal plane.

So right now you have two series, a blue line and a green area. We never mentioned anything about colors, though, so how can that be? You're about to discover that little secret.

10.8   *Custom themes*

Charts, as a visual representation of data, rely on graphical shapes and color. Axes and series fulfill the need for shapes, but how do you control the color? The answer lies within the `Ext.chart.theme` package.

The package has two main classes: `Ext.chart.theme.Base` and `Ext.chart.theme.Theme`. `Base` is private, and it holds the default theming configuration. The `Theme` class is used to define new themes.

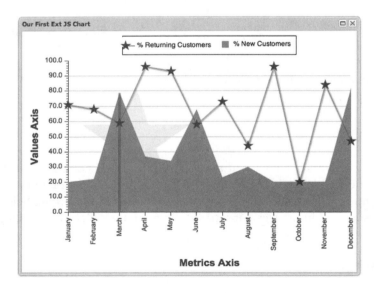

Figure 10.17   Legend in a mixed chart

To better explain the configuration, we'll go over the default settings. The following listing shows the default configuration object. This listing is really long, so please stick with us. As you've already seen, configuring charts takes quite a bit of work, and theming adds to the effort.

Listing 10.15 Theme configuration

```
{
    background: false,
    axis: {
        stroke: '#444',
        'stroke-width': 1
    },
    axisLabelTop: {
        fill: '#444',
        font: '12px Arial, Helvetica, sans-serif',
        spacing: 2,
        padding: 5,
        renderer: function(v) { return v; }
    },
    axisLabelRight: {
        fill: '#444',
        font: '12px Arial, Helvetica, sans-serif',
        spacing: 2,
        padding: 5,
        renderer: function(v) { return v; }
    },
    axisLabelBottom: {
        fill: '#444',
        font: '12px Arial, Helvetica, sans-serif',
        spacing: 2,
        padding: 5,
        renderer: function(v) { return v; }
    },
    axisLabelLeft: {
        fill: '#444',
        font: '12px Arial, Helvetica, sans-serif',
        spacing: 2,
        padding: 5,
        renderer: function(v) { return v; }
    },
    axisTitleTop: {
        font: 'bold 18px Arial',
        fill: '#444'
    },
    axisTitleRight: {
        font: 'bold 18px Arial',
        fill: '#444',
        rotate: {
            x:0, y:0,
            degrees: 270
        }
    },
    axisTitleBottom: {
```

```
        font: 'bold 18px Arial',
        fill: '#444'
    },
    axisTitleLeft: {
        font: 'bold 18px Arial',
        fill: '#444',
        rotate: {
            x:0, y:0,
            degrees: 270
        }
    },
    series: {
        'stroke-width': 0
    },
    seriesLabel: {
        font: '12px Arial',
        fill: '#333'
    },
    marker: {
        stroke: '#555',
        radius: 3,
        size: 3
    },
    colors: [ "#94ae0a", "#115fa6","#a61120", "#ff8809", "#ffd13e",
     "#a61187", "#24ad9a", "#7c7474", "#a66111"],
    seriesThemes: [{
        fill: "#115fa6"
    }, {
        fill: "#94ae0a"
    }, {
        fill: "#a61120"
    },
    ...
    ],
    markerThemes: [{
        fill: "#115fa6",
        type: 'circle'
    }, {
        fill: "#94ae0a",
        type: 'cross'
    },
    ...
    ]
}
```

You already know that charts are a bunch of sprites on a surface, so laying out a new theme will require a bit of skill with Ext.draw. Let's review the configuration properties:

- background—A fill that always stays in the back and has the lowest z-index
- axis—The line that represent an axis
- axisLabelTop, axisLabelRight, axisLabelBottom, axisLabelLeft—Labels on each axis location
- axisTitleTop, axisTitleRight, axisTitleBottom, axisTitleLeft—Axis titles

- `series`—Default series configuration
- `seriesLabel`—Label for each value in the series
- `marker`—Default marker
- `colors`—Color hex where the array index of the series equals the array index of the color
- `seriesThemes`—Draw configuration for series; same array rule as with colors
- `markerThemes`—Marker style; same array rule as with colors

Sure enough, understanding the `Ext.draw.Sprite` configuration will make your life easier when setting up a new theme. Let's implement a custom theme for your chart and show this in action in the next listing.

Listing 10.16 Configuring the Spring theme

```
Ext.define('Ext.chart.theme.Spring', {          ← Defines Spring ❶
    extend: 'Ext.chart.theme.Base',                theme class
    constructor: function(config) {             ← Extends Base ❷
        var axisColor = '#610519';                 theme class

        config = Ext.apply({
            axis: {
                fill: axisColor,
                stroke: axisColor
            },
            axisLabelLeft: {
                fill: axisColor
            },
            axisLabelBottom: {
                fill: axisColor
            },
            axisTitleLeft: {
                fill: axisColor
            },
            axisTitleBottom: {
                fill: axisColor
            },
            colors: ['#6695CC', '#65ed73'],

            seriesThemes: [{
                fill: "#CC7200",
                stroke: '#3FCC00'
            }, {
                fill: "#610519"
            }],
            markerThemes: [{
                stroke: '#f00'
            }]
        }, config);

        this.callParent([config]);
    }
});
```

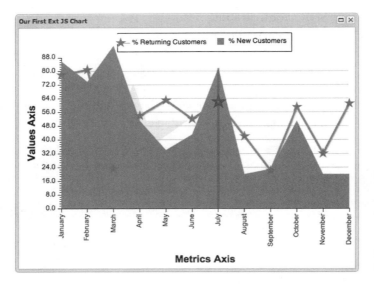

Figure 10.18   The new theme in action

Call this theme Spring ❶. It's mandatory that the new class extend `Ext.chart.theme`
`.Base` ❷. After that, things become straightforward. Most of the magic (see figure 10.18)
was accomplished using fill and stroke colors.

Ever since we began talking about charts, we've been discussing the Cartesian types.
They share a similar configuration and all have axes in common. Next you'll conduct
an experiment with charts without axes.

10.9   *Pie charts*

When a ratio between a value and a gross total is observed, we often turn to pie charts.
They don't benefit from axes, but they interact with other values in the data set. In this
example, you'll reuse the same data store but limit the amount of data. Too many data
values in the same series will give you an untidy chart.

Your pie chart will have a legend and labels written inside of each slice. Slices will
react on mouseover to move the selected slice outside the perimeter, as shown in the
following listing.

Listing 10.17   Setting up the data store and rendering the chart

```
var store = Ext.create('Ext.data.JsonStore', {
    fields: ['name', 'data1'],
    data: generateData(4,30)
});

Ext.create('Ext.chart.Chart', {
    animate      : true,
    store        : store,
    shadow       : true,
    insetPadding : 10,
```

❶ Generates small dataset

❷ Sets chart padding

```
    legend      : {
        position : 'bottom'
    },
    background   : {
        fill : '#fff'
    },
    series       : [
        {
            type          : 'pie',
            field         : 'data1',
            donut         : 40,
            showInLegend  : true,
            tips          : {
                trackMouse : true,
                width      : 150,
                height     : 28,
                renderer   : function (record, item) {
                    this.setTitle(record.get('name')
                            + ': ' + record.get('data1'));
                }
            },
            highlight     : {
                segment : {
                    margin : 20
                }
            },
            label         : {
                field    : 'name',
                display  : 'rotate',
                contrast : true,
                font     : '18px Arial'
            }
        }
    ]
});
```

3 Configures pie chart type

4 Connects with model

5 Adds "hole" inside pie

6 Shows categories in legend

Using the data generator you created earlier in the chapter, you create a smaller random set of data **1**. Then you create a chart and make sure the pie leaves enough room **2** for mouseover effects. You didn't set up any axes, which is okay, given the series type is pie **3**. X- and Y-axes don't exist, so there's no xField or yField, just field to assign the model field name to it **4**. The "hole" is referred to as donut, assigning a value for the radius in pixels **5**. Finally, you instruct this series to show in the legend **6**.

It looks like a lot of effort, but once you've learned to create a basic chart, you can use that knowledge as a basis to create any other type. Pie charts differ from the Cartesian types mostly in the relationship with axes. Configuration-wise, that makes them simpler. Let's see what you just made (figure 10.19).

There, it wasn't that hard, and it looks beautiful. You can clearly see that January yielded little value in the first trimester, and if you work a bit more with the labels, you can even see how much. We'll leave that to you as homework.

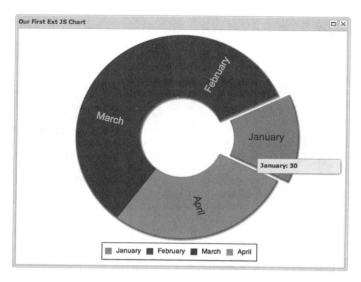

Figure 10.19   Pie chart

10.10 Summary

In this chapter we covered the basics of drawing. Drawing is a new concept introduced in Ext JS 4, a feature often used with Flash to ensure consistency in browsers. Ext.draw proves that cross-browser-friendly drawings can be created easily, following a simple API.

Drawing is a good foundation for learning to create stunning charts. Not only do charts depend on the Ext.draw package, but advanced chart creation heavily depends on familiarity with drawing concepts. You saw that quite clearly when you created your first theme.

Building a chart slowly and progressively throughout most of the chapter demonstrated the main concepts behind configuring an Ext.chart chart. You started from a small and simple example and built up to a custom-themed, animated, and interactive chart. These principles can be shared with any series type.

Furthermore, you learned about a number of tricks hidden in the Ext.draw and Ext.chart source code. If you get stuck with something, don't be afraid to jump into the source code. This is something that holds true for all issues you might encounter in Ext JS.

The next chapter addresses one of our favorite topics, Ext Direct. You'll dive into a technique called *direct remoting* with Ext JS.

Remote method invocation with Ext Direct

11

This chapter covers

- Setting up Ext Direct servers and clients
- Invoking methods directly
- Using Ext Direct with `Ext.data.Store`

In previous chapters, you exchanged data from servers with widgets like grids, trees, forms, and even XTemplates. You used `Ext.data.Stores` and `Ext.Ajax.requests` for communicating with a server. If you've spent some time working with Ext JS 4, you know that setting up Ajax requests for creating, reading, updating, and destroying data allows for great precision in configuring processes, but it can also be cumbersome. Writing blocks for each operation with separate success and failure callbacks will take up quite a few lines of code on both server and client sides, not to mention the amount of code required to dedicate URL paths or variables to distinguish between operations.

A common way to reduce the amount of code on the server side is to employ a RESTful interface. On the client side, stores and `Ext.data` packages are there to automate most of the CRUD process and make your life much simpler. But the clever developers from Redwood City have gone a step further.

251

Remote procedure call (RPC), also known as remote method invocation, is a well-known technique of sharing program code among platforms. Ext Direct is a platform that brings remote server-side methods to the client side. This flexible and highly extensible technology is compatible with virtually any server-side platform that powers your web application.

As a layer that exists on its own, Ext Direct is beautifully integrated into the rest of the framework. Although its service is frequently provided for data stores (`Ext.data.proxy.Direct`), remotely invocable methods are also accessible for direct execution.

In this chapter, you'll see how to set up the server-side environment and make use of the platform's benefits within your Ext JS web applications. You'll also explore Ext Direct, which will allow you to reduce coding efforts for the data-management portion of your applications.

11.1 *Making the two ends meet*

The Ext Direct package in Ext JS 4 exists on the client side, but it's dependent on server-side support. The client end is mainly responsible for constructing requests and processing responses. It does so through various interfaces, such as `Ext.data.Store` or direct method invocation. The part that makes Ext Direct special over more traditional communication mechanisms sits on the server end. Let's see a broader view of how the communication flow works (see figure 11.1).

It all starts from a method call on the client side of your web application ❶. Ext Direct wraps it into a JSON object ❷ and sends it to the router ❸. The router is a special mechanism in the workflow. It knows how to talk to Ext Direct, and it also knows where the exposed methods are on the server side and how to communicate with them. It listens for requests coming from the client side, finds the needed method, and forwards the arguments to it ❹. The method ❺ will do its work and return ❻ values back to the router ❼. The router constructs another JSON object ❽, which is similar to the one previously received. The new object contains data returned by the remote method ❺. Finally, Ext Direct receives the response ❾ asynchronously and returns the values to the original caller through a callback system. Remember, the whole process is asynchronous.

This is a simplified explanation of how the process works. There's much more to each of the nine steps, and we'll discuss each one in this chapter. These principles show how RPC in Ext Direct is special, stressing the router's role. Ext JS 4 is well equipped with support for other communication types, one of them being the famous RESTful interface. Let's see how developers weigh the two and choose which to use for their projects.

11.2 *Ext Direct vs. REST*

Before you go deeper into Ext Direct, let's take a step back and observe RPC from the REST point of view. Many developers have used a form of RESTful interface before. If you have, you may notice both similarities and differences.

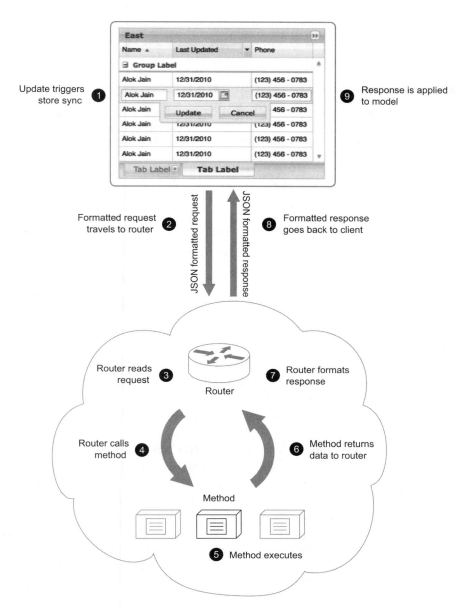

Figure 11.1   Communication flow in Ext Direct

In Ext JS 4, support for both REST and Ext Direct has been taken to the next level. If your project operates with data stores for all data-management purposes, then you won't see a significant difference between using REST and Ext Direct. That's because the framework has made them equal, or almost equal.

Differences exist mostly due to the architectural design of each concept. Table 11.1 compares Ext Direct and REST, emphasizing key features you should consider before choosing the technology for your new project.

Table 11.1   Differences between Ext Direct and REST in Ext JS 4

Feature	Ext Direct	REST
Server-side configuration	Router setup and configuration	Router-like behavior, various implementations
Client-side configuration	Needs separate configuration for RPC provider instantiation	No configuration needed
Cross-domain support	Not supported (Ajax-based)	Supported
File uploads	Supported through iFrame	Per application design
Batching requests (server side)	Managed by the router	Needs to be implemented
Writer API	CRUD methods	CRUD paths
Direct method invocation (client side)	Fully automatized	Not by default; methods need to be created manually

The most significant difference between Ext Direct and REST lies in their definitions. REST exists as an interface or, in other words, as URLs you can use to commit CRUD operations. Ext Direct is a two-way platform that needs to exist on both the server and client side for communication to take place successfully. They're both able to expose methods, but Ext Direct makes the server-side methods visible on the client side. More important, it makes them executable.

Ext Direct calls remote methods through Ajax calls. The only exception is for file uploads, which are sent through an iFrame using regular form posting. A limitation of such an approach is that it's not cross-domain capable. Because REST is an interface that belongs to the server side, it can be used with any method of communication available in the framework and browsers.

Batching requests is an interesting feature. Although it needs to be supported in the router, its implementation is centralized, so server-side developers don't need to worry about it. REST developers, though, may need to work this out on their own, and it depends on their application layout. In some scenarios, every URL path has its own batching support. In such a case, Ext Direct is a huge win.

In an Ext.data package using proxies and writers, your setup won't differ significantly. You can even benefit from batching requests in REST. But you'll need to implement them with your server-side code. Ext Direct wins there, because batching support is implemented for any call, whereas RESTful interfaces will either need to implement batching support for every call or create a router-like before/after behavior.

Another important difference between Ext Direct and REST is ease of use in other scenarios. With Ext Direct, it's easy to call a remote method by calling it in JavaScript, whereas working with REST will require custom-created, Ajax-enabled wrappers to perform a similar task. Having too many of those in application code can become a developer's nightmare, complicating both the development and maintenance of an app.

So far you've explored the theory behind Ext Direct and how it compares to the popular RESTful interface. Their differences are also their strengths. Let's discuss each one in more detail, starting with the server-side setup.

11.3 Server-side setup

Exposing server-side methods is fairly simple and isn't typically complicated to set up. If you're comfortable developing in your server platform, it's a great idea to go ahead and try to develop your own support for Ext Direct. Not only will you be able to tailor it for the needs of your app, but you'll also understand the core principles much better. In addition, you'll get a chance to enjoy all the benefits of extending Ext Direct and expanding its power.

Otherwise, feel free to explore and choose from more than 30 available server-side stacks for nine languages at http://mng.bz/8WkO. It's worth noting that each one of the stacks is different. Trying a few will help you choose the best fit for the existing application and will also help you understand certain concepts. It might even spur you to create your own stack.

11.3.1 How it works

The server-side stack is responsible for three roles. It needs to

- Understand which methods should be exposed
- Use that information to generate the API descriptor to be given to Ext Direct
- Listen for requests, route them, and return them to the client side

In order for the web application to invoke remote methods, a server will need a router script that understands both sides. A router will know how to reach the methods you've decided to expose and will also manage the translation between the two sides.

11.3.2 Remote method configuration

The first step in RPC-enabling your web applications is to let your router know which methods are available and how to execute them. Router developers have been creative in choosing their preferred methodology. These are a few methods:

- Using configuration file(s) (no automation; least creative)
- Expecting entire classes to be exposed, using class statics to define how to communicate with the class
- Parsing comments placed straight above methods and looking for API-style keywords
- Using fully automatic introspection in available methods

Depending on the language, some features may not be available. Specific languages dictate ways of associating the methods to configuration and thus dictate the router itself. The minimum information a router needs is the method's name and the number of arguments accepted. Any additional information could include security measures, before/after execution actions, type conversion, and filter-based triggers.

11.3.3 Routing

The router accepts requests from the client, to be forwarded to the appropriate method along with the supplied arguments. The client can send a request either via JSON-formatted raw HTTP post payload or as a form post. The latter is required when uploading files and also needs to dispatch multiple requests.

Each transaction coming from the client side can be bundled with a mixture of properties:

- `action`—The class where the requested method resides
- `method`—The name of the method to execute
- `data`—The arguments to be passed on to the method
- `type`—Currently set to `'rpc'`
- `tid`—The transaction ID with which to associate the request; essential in batched requests

Form posts reuse the field names but prepend the `ext` keyword to them:

- `extAction`
- `extMethod`
- `extTID`
- `extUpload` (optional field; used for file uploads)

Any further fields are considered to be arguments for `extMethod`.

In most cases, a function that's being executed remotely by the router will return data. Depending on the language used and how the router is designed, it'll either capture the output of the method called or receive data returned from it. The data is processed to JSON format if necessary, and the router appends additional metadata:

- `type`—Set to `'rpc'`
- `tid`—The transaction ID, used to identify the data returned
- `action`—The class in which the method resides
- `method`—The name of the method executed
- `result`—The root for the result data object

If the request was initially batched, it'll combine results and return an array of responses. If the request was a form post and uploaded a file, the response would be a properly formatted HTML file with only a text area in the document body, containing the same formatted JSON object. Because form posts don't support batching, only a single response is returned.

Exceptions should be caught by the router and forwarded as a properly structured response. It's often a good idea to additionally enable the router with a configurable debugging mode that would decide whether to transmit the exceptions. Sending server-side exceptions to the client side in a production environment is considered a security issue.

In most cases, you'll likely use one of the available server-side stacks and not worry too much about how they work internally with data. But some languages (like Node.js) don't have stacks that are as advanced as those existing in other languages. In such cases, you may end up developing your own or extending similar packages (like socket.io or dnode).

> **NOTE** Calling remote methods in Node.js feels natural due to the same language being in use and the architecture of Node itself. But the lack of a good server stack shouldn't discourage you. We're sure you could create your own basic router in a matter of hours. *Node.js in Action* (Manning, 2013) is a wonderful resource for such an endeavor. We highly recommend reading it because Node.js also provides a valuable method for reusing your JavaScript code.

In other cases, you may need to override or extend existing stacks to play nicely with your MVC or session management. What you just learned would be essential for the task.

You now have a working stack ready. Think of it as a football coach. You can't do without one, but you also need players to play the game, or methods to perform your business logic. In the next section, you'll add the players (or rather, methods) to the system.

11.4 Working with remote methods

Now that you know how to make the server-side code available, it's time to make use of it. You'll create a sample application that'll do two things:

- Retrieve a server-side timestamp through a direct method call
- Enable complete CRUD through an `Ext.grid.Panel` with the help of `Ext.data.writer.Writer`

Later in the examples, you'll make use of one of the server-side stacks available at the Sencha forums. Our flavor of choice is the excellent J. Bruni's (a Sencha community member) Extremely Easy Ext Direct Integration with PHP.

11.4.1 Setting up the router

Even before setting up the router, make sure that your server-side methods are available. For the sake of simplicity, in this example you'll create two PHP classes. You'll save both classes in a single file, rpc.php, as shown in the next listing.

> **Listing 11.1 A simple remote method**

```php
<?php
class Util {
```

```
    public function date( $format ) {
        return date( $format );
    }
}
```

In listing 11.1 you create a new PHP class called Util. Only one method belongs to it: date. This method is public, meaning that it's accessible to the outside, and it expects a single argument, $format. The only purpose of this method is to return a string representing the current date and time, according to the pattern specified in the only argument.

This method will justify the need for your server-side timestamp generation through a direct method call. In the following listing, you'll create another class that supports CRUD methods for the grid.

Listing 11.2   A remote CRUD class

```
class Actors {
    public function create($config) {
        return Array(
            "success"=> true,
            "data"=>Array("name"=>"New Actor", "id" => rand(1,22000))
        );
    }

    public function read( $config ) {
        return Array("success"=> true, "data"=>Array(
            Array(
                "id"     => rand(1,22000),
                "name"   => "John Travolta"
            ),
            Array(
                "id"     => rand(1,22000),
                "name"   => "Benny Hill"
            ),
            Array(
                "id"     => rand(1,22000),
                "name"   => "Bruce Willis"
            ),
            Array(
                "id"     => rand(1,22000),
                "name"   => "Rowan Atkinson"
            )
        ));
    }

    public function update( $config ) {
        return Array("success"=>true, "data"=>$config);
    }

    public function destroy( $config ) {
        return Array("success"=>true);
    }
}
```

In listing 11.2, you create a new class with four public methods inside it: create, read, update, destroy. None of the methods will do any real work, other than to return a minimum of required information to your client side. In reality, these four methods perform validation where needed, talk to a database, and then return the database's response on completion of the transaction.

If you've downloaded the PHP router, it's time to plug it in. You'll include the server-side stack API in your newly created router and configure it, as shown in the next listing.

> **Listing 11.3   Router configuration**

```
<?
require 'ExtDirect.php';

ExtDirect::$namespace = 'RPC';
ExtDirect::$descriptor = 'RPC.REMOTING_API';
ExtDirect::$enableBuffer = 200;
```

This router's configuration is extremely straightforward. You're moving back to the beginning of your rpc.php file and appending the reference to the ExtDirect.php file. You're right; ExtDirect.php is this stack's router file. By including the router in rpc.php, you're making sure that the router's API is available for use.

The router has quite a few configuration options. But at this point you only need to set up the namespace to be used on the client side and the Ext Direct descriptor. The latter will be used to inform Ext Direct of the methods you've made available.

Because you'll want to make your application a bit smarter and reuse resources by batching requests, you'll also enable a buffer and set it to 200ms.

You've now successfully set up your RPC server-side router. This particular installation will understand that all public methods are made available, gather the number of arguments required, and reconfigure the API description every time the web application requests it.

The journey continues on the client side. Ext Direct needs to know how to behave, where the router is, and which methods it can call remotely. It'll make use of the configuration you just explored, and you're about to see how.

11.4.2 *Enabling Ext Direct*

Ext.direct.Manager is in charge of Ext Direct on the client side. Its job is to create, cache, and manage the instances for each provider you want to use. Two different providers exist: PollingProvider and RemotingProvider.

Ext.direct.PollingProvider has one responsibility: to execute a single remote method in configurable intervals. It'll also process the information according to predefined rules, specified in a callback function. An example scenario would be checking in with the server to let it know that a user is still online, while also refreshing the availability of messages that need to be delivered for the user.

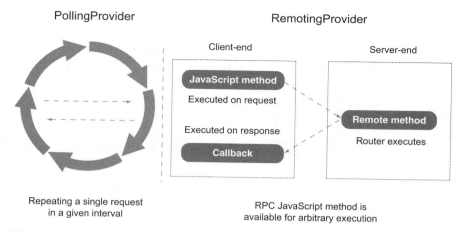

Figure 11.2   `PollingProvider` vs. `RemotingProvider`

`Ext.direct.RemotingProvider`, on the other hand, invokes remote methods as needed. It's particularly useful for connecting with `Ext.data.Store`, including both the reader and writer. Its usage pattern is similar to that of the `PollingProvider`, which is what we'll concentrate on in further examples.

Let's examine the core differences between the two providers in figure 11.2. Most notably, the `PollingProvider` repeats a request in given intervals. It'll repeat this way until forcibly stopped. `RemotingProvider` creates a remote method's synonym on the client side. Only when the client-side method is executed will Ext Direct send a request to a server and process the response through a callback. The same client-side method can be executed manually (programmatically), or by an `Ext.data.Store` `load()` or `sync()` call.

Now that you've specified the remoting provider, you'll retrieve your API description and process it through `Ext.direct.Manager`. To do so you'll add an extra `<script>` tag, right after the one that references the framework:

```
<script type="text/javascript" src="rpc.php?javascript"></script>
```

Now would be a good time to look at the example code in rpc.php found in examples/ch11/direct_app/rpc.php.

The router will automatically return a configuration and create an instance of `Pro-vider` by appending a special line to the end of the received JavaScript file:

```
Ext.Direct.addProvider(RPC.REMOTING_API);
```

In this step, Ext Direct will automatically initialize the `namespace` and `create` methods. Then all remotely available methods will be accessed through a previously configured namespace. `Util.date` becomes `RPC.Util.date`, and `Actors.read` becomes `RPC.Actors.read`.

Take a look at listing 11.4, which shows a sample API description.

Additional JavaScript calls before instantiating a provider

If your project makes use of `Ext.Loader`, you'll need to require `Ext.direct.Manager` before `Ext.Direct.addProvider` is called by adding `Ext.syncRequire( 'Ext .direct.Manager' )`. Additionally, if your application hasn't previously been defined, you'll need to do that as well by issuing `Ext.ns( 'RPC' );`, where `RPC` is your namespace as defined in the API description.

Listing 11.4 Sample API description

```
RPC.REMOTING_API = {                                              ❶ Adds path to
    "url"            :"\/extdirect\/rpc.php",                          router URL
    "type"           :"remoting",
    "namespace"      :"RPC",                                       ❷ Sets type
    "descriptor"     :"RPC.REMOTING_API",                             of service
    "enableBuffer"   :1000,
    "actions":{                                                    ❹ Configures
        "Actors":[                                                    batching buffer
            {"name":"create",    "len":1},
            {"name":"read",      "len":1},                         ❺ Adds classes
            {"name":"update",    "len":1},                            and methods
            {"name":"destroy",   "len":1}
        ],
          "Util":[
            {"name":"date",      "len":1}
        ]
    }
};
```

Sets namespace root for API ❸

The server end responds with a variable that's going to be known to Ext Direct later in execution. The variable will reference an object consisting of a minimum of three parameters:

- The URL to the router ❶
- The type of service (remoting/polling) ❷
- Actions, representing classes, methods, and the number of arguments accepted for each method ❺

Anything more accounts for special configuration options. Because you shouldn't pollute a global namespace, you're configuring it to RPC ❸. You can choose your application namespace or something particular for Ext Direct—that's based on the developer's preference. You've also chosen to enable the batching buffer and set it to 1000ms (1s) ❹. That means Ext Direct will delay the first request by one second and wait for any consecutive calls in order to batch them together as a single request. Such a feature needs to be supported by the router because requests will be sent combined in an array of uniquely identified calls.

The next listing contains a sample API description configuration object for Sencha Architect users.

Listing 11.5   Sample API description for Sencha Architect

```
{
    "url"            :"\/extdirect\/rpc.php",
    "type"           :"remoting",
    "namespace"      :"RPC",
    "descriptor"     :"RPC.REMOTING_API",          Specifies API
    "enableBuffer"   :1000,                      ① descriptor name
    "actions":{
        "Actors":[
            {"name":"create",   "len":1},
            {"name":"read",     "len":1},
            {"name":"update",   "len":1},
            {"name":"destroy",  "len":1}
        ],
        "Util":[
            {"name":"date",     "len":1}
        ]
    }
}
```

If you're a Sencha Architect user, you'll appreciate Architect's ability to import API descriptions for further use with stores and widgets. The major difference is that the description needs to be in JSON format and contain the API descriptor name ①. Other than the format change, the information is exactly the same as in the previous listing.

You've reached a major milestone—all the prep work is now completed. You've created a router, described the API, and included it in the web application. Ext Direct has created a provider instance, and you're ready to start using remote methods. Later in this chapter, you'll see two main RPC uses in an Ext JS application: direct method invocation through JavaScript and CRUD operations through Ext.data.Store.

11.5   *Directly invoking remote methods*

As mentioned earlier in this chapter, Ext Direct will process calls by issuing Ext.Ajax requests. This means that the process is asynchronous; callbacks are needed in order to do anything with response data. Every client-side remote method will have the same number of arguments as its remote counterpart, plus callback and scope. You'll try RPC.Util.date in the next listing.

Listing 11.6   Directly invoking a remote method

```
var callbackFn = function(res) {
    this.log(res);
    this.timeEnd('DirectTiming');
}

console.time('DirectTiming');
RPC.Util.date('d/m/Y', callbackFn, console);
```

In your callbackFn, you're outputting the end result only to the console. To demonstrate round-trip speed, you'll define a new console timer, only to be terminated when callback is called. Now that the callback is prepared and the console is ready to benchmark, it's time to execute `RPC.Util.date`. Date pattern `'d/m/Y'` is sent to the router and forwarded to the target method, which returns the formatted date back to the router. Data is encapsulated in a JSON object and sent back to the browser. Ext Direct receives the data, identifies it against the `tid` property, and then calls the callback function, passing returned data as the first argument:

```
25/01/2013
DirectTiming: 151ms
```

`RPC.Util.date` nicely output two lines in the browser's console: the date, exactly in the form you wanted, and the time needed for the entire operation to complete. The test was executed from a remote location, using a mobile network.

So far, so good. Now let's spice it up with consecutive requests in the following listing. You'll call the same method three times but with different arguments. It'll be particularly interesting to observe the Web Inspector's Network tab.

Listing 11.7   Batching requests

```
RPC.Util.date('d/m/Y', console.log, console);
RPC.Util.date('H:i', console.log, console);
RPC.Util.date('U', console.log, console);
```

All the requests are sent at about the same time. You'll notice that the callback is a simple console.log, meaning it'll output the returned result in the console. As intended, all results returned at the same time, after 1000ms along with the remote processing time and the round-trip time.

But how does Ext Direct differentiate requests on client and server sides? Let's look at the next listing.

Listing 11.8   Batched request payload

```
[
    {
        "action":"Util",
        "method":"date",
        "data":["d/m/Y"],
        "type":"rpc",
        "tid":2
    },
    {
        "action":"Util",
        "method":"date",
        "data":["H:i"],
        "type":"rpc",
        "tid":3
    },
    {
        "action":"Util",
        "method":"date",
        "data":["U"],
```

```
            "type":"rpc",
            "tid":4
        }
]
```

The only major difference between a single request and a batched one is that the latter is sent in the form of an array of request objects. Each request object is identified with a `tid` that's used to differentiate calls on the server end. The router will also need to return the same ID for an array of responses, but we'll get back to that in a minute.

Arguments to be used with remote methods are sent as an array. In the future, Sencha may allow key/value pairs, but right now make sure that arguments are called in the right order.

Every request should be politely returned with a response. Let's see what that looks like in the next listing.

Listing 11.9 Batched response

```
[
    {
        "type":"rpc",
        "tid":2,
        "action":"Util",
        "method":"date",
        "result":"27\/01\/2013"
    },
    {
        "type":"rpc",
        "tid":3,
        "action":"Util",
        "method":"date",
        "result":"03:08"
    },
    {
        "type":"rpc",
        "tid":4,
        "action":"Util",
        "method":"date",
        "result":"1327633709"
    }
]
```

The request and response may look like twins, but there's a single key difference between them. Although arguments belonged to `data` key in the request, the returned value now matches the `result` key. Note that the response is also an array of objects, all containing the `tid` property to match the appropriate request.

You've learned how to execute RPC methods directly and how to debug and even benchmark them. You'll often use Ext Direct through `Ext.data.Store` and use the data in a widget. Let's see how Ext Direct makes it easier and faster to write such code. You'll also use Ext Direct to perform the full CRUD process in an `Ext.grid.Panel`. Fire away!

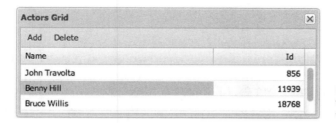

Figure 11.3 An editable grid that automatically syncs data with the remote end

11.6 CRUD-enabled Ext.data.DirectStore

Next you'll create an instance of `Ext.grid.Panel` (figure 11.3) that's editable and uses the writer configuration in `Ext.data.Store` to take advantage of automatic data syncing on the remote end. It looks like a lot to do, but jobs like this are a piece of cake for Ext JS 4 and Ext Direct.

This example can share the same index.html file and the same API descriptor that you used in the first example. This means you already know how to initialize Ext Direct and let it know which remote methods are available. Also, take another look at listing 11.2, where you created the methods for the second example in PHP.

You'll get the hardest part done first: your `Ext.data.Model` workhorse, as shown in the following listing. `Ext.data.Model` is in charge of virtually everything data-wise: pulling records from the server, creating new records, updating and deleting, calling Ext Direct methods, and handling callbacks.

Listing 11.10 Setting up `Ext.data.Model`

```
Ext.define('Actor', {
    extend  : 'Ext.data.Model',

    fields  : [
        'name',
        'data'
    ],
    proxy: {
        type : 'direct',                              ❶ Adds Direct proxy
            api  : {
                create  : RPC.Actors.create,          ❷ Sets CRUD API methods
                read    : RPC.Actors.read,
                update  : RPC.Actors.update,
                destroy : RPC.Actors.destroy
            },
            writer  : {
                type: 'json',
                writeAllFields: true
            },
            reader  : {
                root            : 'data',
                idProperty      : 'id',
                type            : 'json',
                successProperty : 'success'
```

```
        }
      }
});
```

You've already dealt with stores, proxies, readers, and writers, so you should be comfortable with most parts of this example. The two distinct configuration options are the proxy type ❶ and the CRUD API ❷. In the API configuration property, you've told the proxy which methods to use for each CRUD action. That's all the Ext Direct you'll need to set up. Now you must create some handlers for adding and deleting data, as shown in the next listing.

Listing 11.11   Supporting handlers and instances

```
var editing = Ext.create('Ext.grid.plugin.CellEditing'),        ◁──┐  Instantiates
    grid,                                                        ❶  CellEditing plug-in
    onAdd,
    onDelete;

    onAdd = function() {                                         ◁──┐  Adds new
        var record = Ext.create('Actor');                       ❷  records
        editing.cancelEdit();
        grid.getStore().insert(0, record);
        editing.startEditByPosition({
            row: 0,
            column: 0
        });
}
onDelete = function(){                                           ❸  Deletes
    var view       = grid.getView(),              ◁──┐            records
        selection = view.getSelectionModel().getSelection()[0];
    if (selection) {
        grid.getStore().remove(selection);
    }
}
```

The first step is instantiating the CellEditing plug-in ❶, which you chose to be your editing option for the grid. You'll use this reference with the grid shortly. Next, you set up the onAdd ❷ and onDelete ❸ handlers for toolbar buttons. Each one will work with the store directly; they won't be working with Ext Direct in any way. Ext.data.Store will do the job for you.

> **NOTE** You aren't polluting the global namespace because you've included the whole code in Ext.onReady.

Finally, you'll create the grid in the next listing. This will be fun!

Listing 11.12   Grid setup

```
grid = Ext.create('Ext.grid.Panel', {
        height      : 350,
        width       : 600,
        title       : 'Actors Grid',
```

```
renderTo    : Ext.getBody(),
selType     : 'cellmodel',
store       : {
    model   : 'Actor',
    autoLoad: true,
  autoSync: true                     ❶ Syncs data
},                                       with server
columns     : [{
    dataIndex   : 'name',
    flex        : 1,
    text        : 'Name',
      field         : {
          type    : 'textfield'
      }
}, {
    dataIndex   : 'id',
    align       : 'right',
    width       : 120,
    text        : 'Id'
}],
  plugins     : [
      editing
  ],
  dockedItems : [
      {
          xtype   : 'toolbar',
          dock    : 'top',
          items: [
              {
                  text    : 'Add',          ❷ Assigns onAdd
                  handler : onAdd              handler
              },
              {
                  text    : 'Delete',
                  handler : onDelete   ←      Assigns onDelete
              }                          ❸  handler
          ]
      }
  ]
});
```

The key configuration option goes into store setup ❶. You set autoSync to true, which means that Ext.data.Store will monitor for data changes and push them to the server. With that set, your grid is finished and renders as shown in figure 11.4.

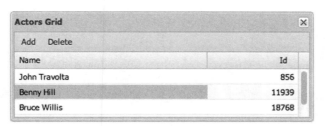

Figure 11.4 Your data grid with Ext Direct in action

With every response, you should return an object with the success: true property to let the store know that everything is okay. Otherwise, you'll describe a failure. This is true for reads, updates, and destroys, whereas adding data will have an additional bit of information returned: the ID of the new record. Once the user clicks the Add button ❷, the store will create a new record and confirm it with the server. The user will continue editing the new record, and Ext.data.Store will update the record's ID as soon as it's received. Should changes happen in the meantime, the store will mark the unsaved fields with a red triangle and wait for the next sync to send changes.

In fewer than 100 lines of codes, you've created a grid that reads data from a server, yet allows creating, editing, and deleting of records ❸. It'll also buffer requests for those who type quickly and are able to modify several columns in short periods of time. That's a great bandwidth saver and, in some cases, a performance booster.

11.7 *Summary*

Ext Direct is a powerful mechanism for invoking remote methods. Its main purpose is to streamline the communication between a server and a client while reducing the amount of code needed for the job. True, there are a few APIs, like dnode, that do something similar, but none is so nicely integrated with Ext JS's data stores, providing complete CRUD workflow to new and existing applications. The easy scoping control is another ingenious advantage of the package.

Now that you've seen how data can be transferred between the server and the client end, let's continue transferring data interactively between user interface elements. In the next chapter, you'll drag-and-drop empower your applications.

Drag-and-drop

This chapter covers

- Understanding the drag-and-drop workflow
- Dissecting the Ext JS drag-and-drop classes
- Implementing drag-and-drop override methods
- Understanding the drag-and-drop life cycle
- Using the drag-and-drop plug-ins

One of the greatest advantages of using a graphical user interface is the ability to easily move items around the screen with simple mouse gestures. This interaction is known as *drag-and-drop*. You use drag-and-drop without giving it a second thought just about every time you use a modern computer. If you step back and think about it, you'll realize how this feature makes your life a lot easier.

Want to delete a file? Click and drag the file icon and drop it on the trash or Recycle Bin icon. Easy, right? What if you didn't have drag-and-drop? How would you move a file from its location to the Recycle Bin? Let's ponder the possibilities. You'd first click the file to provide it focus. You could then use a keyboard key combination to "cut" the file. You'd then have to find and focus the Recycle Bin window and use the keyboard key combination to "paste" it in. Another option would be to click to select the file to focus it and press Delete on your keyboard, but if you're right-handed, doing so would require you to take your hand off your mouse. In contrast, drag-and-drop is much simpler, isn't it? Now put yourself in the world of RIA users. What if you could use drag-and-drop to simplify their experiences?

Fortunately, Ext JS provides a means for you to do that. In this chapter, you'll see that with a bit of elbow grease and determination you can achieve the goal of adding drag-and-drop to your applications. You'll start off by learning to apply drag-and-drop to basic DOM elements, which will give you the foundation for applying these behaviors to widgets such as the grid and tree panels.

12.1   The drag-and-drop workflow

Before drag-and-drop can take place, the computer must decide what can and can't be dragged, and what can or can't be dropped on. For instance, icons on your desktop can generally be dragged around, but other items, such as the clock on your taskbar (Windows) or menu bar (Mac OS X) can't. This level of control is necessary to allow the enforcement of certain workflows, as we'll discuss in a bit.

To use drag-and-drop effectively, you need to understand the entire workflow. This section divides the workflow into the *drag-and-drop life cycle*, which can be broken up into three major categories: start of drag, the drag operation, and drop.

12.1.1   The drag-and-drop life cycle

Using the desktop paradigm, any icon on the desktop can be dragged around, but only a select few can be dropped on (generally disk or folder icons, the trash or Recycle Bin, or icons for executables [applications]). In Ext JS, the same registrations must occur for drag-and-drop to be possible. Any element that can participate in drag-and-drop must be initialized as such. For elements in the DOM to participate in drag-and-drop, they must, at the least, be registered as drag items and as drop targets. Once the items are registered, drag-and-drop can take place.

Drag operations are initiated by clicking and holding a mouse button over a UI element, followed by mouse movement while the mouse button is being held. The computer decides, based on the registration described previously, whether the item that's being clicked is draggable. If it isn't, then nothing happens. The user can click and attempt a drag operation, but with no results. But if an element is allowed to be dragged, the UI generally creates a lightweight duplicate of that object, known as a *drag proxy*, that's anchored to the movements of the mouse cursor. This gives the user the feeling that they're physically moving or dragging that item onscreen.

During each tick (or X-Y coordinate change) of the mouse cursor during the drag operation, the computer determines whether you can drop the item at that given position. If a drop is possible, then some sort of visual invitation for a drop operation is displayed. In figure 12.1, you see a form of drop invitation where a file icon proxy is dragged over a folder icon on the desktop.

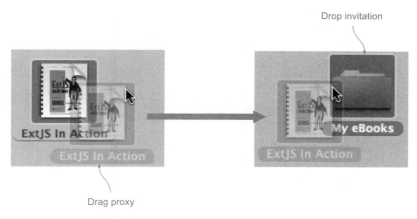

Figure 12.1   Desktop drag-and-drop interaction as seen in Mac OS X, where a drag proxy (left) is created upon an item drag event and a drop invitation is being displayed (right)

The drag-and-drop life cycle ends when a drop operation occurs, which happens when the mouse button is released after a drag operation has occurred. At this time, the computer must decide what to do with the drop operation. Did the drop event occur on a valid drop target? If so, is the drop target part of the same drag-and-drop group as the drag element? Does it copy or move the item that was dragged? This decision is generally left to the application logic to decide, and it's where you'll do most of your coding.

Although it's relatively easy to describe how drag-and-drop should behave, it's infinitely more difficult to implement, although not impossible. One of the keys to being able to effectively implement drag-and-drop is a basic understanding of the class hierarchy and the jobs that each class performs. This holds true from implementing drag-and-drop at the basic DOM level, as you'll see in a bit, all the way to implementing it on Ext JS UI widgets.

Throttle up. We're going to climb up to 30,000 feet and take a bird's-eye view of the drag-and-drop class hierarchy.

12.1.2 *A top-down view of the drag-and-drop classes*

At first glance, the list of drag-and-drop classes can be a bit overwhelming. When I (Jay) first glanced at the list of classes in the API, I was taken aback by the options. With 11 classes, it can be considered a framework within a framework that provides functionality from the basic, such as the ability to make any DOM element draggable, to more complex features, such as the ability to drag and drop multiple nodes using what is called a *proxy*. The cool thing is that once you take a high-level look at the classes it isn't that difficult to organize the supporting classes and understand their roles.

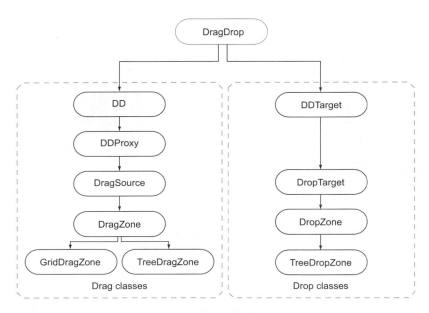

Figure 12.2   The drag-and-drop class hierarchy can be broken up into two major sections: drag (left), and drop (right).

This is where we'll start our exploration. Figure 12.2 shows what the class hierarchy looks like. In this figure, you see the 11 drag-and-drop classes. All of the drag-and-drop functionality for the entire framework starts with the DragDrop class, which provides the base methods for everything drag-and-drop and is *meant* to be overridden. It provides only the basic tools for you to implement this behavior. It's up to you to write the code for the entire spectrum of the implementation.

This is the fundamental key to understanding how drag-and-drop works, because this design pattern is repeated throughout the drag-and-drop class hierarchy. This concept is extremely powerful, because by having the basic tools to add this behavior to your application you can easily ensure that drag-and-drop works for your application's needs.

As you look down the chain of inheritance you can see a split, which starts with DD (left) and DDTarget (right). DD is the base class for all drag operations, and DDTarget is the base class for all drop operations. Both provide the base functionality for their respective behaviors. This split in functionality allows you to focus on specific behaviors. You'll see this in action when we look at implementing drag-and-drop with DOM nodes a little later on.

As you move down the chain, you can see that Ext JS adds features progressively for the intended behavior. Table 12.1 enumerates the classes and provides a brief description of their designated tasks.

Table 12.1 Drag-and-drop classes

Drag classes		Drop classes	
Name	Purpose	Name	Purpose
DD	A basic drag implementation where an element can be dragged around and dropped anywhere. This is where most DOM-level drag implementations take place.	DDTarget	The basic class to allow any element to participate in a drag-and-drop group, but it can't be dragged around, meaning it can only have items dropped on it.
DDProxy	A basic drag implementation where a lightweight copy of the drag element, known as a *drag proxy*, is dragged around instead of the source element. It's common practice to use this class for drag operations where a drag proxy is desired.	DropTarget	A base class that provides the empty plumbing for an element to take action when a draggable element is dropped onto this one. It's left up to the developer to finish the implementation by overriding the notify methods.
DragSource	Provides a base implementation for drag-and-drop using status proxies, and is the base class for DragZone. This can be used directly, but it's more common to use the DragZone class (see the next item).	DropZone	A class that provides the means for multiple nodes to be dropped onto this element; it works best with the DragZone class. There's a grid panel–specific implementation in Ext.grid .header.DropZone. A tree panel–specific implementation is known as the Ext.tree .ViewDropZone.
DragZone	This class allows for the drag of multiple DOM elements at a time and is commonly used with the view widgets. To provide drag-and-drop with the grid and tree panels, each has its own implementation of this class, known as Ext.grid .header.DragZone and Ext.tree.ViewDragZone, respectively.		

There you have it: each of the drag-and-drop classes and what they're designed to do. A drag item (DD class or subclass) can be a drop target, but a drop target (DDTarget or subclass) can't be a drag item. It's important to know this, because if you ever decide to have an element be a drag item *and* a drop target, you must use one of the drag classes.

If you're implementing drag-and-drop with generic DOM nodes and you need to allow for one drag node at a time, use DD or DDProxy. If you need to drag more than one element, you'll want to use either the `DragSource` or `DragZone` class. This is why the tree panel and grid panel have their own respective extensions or implementations of the `DragZone` class.

Likewise, if you're going to drop a single node, `DDTarget` will be your drop class of choice. For multiple-node drops, `DropTarget` or `DropZone` is required because those classes have the necessary plumbing to interact with `DragSource` and `DragZone` and their descendant classes.

Knowing what the classes are is one piece of the puzzle. The next piece that you need to know is what methods should be overridden. This is the biggest key to successful deployment.

12.1.3 *It's all in the overrides!*

As we discussed earlier, the various drag-and-drop classes were designed to provide a base framework for drag or drop behaviors and are only part of what's needed to make drag-and-drop useful. Each of the drag-and-drop classes contains a set of abstract methods that are meant to be overridden by you, the end developer (see table 12.2).

Table 12.2   Commonly used abstract methods for drag-and-drop

Method	Description
onDrag	Called for each onMouseMove event while the element is being dragged. If you plan to do something before an item is dragged, you may elect to override the b4Drag or startDrag method.
onDragEnter	Called when a drag element first intersects another drag/drop element within the same drag/drop group. This is where you can code for drop invitation.
onDragOver	Called while a drag element is being dragged over.
onDragOut	Called when a drag element leaves the physical space of an associated drag or drop element.
onInvalidDrop	Called when a drag element is dropped on anything other than an associated drag or drop element. It's a great place to inject notification to users that they dropped a drag element in the wrong place.
onDragDrop	Called when a drag element is dropped on another drag/drop element within the same drag/drop group.

Although all of these methods are listed in the framework API for each drag/drop class, it's a good idea to briefly discuss a few of the more commonly used abstract methods that are to be overridden for the `Ext.dd.DD` class. This way, you get a sense of what to look for in the API.

Remember that `Ext.dd.DD` is the base class for all drag-specific elements, and as you move down the hierarchy more features get added. The features added by the subclasses progressively override these methods for you.

For instance, there are a few b4 (before) methods that Ext.dd.DD provides that allow you to code a behavior to occur before something happens, such as before the mousedown event fires (b4MouseDown) and before the drag of an element occurs (b4StartDrag). Ext.dd.DDProxy, the first subclass of Ext.dd.DD, overrides these methods to create a draggable proxy just before the drag code begins to execute.

To figure out which methods you need to override to achieve a specific implementation, you'll need to consult the API for that specific drag or drop class. Because Ext JS has a more aggressive release cycle, some methods may be added, renamed, or removed, so looking at the API regularly will help you stay fresh with the current changes.

The last bit of drag-and-drop theory we need to discuss is the use of drag-and-drop groups and what they mean for implementing this behavior in your application.

12.1.4 Drag-and-drop always works in groups

Drag-and-drop elements are associated with groups, which is the basic constraint that governs whether a drag element can be dropped on another element. A group is a label that helps the drag-and-drop framework decide whether a registered drag element should interact with another registered drag or drop element.

Drag or drop elements must be associated with at least one group but can be associated with more than one. They're generally associated with a group upon instantiation and can be associated with more via the addToGroup method. Likewise, they can be unassociated via the removeFromGroup method.

This is the last piece of the puzzle needed to understand the basics of drag-and-drop with Ext JS. It's time to start using and reinforcing what you've learned. You'll start out by implementing drag-and-drop with DOM elements.

12.2 Drag-and-drop: a basic example

You'll begin your exploration with a setup that mimics a swimming pool setting, complete with locker rooms, a swimming pool, and a hot tub. There are constraints that you must follow. For instance, men and women nodes can only be in their respective locker rooms. All can go in the swimming pool, but only a few like to go into the hot tub. Now that you understand what you must create, you can begin coding.

As you'll see, it's extremely simple to configure an element to be dragged around the screen. But before you can do that, you must create a workspace to manipulate. You'll do this by creating some CSS styles that govern how a specific set of DOM elements look, and then you'll apply drag logic to them. We'll keep things as simple as possible to focus on the subject matter.

12.2.1 Creating a small workspace

First you create the markup to represent the locker rooms and people inside them, as shown in the next listing. This listing is rather lengthy because of the HTML required to achieve the desired style and layout.

Listing 12.1   Creating your drag-and-drop workspace

```
<style type="text/css">
    body  {
        padding: 10px;
    }
    .lockerRoom {
        width:              150px;
        border:             1px solid;
        padding:            10px;
        background-color:   #ECECEC;
    }
    .lockerRoom div {
        border:             1px solid #FF0000;
        background-color:   #FFFFFF;
        padding:            2px;
        margin:             5px;
        cursor:             move;
    }
</style>
<table>
    <tr>
        <td align='center'>
            Male Locker Room
        </td>
        <td align='center'>
            Female Locker Room
        </td>
    </tr>
    <tr>
        <td>
            <div id="maleLockerRoom" class="lockerRoom">
                <div>Jack</div>
                <div>Aaron</div>
                <div>Abe</div>
            </div>

        </td>
        <td>
            <div id="femaleLockerRoom" class="lockerRoom">
                <div>Sara</div>
                <div>Jill</div>
                <div>Betsy</div>
            </div>
        </td>
    </tr>
</table>
```

① Configures drag element container styles

② Makes child nodes look different

③ Sets HTML for our drag items

In listing 12.1, you create the CSS styles and markup to set the stage for your exploration of basic DOM drag-and-drop. You begin by defining the CSS that'll control the styles for the lockerRoom ① element containers and their child (people) nodes ②. Then you set up the markup ③ to use the CSS.

Figure 12.3 shows what your locker HTML looks like when rendered onscreen. Notice that when you hover the mouse cursor over a child node of a locker room element, the arrow will change into a cross. This is due to the CSS styling that you configured earlier, and it provides a nice means of inviting a drag operation.

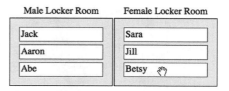

Figure 12.3   The locker room HTML rendered onscreen

Next you'll configure the JavaScript to allow these elements to be dragged around.

12.2.2   Configuring items to be draggable

In listing 12.2, you configure the locker room child items to be dragged around the screen. To accomplish this you gather a list of child elements in the `maleLockerRoom` element by chaining a `select` call (DOM query) to the results of the `Ext.get` call. You then utilize `Ext.each` to loop through the list of child nodes and create a new instance of `Ext.dd.DD`, passing the `element` reference, which enables that element to be dragged around the screen. You do the same thing for the elements in the `femaleLockerRoom`.

Listing 12.2   Enabling drag for your elements

```
var maleElements = Ext.get('maleLockerRoom').select('div');
Ext.each(maleElements.elements, function(el) {
    new Ext.dd.DD(el);
});
var femaleElements = Ext.get('femaleLockerRoom').select('div');
Ext.each(femaleElements.elements, function(el) {
    new Ext.dd.DD(el);
});
```

After refreshing the page, you can easily drag-and-drop the elements around the screen. As you can see in figure 12.4, you can drag any of the child `div`s around the screen without constraints.

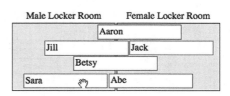

Figure 12.4   Drag is now enabled on the locker room elements without constraints.

Let's examine how `Ext.dd.DD` works and what it does to your DOM elements. To do this, you'll need to refresh the page again and open Firebug's live HTML inspection tool. We'll focus on `Jack`.

12.2.3   Analyzing the Ext.dd.DD DOM changes

Figure 12.5 shows the HTML of the drag elements immediately after a page refresh, along with the DOM inspection view in Firebug.

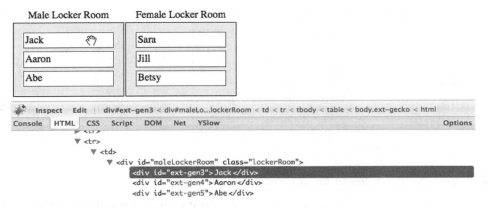

Figure 12.5   Inspecting the DOM for the `Jack` element (highlighted) before a drag operation takes place

When looking at the `Jack` element (highlighted in figure 12.5), the first thing you might notice is that it's assigned a unique ID of `"ext-gen3"`. Recall that in your markup you didn't assign an ID to this element. If the element already had its own unique ID, `Ext.dd.DD` would use it. But instead, in order to track this element by ID, it's assigned one by `Ext.dd.DD`'s superclass, `Ext.dd.DragDrop`.

> **WARNING**   If the `id` of the element is changed after it has been registered for drag, the drag configuration for that element will cease to function. If you plan to change the `id` for a particular element, it's best to call the `destroy` method on the instance of `Ext.dd.DD` for that element and create a new instance of `Ext.dd.DD`, passing the new element `id` as the first parameter.

Another thing that you'll notice in the HTML inspection is that no other attributes are assigned to that element. Now you'll drag the element a little and observe the changes, as shown in figure 12.6.

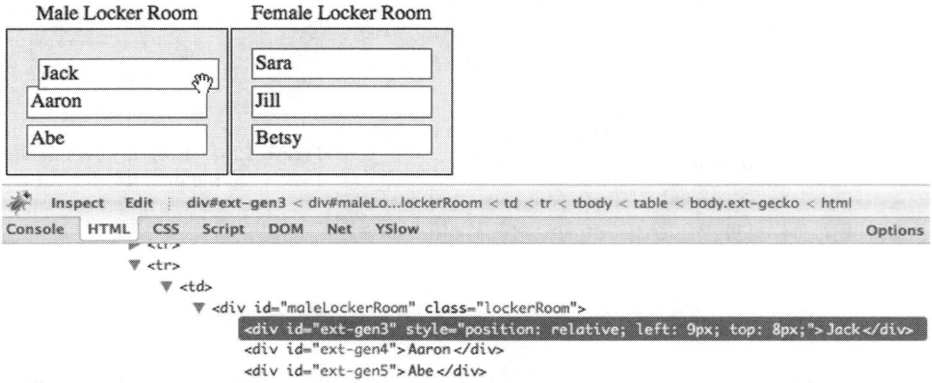

Figure 12.6   Observing the changes that the drag operation makes on the `Jack` element

You can see that you dragged the `Jack` element a little. `Ext.dd.DD`, in turn, added a `style` attribute to the element, which changes the `position`, `top`, and `left` CSS properties. This is important to know because using `Ext.dd.DD` will result in a change of positioning for the element onscreen, and this is one of the key differences between using `Ext.dd.DD` and `Ext.dd.DDProxy`, which we'll explore later.

The last observation that we'll discuss is the ability for the dragged elements to be seemingly dropped anywhere. At first, this may seem cool, and it is! But it's hardly useful. To make this useful, you'll have to apply constraints.

To do this, you'll need to create some containers to drop them onto. This is where you'll generate the pool and hot tub for these people to enjoy.

12.2.4 *Adding the pool and hot tub drop targets*

As before, you'll add some CSS to stylize the HTML. Insert the following CSS inside the `style` tags of your document. They'll set the background color of the pool and hot tub to blue and red, respectively:

```
.pool {
    background-color: #CCCCFF;
}
.hotTub {
    background-color: #FFCCCC;
}
```

Now you'll need to add the HTML to the document body. Append the following HTML markup below the locker room HTML table:

```
<table>
    <tr>
        <td align='center'>
            Pool
        </td>
        <td align='center'>
            Hot Tub
        </td>
    </tr>
     <tr>
        <td>
            <div id="pool" class="lockerRoom pool"/>
        </td>
        <td>
            <div id="hotTub" class="lockerRoom hotTub"/>
        </td>
    </tr>
</table>
```

This code will give you the elements you'll need to set up drop targets. Figure 12.7 shows how the HTML now renders.

You've added all the HTML that you need for now. Next you must set up the `'pool'` and `'hotTub'` elements as `DropTargets`, which will enable them to participate in the

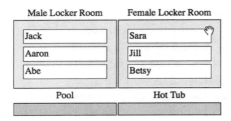

Figure 12.7   **The pool and hot tub HTML rendered onscreen**

drop portion of the drag-and-drop. You'll add this code just after the JavaScript in listing 12.2:

```
var poolDDTarget    = new Ext.dd.DDTarget('pool', 'males');
var hotTubDDTarget  = new Ext.dd.DDTarget('hotTub', 'females');
```

Here you set up one instance of `Ext.dd.DDTarget` each for the `'pool'` and `'hotTub'` elements. The first parameter for the `DDTarget` constructor is the ID of the element (or DOM reference). The second parameter is the group the `DDTarget` is to participate in.

Now refresh your page and drag-and-drop a male node onto the pool node or a female node onto the hot tub node. What happens when you drop the item onto the target? That's right: nothing happens. Why is that? Well, you set up drag items and the drop targets, which set the stage for complete drag-and-drop, but remember that it's up to you to follow through with the rest of the implementation. You must develop the code for the drop invitation and for valid and invalid drops. As you'll see, this is precisely where most of the drag-and-drop implementation code will take place, and it's what you'll do next.

12.3   *Finishing your drag-and-drop implementation*

As you just saw, setting up an element to be dragged around is simple, as is setting up a drop target. But unless you connect the dots, you're left with a source and destination but no way to get there.

To add the drop invitation and valid and invalid behaviors, you need to refactor how you configure the elements to be dragged around. You'll begin by adding one last CSS class, which you'll use to turn the drop target green for the drop invitation:

```
.dropZoneOver {
    background-color: #99FF99;
}
```

As you can see, this CSS is simple. Whatever element has this class will have a green background. Next you'll work on refactoring the way you set up the male and female elements to be dragged around by setting up an `overrides` object that gets applied to each instance of `Ext.dd.DD`.

12.3.1 Adding the drop invitation

To add the drop invitation, you'll have to completely replace how you initialized the drop targets. The following listing shows what you'll use, and it'll set the stage for the valid and invalid drop behaviors.

Listing 12.3   Refactoring your implementation of `Ext.dd.DD`

```
var overrides = {                                             Creates
    onDragEnter : function(evtObj, targetElId) {     Adds drop   overrides
        var targetEl =  Ext.get(targetElId);       2 invitation 1 object
        targetEl.addCls('dropZoneOver');
    },
    onDragOut : function(evtObj, targetElId) {       Removes drop
        var targetEl =  Ext.get(targetElId);       3 invitation
        targetEl.toggleCls('dropZoneOver');
    },
    b4StartDrag    : Ext.emptyFn,
    onInvalidDrop  : Ext.emptyFn,
    onDragDrop     : Ext.emptyFn,
    endDrag        : Ext.emptyFn
};
var maleElements = Ext.get('maleLockerRoom').select('div');  4 Sets male
Ext.each(maleElements.elements, function(el) {                  elements to
    var dd = new Ext.dd.DD(el, 'males', {                       be drag items
        isTarget  : false
    });                                              Overrides methods
    Ext.apply(dd, overrides);                      6 to DD instance
});
var femaleElements = Ext.get('femaleLockerRoom').select('div');
Ext.each(femaleElements.elements, function(el) {
    var dd = new Ext.dd.DD(el, 'females', {
        isTarget  : false
    });
    Ext.apply(dd, overrides);
});
```

Adds
drop
logic 5

In listing 12.3, you create an object, `overrides`, which will be applied to the instances of `Ext.DD` that'll be created. You'll override a total of five methods to achieve the desired results, but for now you'll override only `onDragEnter` **1** and `onDragOut` **2**.

Remember that `onDragEnter` will be called only when a drag element first intersects a drag or drop element with the same associated group. Your implementation of this method will add the `'dropZoneOver'` CSS class, which changes the background color of the drop element to green and provides the drop invitation that you want.

Likewise, the `onDragOut` method gets called when the drag element first leaves a drag-and-drop object with the same associated group. You use this method to remove the invitation from the background of the drop element **3**.

You then stub four methods, `b4StartDrag`, `onInvalidDrop`, `onDragDrop`, and `endDrag`, which you'll fill in later on. We won't cover these right now because we want you to be able to focus on the behaviors and constraints that you add in layers. But in case you're curious, you'll use `b4StartDrag` to get the original X and Y coordinates of the drag element. These coordinates will be used in the `onInvalidDrop` method, which will set a local property to indicate that this method was fired. The `onDragDrop` method will be used to move the drag node from its original container to the dropped container. Finally, the `endDrag` method will reset the position of the drag element if the `invalidDrop` property is set to `true`.

To use this `overrides` object, you have to refactor how you're initializing the drag objects ❹ for both male and female elements. You do this because you need to prevent the drag element from being a drop target: this is why you add a third argument to the `DD` constructor, which is meant to be a somewhat limited configuration object. You'll see what we mean by *limited* in a bit. In that configuration parameter you set `isTarget` ❺ to `false`, which sets the controlling behavior for this drag item to not be a drop target.

Finally, you apply the `overrides` object to the newly created instance of `Ext.DD` ❻. Earlier we said that the configuration object is used only to set a limited number of properties. We said this because the drag-and-drop code that exists in Ext JS today was written back in the early Ext JS 1.0 days, before most constructors applied configuration properties to themselves. This is why you have to use `Ext.apply` to inject the override methods, instead of setting them on the configuration object as you would for most constructors in the framework.

You've added the code for the invitation. Let's see what happens when you try to drag a male node over the pool or hot tub (figure 12.8).

As your knowledge of drag-and-drop and code dictates, dragging a male node over a drop target (think `onDragEnter`) with the same associated group will result in a drop invitation, which is the background of the drop target turning green, as shown in the figure. When you drag the element out of the same drop target (think `onDragOut`), the background will return to its original state, removing the drop invitation.

Conversely, dragging a male element over any other drop target, such as the hot tub, will result in no invitation. Why does this happen? There's no drop invitation on the `'hotTub'` element because the hot tub isn't associated with the `males` drop group.

Another thing you'll notice is that dragging a female element over the hot tub results in a drop invitation on the `'hotTub'` element but not the pool, as shown in figure 12.9. That's because the hot tub is associated only with `females`.

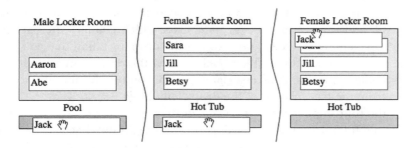

Figure 12.8   Conditional drop invitation for the male nodes

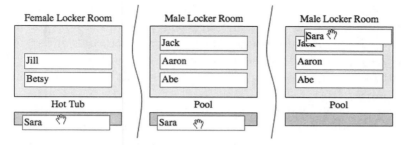

Figure 12.9   Conditional drop invitation for the female nodes

Although this demonstrates the drop invitation well, you still have the issue of the pool and the hot tub needing to be able to receive both male and female nodes. To do this you must register them with an additional group. You need to call the `addToGroup` method, passing in an alternate group. Here's what the `'pool'` and `'hotTub'` element `DDTarget` registration looks like with the addition of `addToGroup` calls:

```
var poolDDTarget = new Ext.dd.DDTarget('pool', 'males');
poolDDTarget.addToGroup('females');
var hotTubDDTarget = new Ext.dd.DDTarget('hotTub', 'females');
hotTubDDTarget.addToGroup('males');
```

After injecting this into your example, refresh the page. You can see that the `'pool'` and `'hotTub'` drop elements now invite the drop, but what happens when you drop a drag element onto a valid drop target? Absolutely nothing. That's because you didn't code for the valid drop operation.

You'll do this next.

12.3.2 Adding a valid drop

To add the valid drop behavior to your drag-and-drop implementation, you must replace the `onDragDrop` method in your `overrides` object, as shown in the following listing.

Listing 12.4   Adding a valid drop to your `overrides`

```
onDragDrop : function(evtObj, targetElId) {
    var dragEl = Ext.get(this.getEl());
    var dropEl = Ext.get(targetElId);
    if (dragEl.dom.parentNode.id != targetElId) {
        dropEl.appendChild(dragEl);
        this.onDragOut(evtObj, targetElId);
        dragEl.dom.style.position ='';
    }
    else {
        this.onInvalidDrop();
    }
}
```

In your `onDragDrop` method, you set up the code for a successful or valid drop operation. To do this, you first need to create local references for the drag and the drop elements.

Next, you hit a conditional `if` statement, where you test to see if the `id` of the drag element's parent node is the same as the drop target `id`. This ensures you don't perform a drop operation on a drop target where the drag element is already a child. If the drop target element isn't the same as the drag element's parent, you allow the drop operation to occur; otherwise, you call the `onInvalidDrop` method, which you'll code shortly.

The code to physically move the drag element from one parent container to another is simple. Call the drop element's `appendChild` method, passing in the drop element. Remember that even though `Ext.dd.DD` allows you to move the drag element onscreen, it only changes the X and Y coordinates. If you don't move the drag element to another parent node, it will still be a child of its original container element.

Next you call the `onDragOut` override, which will clear the drop invitation. Notice that you're passing the `eventObj` and `targetElId` arguments to the `onDragOut` method. This is so the `onDragOut` method can do its job as designed.

Finally, you clear the element's `style.position` attribute. Recall that `DD` sets the position to `relative`, which isn't needed after the node has been moved from one parent container to another.

This ends the override of the `onDragDrop` method. Figure 12.10 shows what this does to your page. As illustrated in this figure, you can successfully drop male and female elements onto both the `'pool'` and `'hotTub'` drop elements, which successfully demonstrates your `OnDragDrop` method in action.

Although it's nice that males and females can now be dropped into the pool or hot tub, you can't let them stay in there forever or they'll prune. You need to be able to pull them out and put them back in the locker room. What happens if you try to drag them over

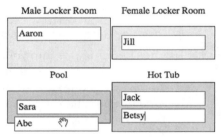

Figure 12.10   Male and female nodes can now be dropped onto the pool and hot tub drop targets.

their respective locker room? No invitation. Why? Correct: it's because you haven't registered the locker room elements as `DDTargets`. Do that now:

```
var mlrDDTarget = new Ext.dd.DDTarget('maleLockerRoom', 'males');
var flrDDTarget = new Ext.dd.DDTarget('femaleLockerRoom', 'females');
```

Adding this code to the bottom of your drag/drop implementation allows the male drag elements to be invited and dropped on every drop target except for the female locker room. Likewise, female drag elements can be dropped on any drop target except the male locker room. This follows the paradigm where most public places don't have coed locker rooms.

You now have the drop operations completely developed. The last piece to this implementation is the invalid drop behavior set, which is what you'll work on next.

12.3.3 Implementing an invalid drop

You've probably noticed that when you drop a node anywhere onscreen other than a valid drop point, the element stays stuck where it was dropped. This is because you need to set up the invalid drop behavior that'll place the element back in its original position. You'll do this with style using the Ext.fx class. The following listing replaces the b4StartDrag and onInvalidDrop methods in the overrides object.

Listing 12.5 Cleaning up after an invalid drop

```
b4StartDrag : function() {
    var dragEl = Ext.get(this.getEl());          ◁──┐  Overrides
    this.originalXY = dragEl.getXY();                ❶ b4StartDrag method
},
onInvalidDrop : function() {                       ◁──┐  Sets this.invalidDrop
    this.invalidDrop = true;                          ❷ to true
},
endDrag : function() {                             ◁──┐  Animates drag
    if (this.invalidDrop === true) {                  ❸ element return
        var dragEl = Ext.get(this.getEl());
        var animCfgObj = {
            easing   : 'elasticOut',
            duration : 1,
            callback : function() {                    ❹ Resets drag
                dragEl.dom.style.position = '';   ◁──┘  element's position
            }
        };
        dragEl.moveTo(this.originalXY[0], this.originalXY[1], animCfgObj)  ◁──┐
        delete this.invalidDrop;
    }                                                      Animates reset
}                                                          of drag element ❺
```

In listing 12.5, you first override the b4StartDrag ❶ method, which is called the moment a drag element is dragged. At this point you can store the drag element's original X and Y coordinates, which will be used for the repair operation. To *repair* an invalid drop means to reset the position of the drag element or proxy (as you'll see in a bit) to its position before the drag operation took place.

Next you override onInvalidDrop ❷, which is called when the drag item is dropped on anything other than a valid drop point that's associated with the same group. In that method, all you do is set the local invalidDrop property to true, which will be used in the next method, endDrag.

Last, you override the endDrag ❸ method, which will perform the repair operation if the local invalidDrop property is set to true. It also uses the local originalXY property set by the b4StartDrag method. This method creates a configuration object for the animation.

In the configuration object you set easing to 'elasticOut', which will give the element a nice springy or elastic end to the animation, and set duration to one second. This ensures that the animation is smooth and not jerky. You also create a callback method to reset the drag element's `style.position` attribute ❹, which ensures that the drag element fits exactly where it needs to go.

> **NOTE** If you want to forgo the animation and just reset the position of the drag element, all `onInvalidDrop` has to do is set the `style.position` to an empty string, like so: `dragEl.dom.style.position = '';`.

Next you call the drag element's `moveTo` method, passing in the X and Y coordinates as the first and second parameters and the animation configuration object as the third. This invokes the animation on your drag element.

Last, you delete the local `invalidDrop` reference, because it's no longer needed. You'll need to refresh the page to see these three override methods at work.

When you drag an element and drop it anywhere other than an associated drop element, you see that it slides back to its original position and has a springy effect when it gets to its target X and Y coordinates ❺.

You've now seen what it takes to implement drag-and-drop with the `Ext.dd.DD` and `Ext.DD.DDTarget` classes. Next you'll see how to implement the similar `DDProxy` class.

12.4 Using DDProxy

The use of drag proxies in a drag-and-drop implementation is common and is worth going over, because the implementation is similar to `DD` but not quite the same. This is because the `DDProxy` class allows you to drag around a lightweight version of the drag element, which is known as the *drag proxy*. Using `DDProxy` can result in huge performance savings if the drag element is complex. Part of the performance savings comes from the fact that every instance of `DDProxy` uses the same proxy `div` element in the DOM. Remembering that the drag proxy is the element being moved around onscreen will help you understand your implementation code.

In this example, you'll use the same HTML and CSS that you used before, and we'll provide the pattern that you'll need to use if you plan on using drag proxies in your drag-and-drop implementations.

The first thing you'll do is add one more CSS rule to your page, which will style the drag proxy with a yellow background:

```
.ddProxy {
    background-color: #FFFF00;
}
```

You'll follow the same flow as you did when implementing the `DD` class. In doing so, you'll see that implementing the `DDProxy` class takes a bit more code than the `DD` class.

12.4.1 Implementing DDProxy and the drop invitation

The `DDProxy` class is responsible for creating and managing the X and Y coordinates of the reusable proxy element, but it's up to you to style it and fill it with content. You'll do so by means of overriding the `startDrag` method, instead of the `b4Drag` method as you did with the `DD` implementation.

In the next listing, you'll create the `overrides` object along with the instance of `DDProxy`. The following CSS is required to get this listing to work properly:

```css
.lockerRoom div, .lockerRoomChildren {
    border            : 1px solid #FF0000;
    background-color  : #FFFFFF;
    padding           : 2px;
    margin            : 5px;
    cursor            : move;
}
```

This listing is rather long, but you're accomplishing quite a bit.

Listing 12.6   Implementing the drop invitation

```javascript
var overrides = {
    startDrag : function() {
        var dragProxy = Ext.get(this.getDragEl());
        var dragEl = Ext.get(this.getEl());
        dragProxy.addClass('lockerRoomChildren');
        dragProxy.addClass('ddProxy');
        dragProxy.setOpacity(.70);
        dragProxy.update(dragEl.dom.innerHTML);
        dragProxy.setSize(dragEl.getSize())
        this.originalXY = dragEl.getXY();
    },
    onDragEnter : function(evtObj, targetElId) {
        var targetEl = Ext.get(targetElId);
        targetEl.addClass('dropzoneOver');
    },
    onDragOut : function(evtObj, targetElId) {
        var targetEl = Ext.get(targetElId);
        targetEl.removeClass('dropzoneOver');
    },
    onInvalidDrop : function() {
        this.invalidDrop = true;
    },
    onDragDrop : Ext.emptyFn
};
var maleElements = Ext.get('maleLockerRoom').select('div');
Ext.each(maleElements.elements, function(el) {
    var dd = new Ext.dd.DDProxy(el, 'males', {
        isTarget  : false
    });
    Ext.apply(dd, overrides);
});
var femaleElements = Ext.get('femaleLockerRoom').select('div');
Ext.each(femaleElements.elements, function(el) {
    var dd = new Ext.dd.DDProxy(el, 'females', {
        isTarget  : false
    });
    Ext.apply(dd, overrides);
});
```

① Overrides **startDrag** method

② Stylizes **DragProxy**

③ Adds drop invitation

④ Adds **onDragDrop** stub

In listing 12.6, you accomplish the tasks of stylizing the proxy, adding the drop invitation, and instantiating the instances of `Ext.dd.DDProxy` for each of the elements. Here's how this works.

The `startDrag` method ❶ takes care of stylizing the drag element by first adding the `lockerRoomChildren` and `ddProxy` CSS classes ❷ to the `DragProxy` element. Next, it sets the proxy's opacity to 70% and duplicates the HTML contents of the drag element. It then sets the size of `DragProxy` to the size of the drag element. Then the `originalXY` property is set, which will be used for an invalid drop repair operation down the road.

Next, you add the drop invitation by means of overriding the `onDragEnter` and `onDragOut` methods ❸. This is exactly the same as the prior implementation. The `onInvalidDrop` override is also the same as before. The last override is a stub for the `onDragDrop` method ❹, which you'll fill out in just a bit.

Before you can use the drop invitation, you have to set up the drop targets for the pool, hot tub, and locker room elements:

```
var poolDDTarget = new Ext.dd.DDTarget('pool', 'males');
poolDDTarget.addToGroup('females');
var hotTubDDTarget = new Ext.dd.DDTarget('hotTub', 'females');
hotTubDDTarget.addToGroup('males');
var mlrDDTarget = new Ext.dd.DDTarget('maleLockerRoom', 'males');
var flrDDTarget = new Ext.dd.DDTarget('femaleLockerRoom', 'females');
```

Now that you have those set up, try out the `DDProxy` implementation you've cooked up so far. Refresh your page, and drag around a drag element. Figure 12.11 illustrates what the drag proxy looks like in action.

As you can see, performing a drag gesture on a draggable element produces `DragProxy`, which is dragged around while the drag element itself remains stationary. You can also see that the drop invitation works. What happens when you drop the drag element on a valid or invalid drop target?

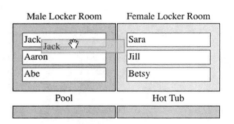

Figure 12.11   `DDProxy` in action with one of your male drag elements

In both cases, the drag element is moved to `DragProxy`'s last known coordinates, which mimics the behavior of the `DD` class without the valid and invalid drop behavior constraints.

You'll add those next. The following listing wraps up the `DDProxy` implementation.

Listing 12.7   Adding the valid and invalid drop behaviors

```
onDragDrop : function(evtObj, targetElId) {
    var dragEl = Ext.get(this.getEl());
    var dropEl = Ext.get(targetElId);
    if (dragEl.dom.parentNode.id != targetElId) {
```

❶ Overrides `onDragDrop` method

```
        dropEl.appendChild(dragEl);
        this.onDragOut(evtObj, targetElId);
        dragEl.dom.style.position ='';
    }
    else {
        this.onInvalidDrop();
    }
},
b4EndDrag : Ext.emptyFn,
endDrag : function() {
    var dragProxy = Ext.get(this.getDragEl());
    if (this.invalidDrop === true) {
        var dragEl = Ext.get(this.getEl());
        var animCfgObj = {
            easing   : 'easeOut',
            duration : .25,
            callback : function() {
                dragProxy.hide();
                dragEl.highlight();
            }
        };
        dragProxy.moveTo(this.originalXY[0],
                this.originalXY[1], animCfgObj);
    }
    else {
        dragProxy.hide();
    }
    delete this.invalidDrop;
}
```

② Prevents proxy from hiding before drag ends

③ Overrides endDrag method

④ Executes repair animation

⑤ Hides drag proxy if valid drop

In listing 12.7, you finish up the rest of the DDProxy implementation by adding the onDragDrop, b4EndDrag, and endDrag overrides.

The onDragDrop **①** method is exactly the same as the DD implementation, where if the drop element isn't the same as the drag element's parent, you allow the drop to occur, moving the node to the drop element. Otherwise you call the onInvalidDrop method, which sets the invalidDrop property to true.

The b4EndDrag method **②** is an intentional override using the Ext.emptyFn (empty function) reference. You do this because the DDProxy's b4EndDrag method will hide DragProxy before the endDrag method is called, which conflicts with the animation that you want to perform. And because it'd be wasteful to allow DragProxy to be hidden and then show it, you prevent it from hiding by overriding b4EndDrag with a function that does nothing.

As in the DD implementation earlier, the endDrag method **③** is tasked with doing the repair if the invalidDrop property is set to true **④**. But instead of animating the drag element itself, it animates DragProxy. The animation uses easeOut easing to allow for a smoother finish animation. The callback will hide DragProxy and then call the highlight effect method of the drag element, animating the background from yellow to white.

Finally, if endDrag was called with the invalidDrop property not set, it hides **⑤** the proxy element from view, completing your DDProxy implementation.

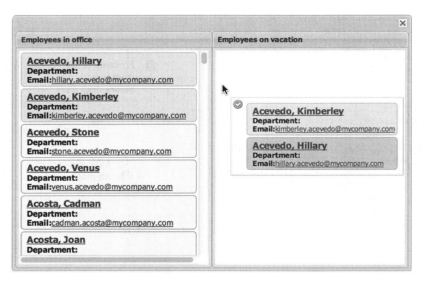

Figure 12.12   The two views

As you've seen, implementing the full gamut of drag-and-drop with generic DOM elements requires some work and an understanding of the basics of the drag-and-drop class hierarchy. The reward is a cool way to drag and drop elements across the screen, adding that extra bit of functionality for your users.

Let's continue to explore drag-and-drop functionality in the Ext JS components. You can build on the basic ideas we've covered so far. You'll start with drag-and-drop with views.

12.5   *Drag-and-drop with views*

Say you've been tasked to develop something that'll allow managers to track employees who are in the office or on vacation using simple drag-and-drop gestures. For this you'll construct two views, both of which are similar to the ones you constructed earlier. To use them you'll make some slight modifications, which will include enabling multiple-node selection. This should be an excellent first example of how to use drag-and-drop inside components. Figure 12.12 shows the two views encapsulated in an instance of `Ext.Window`.

Now that you know what you going to build, let's begin.

12.5.1   *Constructing the views*

You'll start by creating the CSS required to style the elements within the view. The drag-and-drop CSS will be included, so let's get it out of the way in the next listing.

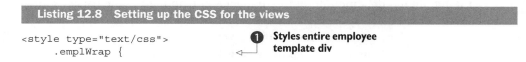

Listing 12.8   Setting up the CSS for the views

```
<style type="text/css">
    .emplWrap {
```
❶ Styles entire employee
template div

```
        border: 1px #999999 solid;
        -moz-border-radius: 5px;
        -webkit-border-radius: 5px;
        margin : 3px;
        padding : 3px;
        background-color: #ffffcc;
    }

    .emplOver {
        border: 1px #9999ff solid;
        background-color: #ccccff;
        cursor: pointer;
    }

    .emplSelected {
        border: 1px #66ff66 solid;
        background-color: #ccffcc;
        cursor: pointer;
    }

    .emplName {
        font-weight: bold;
        margin-left: 5px;
        font-size: 14px;
        text-decoration: underline;
        color: #333333;
    }

    .emplAddress {
        margin-left: 20px;
    }
</style>
```

② Styles on mouseover

③ Sets selected employee style

In the CSS in listing 12.8, you style how each employee `div` will look in the views. An unselected employee element will have a yellow background **①**, similar to that of a manila folder. When the mouse hovers over the name of an employee, it'll use the `emplOver` **②** CSS class to style it blue. When selected, the employee will be colored green using the `emplSelected` **③** CSS class.

You now have the CSS in place for your future views to use. In the following listing, you'll configure the two stores that will be consumed by the different views.

Listing 12.9 Configuring the stores for the data views

```
Ext.define('Employee', {
    extend     : 'Ext.data.Model',
    idProperty : 'id',
    fields     : [
        {name : 'departmentName', type : 'string' },
        'departmentName',
        'email',
        { name : 'firstName', mapping : 'firstname' },
        { name : 'lastName',  mapping : 'lastname'  }
    ]
});
```

① Creates Employee model

```
var inOfficeStore = Ext.create('Ext.data.Store', {
    model     : 'Employee',
    autoLoad  : true,
    proxy     : {
        type    : 'jsonp',
        url     : 'http://extjsinaction.com/getEmployees.php',
        reader : {
            type       : 'json',
            root       : 'records',
            idProperty : 'id'
        }
    }
});

var onVacationStore = Ext.create('Ext.data.Store', {
    model: 'Employee'
});
```

❷ Configures remote store

❸ Creates local store

In listing 12.9, you create the employee model ❶ and two configuration objects for the stores. The first store ❷ uses an Ajax proxy to fetch the list of employees, whereas the second `JsonStore` ❸ sits quietly waiting for records to be inserted upon a drop gesture.

Now that you have the data stores configured, you can create the views, as shown in the following listing.

Listing 12.10 Constructing the two views

```
var dvTpl = new Ext.XTemplate(
    '<tpl for=".">',
        '<div class="emplWrap" id="employee_{id}">',
            '<div class="emplName">{lastName}, {firstName}</div>',
            '<div>',
                '<span class="title">Department:</span>',
                ' {departmentName}',
            '</div>',
            '<div>',
                '<span class="title">Email:</span>',
                '<a href="#">{email}</a>',
            '</div>',
        '</div>',
    '</tpl>'
);

var inOfficeDv = Ext.create('Ext.view.View', {
    tpl              : dvTpl,
    store            : inOfficeStore,
    loadingText      : 'loading..',
    multiSelect      : true,
    overItemCls      : 'emplOver',
    selectedItemCls  : 'emplSelected',
    itemSelector     : 'div.emplWrap',
    emptyText        : 'No employees in the office.',
    style            : 'overflow:auto; background-color: #FFFFFF;'
});
```

❶ Provides XTemplate for views

❷ Creates in-the-office view

```
var onVacationDv = Ext.create('Ext.view.View', {
    tpl             : dvTpl,
    store           : onVacationStore,
    loadingText     : 'loading..',
    multiSelect     : true,
    overItemCls     : 'emplOver',
    selectedItemCls : 'emplSelected',
    itemSelector    : 'div.emplWrap',
    emptyText       : 'No employees on vacation',
    style           : 'overflow:auto; background-color: #FFFFFF;'
});
```

Creates on-vacation view ❸

In listing 12.10, you configure and construct the two views, starting with a common XTemplate instance ❶. inOfficeDv ❷ will consume the data from inOfficeStore to load the list of employees currently in the office, whereas onVacationDv ❸ will use the unpopulated onVacationStore.

You could render the views onscreen, but they'd look better inside a window and standing side by side with an HBoxLayout, as in the next listing.

Listing 12.11 Placing the views inside a window

```
new Ext.Window({
    layout       : 'hbox',
    height       : 400,
    width        : 550,
    border       : false,
    layoutConfig : { align : 'stretch'},
    items        : [
        {
            title : 'Employees in the office',
            frame : true,
            layout : 'fit',
            items : inOfficeDv,
            flex  : 1
        },
        {
            title : 'Employees on vacation',
            frame : true,
            layout : 'fit',
            id    : "test",
            items : onVacationDv,
            flex  : 1
        }
    ]
}).show();
```

Instantiates window for views ❶

Places data views inside panels ❷

In listing 12.11, you create an instance of Ext.Window ❶ that uses the HBoxLayout to place two panels side by side with equal widths and their heights stretched to fit the window's body. The panel on the left will contain the in-the-office data view ❷, and the panel on the right will contain the data view for those on vacation, as shown in figure 12.13.

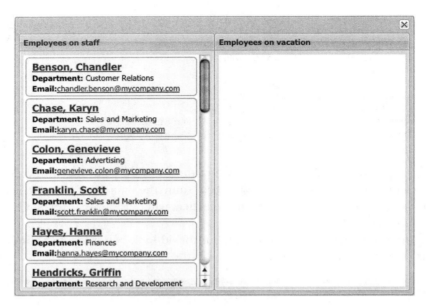

Figure 12.13 The rendered views inside an `Ext.Window`

You can see that the views have rendered properly, with employees in the office appearing on the left and no one currently on vacation. With that, you've set the stage for applying drag-and-drop.

12.5.2 *Adding drag gestures*

The application of drag-and-drop with views requires more effort than applying drag-and-drop to the grid and tree panels. This is because unlike those widgets, the `View` class doesn't have its own `DragZone` implementation subclass for you to build on, which means you'll have to craft your own implementation of `DragZone`. Also, you'll have to develop an implementation of `DropZone` to manage the drop gestures.

The `DragZone` class uses a special proxy known as `StatusProxy`, which will use icons to indicate whether a successful drop is possible. Figure 12.14 shows what they typically look like.

The default `StatusProxy` is extremely light-weight and efficient but somewhat boring. Although it provides useful information, it's far from fun to use. You'll take advantage of the ability to customize the `StatusProxy` look to spice up the drag gestures and make them much more enjoyable and informational. Another feature that `DragZone`

Figure 12.14 The `StatusProxy`, indicating that a drop is possible (left) or not (right)

adds is automated repair of an invalid drop scenario, which reduces the amount of code that you need to generate to get this stuff working.

You'll begin by creating the overrides that'll be applied to the instance of DragZone that you'll create afterward. Because the data views *must* be rendered in order to have drag-and-drop applied, you'll need to insert the code in the following listing below that of listing 12.11.

Listing 12.12 Creating the DragZone overrides

```
var dragZoneOverrides = {                    ❶ Scrolls destination
    containerScroll : true,           ◄──┘      container
    scroll          : false,               ◄──────── ❷ Prevents document.body
    getDragData     : function(evtObj){                from scrolling
        var dataView = this.dataView;          ◄───── ❸ Overrides getDragData method
        var sourceEl = evtObj.getTarget(dataView.itemSelector, 10);
        if (sourceEl) {
            var selectedNodes = dataView.getSelectedNodes();
            var dragDropEl = document.createElement('div');
                                                    ❺ Creates, returns
            if (selectedNodes.length < 1) {    ◄─────   drag data object
                selectedNodes.push(sourceEl);
            }

            Ext.each(selectedNodes, function(node) {   ◄──┐ Loops through
                dragDropEl.appendChild(node.cloneNode(true)); │ selectedNodes
            });                                         ❻   │ list

            return {
                ddel            : dragDropEl,
                repairXY        : Ext.fly(sourceEl).getXY(),
                dragRecords     : dataView.getSelectionModel()
                                        .getSelection(),
                sourceDataView  : dataView
            };
        }
    },
    getRepairXY: function() {
        return this.dragData.repairXY;
    }
};
```

Caches drag gesture element ❹

In listing 12.12, you create the override properties and methods that will be applied to the future instances of DragZone. Even though the amount of code is relatively small, there's a lot going on that you need to be aware of. Here's how this all works.

Initially you set two configuration properties that help manage scrolling when a drag operation is under way. The first is containerScroll ❶, which is set to true. Setting this property to true instructs the DragZone to call Ext.dd.ScrollManager.register, which will help manage the scrolling of a DataView when scrolling operations are in effect. You'll examine this in detail when you look at the DataView after the application of DragZone.

The next property, scroll ❷, is set to false. Setting this to false prevents the document.body element from scrolling when the drag proxy is moved out of the browser's viewport. Keeping the browser canvas fixed during drag-and-drop operations will increase its effectiveness.

Next you override getDragData ❸, which is an extremely important method for the multinode drag-and-drop application. The purpose of getDragData is to construct what's known as the *drag data object* that you'll see returned toward the end of this method. It's important to note that the drag data object that will be generated and returned by the getDragData method will be cached on the instance of dropZone and can be accessed via the this.dragData reference. You'll see this in action in the getRepairXY method later on.

In this method, you first set a reference to the element that the drag gesture was initiated with ❹ sourceEl. You'll use it later to update the StatusProxy if the number of selected nodes the DataView thinks it has is wrong. You also create a container element, dragDropEl, that will be used to contain copies of the selected nodes during drag, and it will be placed in the StatusProxy.

> **NOTE** The presence of sourceEl is tested in order for the rest of the method to continue. getDragData is called during the mouse-down event of the element that's registered with the DragZone. This means that getDragData will be called even if the View element itself is clicked instead of a record element, which would cause the method to fail.

Next you interrogate the number of items the View thinks are selected during the drag operation. If the number of selectedNodes ❺ is less than 1, you append the element with which the drag gesture was started. You do this because sometimes a drag gesture is initiated before the View can register an element as visually selected. This is a quick fix to this odd behavior.

You then use Ext.each ❻ to loop through the selectedNodes list, appending it to the dragDropEl. This will help customize the StatusProxy and give the appearance that the user is dragging over a copy of the selected node(s).

In the last chunk of this override, you return an object that will be used to update the StatusProxy and any drop operations. The only required property that's to be passed in this object is ddel, which will be placed inside the StatusProxy.

For this implementation you add a few other useful properties to the custom drag data object. First is repairXY, which is an array of the X and Y coordinates of the element on which the drag gesture was initiated. This will be used later to help the invalid drop repair operation.

Also included is dragRecords, which contains a list of instances of Ext.data.Record for each of the nodes selected and being dragged. Last, you set sourceDataView as the reference of the DataView for which this DragZone is being used. Both dragRecords and sourceDataView properties will help the application of DropZone to remove the dropped records from the source DataView.

The last method in the list of overrides is getRepairXY, which returns the locally cached data object's repairXY property and helps the repair operation know where to animate the StatusProxy on an invalid drop.

You've now set your overrides, so it's time to instantiate instances of `DragZone` and apply them to the views, as shown in the following code.

Listing 12.13   Applying `DragZone` to the views

```
var inOfficeDragZoneCfg = Ext.apply({}, {          Custom copy of
    ddGroup        : 'employeeDD',             ❶  dragZoneOverrides
    dataView       : inOfficeDv
}, dragZoneOverrides);

new Ext.dd.DragZone(inOfficeDv.getEl(), inOfficeDragZoneCfg);

var vacationDragZoneCfg = Ext.apply({}, {
    ddGroup        : 'employeeDD',
    dataView       : onVacationDv
}, dragZoneOverrides);

new Ext.dd.DragZone(onVacationDv.getEl(), vacationDragZoneCfg);
```

In listing 12.13, you use `Ext.apply` to create a custom copy of the `dragZoneOverrides` object for the custom `DragZone` targeted in the office `View` ❶. The custom copy of the overrides will include a `ddGroup` property. Both `DragZone` implementations will share this. What makes each copy special is the `dataView` property, which references the `DataView` that's attached to the `DragZone` and which is used by the `getDragData` method you created earlier. The same pattern is used to set up the `DragZone` for the vacation `DataView`.

One thing you may notice is that, unlike the implementation of `DDTarget`, you don't apply the overrides to the instance of `DragZone`. This is because `DragZone`'s superclass, `DragSource`, takes care of that for you automatically, as `Ext.Component` does.

Refreshing your project page will allow you to exercise drag operations. You can also see your customized `StatusProxy` in action. Mine is shown in figure 12.15.

You can see that selecting and dragging one or more `Records` in the office `View` reveals the `StatusProxy` with the copies of the selected nodes, which makes the drag operation nicer and much more fun to use.

You can also see the `getRepairXY` method in action by dropping the drag proxy anywhere on the page. The animation will make the drag proxy slide toward the X-Y coordinates of the element on which the drag operation was initiated.

You've probably already noticed that when you drag the nodes above the vacation `View`, the `StatusProxy` shows an icon indicating that the drop won't be successful. This is because you haven't employed a `DropZone`, which is what you'll do next.

12.5.3   *Applying drop*

Just like for your previous drag-and-drop applications, you must register a drop target of sorts for the drag classes to interact with. As we discussed before, you'll use the `DropZone` class. Following the pattern for this, you'll create an `overrides` object in the next listing, which will handle the drop gestures and which is much easier to implement relative to drag gestures.

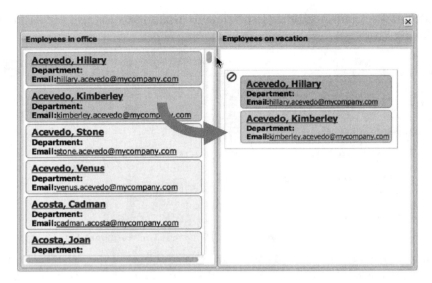

Figure 12.15 `DragZone` **with a custom** `DragProxy`

Listing 12.14   Creating the `DropZone` **overrides**

```
var dropZoneOverrides = {
    onContainerOver : function() {
      return this.dropAllowed;                              ◁─┐  Updates
    },                                                        ❶  StatusProxy
    onContainerDrop : function(dropZone, evtObj, dragData) {
        var dragRecords = dragData.dragRecords;
        var store = this.dataView.store;
        var dupFound = false;
        Ext.each(dragRecords, function(record) {          ◁─┐  Searches for
            var found = store.findBy(function(r) {          ❷  duplicate records
                return r.data.id === record.data.id;
            });
            if (found > -1 ) {
                dupFound = true;
            }
        });                                                      ❸  Removes
        if (dupFound !== true) {                                     all records
            Ext.each(dragRecords, function(record) {      ◁─       from source
                dragData.sourceDataView.store.remove(record);
            });                                                 ❹  Adds records
            this.dataView.store.add(dragRecords);         ◁─       to destination
            this.dataView.store.sort('lastname', 'ASC');  ◁─┐  Sorts records
        }                                                   ❺  by last name
        return true;                 ◁─┐  Indicates
    }                                  ❻  successful drop
};
```

In listing 12.14, you create an override object with two methods, to enable drop gestures to successfully occur in the two views. The first method is `onContainerOver` ❶, which is used to determine whether the drop should be allowed. In this application no processing is needed, but you need to at least return the `this.droppedAllowed` reference, which is a reference to the CSS class `x-dd-drop-ok` that provides the green check icon. If you wanted to use a custom icon, this is where you'd return a custom CSS class.

The next method, `onContainerDrop`, is where you'll process the dropped nodes, and it will be called by the instance of `DragZone` when the `mouseup` event fires. Remember that `DragZone` won't interact with `DropZone` if both aren't participating in the same drag/drop group.

In this method you use the `dragData` object that you created in your `DragZone` `getDragData` override. A local reference to the selected records (`dragRecords`) and the destination view's store (`store`) are created for later utilization.

Next, `onContainerDrop` searches for duplicate `Records` ❷. This is useful if you're attempting a copy instead of a move. If no duplicates are found, `Ext.each` is used to loop through the drag `Records` to remove them from the `sourceDataView`'s store ❸. The records are then added ❹ to the destination view's store and sorted ❺ by last name in ascending order.

After all of the `Record` management has taken place, the `onContainerDrop` returns the Boolean value `true`. By returning `true`, you convince the `DragZone` that the drop was successful ❻, and it doesn't initiate a repair animation. Any other value would indicate that the drop was unsuccessful, and a repair would occur.

Now that the overrides are in place, it's time to apply them to the views, as shown in the following listing.

Listing 12.15 Creating the `DropZone` overrides

```
var inOfficeDropZoneCfg = Ext.apply({}, {
    ddGroup         : 'employeeDD',
    dataView        : inOfficeDv
}, dropZoneOverrides);

new Ext.dd.DropZone(inOfficeDv.ownerCt.el, inOfficeDropZoneCfg);

var onVacationDropZoneCfg = Ext.apply({}, {
    ddGroup         : 'employeeDD',
    dataView        : onVacationDv
}, dropZoneOverrides);
new Ext.dd.DropZone(onVacationDv.ownerCt.el,  onVacationDropZoneCfg);
```

In listing 12.15, you create custom copies of the `dropZoneOverrides` object for the implementation of `DropZone` for each of the views and follow the same pattern that you used in listing 12.13, where you created instances of `DragZone`.

You can now see your end-to-end drag/drop application in action. Refresh your page, and attempt a drag operation from the office data view to the vacation data view, as shown in figure 12.16.

Dragging nodes from the employee view to the vacation view produces a `Status-Proxy` that contains a green checkmark to indicate a drop invitation. Dropping the

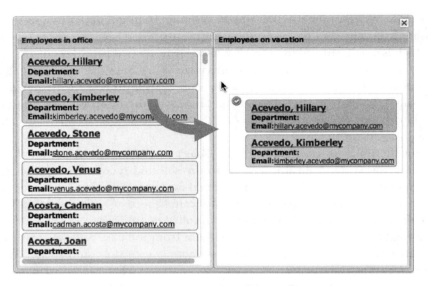

Figure 12.16   The `StatusProxy` now shows that a drop gesture can occur on the drop zone.

nodes invokes the `onContainerDrop` method, moving the `Records` from left to right, as shown in figure 12.17.

There you have it, drag-and-drop from one view to another with a good-looking `StatusProxy`. Because each data view has its own attached instance of `DragZone` and

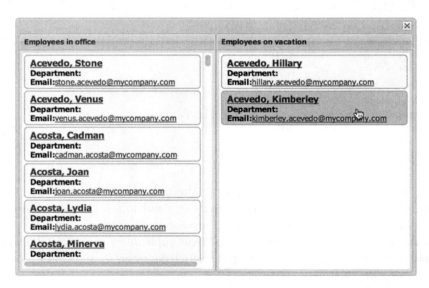

Figure 12.17   You've successfully dragged and dropped two `Records` from the left view to the right.

DropZone, you can drag-and-drop items from one to the other and the Records will automatically be sorted by last name.

You've learned how to apply drag-and-drop to two views, and learned that you're responsible for employing the full end-to-end code for both gestures. Next we'll dive into the world of drag-and-drop with grid panels, where you'll learn that the implementation pattern is different from that of the view. Here you'll use the drag-and-drop plug-ins available in Ext JS 4.

12.6 *Drag-and-drop with grid panels*

Say you've been asked to create a program that'll allow managers to track whether departments need computer upgrades. They want to be able to flag the departments that require an upgrade and change the order in which the departments will be upgraded.

To get the job done, you'll use two grid panels side by side, as you did with the views. You'll put drag-and-drop into practice from grid panel to grid panel and allow for the reordering of departments in the list.

In this exercise, you'll learn that the application of drag-and-drop between two grid panels is much simpler than for the view. You'll use `Ext.grid.plugin.DragDrop` to set up a specialized `Ext.dd.DragZone` that works well with grid panels.

You'll start by constructing two grid panels that will live in a window. The window will manage the grid panel dimensions by means of `HBoxLayout`.

12.6.1 *Constructing the grid panels*

By now you should be comfortable with creating grid panels and configuring their supported classes. In the following listing you'll create the first grid panel for this example.

Listing 12.16   Creating the first grid panel

```
Ext.define('PCStats', {
    extend: 'Ext.data.Model',
    fields: [
        { name: 'department',    type: 'string'},
        { name: 'workstationCount',  type: 'int'}
    ]
});

var remoteJsonStore = {                           ❶ Creates remote
    xtype    : 'json',                              JSON store
    model    : 'PCStats',
    autoLoad : true,
    proxy    : {
        type : 'jsonp',
        url  : 'http://extjsinaction.com/getPCStats.php',
        reader : {
            type : 'json',
            root : 'records'
        }
    }
};
```

```
var depsComputersOK = Ext.create('Ext.grid.Panel', {          Instantiates
    title       : 'Departments with good computers',    ❷    first grid panel
    store       : remoteJsonStore,
    multiSelect : true,
    viewConfig  : {
        plugins : {
            ptype : 'gridviewdragdrop'
        }
    },
    columns     : [
        {
            header    : 'Department Name',
            dataIndex : 'department',
            flex      : 1
        },
        {
            header    : '# PCs',
            dataIndex : 'workstationCount',
            width     : 40
        }
    ]
});
```

In listing 12.16, you create a remote store ❶ using a JsonP proxy. Next, you instantiate a grid panel ❷, which will use your store to display the departments.

In the next listing, you'll create the second grid panel, which will be used to list the departments in need of an upgrade.

Listing 12.17   Creating the second grid panel

```
var needUpgradeStore = {                          Configures
    xtype : 'json',                          ❶    local store
    model : 'PCStats'
};

var needUpgradeGrid = Ext.create('Ext.grid.GridPanel', {   Configures
    title          : 'Departments that need upgrades',     second
    store          : needUpgradeStore,               ❷     grid panel
    multiSelect    : true,
    viewConfig     : {
        plugins: {
            ptype: 'gridviewdragdrop'                       Configures
        }                                               gridviewdragdrop
    },                                              ❸    plug-in
    columns        : [
        {
            header    : 'Department Name',
            dataIndex : 'department',
            flex      : 1
        },
        {
            header    : '# PCs',
            dataIndex : 'workstationCount',
            width     : 40
        }
```

```
        ]
    });
```

In listing 12.17, you configure a local store ❶ with the PCStats model. Next, you create the second grid panel ❷ for the departments that need to be upgraded. Finally, you configure the gridviewdragdrop plugin ❸.

These grid panels need a home. The following listing shows how to create an Ext.Window to display them in.

Listing 12.18 Giving the grid panels a home

```
new Ext.Window({
    width     : 500,
    height    : 300,
    border    : false,
    defaults  :  {
        frame : true,
        flex  : 1
    },
    layout : {
        type   : 'hbox',
        align : 'stretch'
    },
    items        : [
        depsComputersOK,
        needUpgradeGrid
    ]
}).show();
```

In listing 12.18, you create an Ext.Window, which uses HBoxLayout to manage the two grid panels. It's time to take your panels out for a test drive. The results are shown in figure 12.18.

Departments with good computers		Departments that need upgrades	
Department Name	# PCs	Department Name	# PCs
Accounting	114		
Advertising	151		
Asset Management	106		
Customer Relations	124		
Customer Service	141		
Finances	176		
Human Resources	120		
Legal Department	144		
Media Relations	146		
Payroll	117		

Figure 12.18   The two department grid panels side by side

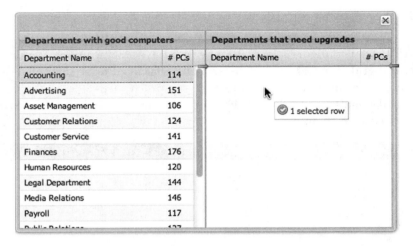

Figure 12.19   Drag gestures enabled in the grid panel

If you select an entry in the left grid and drag and drop it to the right grid, the result will look something like figure 12.19.

When attempting a drag gesture with the grid panel on the left, you can see the `StatusProxy` appear with the number of rows selected. This is how the `Grid DragZone` class uses the `getDragData` method, where it displays the number of selected rows for the `ddel` property of the drag data object. Sound familiar? You took a shortcut here by using the `gridviewdragdrop` plug-in, but if you dig deep into the code you find the same drag-and-drop framework you've used previously. That was easy, right? It turns out that there's also a drag-and-drop plug-in for the tree panel. You can use it in a similar manner, but let's dive into the details for drag-and-drop with tree panels without using the plug-ins.

12.7   *Drag-and-drop with tree panels*

Your company has purchased another company, and management needs a way to track how to absorb employees from the purchased company's various departments. They requested that you develop something that will allow them to track the reassignment of employees using tree panels and drag-and-drop.

The most important requirement is the ability to allow associates to be relocated to a specified set of similar departments. For instance, any associate from Accounting, Finances, or Payroll can be reassigned to any of those departments. Likewise, associates from Customer Relations, Media Relations, Customer Service, or Public Relations can be reassigned to any of those. Instead of building a valid drop matrix in JavaScript, the node list returned from the server will report a list of valid departments for each node. It will be up to you to somehow use that data to satisfy the requirements.

To give you a sense of how you're going to power these constraints, here's what an employee record looks like for the tree panel:

```
{
    "text": "Kemp, Sawyer",
    "leaf": true,
    "validDropPoints": [
        "Accounting",
        "Finances",
        "Payroll"
    ]
}
```

As you dive into the implementation of the drop operations, you'll use the `valid-DropPoint` array to drive the decision-making process for the UI. For this record, this employee can only move to the Accounting, Finances, or Payroll departments.

OK, let's move on to constructing the tree panels. Afterward you'll add in the appropriate drag-and-drop functionality.

12.7.1 Constructing the tree panels

As with the previous view and grid panel exercises, you'll configure two tree panels, both of which will be managed by an instance of `Ext.Window` using the `HBoxLayout`.

Because you've built a few tree panels already, we're going to move through this pretty fast. The following listing sets the stage.

Listing 12.19 Setting the stage for tree panel drag-and-drop

```
var leftTree = Ext.create('Ext.tree.Panel', {        ◁───┐   Their company's
    autoScroll : true,                                    ❶ tree panel
    title      : 'Their Company',
    animate    : false,
    store      : Ext.create('Ext.data.TreeStore', {
        proxy : {
            type   : 'jsonp',
            url    : 'http://extjsinaction.com/theirCompany.php',
            reader : {
                root : 'records'
            }
        },
        root  : {
            text     : 'Their Company',
            id       : 'theirCompany',
            expanded : true
        }
    })
});
                                                      ❷  Your company's
var rightTree = Ext.create('Ext.tree.Panel', {       ◁───┘  tree panel
    title      : 'Our Company',
    autoScroll : true,
    animate    : false,
    store      : Ext.create('Ext.data.TreeStore', {
        proxy : {
            type   : 'jsonp',
            url    : 'http://extjsinaction.com/ourCompany.php',
            reader : {
```

```
                root : 'records'
            }
        },
        root   : {
            text       : 'Our Company',
            expanded : true
        }
    })
})
});

// Drag and drop code will go here                    ❸  Window to contain
Ext.create('Ext.Window', {                           ◁─┘   the tree panels
    height    : 350,
    width     : 450,
    border    : false,
    layout    : {
        layout : 'hbox',
        align  : 'stretch'
    },
    defaults : {
        flex : 1
    },
    items    : [
        leftTree,
        rightTree
    ]
}).show();
```

In listing 12.19, you create two tree panels and an `Ext.Window`, which will contain them and manage their sizes using the `HBoxLayout`. The left tree panel ❶ will load a list of departments for the other company. Each department will have to be expanded to reveal the child items.

The right tree panel ❷ will load up a list of departments for the company, which, lucky for you, aligns with the company being sold. For simplicity, we won't display the employees currently in the company's departments.

Finally, the `Ext.Window` is created ❸ to manage the two tree panels side by side. Figure 12.20 shows the tree panels rendered onscreen.

You have the two tree panels rendered within the `Ext.Window`. It's time to get the party started with drag-and-drop.

12.7.2 *Enabling drag-and-drop*

When exploring how to employ drag-and-drop with data views, you were required to implement both the `DragZone` and `DropZone` classes. When applying this feature to grid panels, you learned that you were required to implement only `DropZone`, because the grid view automatically creates `GridDragZone` if the grid panel has the `enableDragDrop` property set.

With a tree panel, you could enable drag-and-drop easily by enabling the View-DragDrop plug-in. You do this by adding the following configuration property on a tree panel:

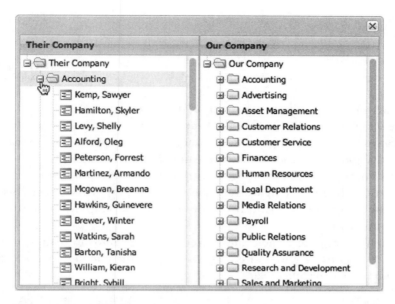

Figure 12.20 The two tree panels

```
viewConfig : {
    plugins : { ptype : 'treeviewdragdrop' }
}
```

By enabling drag-and-drop in this way, you allow drag-and-drop to operate easily on the tree panel. Everything can be dragged and dropped, which can be useful for, let's say, a filesystem management tool; but for what you need, the basic drag-and-drop implementation won't cut it. Adding constraints to the out-of-the-box drag-and-drop plug-in becomes a rather difficult task.

In order to apply constraints, you're going to need to implement your own instances of the ViewDragZone and ViewDropZone classes. You'll tackle this intense procedure next. Are you ready?

12.7.3 Employing flexible constraints

You're going to tackle this task in two phases: enabling drag on the left tree panel, and adding drop enablement to the right tree panel. Enabling drag operations on the left tree panel is the easiest of the two operations, which is demonstrated in the next listing. The following code is to be placed immediately before the Window instance you created in listing 12.19.

Listing 12.20 Applying better drop constraints

```
leftTree.getView().on('render', function(view) {           ◁─────  ❶ Adds a
    Ext.create('Ext.tree.ViewDragZone', {        ◁──  ❷ Creates the    render
        view         : view,                          ViewDragZone      listener
        dragText     : 'schedule vacation',
```

```
            ddGroup       : 'myTreeDDGroup',
            onBeforeDrag : function(dragData) {
                return view.getNode(dragData.item).attributes.leaf;
            }
        });
    });
```

Enables drag on leaf items only ❸

To enable drag, you register a render listener on the left tree view class ❶. This listener is responsible for creating an instance of the `ViewDragZone` class ❷. This `ViewDragZone` class requires some basic configuration parameters that are pretty self-explanatory, but I want to talk about the `onBeforeDrag` function ❸ for a moment.

In this pattern, you're implementing your own `onBeforeDrag` function that essentially returns true if the item being dragged has a leaf property set to `true`. This effectively only allows drag operations to occur on leaf nodes (employees) and not the branch (department) nodes.

With the drag operation armed and locked, you can move to getting the drop operation for the right tree panel wired in. You'll place the code for the next listing right under the code for listing 12.20.

Listing 12.21   Applying better drop constraints

Adds a render listener ❶

```
rightTree.getView().on('render', function(view) {
    Ext.create('Ext.tree.ViewDropZone', {
        view               : view,
        ddGroup            : 'myTreeDDGroup',
        isValidDropPoint : function(node, pos, dz, e, data) {

            var dropNode   = view.getRecord(data.item),
                targetNode = view.getRecord(node),
                dragNode   = data.records[0],
                validDropPoints,
                targetNodeText;

            if (! dropNode || !targetNode) {
                return false;
            }

            if (targetNode.raw.leaf) {
                return false;
            }

            if (pos != 'append') {
                return false;
            }

            validDropPoints = dragNode.raw.validDropPoints;
            targetNodeText = targetNode.get("text");

            return Ext.Array.contains(validDropPoints, targetNodeText);
        }
    });
});
```

Creates the ViewDropZone ❷

Overrides isValidDropPoint ❸

Adds a validation test ❹

Listing 12.21 contains all that you need to ensure that drop operations occur only on branch nodes that are associated. In order to create the ViewDropZone at the right time, you have to register a render event listener on the right tree View class ❶.

The event listener has a sole purpose, which is to create the instance of the View-DropZone class ❷. In order to add the proper drop constraints, you had to override the isValidDropPoint method ❸.

In this method, you gather some data up front in the form of lexically scoped references. Then you have a few if conditions, which return false if met, applying the bulk of the constraints. If no constraint is met, you return the result of a test where you verify that the targetNodeText is within the validDropPoints array ❹. These constraints include attempting to drop on

- Anything that is not a tree view node
- Any node that is a leaf node
- Any node where the position (pos) property is not append.

Assuming the drop operation passes all of those tests, you then return the result of an Ext.Array.contains method call, where you're looking to see if the targetNode (node being dropped on) has a title that is a match in the drop node's (node that is being dragged) validDropPoints array. If there's a match, the drop is allowed, as shown in figure 12.21.

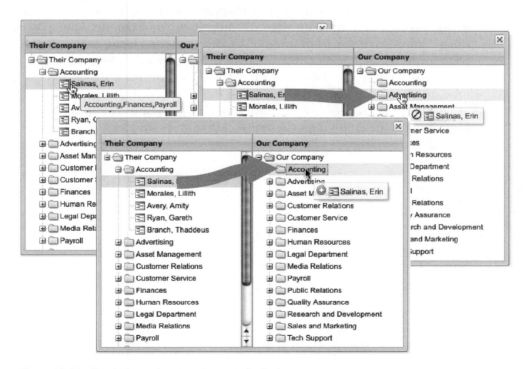

Figure 12.21 Testing your drop target constraint logic

You can test your constraint logic by attempting to drag a department branch node. You'll see that it's impossible. This tells you that the onBeforeDrag override method is working as designed.

To determine where the associate can be dragged, hover over it, and you'll see a ToolTip appear with the values that are in the validDropPoints array. In hovering over Erin, you'll find that she can be dropped on Accounting but not Advertising. When you drag Erin over Accounting on the right-hand tree panel, the StatusProxy displays a valid drop icon. But if you hover her over Advertising, you see an invalid drop icon in the StatusProxy. As extra credit, you can try to hover Erin over Finances and Payroll, and you'll see a valid drop icon there too.

The last test you can perform is to drop an associate or two onto a valid department. You can test the ability to drop leaf nodes above or below other leaf nodes within a valid department as well.

There you have it: drag-and-drop with two tree panels, with a complex but somewhat flexible drop constraint system. I'm sure your managers will be pleased that you delivered what they were asking for.

12.8   Summary

This chapter explored various ways of implementing drag-and-drop with the three most commonly used widgets within the framework. You started with implementing drag-and-drop on DOM elements. This chapter covered the basics of the drag-and-drop framework and moved on to views as a more complex example. Then you explored using a plug-in as a shortcut for setting up drag-and-drop between grid panels. Finally, you learned about drag-and-drop with tree panels. In this implementation, you discovered that enabling this behavior with tree panels is the easiest task, and the application of somewhat complex constraints on the drop gestures is the most difficult task.

In the next chapter, you'll learn about plug-ins and extensions and how they work. You'll start to use object-oriented techniques with JavaScript—and you'll have a lot of fun.

Part 3

Building an application

In this part of the book, you'll get to know how Ext JS works and learn some best practices for building MVC applications.

Chapter 13 dives into class system foundations used for enhanced reusability by focusing on prototypal inheritance, class definition, subclassing components, framework extensions, shared plug-ins, and dynamic class loaders including a composite grid panel with context menus that can be applied to any data view. Chapter 14 shows how to build complex applications based on the MVC architecture with controllers; coding conventions for Ext JS, JavaScript, and CSS; and recommended development processes with Sencha Cmd tools using all the knowledge gathered throughout this book.

This part enables you to use more advanced features of the framework such as custom extensions, plug-ins, and class loaders, as well as to learn solid principles for building and managing web applications.

Class system foundations

This chapter covers

- Understanding prototypal inheritance
- Developing your first extension
- Working with plug-ins
- Exploring the Ext JS class loader

Every Ext JS developer faces challenges where reusability is an issue. Often a component must appear more than once within the application's lifetime. Without mastering certain techniques, you could end up with what's known as "function soup," or unmaintainable code. This is why we'll focus on the concept of reusability with the use of framework extensions and plug-ins.

In this chapter, you'll learn the basics of extending (subclassing) with Ext JS. You'll begin by learning how to create subclasses with JavaScript, and you'll see what it takes to get the job done with the native language tools. This knowledge will give you the foundation to refactor your newly created subclass in order to use the Ext JS class system.

Once you're familiar with creating basic subclasses, we'll focus our attention on extending Ext JS components. You'll learn the basics of framework extensions, and you'll solve a real-world problem by extending the grid panel widget.

Next, you'll see that though extensions solve problems, they can create inheritance issues when similar functionality is desired across multiple widgets. Once you understand the basic limitations of extensions, you'll convert your extension into a plug-in, where its functionality can easily be shared across the grid panel and any of its descendants.

Once you've built a solid foundation in the Ext JS class system, we'll look at the dynamic class loader that Ext JS provides. We'll discuss three popular patterns for using the dynamic class loader and the caveats that accompany each one. Note that it will be a good idea to download the example code for this chapter and follow along while reading the text.

13.1 *Classic JavaScript inheritance*

JavaScript provides all the necessary tools for prototypal inheritance, but it falls short in giving you the ability to easily set up multiple-class inheritance. Ext JS makes multiple-class inheritance much easier with the class system. To begin learning about inheritance you'll create a base class.

To help you along, imagine you're working for an automobile dealership that sells two types of car. The first is the base car, which serves as a foundation to construct the premium model. Instead of using 3D models to describe the two car models, you'll use JavaScript classes.

> **NOTE** If you're new to object-oriented JavaScript or are feeling a bit rusty, the Mozilla foundation has an excellent article to bring you up to speed or polish your skills. You can find it at http://mng.bz/R9BB.

13.1.1 *Creating a base class*

Start by constructing a class to describe the base car, as shown in the next listing.

Listing 13.1 Constructing the base class

```
var BaseCar = function(config) {                            Creates
    this.octaneRequired = 86;                         1  constructor
    this.shiftTo = function(gear) {
        this.gear = gear;
    };
    this.shiftTo('park');
};
BaseCar.prototype = {                                       Assigns
    engine    : 'I4',                                2  prototype object
    turbo     : false,
    wheels    : 'basic',
    getEngine : function() {
        return this.engine;
    },
    drive     : function() {
        console.log("Vrrrrooooooom - I'm driving!");
    }
};
```

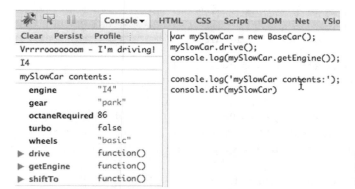

Figure 13.1 Instantiating an instance of `BaseCar` and exercising two of its methods

In listing 13.1 you create the `BaseCar` class constructor ❶, which when instantiated sets the instance's local `this.octaneRequired` property, adds a `this.shiftTo` method, and calls it, setting the local `this.gear` property to `'park'`. Next you configure the `BaseCar` class's `prototype` object ❷, which contains three properties that describe the `BaseCar` class and two methods.

Use the following code to create an instance of `BaseCar` and inspect its contents with Firebug:

```
var mySlowCar = new BaseCar();
mySlowCar.drive();
console.log(mySlowCar.getEngine());
console.log('mySlowCar contents:');
console.dir(mySlowCar)
```

Figure 13.1 shows what the output of this code looks like in the Firebug multiline editor and console.

You can now focus on subclassing the `BaseCar` class. First you'll do it the traditional way. This will give you a better understanding of what's going on under the hood when you use `Ext.define` later on.

13.1.2 Creating a subclass

You can create a subclass using native JavaScript in several steps. Rather than simply describing them, we'll walk through the steps together. The next listing shows you how to create `PremiumCar`, a subclass of the `BaseCar` class.

Listing 13.2 Creating a subclass the old-school way

```
var PremiumCar = function() {                              Configures subclass
    PremiumCar.superclass.constructor.call(this);    ❶  constructor
    this.octaneRequired = 93;
};
PremiumCar.prototype    = new BaseCar();                        Sets subclass
PremiumCar.superclass   = BaseCar.prototype;              ❸  prototype
PremiumCar.prototype.turbo  = true;
PremiumCar.prototype.wheels = 'premium';
```

Calls superclass constructor ❷

Sets subclass's superclass reference ❹

```
PremiumCar.prototype.drive = function() {
    this.shiftTo('drive');
    PremiumCar.superclass.drive.call(this);
};
PremiumCar.prototype.getEngine = function() {
    return 'Turbo ' + this.engine;
};
```

To create a subclass you begin by creating a new constructor, which is assigned to the reference PremiumCar ❶. Within this constructor is a call to the constructor method of PremiumCar.superclass; within the scope of the instance of PremiumCar ❷ you're creating (this).

You do this because, unlike other object-oriented languages, JavaScript subclasses don't natively call their superclass constructor. Calling the superclass constructor gives it a chance to execute and perform any constructor-specific functions that the subclass might need. In this case, the shiftTo method is being added and called in the Base-Car constructor. Not calling the superclass constructor would mean that your subclass wouldn't get the benefits provided by the base class constructor.

Next you set the prototype property of PremiumCar to the result of a new instance of BaseCar ❸. Performing this step allows PremiumCar.prototype to inherit all of the properties and methods from BaseCar. This is known as *inheritance through prototyping* and is the most common and robust method of creating class hierarchies in JavaScript.

In the next line you set the PremiumCar's superclass reference to the prototype value of the BaseCar class ❹. You then can use this superclass reference to do things like create so-called *extension methods*, such as PremiumCar.prototype.drive. This method is known as an extension method because it calls the like-named method from the superclass prototype, but from the scope of the instance of the subclass it's attached to.

> **TIP**   All JavaScript functions (JavaScript 1.3 and later) have two methods that force the scope execution: call and apply. To learn more about call and apply, visit www.webreference.com/js/column26/apply.html.

With the subclass you can test things by instantiating an instance of PremiumCar with the following code entered into the Firebug editor:

```
var myFastCar = new PremiumCar();
myFastCar.drive();
console.log('myFastCar contents:');
console.dir(myFastCar);
```

Figure 13.2 shows what the output would look like in Firebug. This output shows that your subclass performed as desired. From the console.dir output, you can see that the subclass constructor set the octaneRequired property to 93 and the drive extension method even set the gear method as "drive."

Figure 13.2 Your `PremiumCar` subclass in action

This exercise shows that you're responsible for all of the crucial steps in order to achieve prototypal inheritance with native JavaScript. First you had to create the constructor of the subclass. Then you had to set the prototype of the subclass to a new instance of the base class. Next, for convenience, you set the subclass's superclass reference. Last, you added members to the prototype one by one.

You can see that quite a few steps need to be followed in order to create multiple classes with the native language constructs. Luckily there's an easier way to achieve this result. Next, you'll see how the Ext JS class system makes creating classes and multiple inheritance much easier.

13.2 Inheritance with Ext JS

The Ext JS class system takes JavaScript's prototypal inheritance to another level, adding features like dependency injection, automatic setter and getter method creation, statics, and mixin support (multiple inheritance). All of these features require the use of Ext JS class-specific methods, such as `Ext.define`, `Ext.create`, and `Ext.require`, as you'll learn later. As you read this section you'll learn why the Ext JS class system is a great solution for developing your applications.

13.2.1 Creating a base class

You've seen what it takes to implement JavaScript prototypal inheritance. You had to do quite a bit of work to just get a single level of inheritance set up. With complex software like these applications, you'd have to do quite a bit of typing to get inheritance going. This means that you'd have redundant code in your projects, resulting in bloat.

Ext JS is in the perfect position to take on the heavy lifting for you. To see what we mean, take a step back to the first two classes you created. Listing 13.3 shows how the `BaseCar` and `PremiumCar` classes look when you start using Ext JS to define the `Base-Car` class. You'll then extend the `BaseCar` class to create `PremiumCar`. Instead of just using simple class names, you'll define your class names using properly namespaced packages, much like you find in classic languages such as Java.

Listing 13.3   Defining the base class with Ext JS

```
Ext.define('MyApp.car.BaseCar', {                          Defines
    engine : 'I4',                                      ❶  BaseCar class
    turbo  : false,
    wheels : 'basic',                          Specifies class
                                            ❷  primitives

    constructor : function(config) {           Defines
        this.octaneRequired = 86;           ❸  constructor

        this.shiftTo = function(gear) {
            this.gear = gear;
        };

        this.shiftTo('park');
    },
    getEngine : function() {
        return this.engine;
    },
    drive      : function() {
        console.log("Vrrrroooooooom - I'm driving!");
    }
});
```

Listing 13.3 demonstrates the most basic use of `Ext.define`, where you define the
BaseCar class ❶. The first thing that might strike you as strange is the way you define
the class names: by string. This is because Ext JS gives you an opportunity to define a
class and namespace together. Ext JS will create the `MyApp.car` namespace for you if it
wasn't previously defined, and it'll place the `BaseCar` class in that namespace. This
pattern paves the way for our look at the class loader system later in this chapter,
where you'll learn how important it is to organize your classes in your project's filesystem according to the namespace for which they're defined.

In the class definition you set the primitives for the class's prototype ❷, and then
you create the constructor ❸. This class will behave exactly like the one that you
defined in listing 13.1, but you're using Ext JS to define it.

To instantiate this class, you'll have to use `Ext.create` instead of the JavaScript `new`
keyword. By now you're used to using `Ext.create` for Ext JS classes, but we want you
to use it within the context of your own class. Here's how you do it:

```
var mySlowCar = Ext.create('MyApp.car.BaseCar');
mySlowCar.drive();
console.log(mySlowCar.getEngine());
```

Figure 13.3 shows the results.

**Figure 13.3   The results of your
first Ext JS class**

As figure 13.3 demonstrates, you get the results you expect from your implementation of the `MyApp.car.BaseCar` class you just created. This sets the stage perfectly for you to extend this class using `Ext.define`.

13.2.2 *Creating a subclass*

The next listing shows how you extend `BaseCar`. You create the `MyApp.car.PremiumCar` class, which is an extension (subclass) of the `MyApp.car.BaseCar` superclass, using the `Ext.define` method. Here's how it works.

> **Listing 13.4   Extending `BaseCar` with `Ext.define`**

```
Ext.define('MyApp.car.PremiumCar', {        ← Defines
    extend      : 'MyApp.car.BaseCar',      ❶ PremiumCar class

    turbo       : true,                     ← Overrides BaseCar
    wheels      : 'premium',                ❸ prototypal primitives
    stereo      : '5.1',

    constructor : function() {              ← Defines PremiumCar
        this.callParent(arguments);         ❹ constructor
        this.octaneRequired = 93;
    },
    getEngine   : function() {
        return 'Turbo ' + this.engine;
    },                                      ❺ Extends drive
                                              method of superclass
    drive       : function() {              ←
        this.callParent();
        this.shiftTo('drive');
        console.log('The turbo makes a big difference!');
    }
});
```

Extends BaseCar class ❷

First you call on `Ext.define` to define the class for the `MyApp.car.PremiumCar` ❶ extension class. You instruct Ext JS to extend your previously defined `MyApp.car.BaseCar` class by naming it via `string` set to the `extend` keyword ❷. Next you set the prototype overrides, making this class's `turbo`, `wheels`, and `stereo` properties different from the base.

When thinking about extending classes, you must consider whether prototypal methods in the subclass will share the same name as prototypal methods in the base class. If they'll share the same symbolic reference name, decide whether they'll be extension methods or overrides.

An extension method is a method in a subclass that shares the same reference name as another method in a base class. What makes this an extension method is the fact that it includes the execution of the base class method within itself. The reason you'd want to extend a method would be to reduce code duplication; you reuse the code in the base class method.

The constructor ❸ for this class is an extension method. It's an exact duplicate of the previously created `PremiumCar` constructor ❹, with the addition of a call to the

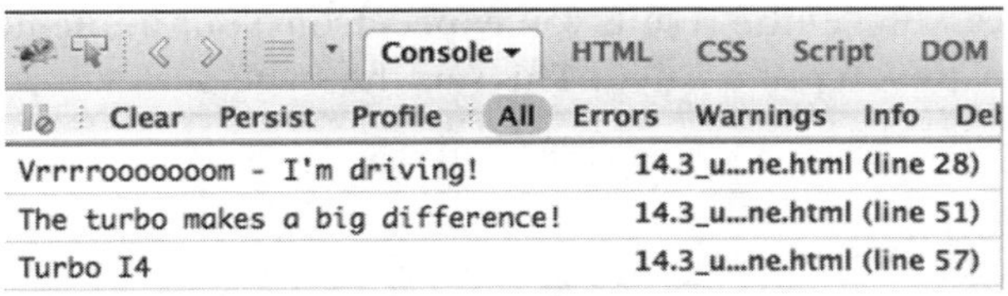

Figure 13.4   **The results of the instantiation of the** `PremiumCar` **class**

parent class constructor ❺ via `this.callParent(arguments);`. This statement allows the subclass to chain the constructor method calls, effectively allowing the `MyApp.car.BaseCar` superclass constructor to execute within the scope of new instances of your `MyApp.car.PremiumCar` subclass.

An *override method* is a method in a subclass that shares the same reference name as another method in a base class but doesn't chain method calls up to the superclass via `this.callParent()`. You override a method if you wish to completely discard the code that's in the like-named method in the base class. Therefore, you just don't call `this.callParent()` within your override method.

Now that you have your `PremiumCar` configured using `Ext.define`, you can see it in action using Firebug. You can do so using the same code you used when you tested your manually created subclass:

```
var myFastCar = Ext.create('MyApp.car.PremiumCar');
myFastCar.drive();
console.log(myFastCar.getEngine());
```

Figure 13.4 shows what it looks like in the Firebug console.

You've just successfully extended a class using `Ext.define`. You created a class from scratch (`MyApp.car.BaseCar`) and extended it (`MyApp.car.PremiumCar`). You can extend the `MyApp.car.PremiumCar` class and create a `MyApp.car.SportsCar` class that adds features like `drift()`-ing and `dragRace()`-ing.

Now that you've learned about prototypal inheritance with JavaScript and `Ext.define`, you can start extending Ext JS.

13.3   *Extending Ext JS components*

Extensions to the framework are developed to introduce additional functionality to existing classes in the name of reusability. The concept of reusability drives the framework, and when used properly it can enhance the development of your applications.

Some developers create preconfigured classes, which are constructed mainly as a means to reduce the amount of application-level code by stuffing configuration parameters into the class definition itself. Having such extensions alleviates the application-level code from having to manage much of the configuration, requiring only the simple instantiation of such classes. This design pattern is okay but should be used only if you're expecting to stamp out more than one instance of the preconfigured class. It's considered wasteful to define a class just as a home for a collection of configuration parameters.

Other extensions add features such as utility methods or embed behavioral logic inside the class itself. An example of this would be a form panel that automatically pops up a message box whenever a save operation failure occurs. I (Jay) often create extensions for applications for this very reason, where the widget contains limited built-in behavioral logic. I say limited, because with Ext JS 4.0 you now have an MVC architecture for which you can abstract business logic to controllers. This is something we'll explore in the next chapter.

My favorite kind of extension is what I like to call a composite widget, which combines one or more widgets into one class. An example of this would be a window that has an embedded grid panel, or a form panel that embeds a tab panel to spread its fields over multiple tabs.

This is the type of extension that we'll focus on now. You'll merge a grid panel with a menu.

13.3.1 *Thinking about what you're building*

When building an extension, you may want to take a step back and analyze the problem from all facets. Sometimes a problem can be extremely complex, such as the creation of a dynamic wizard-like widget that has numerous workflow rules that must be controlled by the UI. Often, extensions can be used to solve the problem of reusability. This will be our focus for the rest of this chapter.

Think back to chapter 8, when we explored the creation of a grid panel. You attached a menu and configured it to display when the grid's contextmenu event fired. Recall that you had to manually configure the menu to destruct upon the grid panel's destruction. If you extrapolate this task over the span of an application where several grid panels coupled with menus are to be rendered onscreen, you can easily visualize the amount of code duplication required to make this work. Before you start coding, let's take a moment to analyze the problem and come up with the best possible solution.

To mitigate this code-duplication risk, you'll create an extension to the grid panel that'll automatically handle the instantiation and destruction of the menu. What other features can you add to this extension to make it more robust?

The first thing that comes to mind is the differences in the selection getter and setter methods for RowSelectionModel and CellSelectionModel. RowSelectionModel has selectRow and getSelected, whereas CellSelectionModel has selectCell and getSelectedCell. It would be great if your extension could handle this variation in the grid panel's selection models. Such a feature would reduce the amount of code in the application layer.

When considering the design of your class, you must take into account multiple possibilities for implementations. For example, you should be able pass a configuration object that'll get transformed into a Menu instance:

```
Ext.create('MyApp.grid Panel', {
    // ... (other configuration options)
    menu : {
        items : [
```

```
            { text : 'menu item 1' },
            { text : 'menu item 2' }
        ]
    }
});
```

Or you could pass an array of menu.Item configuration objects

```
Ext.create('MyApp.grid Panel',
    // ... (other configuration options)
    menu :[
        { text : 'menu item 1' },
        { text : 'menu item 2' }
    ]
});
```

or an instance of Ext.menu.Menu as the menu configuration:

```
var myMenu = Ext.create('Ext.menu.Menu', {
items : [
    { text : 'menu item 1' },
    { text : 'menu item 2' }
    ]
});
Ext.create('MyApp.grid Panel', {
    // ... (other configuration options)
    menu : myMenu
});
```

Having this type of flexibility for the implementation of the subclass plays into the framework's culture and will allow the subclass to be used in more ways than one. It's important to keep in mind as you design your classes for your own application. With a clear picture of the issues you're going to solve you can begin the construction of your first Ext JS extension.

13.3.2 *Extending GridPanel*

To extend the GridPanel class you'll use Ext.define. The following listing contains the template for the extension that you'll create. The best place to put this code is in a separate file included in your HTML. Because you're not using a loader, you can name it ContextMenuGridPanel.js.

> **Listing 13.5 The grid panel extension**

```
Ext.define('MyApp.grid.ContextMenuGridPanel', {
    extend : 'Ext.grid.GridPanel',
    alias : 'widget.contextmenugrid',

    constructor : function() {                                    ❶ Defines
        this.callParent(arguments);                                  constructor
        if (this.menu) {
            if (! (this.menu instanceof Ext.menu.Menu)) {         ❷ Constructs
                this.menu = this.buildMenu(this.menu);               menu
            }
```

```
            this.on({
                scope               : this,
                itemcontextmenu : this.onItemContextMenu
            });
        }
    },
    buildMenu : function(menuCfg) {
        if (Ext.isArray(menuCfg)) {
            menuCfg = {
                items : menuCfg
            };
        }

        return Ext.create('Ext.menu.Menu', menuCfg);
    },
    onItemContextMenu : function(grid, model, row, index, evt) {
        evt.stopEvent();
        this.menu.showAt(evt.getXY());
    },

    onDestroy : function() {

        if (this.menu && this.menu.destroy) {
            this.menu.destroy();
        }

        this.callParent(arguments);
    }
});
```

Hooks
itemcontextmenu
❸ **event**

Adds Menu
❹ factory method

**Handles
itemcontextmenu
event** ❺

Destroys menu
❻ **if it exists**

Listing 13.5 contains the code for the extension and provides three methods that will be applied to the subclass's prototype. First is the constructor method ❶, which will be the vector to extend the grid panel. In this method you first call the superclass's constructor and then move on to test for the presence of this.menu ❷. If it's present and not an instance of Ext.menu.Menu already, you construct a menu using the build-Menu factory method ❹, passing in the this.menu reference.

In the buildMenu factory method you determine whether menuCfg points to an existing instance of Ext.menu.Menu. If it doesn't, you test to see if it's a plain array using Ext.isArray. If it's an array, you have to wrap an object around the array in order for the constructor for Menu's superclass, Container, to properly do its job.

The last bit of the extension's constructor handles registering the itemcontext-menu event listener ❸, which is onItemContextMenu ❺. This listener is responsible for invoking stopEvent() on the Ext.EventObject reference (evt). This will prevent the browser's own context menu from appearing. It then instructs the menu to display at the event's own X and Y coordinates.

Last, the onDestroy method ❻ extends the GridPanel class's own onDestroy method. This is where you'll code the automatic destruction of the menu if it exists and has a destroy method attached to it.

You now have your custom extension all set up. Let's move forward with its implementation.

13.3.3 *Your extension in action*

When discussing the constructor for the grid panel extension, we mentioned three patterns for implementation: the menu reference for the configuration object can be set to an array of menu.Item configuration objects, an instance of Menu, or a configuration object designed for an instance of Menu. For this implementation you'll choose the first pattern, an array of menu.Item configuration objects. This way, you can see an automatic instantiation of Menu as coded in your extension's constructor.

The following listing contains the implementation code and is quite lengthy because of the configuration that has to be put in place to get the grid panel to work. By now you're familiar with data stores and grid panels, so it should be a relatively light read.

Listing 13.6   Creating the remote JSON store for the extension implementation

```
Ext.define('MyModel', {                                          ◁──┐  ❶ Defines
    extend : 'Ext.data.Model',                                      └──  model
    fields : [
        'firstname',
        'lastname'
    ]
});
                                                                          ❷ Configures remote
var remoteJsonStore = Ext.create('Ext.data.Store', {   ◁──┐             JSON store
    autoLoad : true,                                      └──
    model    : 'MyModel',
    proxy    : {
        type   : 'jsonp',
        url    : 'http://extjsinaction.com/dataQuery.php',
        reader : {
            type : 'json',
            root : 'records'
        }
    }                                                                  ❸ Sets up click
});                                                                       handler

var onMenuItemClick = function(menuItem) {             ◁──┐
    var gridPanel   = Ext.ComponentQuery.query('contextmenugrid')[0],
        selModel    = gridPanel.getSelectionModel(),
        selectedRec = selModel.getSelection()[0],
        msg         = Ext.String.format(
            '{0} : {1}, {2}',
            menuItem.text,
            selectedRec.get('lastname'),
            selectedRec.get('firstname')
        );

    Ext.MessageBox.alert('Feedback', msg);
};                                                                     ❹ Configures
                                                                          custom grid
var grid = {                                            ◁──┐
    xtype   : 'contextmenugrid',
    store   : remoteJsonStore,
    columns : [
```

```
        {
            header    : 'Last Name',
            dataIndex : 'lastname',
            flex      : 1
        },
        {
            header    : 'First Name',
            dataIndex : 'firstname',
            flex      : 1
        }
    ],
    menu      : [                              ❺  Defines menu
        {                                          configuration
            text    : 'Add Record',
            handler : onMenuItemClick
        }
    ]
};
new Ext.Window({                               ❻  Implements custom
    height : 300,                                  grid in a window
    width  : 300,
    border : false,
    layout : 'fit',
    items  : grid
}).show();
```

Listing 13.6 does quite a bit of work to configure an instance of your custom `Grid-Panel` class. You begin by configuring the model ❶ and the remote JSON store ❷. Next, you set the menu click handler, `onMenuItemClick` ❸, to show an alert message box displaying the data for the row that was right-clicked.

Next you configure a simple JavaScript object ❹ that'll be used by Ext JS to configure an instance of your custom `ContextMenuGridPanel` class. You accomplish this by setting the `xtype` property to `'contextmenugrid'`. Notice how you're configuring an array with a simple object as the menu property ❺. This will be used by your `Context-MenuGridPanel` class to create an instance of `Menu` and display it via the registered `itemcontextmenu` event handler.

Finally, you render the component inside a `Window` instance ❻. Figure 13.5 shows how it looks onscreen.

You can see that your custom grid panel works exactly as expected. You could import this code into your project and it'd work like a charm. But there are some cases where you might want to choose a plug-in instead of directly extending the grid panel to add this functionality. For example, what if you have an application that you're already developing or that's already in production? How do you inject this extension into your inheritance chain without inducing risk?

Or say you want to include this functionality in all types of data-bound views: grid, tree, and generic views. To accommodate this requirement, you'd have to create an extension to each of these classes, which would inject a lot of duplicate code.

The only real solution to this problem is a plug-in.

Figure 13.5   Using your custom grid panel extension for the first time

13.4   *Plug-ins to the rescue*

Plug-ins, which were introduced in Ext JS version 2.0, solve this problem by allowing you to distribute functionality across widgets without having to create extensions. What also makes plug-ins powerful is the fact that you can have any number of them attached to a component.

> **Component life cycle refresh**
>
> In case you don't remember when plug-ins are created and initialized, now would be an excellent time to brush up on the initialization phase of the component life cycle, which we covered in chapter 3.

Before we dive into creating plug-ins, let's have a quick chat about how plug-ins work.

13.4.1   *The anatomy of a plug-in*

The basic anatomy of a plug-in is simple. It starts out by defining your class and extending the `AbstractPlugin` class:

```
Ext.define('MyPlugin', {
  extend : 'Ext.AbstractPlugin',
  alias : 'plugins.myplugin'
  // do stuff
});
```

This snippet demonstrates the basics of creating a plug-in using `Ext.define`. When creating plug-ins, you'll find it best to extend the `Ext.AbstractPlugin` class, because it provides the necessary functionality to manage the destruction of plug-ins after their parent self-destructs.

In the template you set up an `alias` as `'plugins.myplugin'`. You prefix your plug-in alias with `plugins` to allow the Ext JS class-management system to route the registration of this class with `PluginManager`, which will be responsible for creating instances of your classes via lazy objects—much like XTypes, except they're known as PTypes in this case.

Here's an example of how you'd use a lazy object to configure this plug-in in a generic component instance:

```
Ext.create('Ext.Component', {
    plugins : [
        {
            ptype : 'myplugin'
        }
    ]
});
```

In this code you create an instance of `Ext.Component` and set its `plugins` property to an array with a single object. The single object has a `ptype` property set as `'myplugin'`. When the component nears the end of its initialization phase, it'll create an instance of your custom plug-in via this PType shortcut.

Extending `AbstractPlugin` is considered to be best practice by the Sencha core development team, so you'll use it when you create your custom plug-in.

13.4.2 Developing a plug-in

We just discussed the anatomy of a plug-in class. We showed you the basics of how to register a plug-in and configure it via a simple PType configuration object. You'll use this knowledge to create your custom `ViewContextMenu` plug-in class in the next listing.

Listing 13.7 Your custom view plug-in

```
Ext.define('MyApp.plugin.ViewContextMenu', {          ← Defines ViewContextMenu
    extend : 'Ext.AbstractPlugin',                    ❶ plug-in
    alias  : 'plugin.viewcontextmenu',

    init : function() {
        if (this.menu) {                                        ← Defines init
            if (! (this.menu instanceof Ext.menu.Menu)) {      ❸ method
                this.menu = this.buildMenu(this.menu);
            }

            this.cmp.on({                                       ← Registers
                scope             : this,                       itemcontextmenu
                itemcontextmenu   : this.onItemContextMenu     ❹ listener
            });
        }
    },
    buildMenu : function(menuCfg) {
        if (Ext.isArray(menuCfg)) {
            menuCfg = {
                items : menuCfg
            };
        }
```

Sets PType alias ❷

```
            return Ext.create('Ext.menu.Menu', menuCfg);
        },
        onItemContextMenu : function(view, model, row, index, evt) {
            evt.stopEvent();
            this.menu.showAt(evt.getXY());
        },
        destroy : function() {
            if (this.menu && this.menu.destroy) {
                this.menu.destroy();
            }
        }
    }
});
```

⟵ ❺ **Destroys instantiated menu**

Looking at listing 13.7, you can see that most of the code is the same as in your extension. The difference is that you're defining a class ❶, which extends `AbstractPlugin`. Following best practice, you set the plug-in alias accordingly ❷.

Next you create an `init` method ❸, which is responsible for detecting the plug-in and registering the view's `itemcontextmenu` event handler ❹. The `destroy` method ❺ is responsible for destroying the instance of the menu that was instantiated.

To use this plug-in, you can reuse almost all of the code that you wrote in listing 13.6. The biggest change is the way you configure the grid panel. The next listing shows the implementation difference.

Listing 13.8   Configuring and showing the grid panel

```
// Model, Store, and Menu click handler from Listing 13.6 go here
var grid = {
    xtype    : 'grid',
    store    : remoteJsonStore,
    columns : [
        {
            header    : 'Last Name',
            dataIndex : 'lastname',
            flex      : 1
        },
        {
            header    : 'First Name',
            dataIndex : 'firstname',
            flex      : 1
        }
    ],
    plugins : [
        {
            ptype : 'viewcontextmenu',
            menu  : [
                {
                    text    : 'Add Record',
                    handler : onMenuItemClick
                }
            ]
        }
    ]
```

⟵ ❶ **Adds grid panel**

⟵ ❷ **Configures plug-in**

```
};
// Window code to display the grid Panel here
```

In listing 13.8 you configure a generic grid panel xtype object ❶ that uses the custom ViewContextMenu plug-in you configured earlier, and you display it via an Ext.Window. In this implementation you configured only one plug-in via the plugins reference. If you had more than one, you'd configure an array of plug-ins ❷, such as plugins : [plugin1, plugin2, etc].

Rendering this onscreen, you can see that you have the same functionality as your grid panel extension, as shown in figure 13.6.

If you want to read the source code for other, more complex plug-ins, you can look at the Ext JS SDK examples/ux folder, which has a few examples. Two plug-ins we'll mention here were initially contributed by this author (Jay) in the early 3.0 days and are now maintained by the Sencha development team.

The first, shown in figure 13.7, is known as TabScrollerMenu (TabScrollerMenu.js). This plug-in adds a menu to scrolling tab panels and allows users to select and focus a

Figure 13.6　Using your custom grid panel extension for the first time

Figure 13.7　The TabScrollerMenu plug-in

Figure 13.8   A plug-in that adds an animated progress bar to the paging toolbar

tab panel much more easily than if they had to scroll. To see this plug-in in action, navigate to the <your extjs dir>/examples/tabs/tab-scroller-menu.html URL in your browser.

The second, shown in figure 13.8, is known as the ProgressBar paging toolbar (ProgressBarPager.js), which adds an animated progress bar to the paging toolbar widget, making the paging toolbar much nicer to look at. To view this plug-in in action, point your browser to <your extjs dir>/examples/build/KitchenSink/ext-theme-neptune/#progress-bar-pager.

This concludes our exploration of plug-ins. You now know how to create plug-ins that'll enhance functionality in your projects. If you have an idea for a plug-in and aren't sure whether it's been done before, visit the Ext JS forums at http://sencha.com/forum. An entire section is dedicated to user extensions and plug-ins. Fellow community members have posted their work there, some of which is completely free to use.

Sencha has a nice collection of user extensions that you can download at its own marketplace. You can visit it at http://market.sencha.com.

Next let's discuss using the Ext JS class loader system. You'll need this information as you start developing your applications. Trust us! It's going to save you a lot of time.

13.5   *Dynamically loading classes with the Ext JS loader*

New to Ext JS 4 is a dynamic class loader system designed to make use of the dependency model. There are a few options to consider when developing your applications. Each option has its pros and cons, so we'll discuss each one in turn.

13.5.1   *Loading everything dynamically*

Ext JS gives you the option to load most JavaScript files dynamically. Loading the framework files dynamically gives you the capability to render an initial page quickly, which is ideal for internet-based applications.

```
(!) [Ext.Loader] Synchronously loading 'Ext.window.Window'; consider adding   ext-debug.js (line 6198)
    Ext.require('Ext.window.Window') above Ext.onReady
▶ GET http://ext4ia/ext4/src/window/Window.js?_dc=1308739656143   200 OK 6ms
▶ GET http://ext4ia/ext4/src/panel/Panel.js?_dc=1308739656160   200 OK 13ms
▶ GET http://ext4ia/ext4/src/panel/AbstractPanel.js?_dc=1308739656185   200 OK 9ms
▶ GET http://ext4ia/ext4/src/container/Container.js?_dc=1308739656203   200 OK 9ms
▶ GET http://ext4ia/ext4/src/container/AbstractContainer.js?_dc=1308739656221   200 OK 4ms
▶ GET http://ext4ia/ext4/src/Component.js?_dc=1308739656235   200 OK 11ms
▶ GET http://ext4ia/ext4/src/AbstractComponent.js?_dc=1308739656257   200 OK 11ms
▶ GET http://ext4ia/ext4/src/util/Observable.js?_dc=1308739656287   200 OK 10ms
▶ GET http://ext4ia/ext4/src/util/Animate.js?_dc=1308739656308   200 OK 11ms
```

Figure 13.9   The console view of Firebug, displaying a warning message from Ext JS as well as a log trace of the dynamically loaded classes

To do this you need to include the ext-all.css and ext-debug.js files. The head of your document should look like this:

```
<link rel="stylesheet" type="text/css"
      href="js/ext4/resources/css/ext-all.css" />
<script type="text/javascript" src="js/ext4/ext-debug.js"></script>
```

Loading ext-debug.js will load the debug version of the Ext JS foundation, which includes the base class system, utilities like observable and element, and the loader framework. This means that the rest of the framework itself isn't in memory; therefore, it needs to be loaded. To test things out, you'll need to render something onscreen.

Here's the code to render an `Ext.Window` onscreen:

```
Ext.onReady(function() {
  Ext.create('Ext.window.Window', {
    height : 100,
    width : 100,
    html  : 'I loaded dynamically.'
  }).show();
});
```

When viewing the page, you'll see that the Ext JS window renders onscreen; but in order to understand what's going on, you'll have to look under the hood. To do so, pop up a debug tool like Firebug (see figure 13.9).

When reading just the filenames of the classes loaded, you'll begin to notice that Ext JS is loading classes in a somewhat backward fashion. This has to do with the dependency system. To help you better understand this, figure 13.10 shows the Ext JS `Window` inheritance model.

The code instantiated an instance of `Ext.window.Window`, yet you see classes like `Panel` being loaded. You see the seemingly reversed loading pattern shown in figure 13.10 because `Window` requires `Panel`, and `Panel` requires

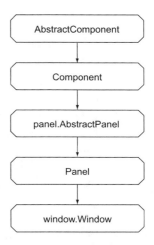

Figure 13.10   The Ext JS `Window` inheritance model

AbstractPanel. Ext JS loaded Window, read its dependencies, and then loaded Panel. It then read Panel's dependencies and loaded AbstractPanel, and so on.

Earlier, Ext JS warned you that it was synchronously loading the Window class. The reason it warns you is because it's loading the classes via synchronous XHR, meaning that the requests are blocking. When Ext JS executed your code to create the window, it churned through all the requirements, and no other JavaScript executed during that time.

This method of loading JavaScript classes is somewhat slower when you're trying to load a large chunk of the framework. We suggest using this approach if you want to use the minimal form of the framework for a quick render of something like a login screen. If the login is successful, you can invoke the loading of the required Ext JS class files.

The one thing we should caution you about regarding this pattern is that the JavaScript that's synchronously loaded by Ext JS can't be debugged due to the fact that scripts loaded via XHR are evaluated at runtime. There's a solution to this problem, but it requires just a tad more work on your end.

13.5.2 *Thou shalt require only what's needed*

Earlier you created an instance of Window within the confines of Ext.onReady. Though this is completely acceptable, you invoked the synchronous loading of the framework classes. The solution to this problem is to instruct Ext JS that you're requiring the use of the Window class but outside of Ext.onReady.

Here's the code to do just that:

```
Ext.require('Ext.window.Window');
Ext.onReady(function() {
    Ext.create('Ext.window.Window', {
        height : 100,
        width  : 100,
        html   : 'I loaded dynamically.'
    }).show();
});
```

Adding the require statement outside the Ext.onReady call instructs Ext JS to immediately load all dependencies for the Window class, and it does so in a manner that's easy to debug and that'll stop Ext JS from barking at you. This means that you should invoke a require statement for every class you'll ever use. Figure 13.11 shows a screenshot of the (live) HTML view in Firebug.

In figure 13.11 you can see a lot of script tags being added to the head of the document. These script tags were injected by Ext JS because you added the require statement before Ext.onReady, allowing Ext JS to load these classes via traditional script tags, which doesn't require the script to be eval'd. The greatest benefit of this technique is that it gives you the ability to debug the Ext JS JavaScript.

This method of using Ext JS gives you the best option for debugging issues because the classes are loaded individually, allowing you to isolate issues to a specific class. But

Figure 13.11   The Firebug live HTML view, demonstrating the dynamic loading of the Ext JS classes

it's slow. In our local development environment, we see over one second of load time for the page. The reason it's slow is because of the sheer number of requests needed for the class files to be loaded one by one. This obviously isn't the best pattern for rapid application development cycles.

You'll have to modify your approach a bit to remedy this situation.

13.5.3   *Taking the hybrid approach*

So far you've seen two approaches to using the loader to load Ext JS class files. Both approaches had their pros and cons. If you're on an intranet, where speed doesn't matter, then using a hybrid approach can give you the best of both worlds. You can load all of Ext JS in one request and then dynamically load your class files.

To explore this hybrid approach, we've included an extremely minimalistic application in the chapter 13 examples folder. The folder structure is shown in figure 13.12. When looking at the folder structure, notice that the files are organized on the disk according to their namespaces, which begin with `MyApp`.

Figure 13.12   The folder structure for our example application

This application contains an interdependency model that requires both Ext JS and classes within the namespace. Figure 13.13 illustrates the dependency model from a high level.

This interdependency model demonstrates that you can configure requirements for the application, which Ext JS will honor. Also, you won't have to write a single script tag for your application code. This is the single greatest benefit to using this approach.

To get this hybrid approach working, you must work through two steps. The first is to include ext-all-debug.js instead of ext-debug.js:

```
<script type="text/javascript" src="js/ext4/ext-all-debug.js"></script>
```

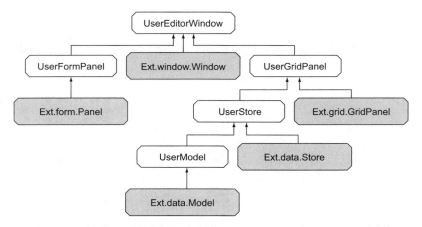

Figure 13.13   The top-level namespaced classes are the ones that you'll develop.

Including ext-all-debug.js will allow the entire Ext JS framework to load at one time, shaving more than half the time of the page load for you. The drawback to this approach is that, by default, the Ext JS loader system is disabled in this version of the framework.

You're going to have to enable the loader system and give it instructions for where your application code lives. To do so, include this code:

```
Ext.Loader.setConfig({
    enabled : true,
    paths    : {
        MyApp : 'js/MyApp'
    }
});

Ext.require('MyApp.view.UserEditorWindow');

Ext.onReady(function() {
    Ext.create('MyApp.view.UserEditorWindow').show();
});
```

In this code you call the `setConfig` method of the `Ext.Loader` singleton, passing in an object that enables the loader and sets up the path for your application. Next you instruct Ext JS to require the `MyApp.view.UserEditorWindow` class, and then the magic happens!

First you'll notice that the mini-application renders onscreen (figure 13.14). Though seeing the application pop up onscreen is cool, the magic is under the hood and can only be seen via the Firebug live HTML tab. What you'll see there is fascinating. Figure 13.15 shows you that all of Ext JS was loaded but your application classes were loaded dynamically. The best part about this is that you didn't have to fuss with script tags in your HTML page.

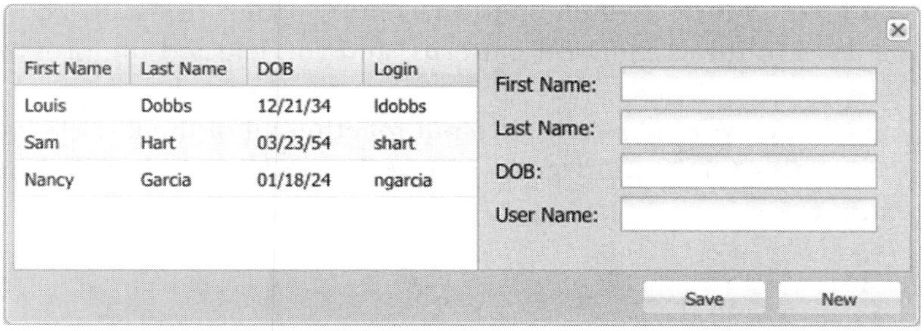

Figure 13.14   The mini-application you dynamically loaded

```
▶ <script type="text/javascript" src="js/MyApp/view/UserEditorWindow.js?_dc=1386253871119">
▶ <script type="text/javascript" src="js/MyApp/view/UsersGridPanel.js?_dc=1386253871179">
▶ <script type="text/javascript" src="js/MyApp/view/UserFormPanel.js?_dc=1386253871179">
▶ <script type="text/javascript" src="js/MyApp/store/UserStore.js?_dc=1386253871201">
▶ <script type="text/javascript" src="js/MyApp/model/UserModel.js?_dc=1386253871218">
```

Figure 13.15   The Firebug live HTML tab shows you that your classes are loaded via Ext JS, without you having to write script tags.

By now you're probably wondering where you go from here. Which loading pattern should you choose? Those are the right questions to be asking.

The truth is that the dynamic loader isn't recommended for production. For our development cycles, we use the third pattern (section 13.5.3). It offers the best performance for loading all of Ext JS in your local development environment as well as the ability to dynamically load all of your application code on demand.

For production, you'll want to use the SDK tools to concatenate and minify your application code in preparation for deployment. We'll discuss those tools in chapter 14.

13.6   Summary

In this chapter you learned how to implement the prototypal inheritance model using the basic JavaScript tools. You saw how this inheritance model is constructed step by step. Using that foundational knowledge, you refactored your subclass using the Ext.define class definition method.

Next, you took all of that foundational knowledge and applied it to the extension of an Ext JS grid panel, and you created a composite grid panel and a menu component. You implemented your custom grid panel extension and saw how cool extending components can be.

You then learned how extensions can be limited when reusability needs to span multiple widgets. To mitigate this problem, you converted the code in your grid panel extension into a plug-in that can be applied to any data view and its subclasses.

Finally, you learned how to implement the Ext JS loader. You saw firsthand how to use the loader with three common patterns, and you learned the pros and cons of each.

In the final chapter, you'll learn how to put together all of the knowledge you've gathered so far in this book, and you'll explore the trade secrets of building complex applications.

Building an application

This chapter covers

- Thinking like a web UI developer
- Understanding the Ext JS architecture
- Writing an MVC-based application
- Building with Sencha Cmd 3

So far in this book we've explained how to define, use, and manage Ext JS components, widgets, and data. We've walked you through creating just about every widget in the framework and discussed each of their intricacies. In the previous chapter we explained how to create custom Ext JS extensions and looked at how the class loader system works.

In this chapter you'll put to work all the knowledge you've gained in this book to create an application. You'll build on chapter 13's lessons and construct an application following the MVC development pattern by implementing the Ext JS App (Application) package. You'll explore how controllers work and learn how they're responsible for responding to events from your application classes. You'll also learn to create both testing and production builds using Sencha Cmd, the Sencha command-line toolset.

Before jumping into source code, let's review the principles of building and managing web applications. Whether your future apps are small or large, you should always follow the same principles described in this chapter.

14.1   Thinking as a web UI developer

Web applications have existed for almost as long as the web itself. The concept was largely popularized with the emergence of Google's Gmail in 2004. In the years that followed, three major principles of building web apps remained:

- Web is mobile
- Design for a single page
- Optimize server-side services (APIs)

The fastest web application is about:blank. Everything you build on top of it adds load and execution time. A "mobile first" way of thinking forces you to pack information lightly in anticipation of users with small screens, weak computers, and the ability to download only through a limited-bandwidth internet connection. We're not implying that you should use Ext JS for developing mobile applications. Instead, we're suggesting picturing a person on an old computer using your application. That will likely be your target user on a target platform.

Single-page apps are also known to be data-driven. To contrast the concept of multipage websites, a server won't prepare HTML views but will just serve data. A browser is responsible for formatting data as a meaningful representation, based on business logic converted into source code by you, the developer. All of this happens without page (re)loading. Modern browsers support this idea like never before, and you'll see how Ext JS can use this pattern.

As just mentioned, data is king in single-page web applications. That should be a good enough reason to pay more attention to how it's served. The best API is built for a purpose. Don't create universal connectors that send loads of data, just in case the app might need it. Send meaningful, targeted chunks that are content-specific, bandwidth-sensitive, and optimized for mobile.

Following the concepts described here, you're about to see how Ext JS can help you create an optimized, data-driven, single-page application. Let's kick things off with a discussion of architecture options.

14.2   Application (infra)structure

Consider an Ext JS application the motherboard of an app. Following the analogy, it's the place where all the components are plugged in. The motherboard uses dedicated controllers to establish communication channels among views, data, and user interactions.

The way an application is initially set up will influence its performance, scalability, and ultimately its maintainability. Using conventions and keeping the right discipline even for small projects will always yield great results and will also help when the project grows into something more serious. Rest assured, trading quality for the urge to save time by using quick-and-dirty implementations is a fantastic recipe for failure. You'll never have the resources to go back and refactor the app, because your little proof-of-concept app will most likely become serious production-level software.

One of the most basic principles when developing an application is to properly define classes. Make sure you do that right.

You're almost ready to start building your first fully featured Ext JS 4 application. Along the way, we'll go over many useful coding conventions, starting with namespacing. What can be a better start than giving your great product a name?

14.2.1 Development within a namespace

As you'll see later in this chapter, one of the first steps of setting up an application is choosing its name. Naming your application in your code isn't necessarily a marketing trick. It's the cornerstone of all further development.

You might already be familiar with the term *global pollution*. It refers to stuffing the global namespace with far too many references (variables). A common pitfall of using global variables in application programming is naming conflicts. What happens if you define two references with the same variable at different sections of the codebase? You have yet another debugging nightmare. That's why developers are encouraged to define a single global variable, called a *namespace*, to create their own little ecosystem. This is one of the base principles of object-oriented programming (OOP).

A browser environment already comes heavily polluted with numerous global variables. Table 14.1 is a breakdown of globally declared variables in several modern browsers in the about:blank page.

Table 14.1 Global pollution in about:blank

Browser	Number of declared variables
Google Chrome 23	559
Apple Safari 6	517
Mozilla Firefox 15	184
Opera 11.64	74
Internet Explorer 7	38

In a forest of declared variables, the last thing you want to do is rewrite one and alter the whole application's behavior. Furthermore, it's not unlikely that your application needs to access additional APIs, such as maps, analytics, other third-party libraries, or even other Ext JS applications.

When defining your namespace, you'll want to make sure it has these characteristics:

- *Concise*—Developers love to type less, and it helps with codebase size.
- *Unique*—Assign a meaningful name, not just *App*.

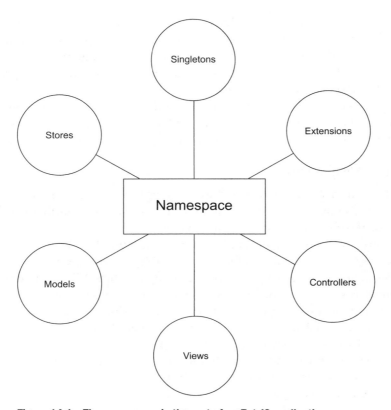

Figure 14.1   The namespace is the root of an Ext JS application.

In the Ext JS world, just as with many other structure-oriented programming frameworks, there are exact patterns you need to follow when forming class names. In this book we'll refer to the pattern as the *Namespace/Package/Class* (NPC) pattern.

The namespace is where application code begins. It's the root reference under which all the application's packages and classes are nested and subnested. Ideally, your whole application will add just two references to the browser's global namespace:

- *Ext JS*—the framework classes
- *Your namespace (for example, App)*—the application's classes

Your application's MVC code, as well as singletons, extensions, or any other code, should exist under the wing of your namespace (figure 14.1). Because you'll use the namespace frequently, it's generally a good idea to keep the name to under four characters. Just be sure not to lose the meaning. For example, names as generic as App could lead to confusion and code conflicts if you ever merge several project files together.

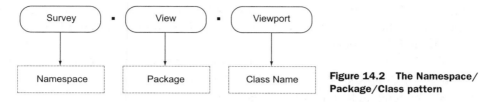

Figure 14.2 The Namespace/Package/Class pattern

As shown in figure 14.2, your newly defined class will form a name that consists of the following:

1. Application namespace (CamelCase)
2. Package name (lowercase, singular)
3. Class name (CamelCase)

Naturally, there will be only a single application namespace. In contrast, any given app is likely to have numerous classes, their number often reaching into the thousands. Packages are an effective solution for breaking apart code.

Packages are also great because you can nest them, as shown in figure 14.3. The first level of packaging will generally be one of the following seven options:

- Model
- View
- Controller
- Store
- Ux
- Util
- Component

All further nested packages should reflect the business logic of the application. You want to break down the app into logical sections, some of which will reflect application modules and submodules or abstraction layers.

The NPC pattern's naming conventions go beyond just naming. The pattern also defines the file and folder structure of a given class. This is where Ext.Loader, one of the most valuable features of Ext JS 4, kicks in.

14.2.2 *Dynamic dependency loading*

In the pre–Ext JS 4 world, you were stuck with hard-coding script tags for each JavaScript file needed for a project to run. We intentionally said *file* and not *class*,

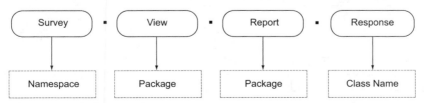

Figure 14.3 Nested packages

because this particular situation discouraged many developers from writing each class into its own file. In such a case, larger applications would have enormous HTML files with hundreds of coded script tags.

Ext JS 4 ships with Ext.Loader, a useful feature that allows for the automatic inclusion of dependencies. Its functionality is twofold:

- On-demand loading when a class is needed
- Boot-time inclusion of specifically outlined dependencies

On demand (or on the fly) is more of a fire extinguisher than a cool feature on which applications should rely. It detects your failure to let the application know of the prerequisites and then loads the missing class files synchronously. Such incidents are also reported in the browser's console, allowing you to go back to code and properly set dependencies.

The new class system offers several methods to directly or indirectly define dependencies. A common thread is that they all belong to the `Ext.define` configuration. Let's take a look:

- `requires`—Dependencies required for a class to be *defined* (blocking)
- `uses`—Dependencies required for a class to be *instantiated* (non-blocking)
- `controllers`—Controllers used by an application
- `models`—Models used by a controller
- `views`—Views used by a controller
- `stores`—Stores used by a controller
- `extend`—The class being extended in `Ext.define`
- `override`—The class being overridden in `Ext.define`

In order for Ext.Loader to load dependencies, you need to properly store class files. By default, the loader will expand full class names, separated by dots. That means each package will become a subfolder, and each class name will be counted as a file with a trailing .js extension. As an exception, the topmost package, more precisely your namespace (`Survey`), will be translated into a predefined folder name: app. Figure 14.4 illustrates the process.

Keeping this principle in mind, you'll find it easy to create the basic file and folder structure. Figure 14.5 shows the structure used in the application you'll create in this chapter.

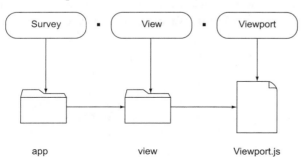

app   view   Viewport.js

Figure 14.4 Conversion of class names into folders and files

Figure 14.5 File and folder structure per naming conventions

Opening an Ext.Loader-enabled application will require access to a web server. This is because it makes use of XHR (Ajax), and browsers don't allow XHR requests to a local file system. But there's a simple trick you can use to make your browser send Ajax requests even without a web server. All you need to do is to start your Google Chrome browser with security turned off and open index.html as a regular local file.

A warning about disabling web security

Disabling web security renders your browser defenseless against malicious scripts. We strongly suggest that you disable web security only with a browser installation dedicated to application testing and debugging. Be aware of the risks involved when browsing external websites.

Here's how you disable Chrome security with various common operating systems.
   Windows (command prompt):

```
chrome.exe -disable-web-security
```

Mac OS X (terminal):

```
open -a Google\ Chrome --args --disable-web-security
```

Linux (terminal):

```
chrome –disable-web-security
```

We'll discuss dependencies in greater depth when you start building your MVC application later in this chapter. Until then, let's explore what the application is going to look like.

14.3 *Kicking off the Survey app*

Every app starts with an idea, followed by a series of wireframes. Through the rest of the chapter you'll follow an idea, build an application based on a wireframe, and finally test the end result.

The idea behind the final project is a survey delivery platform, creatively called Survey. Its sole purpose is to present authenticated users with dynamically generated forms, capture input, and sync with the data source. Concepts you want to embrace here include

- CRUD operations through models and stores
- Data delivery through associations
- Dynamic generation of components from data
- Packaging with Sencha Cmd

14.3.1 *From idea to code*

Survey is a data-driven MVC application. Let's take a moment to investigate the workflow:

1 Users will need to authenticate to receive the applicable surveys and survey data.
2 A user can access more than one survey.
3 Survey questions are grouped into logical sections.
4 Questions are presented one group at a time.
5 Users can jump to surveys and groups as desired.
6 Input data is saved as soon as a new entry is made.
7 Forms are dynamically created based on data received from the server.

Following these guidelines, you'll create a fully functional application. Moreover, you'll have plenty of areas in which to experiment and that you can improve with new features. The final product will look like figure 14.6.

Building user interfaces is like cooking; you spend at least half the time in preparation, gathering all the ingredients and kitchenware to be close at hand when the time to use them comes. We hope your hands are itching with excitement to build this!

To get started, follow the 11-step Sencha Application Workflow (11-SAW) step by step (see figure 14.7). You typically begin by creating some folders and files, but

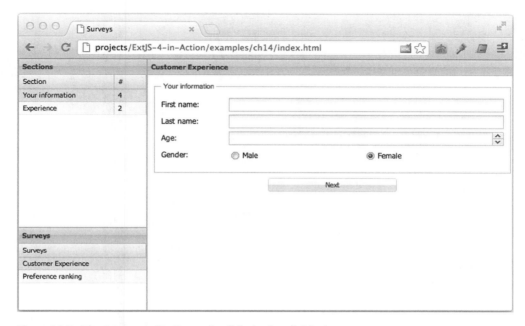

Figure 14.6   The Survey application as it will look when finished

what if we told you that you don't need to do the first three steps manually and can have someone else generate all that for you? You got it: Sencha Cmd can do that for you.

14.3.2 *Moving to the fast track with Sencha Cmd*

Sencha Cmd is a set of command-line utilities that make it easier for a developer to generate an app; add models, views, or controllers; and, most important, create customized builds of the app. Sencha Cmd doesn't ship with the framework, so you'll have to download it from Sencha's website.

To fully utilize Cmd, you'll need to do the following:

1   Download and install a Java Runtime Environment (JRE), version 6 or greater.
2   Download and install the Compass CSS authoring framework (and additional dependencies, such as Ruby, as required).
3   Download and install Sencha Cmd.
4   Download and extract the latest Ext JS SDK package (4.1.2 or later).

Sencha Cmd version

Please note that the Survey application was built using Sencha Cmd v4.0.0.203. Changes in behavior and configuration are possible in any other build.

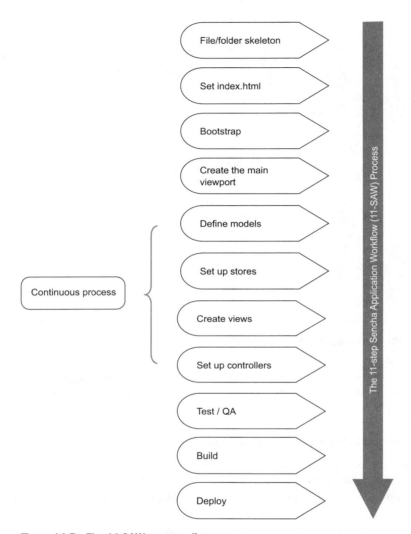

Figure 14.7   The 11-SAW process diagram

The first step you need to take is to generate the app. Open a command-line terminal, and make sure you navigate to the directory that contains the Ext JS SDK package. Now run

```
sencha generate app Survey /path/to/Survey
```

This is all you need to do from the SDK folder right now. Feel free to navigate to /path/to/Survey (change /path/to/ to a path that suits you best, but make sure it's outside of your Ext JS SDK directory), and let's look (figure 14.8).

As you can see in figure 14.8, Sencha Cmd has done quite a bit of work for us:

- Copied the Ext JS SDK files, including only necessary content (no examples or documentation).
- Created a fully functional index.html file.
- Created app.js, a foundation for the application bootstrap.
- Created the MVC skeleton.
- Set up the SASS (Syntactically Awesome Style Sheets) theming project.
- Created a resources folder for storing media files such as images.
- Created empty readme.md files to keep your folders from disappearing in some source control management systems like GIT. Feel free to remove them, but make sure you have at least one file in the respective folder first.
- Set up its private hidden metadata folder and several auto-generated configuration files. Each of them will show a commented message allowing or disallowing manual edits.

Saving you all this work isn't the only benefit of generating the app. Major keys to success in application development are discipline and the ability to stick with conventions.

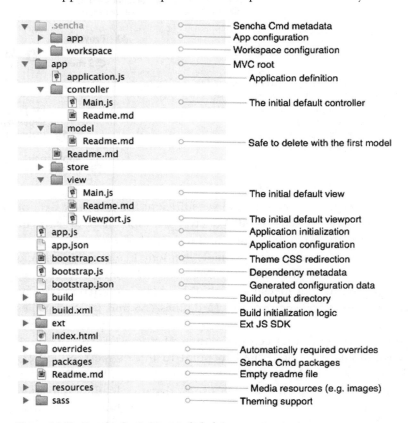

Figure 14.8   Sencha Cmd-generated skeleton

These two points are exactly what you're going to achieve with this application. You'll be disciplined enough to cut corners only where doing so benefits you in the long run. Elsewhere, you'll follow Sencha-suggested application design conventions.

Now that you have some content generated, let's see what you can work with. In the pages to come, you'll go over the application initialization files and decide which data formats you want to use for your models.

14.3.3 Bootstrapping Survey

If you've been following the process on your computer and have generated the app on your own, you've probably already taken a sneak peek at index.html (listing 14.1) and the auto-generated JavaScript files. We encourage everyone to follow the procedure all the way through. Having said that, it's time to explore exactly what the generated app is made of, as shown in the following listing.

Listing 14.1   Generated index.html source

```
<!DOCTYPE HTML>
<html>
<head>
    <meta charset="UTF-8">
    <title>Survey</title>
    <!-- <x-compile> -->
        <!-- <x-bootstrap> -->
            <link rel="stylesheet" href="bootstrap.css">
            <script src="ext/ext-dev.js"></script>
            <script src="bootstrap.js"></script>
        <!-- </x-bootstrap> -->
        <script src="app.js"></script>
    <!-- </x-compile> -->
</head>
<body></body>
</html>
```

❶ HTML5 doctype
❷ Sencha Cmd app bootstrap flag
❸ Provides default CSS sheet
❹ Specifies minimal SDK package
❺ Ext JS dependency mappings
❻ Application initialization

The index page is created to be minimal yet sufficient for your new Ext application. The first thing you'll notice is the HTML5 doctype ❶, which not only saves quite a few bytes, but also helps Ext JS get the most out of modern browsers.

Sencha Cmd also created a few comments that look like opening and closing tags in XML, and that's exactly what they are. Concealed in comments, `<x-compile>` ❷ signals the area that includes special logic that should be modified in the Cmd compilation phase. Within it, `<x-bootstrap>` ❸ defines CSS and JavaScript files used to bootstrap Ext JS.

The bootstrap.css file ❹ redirects to the theme being used. This file should not be edited and is automatically generated to point to the theme CSS. Ext JS is called through the ext-dev.js file ❺, loading a bare minimum of the SDK, and everything else follows dynamically. The dependency list for dynamic loading is located in bootstrap.js ❻, another file that is automatically generated; thus you're advised not to manually edit it. At this point, the browser knows how to support your application with styles and SDK, so it's safe to call for app.js.

The entire block defined with `<x-compile>` is valid for your development environment only. Later in this chapter, we'll discuss application-building steps that will change this block in the interest of performance.

> ### What's minification?
> The internet, as a medium for data distribution, can be provided to end users at a quality beyond your expectations. Reducing the amount of data sent can deliver the information faster and require less bandwidth, potentially incurring lower internet charges for your customers. The process of removing unnecessary parts of JavaScript code without altering its functionality is called *minification*. These parts often include white space, comments, and new-line characters, but minification can go as far as reference renaming and beyond. Although minified code is harder to read, minification shouldn't be confused with obfuscation, a form of cryptography.

For our purposes, you won't rely on index.html beyond what's generated by the Sencha Cmd app-generation process. But what index.html does for web pages, app.js does for Ext JS applications. It's the starting point from which all other code will be executed. Let's move on to see how the app is bootstrapped in the next listing.

Listing 14.2 Generated app.js source

```
Ext.application({                    ❶ Application
    name: 'Survey',                      initialization
    extend: 'Survey.Application',    ❷ Application and
    autoCreateViewport: true             namespace name
});                                  ❸ Inherits from
                                         Survey.Application
                                     ❹ Shows viewport
                                         immediately
```

`Ext.application` ❶ is a special method call that does nothing but load the `Survey` `.Application` ❸ class together with its dependencies and initialize it. It also gets familiar with the application namespace ❷ to help recognize which classes can be dynamically loaded when requested.

This is a great place to review figure 14.4, where we discussed how dependencies are converted to paths for dynamic loading. Because we said that the app's namespace is `Survey`, `Ext.Loader` knows that `Survey.Application` is located in the ./app/Application.js file.

When all the JavaScript is loaded and the document is ready, Ext creates the viewport automatically ❹. Before we jump to the viewport discussion, let's see how to configure the application in the `Survey.Application` class.

Listing 14.3 Application definition

```
Ext.define('Survey.Application', {
    name: 'Survey',                  ❶ Application
                                         name(space)
    extend: 'Ext.app.Application',
```

```
    views: [
        // TODO: add views here
    ],

    controllers: [
        // TODO: add controllers here
    ],

    stores: [
        // TODO: add stores here
    ]
});
```

② MVC dependencies

The Survey.Application class is a natural extension of the Ext.app.Application class that informs the application about models, views, stores, and controllers. The application uses Ext.Loader to load the required files, execute them, and register each according to its functionality, respectively.

Ext.app.Application extends Ext.app.Controller, which makes it the primary controller as well. Thus they share almost all configuration options, apart from the name property. In a few pages you'll learn more about controllers.

You'll notice two gotchas in listing 14.3:

- The name property ❶ is repeated in the Survey.Application and Ext.application calls (listing 14.2). This is more for code organization purposes than functionality. It's safe to omit it in the Survey.Application definition, but it's imperative that the name be stated in the Ext.application call.
- Models aren't listed in the generated class definition ❷. Nevertheless, the application needs to know about them, and you'll add them later.

You'll populate this class with models, controllers, and stores. Only the views, models, and stores that belong to the application globally, or are shared between application sections (modules), should be listed here. In this case, you'll bind views and stores to the respective controller configuration in an effort to produce a more structured and modular application.

VIEWPORT

One special type of view stands out from the crowd: the application viewport. A viewport is the pivotal point for all views in the application. It is, for a single-page application, what <body> is for HTML elements. It often carries central navigational elements as well as a notification console, and it acts as a cradle for all major views in the application. Only one viewport can exist on a page.

As shown in listing 14.2, the viewport can be automatically created when the document becomes ready for DOM manipulations. Ext JS will automatically search for the view.Viewport class. In this case, that's Survey.view.Viewport. So let's provide it.

Before you start building a codebase, spend a few moments thinking about what you want to achieve. Going back to your application requirements, you'll recall that only registered users can access Survey. This means you should offer a registration form. Because the authenticated users will likely sign out at a certain point in time, choose the card layout type for the viewport so that transition from the authentication form and back is faster. The following listing shows how to create your viewpoint (this is only a stub).

Listing 14.4   Viewport stub

```
Ext.define('Survey.view.Viewport', {
    extend : 'Ext.container.Viewport',
    alias  : 'widget.vp',

    layout : {
        type : 'card'
    }
});
```

Usually `Viewport` is an extension of `Ext.container.Viewport`. This is a special class that automatically occupies 100% of the width and height available to the document body. Such a viewport doesn't allow scrolling; individual components will have to specifically enable it. Finally, you give it the XType `vp` for easier access in the future, and set its layout type to `'card'`.

NOTE   Sencha Cmd already created a sample of this file for you. You can modify it per listing 14.3 instead of re-creating it from scratch if you want. Another auto-generated view is in Main.js, which you can safely delete because you won't be using it.

With four steps of the 11-SAW process completed, let's review what you've achieved and prepare for the next step: data modeling.

14.3.4 *Data-driven application model*

If you run the current application in a browser, you'll get nothing but an empty page. This is a good sign: you'll start working on views after you set up data models. After all, it's going to be a data-driven application.

At this point, the 11-SAW process instructs you to define models. Think about this. What kind of models do you anticipate needing? Obviously you'll need a list of surveys, so you should define what a survey looks like. Furthermore, surveys are made of questions, which means you should have a model that defines a question, too. And questions belong to groups, so you should define a group as well. As this quick brainstorming reveals, your models will be

- Survey
- Group
- Question

Before rolling up your sleeves, spend some more time thinking. Only when you reach the essence of an idea can you invent with simplicity. The models you'll create are all connected to one another. A survey has groups, and each group has one or more questions. Because they're all so nicely connected, why not use model associations?

Associations are going to be helpful if you want to download all your data at once and have the topmost model push items to respective models.

It sounds a little ambiguous. In the next listing, you'll create a sample data object, which will help you figure it out.

Listing 14.5   Expected data object

```
[
    {
        id      : 1,
        name    : 'Sample Survey',                    ❶ Adds
        groups  : [                                      association key
            {
                id        : 11,
                name      : 'Sample Group',
                survey_id : 1,                        ❷ Sets
                questions : [                            foreign key
                    {
                        id        : 111,
                        survey_id : 1,
                        group_id  : 11,
                        question  : 'Sample Question',
                        config    : {                 ❸ Configures
                            xtype : 'textarea'           question field
                        }
                    }
                ]
            }
        ]
    }
]
```

In only 20 lines of code, you realize a great deal about the data. Surveys are as plain as it gets; just a name and identification are all you need. Surveys carry a special property, groups ❶, that represents an array of question groups. This is also known as a *has many* association.

Groups are just as simple. Each group has another special property, survey_id ❷. Its purpose is to associate a group with a survey, also known as the *foreign key*. Just like surveys, groups also have a *has many* association with questions.

A question is a bit more complex. It has all the properties needed to configure a field. Notice the config property ❸ that could accept virtually any configuration property for Ext.field.Field or any of its subclasses.

Next you'll set each of the models and its respective stores.

14.3.5   Adding models to the application

The Survey model will consist of just two fields:

- id
- name

In addition to setting up the fields, you'll define associations and the data proxy. The final code is shown in the next listing.

Listing 14.6   Survey model

```
Ext.define('Survey.model.Survey', {
    extend : 'Ext.data.Model',

    requires : [
        'Ext.data.association.HasMany'
    ],
    uses : [
        'Survey.model.Group'
    ],
    associations : [
        {
            type            : 'hasMany',
            model           : 'Survey.model.Group',
            primaryKey      : 'id',
            foreignKey      : 'survey_id',
            autoLoad        : true,
            associationKey  : 'groups',
            name            : 'groups'
        }
    ],

    proxy : {
        type   : 'ajax',
        url    : 'data.json',
        reader : {
            type : 'json'
        }
    },

    fields : [
        {
            name : 'id'
        },
        {
            name : 'name'
        }
    ]
});
```

① Adds associated model

② Populates groups

③ Lists groups data

④ Configures groups method

⑤ Adds proxy configuration

⑥ Sets list of fields

You know that surveys are associated with groups. Thus, you're making sure the class knows that it depends on the model.Group class ①. A survey can have many groups, which means it has a hasMany association type ②. In the association configuration, you use the associationKey property ③ to enable automatic group population. Groups will exist in property groups. Finally, you access the groups through the groups method ④ and listen with the name configuration. You'll return to this model class once you plug it into the views.

Setting up associations was perhaps the most intensive part of defining the Survey model. Next you set up a proxy ❺ so that a `Model` instance knows where the store pulls data from and how to complete the rest of CRUD operations. You won't need to duplicate the proxy setup when configuring the store; it will be automatically shared. Finally, `fields` configuration ❻ takes place with a simple mention of expected field names.

`Survey.model.Survey` is now able to understand where surveys come from and how to identify the fields, and it's aware that groups should be processed through another model, `Survey.model.Group`.

The Group model (listing 14.7) is a lot like Survey, with two major changes:

- There's no communication with a server.
- It receives data from the Survey model and forwards questions to the Question model; thus it has a `belongsTo` and a `hasMany` association.

Listing 14.7   Group model

```
Ext.define('Survey.model.Group', {
    extend : 'Ext.data.Model',

    requires : [
        'Ext.data.association.HasMany',
        'Ext.data.association.BelongsTo'
    ],

    uses : [
        'Survey.model.Survey',
        'Survey.model.Question'
    ],

    fields : [
        {
            name : 'id'
        },
        {
            name : 'survey_id'
        },
        {
            name : 'name'
        },
        {
            name : 'index'
        }
    ],

    associations : [
        {
            type       : 'belongsTo',
            model      : 'Survey.model.Survey',
            primaryKey : 'id',
            foreignKey : 'survey_id'
        },
```

❶ Confirms association with Survey model

```
        {
            type              : 'hasMany',
            model             : 'Survey.model.Question',
            primaryKey        : 'id',
            foreignKey        : 'group_id',
            autoLoad          : true,
            associationKey    : 'questions',
            name              : 'questions'
        }
    ],

    proxy : {
        type    : 'memory'
    }
});
```

❷ Adds hasMany association

❸ Configures memory proxy

Because Survey is associated with Group, the latter needs to return the favor and set a belongsTo association back to Survey ❶. Group acts as the go-between; it receives data from Survey, and then forwards some to Question—hence the hasMany association with Group ❷.

Groups are read-only. They also receive data from another model, which is why it's sufficient to set the memory type of proxy ❸. Setting a proxy is mandatory.

The final model is straightforward, as shown in the following listing. You need to set up the fields and a single belongsTo association, connecting questions to groups.

Listing 14.8   Question model

```
Ext.define('Survey.model.Question', {
    extend : 'Ext.data.Model',

    requires : [
        'Ext.data.association.BelongsTo'
    ],

    uses : [
        'Survey.model.Group'
    ],

    fields : [
        {
            name : 'id'
        },
        {
            name : 'group_id'
        },
        {
            name : 'question'
        },
        {
            name : 'answer'
        },
        {
            name : 'config'
        }
    ],
```

```
    belongsTo : [
        {
            model       : 'Survey.model.Group',
            foreignKey : 'group_id'
        }
    ],

    proxy : {
        type    : 'memory'
    }
});
```

The Question model is the one responsible for dynamic form generation. That's why it essentially consists of properties that determine generated field configuration. The `question` property holds the question label, and you use it as the `fieldLabel` property of an `Ext.field.Field` subclass. Similarly, the `answer` property holds a newly recorded value, or even retrieves a previously saved entry from a server. Any other configuration parameter, including `xtype`, can be specified in the `config` field.

Models do most of the heavy lifting when it comes to data. They represent a collection of data and their fields, are able to normalize and validate data bound to them, and know how to relate to other models through associations. But models represent only a single record definition. You still need to set up the warehouse for all the `Model` instances: stores.

14.3.6   *Adding data stores*

All three stores will mirror the same definition, thanks to the detailed setup of the respective models. Let's take a look at a store in the next listing.

> **Listing 14.9   Surveys store**

```
Ext.define('Survey.store.Surveys', {
    extend : 'Ext.data.Store',

    requires : [
        'Survey.model.Survey'
    ],

    storeId   : 'Surveys',
    autoLoad : true,
    model     : 'Survey.model.Survey'
});
```

By now you're familiar with how data stores work. In this example you're referencing the model name and a `storeId` that'll make it easier to refer to a store with a view. You only have to point a view to the `storeId`, and the view component can instantiate the store if necessary. Otherwise it'll reuse the existing instance.

Defining data structure is a hard job, requiring the architect to plan ahead and make important decisions early in the process. Choosing the right data models will

> **Naming conventions notice**
> Models define the configuration of a single record, whereas stores define the configuration of a set of `Model` instances. For that reason models are always named in the singular and stores in the plural: for example, `Survey.model.Survey` and `Survey.store.Surveys`.

affect the client-side performance, the bandwidth consumed, and, ultimately, the user experience.

Often, server-side limitations will influence client-side data models. For example, server administrators might have limited resources to format their existing API to send the data needed for the Ext JS application to work. In such cases, make sure the compromise will make the least negative impact on the client side. In our example, the server admin should strive to strip unnecessary parts of data objects, format to JSON instead of XML, use compression, lessen recursion, and perform any other tricks that'd benefit the client side. Client computers are likely to be weaker than servers, and you don't want users to experience any holdups.

We're halfway through the 11-SAW process, and you're making great progress. You'll continue building views and controllers so that you can track progress in a browser.

14.3.7 Creating the authentication form

The landing page of the Survey application is the authorization form. The goal is to have users enter their credentials and allow them through to survey selection. The viewport is a card layout container, so you can place the authentication form (see figure 14.9) as the first child of the view. Once the user is successfully signed in, the viewport will switch to the second card, the survey list.

You'll place the authorization form right in the middle of the page. Let's go over the view details:

- It's centered on the screen.
- Fields are enclosed in a fieldset component.
- Fields are anchored at 100%.
- Login button spans the entire available width.

The following listing is a good review of how forms and layouts work.

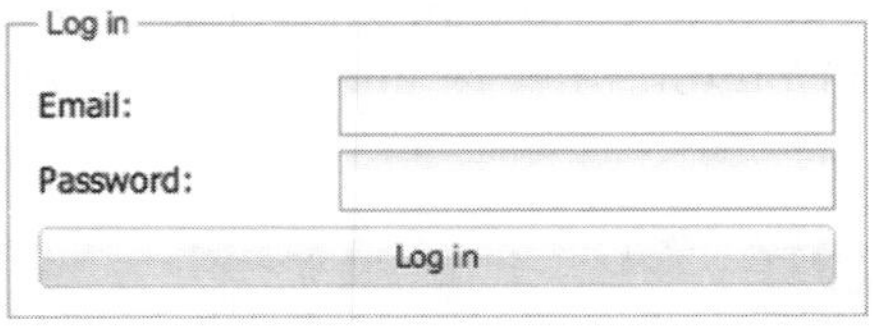

Figure 14.9 Authentication form design

Listing 14.10   Authorization view

```
Ext.define('Survey.view.AuthorizationForm', {
    extend : 'Ext.form.Panel',
    alias  : 'widget.authform',

    requires: [
        'Ext.form.field.Text',
        'Ext.form.FieldSet',
        'Ext.Button'
    ],

    layout : {
        align : 'center',                    ❶ Centers
        pack  : 'center',                      fieldset
        type  : 'hbox'
    },

    items : [
        {                                    ❷ Adds
            xtype : 'fieldset',                fieldset
            width : 300,
            title : 'Log in',
            items : [
                {
                    xtype      : 'textfield',
                    anchor     : '100%',
                    fieldLabel : 'Email'
                },
                {
                    xtype      : 'textfield',
                    anchor     : '100%',
                    inputType  : 'password',
                    fieldLabel : 'Password'
                },
                {
                    xtype  : 'button',
                    anchor : '100%',
                    itemId : 'loginBtn',
                    text   : 'Log in'
                }
            ]
        }
    ]
});
```

The VBox layout ❶ ensures items are both vertically centered and packed to the horizontal center. fieldset ❷ contains the fields used to input the email and password for authentication. Just like the Confirm button, they're anchored to 100% of the available width.

Extra credit

How will the layout be affected if you change VBox to HBox?

The next listing adds an empty component to the main viewport that'll represent the protected area.

Listing 14.11   Adding the form to the viewport

```
items : [
    {
        xtype : 'authform'
    },
    {
        xtype : 'component',
        html  : 'Protected area'
    }
]
```

Add the listing 14.11 code to `Survey.view.Viewport`. The first card, the authorization form, will show by default when the viewport becomes visible. The second one, the protected area component, will only become active upon successful authentication.

Note that the protected view is in another card without further security mechanisms applied. A malicious user could easily replace active cards. Security procedures vary from application to application, so we won't cover them here, but it's a good fact to be aware of.

You'll soon be able to see the changes in a browser. The next step is to create your first controller, which will listen for clicks on the Submit button, process the authentication, and finally show the protected area.

14.3.8   Plugging in the first controller

A controller's main purpose is to establish a communication channel between views, data, and user interaction. Controllers are an important element of the event-based development process. They capture component-fired events and work with them to ensure a fluid user experience. Controllers are aware of views, models, stores, and the application as the four main interaction sources and targets. Also, `Application` is a subclass of `Controller`. The most noticeable difference between the two is that a controller can't instantiate other controllers. That falls under `Application`'s legislation. The following listing is a great representation of a common controller's use.

Listing 14.12   Authentication controller

```
Ext.define('Survey.controller.Authentication', {
    extend : 'Ext.app.Controller',

    views : [                                        ❶ Configures
        'AuthorizationForm'                              views
    ],

    init : function (application) {
        this.control({                               ❷ Creates click
            "button#loginBtn" : {                        handler
                click : this.onLoginClick
            }
```

```
        });
    },
    onLoginClick : function (button) {
        // process authentication...
        button.up('vp').getLayout().setActiveItem(1);
    }
});
```

Although controllers are able to specify views, models, and stores as their dependencies, in this case you only need to specify a single view ❶: the authorization form. Controllers should only specify dependencies they really *control*, which is exactly why you won't specify any further views.

Developers often wonder which models, views, and stores to include in a controller. The rule of thumb says that you should think of those as meaningful, self-sufficient packages. Specify all classes the controller can't do its task without, and nothing more.

Just as `Ext.Component` has `initComponent`, a controller has its counterpart in the `init` method. It's most frequently used to execute the controller's `control` method. Similar to `addListener` in a component, `control` is responsible for finding all components that match a component query and assigning a listener to them ❷. Because controllers instantiate before views, `control` will intelligently work with all future-instantiated components.

Event handlers are usually defined within a controller. According to the convention, all events fired by components should have the firing instance sent as the first argument to the listening callback. Thus, a callback situated in a controller will have an easy way to access the component's instance reference.

This particular component is stripped of a real-life authentication process for simplicity's sake. With current functionality, users are able to input their email and password and click the Submission button, and the controller will send them to the next card in the main viewport. You should now create other views and controllers in this application.

14.3.9 *Survey views*

You're now familiar with the MVC process in Ext JS. Next you'll create view and controller definitions for the remaining classes. Views will be fairly simple, whereas controllers will take on some extra business logic work.

To be able to display the rest of the Survey app, three view types will be needed:

- *Survey list*—The listing of available surveys
- *Group list*—The listing of available groups for the selected survey
- *Questions form*—The host for dynamically created survey form fields

The next listing contains the code for the survey views.

Listing 14.13 Survey views

```
Ext.define('Survey.view.SurveyList', {          ⟵┐  Adds List of
    extend : 'Ext.grid.Panel',                    ❶  surveys
    alias  : 'widget.surveylist',
```

```
    title        : 'Surveys',
    columnLines : false,
    store        : 'Surveys',
    cls          : 'surveylist',
```
◄─── **2** **Hides grid panel header**
```
    columns : [
        {
            xtype      : 'gridcolumn',
            flex       : 1,
            dataIndex : 'name',
            text       : 'Surveys'
        }
    ]
});

Ext.define('Survey.view.GroupList', {
    extend : 'Ext.grid.Panel',
    alias  : 'widget.grouplist',
```
◄─── **3** **Defines GroupList view**
```
    title        : 'Sections',
    columnLines : true,
    store        : 'Groups',
    cls          : 'groupList',

    columns : [
        {
            flex       : 1,
            dataIndex : 'name',
            text       : 'Section'
        },
        {
            xtype      : 'numbercolumn',
            width      : 50,
            text       : '#',
            renderer : function (value, meta, record) {
                return record.questions().getCount();
            }
        }
    ]
});
```
4 **Calculates number of questions** ◄───
```
Ext.define('Survey.view.QuestionsForm', {
    extend : 'Ext.form.Panel',
    alias  : 'widget.questions',
```
◄─── **5** **Defines QuestionsForm class**
```
    requires : [
        'Ext.form.field.Checkbox',
        'Ext.form.field.ComboBox',
        'Ext.form.field.Date',
        'Ext.form.field.Display',
        'Ext.form.field.Hidden',
        'Ext.form.field.HtmlEditor',
        'Ext.form.field.Number',
        'Ext.form.field.Picker',
        'Ext.form.field.Radio',
        'Ext.form.field.Spinner',
        'Ext.form.field.Text',
        'Ext.form.field.TextArea',
```
◄─── **6** **Requires all field types**

```
        'Ext.form.field.Time',
        'Ext.form.RadioGroup',
        'Ext.form.CheckboxGroup'
    ],
    layout : {                          ❼  Centers all
        type  : 'vbox',                    child items
        align : 'center'
    }
});
```

To display the list of available surveys, you use a grid panel ❶ with a single column. Because only names are shown, there is no need for header rows, so you disable them ❷. Quite frankly, all that could be done to remove headers was to hide them through CSS. They'll still be rendered, and headers-specific calculations won't cease to exist.

Next is the Groups list component ❸. It's another simple grid panel, similar to the Survey list. This one has an extra column, fed with the number of questions allocated for a group. The way you get to the number is interesting; you use associations to access a group's questions. Calling for associations generates a `Store` instance loaded with the respective records. You use the `getCount()` method ❹, a member of the `Ext.data.Store` class.

> ### When will a hasMany association store be created?
> When accessing a `Model` instance's (a.k.a. record's) hasMany associated data, such as in the renderer in listing 14.13, Ext JS will create an `Ext.data.AbstractStore` instance, which is a simplified version of `Ext.data.Store`. The instance will stay cached with the record for future use, yet it'll also be destroyed with it.

Even simpler, the `QuestionsForm` class ❺ serves as the parent container for all questions ❻ that'll eventually be dynamically rendered into it. The plan is to add a button under each question group that makes it easier to navigate to the next group, or ultimately to end a survey. To make it more aesthetically pleasing, the button will display horizontally centered onscreen. Setting the layout type to vbox and aligning it to the center ❼ is an easy way to achieve the desired effect. Questions will flex to occupy all of the available width. That part will be done dynamically with controllers, which we'll cover next.

UPDATING THE VIEWPORT
Now you need a home for all the newly defined views. In the `Survey.view.Viewport` class, its layout type is set to card. The first card resolves the authorization screen, which is also the initial screen of the Survey application, according to listing 14.11. As in listing 14.12, the `Authentication` controller will switch to the second card nested under the viewport, which is exactly where you'll place the survey-related views.

Figure 14.6 shows that the group list is stacked right above the survey list. Both lists occupy the left (or west) area of the screen. The larger section is reserved for questions. It makes sense to plug all that into the Viewport class, as shown in the next listing.

Listing 14.14 Updated `Viewport` class

```
Ext.define('Survey.view.Viewport', {
    extend : 'Ext.container.Viewport',
    alias  : 'widget.vp',

    requires : [
        'Survey.view.AuthorizationForm',
        'Survey.view.SurveyList'
    ],

    layout : {
        type : 'card'
    },

    items : [
        {
            xtype : 'authform'
        },
        {
            xtype  : 'container',               ①  Adds Surveys
            itemId : 'mainContainer',               view
            layout : {
                align : 'stretch',
                type  : 'hbox'
            },
            items  : [
                {
                    xtype    : 'container',     ②  Sets left column
                    minWidth : 200,                 container
                    flex     : 1,
                    layout   : {
                        align : 'stretch',
                        type  : 'vbox'
                    },
                    items    : [
                        {
                            xtype : 'grouplist',   ③  Adds
                            flex  : 2,                  GroupList view
                            hidden : true
                        },
                        {                          ④  Adds
                            xtype : 'surveylist',      Survey list
                            flex  : 1
                        }
                    ]
                },
                {                                   ⑤  Adds
                    xtype        : 'questions',         Questions view
                    bodyPadding  : 10,
                    flex         : 3
                }
```

```
        ]
      }
    ]
});
```

All of the views are nested under an HBox layout container **1**. The container splits the screen into four equal vertical sections. Three sections are used by questions **5**, and one section is used by the left navigation bar **2**. The latter is yet another box layout container, but this time it's vertically oriented. Two parts are occupied by the group list **3**, and one part is used by the survey list **4**.

As you can see, grouplist is initialized as hidden to give focus to surveylist. That makes sense, because the user needs to select a survey before going further. Selecting a survey will automatically engage the group list's visible property, recalculating heights to match the desired layout pattern. This automation is controlled through controllers, which leads us to their setup.

14.3.10 *Survey controllers*

From what you just saw, views are basic and simple. That's the way they should be: no data and little if any interaction. Controllers are there to direct all the dynamics to the views.

You used controllers when you defined the Authentication controller class (in listing 14.4). That leads us to the very last couple of items to define: Surveys and Questions controllers. Each will manage its respective area of the application. Let's explore both of the controller classes.

SURVEYS CONTROLLER

The amount of interaction needed for surveys is minimal, but it rounds up all frequently used controller features. As we outlined earlier in this chapter, controllers manage dependencies to a great extent. This one in particular will need to reference all views, models, and stores related to Surveys and Groups. The Surveys controller has an additional task: to wait for users to select a survey in the Survey list view, and show the appropriate groups for further selection. Let's make it happen in the next listing.

Listing 14.15   Surveys controller

```
Ext.define('Survey.controller.Surveys', {
    extend : 'Ext.app.Controller',

    models : [
        'Survey',
        'Group'
    ],
    stores : [
        'Surveys',
        'Groups'
    ],
    views   : [
        'GroupList',
```

1 Sets dependencies

```
            'SurveyList',
            'QuestionsForm'
    ],

    refs : [
        {
            ref      : 'groupList',
            selector : 'grouplist'
        }
    ],

    init : function () {
        this.control({
            surveylist : {
                select : this.loadGroups
            }
        });
    },

    loadGroups : function (grid, record) {
        var groups = this.getGroupList(),
            groupRec,
            questions;

        groups.show();

        groups.reconfigure(record.groups());

        groupRec = groups.getStore().getAt(0);
        if (groupRec) {
            groups.getSelectionModel().select([groupRec]);
        }

        questions = groups.up('#mainContainer').down('questions');
        questions.setTitle(record.get('name'));
    }
});
```

❷ **Listens for selection of SurveyList items**

❸ **Accesses GroupList reference**

❹ **Selects first available group**

The first step is to define dependencies ❶. You'll immediately notice all the models, stores, and views specified. That makes sense, because this controller interacts with both surveys and groups. Also notice that although we talked about the Questions-Form view, you have a dedicated Questions controller planned. This is because QuestionsForm is being accessed further down the controller to set its title dynamically.

In section 14.2.2, we discussed several ways of setting dependencies, mentioning controllers, models, views, and stores. These four types are different because you don't have to specify the full class name. For instance, it's easy to assume that the Group model will have a class name of Survey.model.Group. Thus, you only specify the last bit of the name (for example, Group or package.Group if the class name is Survey.model.package.Group).

Before we go any further let's discuss references. References are used to quickly access the first instantiated component using a defined component query selector. You create a reference to quickly access the GroupList when needed. Refs will automatically create a getter, a convenient method used to call up the referenced instance.

This ref will create the `getGroupList()` method ❷, which is a member of the `Surveys Controller` instance.

The grid selection listener efficiently calls the `loadGroups` callback, which in turn makes a few changes to the user interface. First, it uses the configured ref getter ❸ to make the `GroupList` visible. Making the list visible causes the left column to recalculate the layout, as the 2:1 height ratio between `GroupList` and `SurveyList` is finally enforced.

Next comes reconfiguration of `GroupList`, or in other words, replacing the store with the newly created one. The new store was automatically generated when `record.groups()` was called, and the `hasMany` association was engaged. The new store, or the association if you will, is then accessed to determine its first record, which is also going to be automatically selected ❹. This part is interesting. By selecting a list item, you'll also trigger the `select` event, which you'll later use to load the question. But you're leaving that part for another controller, dedicated to questions. Notice the thin line that separates the two controllers?

Let's move on to the `Questions` controller.

QUESTIONS CONTROLLER

The most comprehensive controller takes charge of rendering questions and saving their values as users are typing or making selections. It looks like it's easier said than done, but the framework does a lot of work here. Take a look at the next listing.

Listing 14.16   `Questions` **controller**

```
Ext.define('Survey.controller.Questions', {
    extend : 'Ext.app.Controller',

    views : [
        'QuestionsForm'                          ◁─┐  Adds Controller
    ],                                             ❶  dependencies

    refs : [
        {
            ref      : 'form',
            selector : 'questions'
        },
        {
            ref      : 'groups',
            selector : 'grouplist'
        }
    ],

    init : function (application) {
        this.control({                                    Establishes
            grouplist : {                              ❷  awareness of
                select : this.showGroupQuestions   ◁─┐      groups switch
            },

            '#groupNext' : {
                click : this.showNextGroup
            },
```

```
            '#surveyFinish' : {
                click : this.finishSurvey
            },

            'questions field' : {
                change : this.saveItem
            }
        });
    },

    showGroupQuestions : function (grid, record, index) {
        var questions = record.questions(),
            form = this.getForm(),
            store = grid.store,
            isLastGroup = (store.getCount() - index) === 1,
            fields = [];

        questions.each(function (question) {
            var field = Ext.apply({
                fieldLabel : question.get('question'),
                value      : question.get('answer'),
                question   : question,
                anchor     : '100%',
                xtype      : 'textfield'
            }, question.get('config'));

            fields.push(field);
        });

        form.removeAll();
        form.add({
            xtype : 'fieldset',
            title : record.get('name'),
            items : fields,
            width : '100%'
        });

        form.add({
            xtype  : 'button',
            text   : isLastGroup ? 'Save' : 'Next',
            itemId : isLastGroup ? 'surveyFinish' : 'groupNext',
            width  : 200
        });
    },

    showNextGroup : function () {
        var grid = this.getGroups(),
            store = grid.getStore(),
            selModel = grid.getSelectionModel(),
            selected = selModel.getLastSelected(),
            curIndex = store.indexOf(selected),
            next = store.getAt(curIndex + 1);

        if (next) {
            selModel.select([next]);
        }
    },
```

❸ Listens for changes in question fields

❹ Processes group selection

❺ Prepares form fields based on questions data

❻ Adds fieldset to contain question fields

❼ Adds convenience group switch button

❽ Sets automation for switching groups

```
finishSurvey : function () {
    var groups = this.getGroups();
    this.getForm().removeAll();
    groups.getSelectionModel().deselectAll();
    groups.hide();
    groups.up().down('surveylist').getSelectionModel().deselectAll();

},

saveItem : function (field) {
    var question = field.question;

    if (!question) {
        field = field.up('[question]');
        question = field.question;
    }

    if (question) {
        question.set('answer', field.getValue());
    }
}

});
```

⑨ Finishes survey, resets Surveys view

⑩ Saves question value

As listing 14.16 shows, the `Questions` controller does a great deal of work. It starts with view dependencies ❶, and you've already defined that view in the `Surveys` controller. Repeating dependencies isn't a bad practice. Rest assured, the loader isn't going to include it twice. Redefining dependencies allows you to create reusable code and, at the same time, make sure another developer knows what the particular class deals with.

The `this.control` section lists four listeners. It completes the interaction with the `Surveys` controller by listening for the `GroupList` item selection event ❷. The `Surveys` controller forces selection of the first group for the previously selected survey. It's that very moment when the `Questions` controller takes over and processes group selection ❹. It'll first iterate through all the questions available in the chosen group and create an array of `Ext.form.Fields`. Then comes the removal of all existing components nested in `QuestionsForm`, if any, to make room for `Ext.form.FieldSet`, which is just a container for the questions ❻. The fieldset's title conveniently equals the selected group name. At this point, `QuestionForm`'s title shows the survey name, and the fieldset's counterpart shows the group name. This will be useful for letting your users know exactly what they're filling out. Of course, the fieldset's `items` property references the array of question fields gathered in step ❺.

A helpful button is added right under the fieldset in ❼. If there are more groups to visit in the active survey, the button will switch to the next one ❽. Otherwise, it'll finish the survey by restoring state to the default views with only the list of surveys populated ❾.

Questions are data-driven, meaning they come from a server. In many cases they'll be associated with a form builder application. You want data to be saved constantly, without users having to click a dedicated save button. This means you need to listen for a generic event that persists in all fields: the `change` event ❸. Its handler simply accesses the `getValue` method of the selected field and stores the value in the model instance of the question ➓. But there's a "gotcha" here. Complex fields, such as `radiogroup` and `checkboxgroup`, act differently for this event. Their nested children fire the change event, but the group container reads and sets the value. In such a case you need to go a step up from the event-firing field to access the `getValue` method.

Voilà, the application is ready for testing. Ready? Let's fire it up. Figure 14.10 shows the client's view of a survey. They selected a survey, which automatically selected the first available group, consequently loading the applicable questions in the middle section of the page. Their changes are automatically saved and previous answers loaded. Moving to another group is seamless, either by clicking the Next button or by selecting another group from the list.

Congratulations, you've completed the target application. As it is, it's a great testing ground for further Ext JS application development. If you're interested in more, here are some ideas on how to enhance the Survey app:

- Set up a whole CRUD workflow with the server.
- Add reports using Ext JS charts.
- Create a survey management interface with a form builder.
- Apply custom styling.

Because we decided to call this a stable version of the app, let's package it for production. To do so, you'll put Sencha Cmd's build process to work.

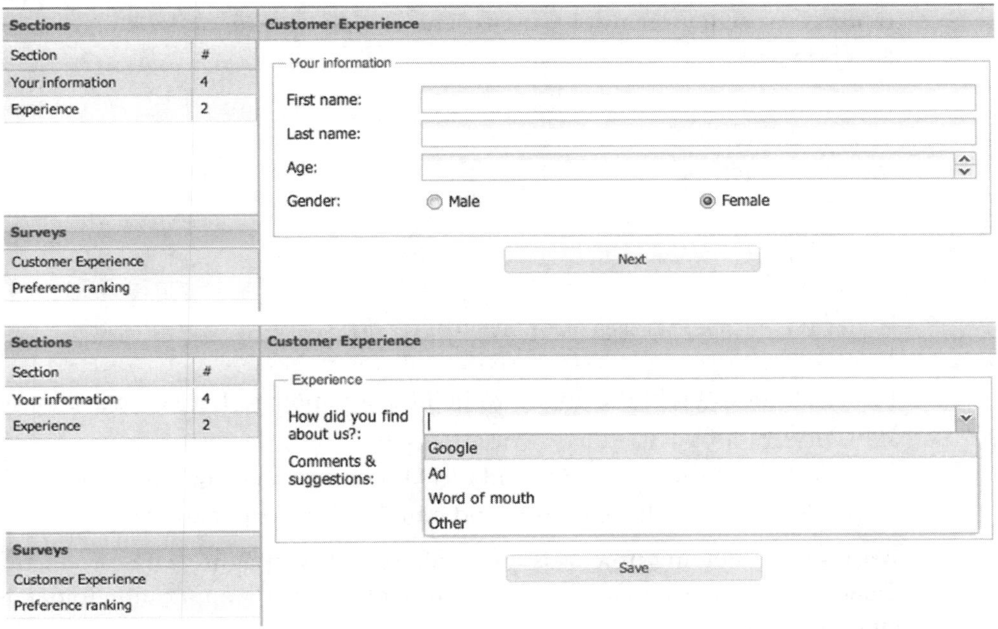

Figure 14.10   Final survey walkthrough

14.4 Packaging

Packaging is a process of preparing a web application for optimum delivery. Sencha Cmd makes packaging quick and easy, and among other great features, it helps to

- Decrease total size for faster transport through a network
- Increase execution speed
- Lower memory footprint

It accomplishes these goals by

- Removing unnecessary parts, such as classes, components, and even method calls
- Concatenating JavaScript and CSS code
- Minifying JavaScript and CSS code

The initial steps of creating the application through Sencha Cmd are going to prove fruitful now that it's time for packaging.

In most cases, an application will be ready for immediate build. But you must include an additional file, data.json, so additional configuration is necessary. Naturally, should you migrate to a RESTful (or similar client-server-based) environment, you can skip this step.

To include the required file in the build process, you'll have to make a minor modification to the app.json file. This JSON object already has a bit of pregenerated content, to which you'll append an array property named `resources`. The `resources` property tells Sencha Cmd to replicate files or folders in the built version of the applications, respecting relative locations. This is what the file will look like when you add data.json to it:

```
{
    "name": "Survey",

    "requires": [
    ],

    "resources": [
        "data.json"
    ],

    "id": "c17ccff8-b8c9-4fb1-80f5-8f818603a5e5"
}
```

You're all set to build the app. Two build types apply to Ext JS applications through Sencha Cmd:

- *Testing*—Concatenated JS and CSS files with minimal optimizations
- *Production*—Fully optimized and minified JavaScript and CSS

Because the building process is identical, we'll skip straight to the production build. Open the terminal, and navigate to the root of the Survey application folder. Now execute the following command:

```
sencha app build production
```

Sit back and relax while your computer gets hot as it checks your JavaScript code for errors, compiles SASS theme, concatenates and minifies code, and does a lot more to optimize your application for best performance and experience.

As figure 14.11 confirms, Sencha Cmd created a new directory structure under the build folder, containing the production version of the Survey application. Let's see how the built version differs from the original, development source code.

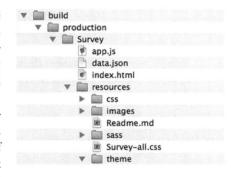

Figure 14.11 Built application files

In terms of speed, the overall benchmark shows the following:

- Unbuilt (development) version execution time: 1764.207 ms
- Fully built (production) version execution time: 472.525 ms

Impressively, the speed more than tripled in the production build. Actually, it's 3.7x faster, a multiplier that would have become even larger had you downloaded the app from a remote location over a poor internet connection. What about the total size?

Using the Network tab in Chrome Inspector (or any other web inspector you favor), you can see how the two versions differ:

- Unbuilt (development) version transfer: 3.8 MB in 274 requests
- Fully built (production) version transfer: 1.2 MB in 4 requests

The production build is indisputably the preferred way of serving your app to the end user. It's faster to execute, and it's also much faster to download and uses far less expensive requests.

In a regular application development cycle, this would be the last test after quality-assurance testing. That makes it a great time to say congratulations! Enjoy testing both locally and remotely to experience the full benefit of the Sencha Cmd build process with the app that you built on your own—from scratch.

14.5 Summary

In this intensive chapter, you explored the major steps of building an application. Whether it's small or huge, the development process is always the same. The 11-SAW process will be a helpful resource when you're planning development steps. Keep in mind that coding conventions are important for the product life cycle. Use the Ext JS conventions described in this chapter, but also use those for developing in JavaScript and CSS.

We covered a great amount of content in this book. You read about the framework's internals, widgets, class system, MVC pattern, Sencha Cmd build process, and more. The framework continues to live, and Sencha will keep on enriching it with new and exciting features. Perhaps the most important skill we hope you learned is the ability to dive into the Ext JS source code, which constantly gives solutions to a myriad of questions.

index

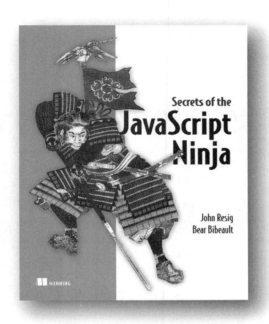

MORE TITLES FROM MANNING

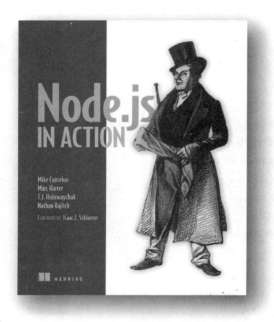

Node.js in Action
by Mike Cantelon
    Marc Harter
    T.J. Holowaychuk
    Nathan Rajlich

ISBN: 978-1-617290-57-2
416 pages
$44.99
October 2013

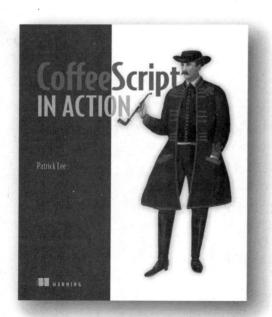

CoffeeScript in Action
by Patrick Lee

ISBN: 978-1-617290-62-6
325 pages
$44.99
May 2014

For ordering information go to www.manning.com